UNBOUND IN WAR?

International Law in Canada and Britain's Participation in the Korean War and Afghanistan Conflict

Unbound in War?

*International Law in Canada
and Britain's Participation
in the Korean War and
Afghanistan Conflict*

SEAN RICHMOND

UNIVERSITY OF TORONTO PRESS
Toronto Buffalo London

© University of Toronto Press 2021
Toronto Buffalo London
utorontopress.com
Printed in Canada

ISBN 978-1-4875-0346-8 (cloth)   ISBN 978-1-4875-1799-1 (EPUB)
                                   ISBN 978-1-4875-1798-4 (PDF)

Library and Archives Canada Cataloguing in Publication

Title: Unbound in war? : international law in Canada and Britain's participation
    in the Korean War and Afghanistan conflict / Sean Richmond.
Names: Richmond, Sean, 1978–, author.
Description: Includes bibliographical references and index.
Identifiers: Canadiana (print) 20210193255 | Canadiana (ebook) 20210193387 |
    ISBN 9781487503468 (hardcover) | ISBN 9781487517991 (EPUB) |
    ISBN 9781487517984 (PDF)
Subjects: LCSH: War (International law) | LCSH: International law – Great Britain. |
    LCSH: International law – Canada. | LCSH: Korean War, 1950–1953 – Great
    Britain. | LCSH: Korean War, 1950–1953 – Canada. | LCSH: Afghan War,
    2001 – Great Britain. | LCSH: Afghan War, 2001 – Canada.
Classification: LCC KZ6385 .R53 2021 | DDC 341.6 – dc23

University of Toronto Press acknowledges the financial assistance to its publishing
program of the Canada Council for the Arts and the Ontario Arts Council, an
agency of the Government of Ontario.

Contents

Acknowledgments

Researching and writing a monograph is a large endeavour, and I have numerous people and organizations to thank for their help along the way. This book expands on doctoral research I completed in the Department of Politics and International Relations at the University of Oxford (Linacre College). Many of the ideas expressed in it are thus a collective product of stimulating debates with classmates and faculty there. In particular, I owe my greatest appreciation to my supervisor, Jennifer Welsh, who provided extensive guidance, wisdom, and support.

Dapo Akande, Rosemary Foot, and Sarah Percy read a number of draft chapters and shared invaluable insights. The project's conceptual contribution and empirical rigour are stronger as a result. Likewise, I will always remember the intellectual warmth and curiosity conveyed by my examiners, Martha Finnemore and Edward Keene, and their encouragement to turn the work into an interdisciplinary book.

I thank Janice Evans, Stephanie Mazza, Daniel Quinlan, Michael Waldin, and the amazing team at the University of Toronto (U of T) Press for guiding the manuscript through the comprehensive review and publication process, particularly during a global pandemic. I also express gratitude to the two anonymous readers who provided thoughtful feedback and enthusiasm for the project, and thank Leah Horlick for creating the detailed index under a tight deadline. Any remaining errors or omissions are, of course, mine alone.

In a time of decreased funding for academic research, I gratefully acknowledge the generous financial assistance of Canada's Social Sciences and Humanities Research Council; the Commonwealth Scholarship; the Canadian Council on International Law; IODE Canada; the Mackenzie King Memorial Trust; Linacre College; the Department of Politics and International Relations at Oxford; and the Department of Law and Legal Studies at Carleton University.

A special thanks is owed to the Chair of the Legal Studies Department at Carleton, Vince Kazmierski, and my wonderful colleagues there for their support, and for showing the world what a commitment to research excellence and social justice looks like in practice. I have also benefitted from discussions over the years with exceptional coworkers in the Legal Branch at Global Affairs Canada; the Law Faculty at the University of Western Australia; the Munk School of Global Affairs at U of T; Sack Goldblatt Mitchell LLP; and the Policy Section of Legal Aid Ontario. In the interest of transparency, this book is based on my academic research.

For first teaching me to think critically, I thank my undergraduate professors at Queen's University. For encouraging me to become an academic, I am grateful to members of the Political Science Department at the University of British Columbia. For training me in international law and fostering fidelity to the rule of law, I owe a debt of gratitude to the legal faculty at the University of Ottawa. For helping to fund these crucial public institutions, and thus helping young people to achieve their potential, I thank the many taxpayers, particularly those who may not have had the same opportunity to pursue higher education.

For valuable discussions and support along the way, I am grateful to Karen Alter, Jutta Brunnée, James Busuttil, Michael Byers, Angela Cameron, Richard Caplan, Christine Cheng, Kamari Clarke, John Currie, Craig Forcese, Catherine Gribbin, Ian Hurd, Andrew Hurrell, the late Nicole LaViolette, Ron Levi, Don McRae, Kim Richard Nossal, Richard Price, Stephen Saideman, Rebecca Sanders, Stephen Smith, Duncan Snidal, Stephen Toope, and Wendy Wong.

This book has also benefitted from the input of participants at the many conferences and workshops where draft sections were presented, including the International Relations Research Colloquium at Oxford, International Studies Association, Canadian Political Science Association, and the Australian and New Zealand Society of International Law. An earlier shorter version of chapter four was published in volume 10/2 of the *Asian Journal of International Law* in 2020, entitled "Unbound in War? International Law and Britain's Participation in the Korean War." I am grateful to the reviewers of that article for their comments.

For feedback, camaraderie or offering a spare bed in Oxford and London, I warmly thank Mjriam Abu Samra, Maja Andjelkovic, Livia Aumand, David Blagden, Anna Bretzlaff, Marco Codevilla, Alissa Cooper, Nicole De Silva, Janina Dill, Amelia Fitzhardinge, Francesca Giovannini, Nina Hall, Elliot Hughes, Patrick Ky, Amy King, Michael Manulak, Linsey McGoey, Travers McLeod, Kate Millar, Chris Mitchell, Ruben Reike, Elina Sinkkonen, Rana Siu Inboden, Vanessa Snyder, Nora Stappert, Landry Subianto, Henning Tamm, and Michael Urban.

For research help, I am indebted to the kind staff of the Bodleian Library at Oxford, the British Library in London, the National Archives in Kew, Library and Archives Canada in Ottawa, and Carleton Library. Matthew Willis, at the Royal United Services Institute, and David Blagden went out of their way to connect me with British military personnel. I thank them both.

This book would not have been possible without the insight and openness of the former government leaders and officials who agreed to be interviewed about Canada and Britain's military involvement in Afghanistan. I am forever grateful to them for their willingness to speak on the record about matters of high politics and internal state decision-making that are often hidden from external scrutiny. Such evidence is particularly important because, as one former Canadian cabinet minister informed me, the documentary record of executive branch decisions has declined. Future historians, I would add, will find this tremendously challenging, and current policymakers should seek to address this gap in the public record. Otherwise, we will ultimately know less about who we are as a country, and why we did or did not go to war.

On a more personal level, I thank my parents, Melodie and Ted, for their love and unwavering support. Throughout the challenges and triumphs of pursuing graduate studies and a university career, they have always had my back, and provided thoughtful editing and a broader perspective. I also appreciate the love and support of my parents-in-law, Jill and Kip Cobbett, who tackle life with humility and enthusiasm, and inspire others to do the same. For helping me remember where I came from, I thank my extended family and old friends. For making my wife, Anne Cobbett, and me feel so welcome when we moved to Perth, Australia, with an infant, I send warm thanks to all the new friends and colleagues we met there.

This book is dedicated to Anne and our children, Anders (7) and Hugh (5). The boys are a source of joy, and we learn more about ourselves each day with them. I hope we inspire them to build a better world, as they inspire us. I asked Anne in the summer of 2009 to go on an adventure overseas in England. Neither of us realized how difficult, memorable, and life changing the following years would be; or how our journey would take our young family around the globe and back again. Through it all, Anne has been patient, encouraging, and very funny. I am lucky to call her my partner, and thank her for her continued love and companionship.

Abbreviations

AIHRC	Afghan Independent Human Rights Commission
ATA	Afghan Transitional Authority
CDS	Chief of the Defence Staff
CF	Canadian Forces
CIIA	Canadian Institute for International Affairs
DPRK	Democratic People's Republic of Korea
ECHR	European Convention on Human Rights
EoL	Exchange of Letters
FCO	Foreign and Commonwealth Office
ICC	International Criminal Court
ICJ	International Court of Justice
ISAF	International Security Assistance Force
JAG	Judge Advocate General
MoU	Memorandum of Understanding
MPCC	Military Police Complaints Commission
NAC	North Atlantic Council
NDS	National Directorate of Security
NGO	Non-Governmental Organization
OEF	Operation Enduring Freedom
OIF	Operation Iraqi Freedom
POW	Prisoner of War
PRT	Provisional Reconstruction Team
ROK	Republic of Korea
UNTCOK	United Nations Temporary Commission on Korea

UNBOUND IN WAR?

International Law in Canada and Britain's Participation
in the Korean War and Afghanistan Conflict

1 Introduction

This is a book about both the power and limits of international law in an area of state activity often assumed to be beyond law's reach – namely, the use of military force and the conduct of war. It is also a story of how two of America's closest allies have sought to reconcile their security concerns with their legal obligations during two of the most significant international conflicts since the Second World War. Following the deaths and atrocities of that war, the use of force and the behaviour of states in armed conflict became subject to extensive legal restrictions in the United Nations Charter (in 1945) and Geneva Conventions (in 1949), respectively. For instance, although the use of force and the conduct of states in war were governed by treaties and customary international law prior to World War II, the Charter and the four Geneva Conventions subjected these fields of activity to international legal rules that were historically unprecedented in nature and scope.

Regarding the Charter, this treaty differed from the 1919 Covenant of the League of Nations in many key ways.[1] While the Covenant was aimed at confronting the narrow concept of "aggression," the Charter was designed to address a broader range of threats to international peace and security. Further, the Charter focused less on prohibiting the formal and specific phenomenon of "war" and more on regulating the general phenomenon of "force," and it regulated such activity in a wide range of circumstances.[2] Finally, if a state resorted to war in breach of the Covenant, the League Council was committed only to

---

1 See Currie 2008: 448–459; Dinstein 2011: 82–100; and Simma et al. 2012: 1–24.

2 See e.g. Article 2(4) of the Charter of the United Nations, 26 June 1945, 1 U.N.T.S. XVI (entered into force 24 Oct. 1945) [hereafter UN Charter], which states that all UN members "shall refrain in their international relations from the threat or use of force against the territorial integrity or political independence of any state, or in any other manner inconsistent with the Purposes of the [UN]").

economic sanctions as a response. In contrast, under the Charter, the Security Council could use force without attempting economic sanctions first, and it was envisioned as taking military measures in its own right, rather than merely recommending action to states.[3] As John Currie notes, the above principles – combined with the broad discretion the Charter gives the Council to maintain peace, and the legal obligation it imposes on states to carry out Council decisions and settle their international disputes peacefully – arguably represent "the single greatest formal surrender of sovereignty, to an international organization, since the emergence of the Westphalian system of international law in the mid-seventeenth century."[4]

Regarding the 1949 Geneva Conventions, these treaties also differed from previous agreements in many key ways.[5] For example, following the abuse of prisoners and civilians in WWII and other conflicts,[6] the treatment of individuals captured in war became subject to increased legal restrictions in these treaties. While the 1929 Prisoners of War (POW) Convention, for instance, contained 97 articles, the 1949 Third Geneva Convention on POWs included 143 articles.[7] Further, under the latter treaty, the categories of persons entitled to POW status were broadened, and the conditions and places of captivity were more precisely defined, including the relief that prisoners are entitled to receive and the judicial proceedings that can be instituted against them. More broadly, the 1949 Conventions affirmed the overriding principle that prisoners and civilians must at all times be treated humanely, and extended this protection to international *and* non-international conflicts.[8] Thus, if another state is unwilling or unable to apply these rules, transferring captured individuals to them is prohibited.[9] Finally, the Third Geneva Convention also established the important principle that POWs shall be released and repatriated without

---

3 Lowe et al. 2010: 10–12.

4 Currie 2008: 459.

5 See Pictet et al. 1960: 3–10, 27–41, 139–142; Best 2002: 80–179; and Roberts and Guelff 2005: 6, 243.

6 Scheipers 2010.

7 Geneva Convention relative to the Treatment of Prisoners of War, signed 12 Aug. 1949, 75 U.N.T.S. 135, 6 U.S.T. 3316 (entered into force 21 Oct. 1950) [hereafter Third Geneva Convention on POWs].

8 See Articles 3 and 13 of the Third Geneva Convention on POWs; and Articles 3 and 27 of the Geneva Convention relative to the Protection of Civilian Persons, 12 Aug. 1949, 75 U.N.T.S. 287 (entered into force 21 Oct. 1950) [hereafter Fourth Geneva Convention on Civilians]. Technically, under the latter treaty, it is "protected persons" who must be treated humanely. These are people who for whatever reason "find themselves … in the hands of a Party to the conflict or Occupying Power of which they are not nationals" (Article 4).

9 Article 12 of the Third Geneva Convention on POWs, and Article 45 of the Fourth Geneva Convention on Civilians.

delay after the cessation of active hostilities.[10] As Geoffrey Best observes, following the horrors of WWII, the above rules asserted the fundamental idea that all human beings must be protected from the misuse of armed power, even in war.[11]

Despite the extensive legal restrictions in the UN Charter and Geneva Conventions, however, the use of force has continued, and millions of people have died and been mistreated in war. One historical survey estimates that between 1945 and 2008, 313 armed conflicts occurred, killing 92–100 million people.[12] Regarding prisoners in these wars, Best notes that since 1950, "Parties to armed conflicts have repeatedly exploited the weaknesses of the POW regime and the vulnerability of its objects in order to serve their own political interests."[13] Reflecting this observation, a 2007 statistical survey found that the humane treatment of POWs has one of the lowest compliance rates compared to other issue areas.[14] The controversies regarding the detention and interrogation of individuals captured in the American-led armed conflicts and anti-terrorist activities that followed the attacks of 11 September 2001 suggest that the foregoing exploitation and questionable compliance have possibly continued or even regressed.[15]

Taken as a whole, the above observations indicate a stark potential gap between the formal law of the UN Charter and Geneva Conventions, on the one hand, and the actual practice of states on the other. Faced with this gap, it can be tempting to draw pessimistic conclusions about the broader irrelevance of international law in world politics, particularly in war when the normative requirements of such law may conflict with the material interests of states. A realist observer, for example, might argue that because there is no true supranational authority able to protect states or control their conduct during hostilities, states, especially powerful ones, are not seriously constrained by the international law on the use of force (*jus ad bellum*) or the international law of armed conflict (*jus in bello*) when they use force, and will indeed violate law if it

---

10 See Article 118 of the Third Geneva Convention on POWs. Earlier treaties stated that prisoners should or shall be repatriated after an armistice or peace treaty was legally concluded, rather than after the factual cessation of hostilities. This left a loophole open for some states to keep prisoners following WWII and WWI. See Pictet et al. 1960: 540–541.

11 Best 2002: 69–72. Indeed, the new Conventions reflected the idea of fundamental human rights operating in war.

12 Bassiouni et al. 2010. The estimate of 92–100 million people killed is twice the number of victims in World Wars I and II combined. The conflicts studied were of an international and non-international nature, as defined by the laws of war, as well as purely internal conflicts, civil wars, and regime victimization.

13 Best 2002: 350.

14 Morrow 2007: 569.

15 See e.g. Brunnée and Toope 2010: 220–270; and Osiel 2009.

conflicts with their political and military concerns in such matters.[16] Similarly, some rational choice views might suggest that the impact of international law will be limited or epiphenomenal to the primacy of states' material interests in contentious zero-sum issues like war.[17]

In response to such pessimism, a small but growing body of International Relations (IR) and International Law (IL) research has sought to challenge its theoretical and empirical accuracy, and demonstrate that international law can impact even "high politics" areas such as security and armed conflict.[18] However, as I elaborate below, this exciting field of research has tended to focus overwhelmingly on America's conduct and recent wars. Moreover, although legal scholars interested in such political topics often assume that the binding, obligatory nature of international law – like all law – helps it play a distinct and significant role in international politics, there is limited empirical work that assesses this fundamental conceptual premise.

To help address these gaps in the literature and advance the interdisciplinary debate, the following study examines the impact and interpretation of international law in the use of force by two important but comparatively understudied countries, the United Kingdom and Canada, during two of the most significant conflicts since 1945 – namely, the Korean War of 1950–53 and the Afghanistan Conflict of 2001–14.[19] It addresses two main questions. First, how, if at all, did international law influence the UK and Canada's conduct regarding the use of force in these conflicts, and the nature and scope of such force? Second, if international law played a role in such conduct, to what extent did policymakers understand it as a distinct and binding set of legal rules, and to what degree did the legal status of these rules affect their decision-making?

To address these questions, key aspects of Britain and Canada's participation in the Korean War and the Afghan Conflict are analyzed. These key aspects touch upon each state's policy and practice regarding (a) whether and how to

---

16 For scholars whose views generally resonate with this realist idea, see e.g. Clausewitz 1966; Kennan 1984; Acheson 1996; Mearsheimer 2003; and Morgenthau 2006.

17 For scholars whose positions tend to reflect this rational choice perspective, see e.g. Guzman 2002; and Goldsmith and Posner 2005.

18 See e.g. Hoyt 1961; Chayes 1974; Henkin 1979; Belt 2000; Byers 2002; Canestaro 2004; Wheeler 2004; Kahl 2007; Dickinson 2010; Brunnée and Toope 2010; Dill 2015; McLeod 2015; and Richmond 2016a.

19 The formal nouns "Korean War" and "Afghanistan Conflict" will be used most often in this book, for the sake of differentiation and consistency, and because such language is often employed by other scholars and leaders themselves. However, note that – depending on the context – other terms will also be used, such as the "Korean crisis" and "Afghan war." Where the *legal* significance of a term is at issue (e.g., whether the situation in Korea was seen as a new collective police action or traditional inter-state war), this will be highlighted. I thank an anonymous reviewer for this clarifying observation.

be involved in the two wars; (b) the major international legal issues related to each crisis; and (c) the treatment of captured enemy prisoners. I draw on constructivist IR theory and "interactional" IL theory, and employ a method of historical reconstruction and process tracing. I describe these theories and methods more later below.

Throughout the book, I centre my analysis on the discourse and practice of the UK and Canada's main political and military leaders during each war, as well as the views and actions of important officials. In conducting this analysis, I examine relevant government archive documents, public and parliamentary statements, private diaries, memoirs, court cases, public inquiries, secondary literature, and original interview data. This last source, it should be emphasized, includes interviews with former Canadian Prime Minister Paul Martin; ex Foreign and Defence Ministers Bill Graham, Arthur Eggleton, and John McCallum; a former Chief of Staff to these leaders, Eugene Lang; and retired Chief of the Defence Staff Ray Henault. It also includes interviews with former senior British diplomat Sir Nigel Sheinwald, and a former national security adviser to Prime Minister Tony Blair, Sir Peter Ricketts.

To my knowledge, no other monograph in the area of international law and international relations has managed to secure access to such high-level leaders, or analysed the breadth of evidentiary sources noted above. I draw on this wide range of evidence to reconstruct and trace (a) the policy options that were considered by leaders and officials about the key aspects of Britain and Canada's involvement in the two conflicts noted earlier; (b) whether and how the thinking and decisions of leaders and officials were influenced by international law; and (c) the extent to which leaders and officials saw this law as a distinct and binding phenomenon.

With the above in mind, the book advances a two-pronged argument. First, contrary to what realist and rationalist IR views might predict, international law helped define and shape each state's possible course of action in the wars, and the justifications that could be made for their behaviour. More specifically, Britain and Canada's involvement in the conflicts illustrates the four roles that I theorize international law can play in the use of force: (1) it helps constitute the identities of actors; (2) it helps regulate their political and military practice; (3) it permits and legitimates certain actions that otherwise might not be permitted; and (4) it helps structure the process by which agents seek to develop and promote new legal rules and legitimate conduct.

Second, however, contrary to what IL scholars might predict, the discourse and actions of UK and Canadian leaders and officials in the Korean War and Afghan Conflict offer mixed support for the hypothesis that, when states use force, policymakers understand international law as a distinct and binding set of legal rules, and the legal status of these rules impacts their decision-making.

Such a study seeks to make a valuable and original contribution to academic knowledge in the IR and IL literature, and to broader policy debates in these fields. For example, existing IR research that examines the role of non-material factors in world politics and the use of force by states has often focused more on moral norms and less on the specific phenomenon of international law.[20] Relatedly, as will be discussed in chapter three, the current political science research on norms has not adequately distinguished legal norms from other types of norms (such as moral and political norms), and scholars have not adequately explained how legal norms operate differently from non-legal norms in world politics.[21] As Martha Finnemore notes, if policymakers do not know and do not care about the legal status of the rules they consider relevant to their decision-making, "what reason do we have to think that 'legalness' matters at all in compliance with norms?"[22] Thus, insofar as the *jus ad bellum* and *jus in bello* are particular forms of international law,[23] and to the extent they contain rules that can and should be analysed as distinct legal phenomena,[24] then asking how such rules influence the use of force, and whether the legal status of these rules matters, poses questions that have not been adequately addressed in existing IR and political science literature.

Moreover, while some IR and IL work *has* analysed the role of law in world politics and found that legal rules can limit and amplify the exercise of state power, this research has often avoided security issues.[25] And this, in turn, has allowed the realist claim to stand that law only affects "secondary" issues in foreign policy, such as trade, and is dispensed with if it impinges on the use of force.[26] To this extent, then, studying law's influence on the use of force addresses a gap in IR and IL research, and addresses an issue that cannot be dismissed as unimportant. If international law is found to play a role in situations where states ought to be purely interested in maintaining their relative

---

20 Price 1997; Thomas 2001; Tannenwald 2007; Percy 2007a; and Petrova 2008.

21 Finnemore 2000: 701–702.

22 Finnemore 2000: 701.

23 For descriptions of the *jus ad bellum* as a branch of international law from the perspective of IL scholars, see Brownlie 1963; Franck 2002; and Gray 2008. For descriptions of the *jus in bello* as a branch of international law, again from an IL viewpoint, see Sassòli and Bouvier 2006; Fleck 2009; and Dinstein 2010.

24 The idea that international law and international legal rules can and should be analysed as phenomena distinct from other factors in world politics is discussed further in the next chapter.

25 See e.g. Kratochwil 1989; Byers 1999; Chinkin 2000; Toope 2000; Slaughter 2000; and Goldstein et al. 2000.

26 Simpson 2000: 457; and Wheeler 2004: 190.

power position, such as decisions about when and how to use force, this suggests that law can play an important role in influencing state decision-making more generally.[27] Or, as Janina Dill usefully puts it, if international law "can regulate war, where social and moral norms against the use of violence have broken down, surely no part of international relations is beyond its [potential] grasp."[28]

Furthermore, as will be discussed in chapter three, while some constructivists *have* argued that legal norms are distinct from non-legal norms,[29] and constructivist theory frequently cites international law and draws on legal philosophy,[30] constructivism has inadequately explained how legal and non-legal norms differ, and what exactly distinguishes international law from other phenomena in world politics. This is because, this study posits, constructivism has not adequately focused on the concept of legal obligation. As I suggest later below, the binding nature of international law is what potentially distinguishes it from other factors in international relations. To this extent, therefore, if this study finds that some British and Canadian policymakers in the Korean War and the Afghanistan Conflict felt bound by *jus ad bellum* and *jus in bello* rules, and that they were influenced in part by this perception of obligation[31] in their decision-making, then this book will help address an analytical and empirical gap in constructivist literature.

Finally, as noted earlier, existing IR and IL research on international law and the use of force by states has tended to focus overwhelmingly on recent conflicts[32] and US conduct.[33] To this extent, then, studying the role of international law in the Korean War – one of the most significant, destructive, and overlooked conflicts of the twentieth century[34] – helps address a historical gap in this research. And examining Britain and Canada – two important democratic

---

27 This point is based on a more general observation made by Sarah Percy about the potential significance of norms in state decisions regarding armed force (Percy 2007a: 10).

28 Dill 2015: 6.

29 Katzenstein 1996; and Arend 1996 and 1999.

30 Onuf 1989; Kratochwil 1989; and Reus-Smit 2004.

31 States have obligations and rights under international law. While both concepts will be seen in the empirical chapters that follow, greater attention is paid to obligations due to the book's conceptual hypothesis that the binding nature of international law is what potentially distinguishes it from other factors in international relations. I thank an anonymous reviewer for this important observation.

32 See e.g. Roberts 1999; Belt 2000; Koskenniemi 2002; Wheeler 2002; Murphy 2004; Kahl 2007; Falk 2012; Lehmann 2012; McLeod 2015; and Richmond 2016a.

33 See e.g. Chayes 1974; Beck 1993; Dunlap 2001 and 2008; Byers and Nolte 2003; Roth 2003; Boyle 2004; Wheeler 2004; Osiel 2009; Carvin 2010; Scharf and Williams 2010; Dickinson 2010; Shue 2011; Warren and Bode 2014; and Dill 2015. For important exceptions to the American and contemporary focus of existing literature, see Peevers 2013 and Hull 2014.

34 Cumings 2001.

countries whose public support for international law is often challenged by their security concerns and US policy wishes – broadens the empirical scope of this work. Further, as elaborated in the next chapter, focusing on Britain and Canada's participation in the Korean War and Afghan Conflict is significant because these cases are empirically puzzling and politically relevant. As such, they offer potential insights for developing and assessing existing understandings of the role – and limits – of international law in world affairs and armed conflict, and for making such understandings more comprehensive and historically informed.

Organization of the Book

With the above in mind, the book is organized as follows. The next chapter situates this investigation within the larger literature that has developed on international law and the use of force, and highlights how I build on and advance this work. Cognizant of this broader context, the study's research design, method, and premises are then further outlined, and the analytical and empirical contributions of this particular approach are discussed. Next, I explain why the book focuses on Britain and Canada's involvement in the Korean War and the Afghanistan Conflict, and I describe the benefits and trade-offs of comparing these two countries and these two wars.

Chapter three then further develops my theoretical framework for assessing the influence and understanding of international law. It addresses four related questions: How should we conceive of international law? How have three major IR theories (realism, neo-liberal institutionalism, and constructivism) engaged with international law? How does an "interactional" lens and the concept of legal obligation respond to the shortcomings of these three theories? And what roles can international law play in the use of force?

I argue that international law is best thought of as a distinct set of binding rules that are generally determinate. Moreover, by prioritizing normative structures and granting international law with "productive" power, constructivism takes us beyond the materialist and state-centred focus of realism and neo-liberal institutionalism, and the weak or functional roles that these theories allocate to law. However, constructivism has inadequately explored the concept of legal obligation and, as a result, has yet to adequately explain the potentially distinct nature and effects of international law in world politics. By contrast, the interactional theory of Jutta Brunnée and Stephen Toope focuses on obligation and thus offers a more compelling account of law's nature and impact.

Finally, by drawing on the analytical insights of constructivism and interactional theory, and employing additional philosophical reflections and historical examples I have derived from the IR and IL literature, I theorize that international law can play four main roles in world politics and the use of force:

1) it helps constitute the identities of actors, whether these are states (i.e., at the macro level of analysis), or individual leaders (i.e., at the micro level of analysis);
2) it helps regulate the political and military practice of actors, where regulate means to govern or control by law;
3) it permits and legitimates certain conduct that otherwise might not be permitted; and
4) it helps structure the process by which agents seek to develop and promote new legal rules and legitimate behaviour for states and other international actors.

The book then applies this framework to its four case studies. Chapter four looks at Britain and the Korean War, and chapter five examines Canada and that conflict. Chapter six looks at Britain's involvement in Afghanistan, and chapter seven analyses Canada's participation in that conflict. These chapters follow a similar structure. After providing a brief background to the wars, I summarize the dominant scholarly views of why Britain and Canada participated in these conflicts, and suggest how this study challenges and advances these views. In the balance of the chapters, I then analyse Britain and Canada's involvement in the wars from the perspective of international law.

By considering key aspects of UK and Canadian policy and practice, I first assess whether and how these aspects reflect the four roles that I posit international law can play in the use of force. I then investigate the extent to which UK and Canadian policymakers understood this law as a binding and distinct set of legal rules, and the degree to which the legal status of these rules impacted their decision-making. With respect to Korea, this is done by examining Britain and Canada's interpretation of the UN Security Council resolutions on the crisis, and their understanding of a key repatriation rule in the 1949 Geneva Convention on POWs. Regarding the conflict in Afghanistan, I assess Britain and Canada's interpretation of their obligations and rights under the UN Charter and the NATO treaty, as well as the UK's understanding of relevant international human rights law and Canada's interpretation of the Geneva Convention on POWs.

In the book's conclusion, I summarize the study's findings and analyse their implications for IR and IL theory. In addition, I offer some suggestions for future research.

Before proceeding, one final point should be made. Although this book ambitiously seeks to make an interdisciplinary contribution to both IL and IR research, some law scholars may engage with the work and ultimately wish it contained more traditional legal analysis. Likewise, some politics scholars may call for more social-science analysis. These potential views highlight the risk of interdisciplinary research. However, it is my hope that the contributions of this book outweigh any perceived shortcomings, and that scholars and non-specialists of different backgrounds will find much value and enjoyment in the chapters that follow.[35]

35 I thank the two anonymous reviewers of this book for the inspiration behind this observation, and for their positive comments and constructive suggestions more generally.

2 Existing Literature, Research Design, and Case Selection

As many readers will know, over the past twenty years, there has been a perceived increase in interdisciplinary research examining the role of international law in world politics.[1] And, as noted earlier, this work has included some studies on the use of force. What is less known, though, is that the above research has a longer history than is usually presumed, and that contemporary studies – such as this book – can and should learn more from this historical work.

As I suggest below, existing literature can be divided into two main groups: early International Law (IL) research from the 1960s and 1970s that looks at law's impact in various world crises; and recent International Relations (IR) and IL work from the 1990s and 2000s that studies the relevance of normative factors in international affairs. Again, the older IL work offers empirical insights and methodological guidance that are often ignored by today's scholars. However, it is also true that this research is theoretically underdeveloped, lacks comparative analysis and examination of *jus in bello* rules, and can be unconvincing about what constitutes evidence of law's distinct influence. Regarding the recent IR and IL work, while it is more conceptually sophisticated than the older IL research, it tends to focus on the United States, and its body of empirical work – particularly its comparative and qualitative research – is still limited and developing. In light of the above, this book will help address the shortcomings of early research, and broaden and advance the debate within contemporary literature.

---

1 For reviews and compilations on the state of this research from a primarily American and rationalist IR perspective, see Slaughter, Tulumello and Wood 1998; Simmons and Steinberg 2006; Hafner-Burton, et al. 2012; and Dunoff and Pollack 2013. For a more critical compilation by a European IL scholar, see Koskenniemi 2011b.

Early International Law Research

Until 1960, there was little scholarly study of the role of international law in state decision-making and the use of force.[2] In 1961, however, Edwin Hoyt examined whether principles of the UN Charter acted as a restraint and an incentive in America's response to the Korean War.[3] He argues convincingly that the US assisted South Korea within the UN framework for political *and* legal reasons.[4] However, while Hoyt is rigorous in his legal-historical method, he focuses on describing the US response from the perspective of international law and does not offer an adequate theoretical account of how this law influenced America's behaviour. Moreover, his findings are based on only one US case study. Although Hoyt notes that during the crisis, Britain disassociated itself from some US positions,[5] one is left wondering why the UK took this view, whether other US allies such as Canada held similar views, and whether international law affected such views. Finally, while Hoyt argues that in war "legal considerations receive low priority,"[6] he does not study the role of *jus in bello* rules in the Korean conflict and offers no evidence for this statement. Considering that some contemporary scholars continue to posit that war is "among the areas least likely to be affected by international law,"[7] one is left pondering whether *jus in bello* rules *do* receive low priority in conflict, whether *jus ad bellum* rules receive higher priority leading up to war, and what this may mean about the relationship between the two branches of law.

Following Hoyt, the American Society of International Law (ASIL) released a series of studies in the 1970s that assessed the effects of law in four world crises.[8] Unfortunately, this rich empirical work is sometimes ignored by contemporary scholars who study law's role in international affairs.[9] By contrast, this book

---

2 Prior to 1960, while a few studies had examined the role of law in state relations and diplomacy (Corbett 1951 and 1959), and the politics and ethics of international law (Visscher 1957), and others saw law wholly as part of the political process (McDougal 1953), this work did not focus on international law and the use of force by states.

3 Hoyt 1961: 45.

4 The political reasons included the fact that US allies might lose confidence in America if it did not help the South Koreans, as well as a desire to show the USSR that the US was willing to fight. The legal factor was the fact that policymakers believed that the North Korean attack was aggression and a clear violation of the UN Charter (1961: 54–55).

5 Hoyt 1961: 69.

6 Hoyt 1961: 67.

7 Guzman 2002: 1885.

8 The four crises are: (1) the Suez Canal crisis of 1956 (Bowie 1974); (2) Cyprus in 1958–67 (Ehrlich 1974); (3) the UN operation in the Congo in 1960–64 (Abi-Saab 1978); and (4) the Cuban missile crisis of 1962 (Chayes 1974).

9 See e.g. Arend 1996: 303.

relies on the ASIL series in two ways. First, it follows the series' methodological warning that, when studying international law's role in the use of force, one should not try to analyse the operation of law *throughout* the event.[10] This study thus examines key aspects of Britain and Canada's participation in the Korean War and the Afghanistan Conflict to assess the impact and interpretation of international law in this participation. Focusing on key aspects is important because leaders in Britain and Canada will have made many decisions about the two wars, and my aim is not to examine all of these choices or the conflicts in their entirety.

Second, this book builds on and advances the ASIL study that is most cited in the literature, namely Abram Chayes's analysis of the 1962 Cuban missile crisis. Despite the security concerns of that dramatic crisis, Chayes argues that US leaders nonetheless "made a considerable effort to integrate legal factors into their deliberations," and "[l]aw and legal institutions played a part in defining and shaping" their possible courses of action.[11] Chayes's study is relevant because, by observing that America's response to the crisis was a naval blockade *instead of* invasion, and this was due in part to legal considerations, it implies that one way to show law constrained a state's use of force is by finding evidence that (a) some leaders or advisers wanted to implement military responses that were broader or more severe than the force that was actually employed; and (b) these broader responses were avoided in part because other leaders or advisers thought this would be more consistent with international law. Like some other contemporary studies,[12] I assume that finding such evidence regarding Britain and Canada's involvement in the Korean War and Afghan Conflict would help suggest that law influenced said involvement.

---

10 For instance, in his study of the Cuban missile crisis of 1962, Abram Chayes "breaks up" the event by examining three US decisions: (1) the choice of the naval blockade against Cuba as opposed to harsher or milder responses; (2) the decision to seek support from the Organization of American States; and (3) America's approach to the UN. Similarly, in his examination of the 1956 Suez Canal crisis, Robert Bowie emphasizes that his goal "is not to recount the history of the crisis in detail," but to "explore what part international law, norms, or agencies played in the decisions and actions of the major protagonists" (Bowie 1974: ix).

11 Chayes 1974: 100–101.

12 For contemporary research that implicitly resonates with this threshold for detecting law's constraining impact, see Scharf 2009; and Scharf and Williams 2010. These studies interview former US legal advisers from the past thirty years, and find multiple examples where – at the urging of such advisers – American policymakers decided to *forgo* the use of force or other policy preferences in order to better comply with international law. See also Franck 1990: 4, who emphasizes that in 1988 the US Defence Department wanted to seize missiles on a ship in the high seas headed to Iran, but the State Department protested because of international legal concerns, and the missiles were allowed to pass.

Despite its insights and influence,[13] there are also limits to Chayes's investigation that this book seeks to address. To show that law constrained the choices of US leaders during the missile crisis, Chayes cites statements indicating that these men were influenced more by *moral* concerns (i.e., that a surprise attack against Cuba would be inconsistent with US values) than by legal factors (i.e., that a surprise attack would be prohibited by international law). While Chayes admits that their concerns were expressed in moral terms, he argues "it is hard to believe" leaders were unaware of the legal overtones of these terms.[14] And, if leaders were unaware of the overtones, Chayes implies this is unimportant because, regarding the use of force, legal norm and moral precept express "the same deep human imperative."[15] However, while it may be "hard to believe" that leaders are unaware of the legal overtones of any moral concerns they express in a crisis, this study assumes more explicit evidence is needed to show they felt bound by international law and were influenced by law in their decision-making. I discuss what this evidence would look like later below. Finally, while legal norms and moral precepts may express a similar "human imperative," I seek in part to assess the extent to which international law is understood by leaders as distinct from moral concerns.[16] One reason for drawing this distinction is to help address the realist criticism, famously leveled against Chayes's study by former US Secretary of State Dean Acheson, that international law is not really law but a "body of ethical distillation."[17]

Another important work in early scholarship is Louis Henkin's book *How Nations Behave*. In it, Henkin assesses the role of international law in four crises.[18] In each case, the legal rules he studies are different, while the effect he examines is the same, namely the influence of law on the national policy and decision-making process of the state at issue.[19] Henkin's method suggests that

---

13 See e.g. Wheeler 2004, which draws on Chayes's study and assesses whether his conclusion about law's constraining effect also applies to the more recent example of NATO's bombing campaign over Kosovo and Serbia in 1999.

14 Chayes 1974: 39–40.

15 As Chayes argues, it does little justice to ourselves or to the leaders who struggled with one another and with their own consciences during the missile crisis "to try to package" the two aspects of legal norm and moral precept "into neat, analytically separate components" (1974: 40).

16 On the differences between international law and morality, see Hart 2012: 227–232.

17 Acheson 1996: 107.

18 The four cases are the Suez crisis of 1956 (where, Henkin argues, the law worked, then failed, but was vindicated); the trial of former Nazi Adolph Eichmann by Israel in 1960 (where the law failed to prevent Israel from kidnapping Eichman in Argentina); US reaction to the Cuban missile crisis (where the law had other influences); and American involvement in Vietnam from 1954 to 1973 (where uncertain law had uncertain effects).

19 1979: 242–243. Put another way, Henkin's "independent variable" is the specific international legal rule that arises in each case, while his "dependent variable" is the national policy and decision-making process of the state at issue.

different rules will often be relevant in different uses of force, and one does not have to study cases with the same rule present in each case to study what role, if any, law played in these cases.[20] This book draws on his approach by analysing key aspects of Britain and Canada's participation in the Korean War and Afghan Conflict. These key aspects involve international legal rules relating to the prohibition on the use of force and its exceptions, and the treatment of captured individuals. However, as we will see, different specific rules from each category are relevant to different aspects of Britain and Canada's involvement in the wars, and to each conflict.

In addition to its methodological insight, *How Nations Behave* is analytically relevant. Unlike the descriptive focus of Hoyt and the ASIL series, Henkin situates his empirical work in a broader theory of law and foreign policy. In essence, he argues that states obey international law because it is in their long-term interest to maintain order and remain respected.[21] This study does not disagree with this view. However, I will argue in the next chapter that rationalist accounts that emphasize the instrumental use of international law by states do not go far enough. Specifically, they cannot adequately explain why states feel obliged to obey international law, or how such law can help constitute the identities of actors and structure the process by which new rules develop.

Recent International Relations and International Law Research

Following the end of the Cold War, a body of IR and IL work developed in the 1990s and 2000s that also addresses, albeit at times indirectly, the role of international law in the use of force by states.[22] In the field of IR, this work can be located within a larger literature that, in its initial phase, aimed to show that contrary to realist predictions, normative factors matter in world politics and can affect state behaviour.[23] More recently, this larger literature has sought to specify and assess *how* and *why* such factors matter.[24] It is in light of these scholarly developments that this study conceives of international law as a type

---

20 This view (i.e., that one does not have to find historical cases with the same international legal rule present in each case to study what role, if any, law played in these cases) is different from some constructivist IR scholars who study the role of moral norms in international politics. In this literature (e.g., Price 1997, Tannenwald 2007, and Percy 2007a), the same norm (the norm against chemical weapons, nuclear weapons, and mercenaries, respectively) is present, to varying degrees, in each historical case that is studied.

21 Henkin 1979: 48, 51–52.

22 See e.g. Beck 1993; Roberts 1999; Belt 2000; Byers 2002; Roth 2003; Canestaro 2004; Kritsiotis 2004; Wheeler 2004; Kahl 2007; Brunnée and Toope 2010; Dickinson 2010; Peevers 2013; Dill 2015; and McLeod 2015.

23 Finnemore 1993; Katzenstein 1996; and Risse, Ropp and Sikkink 1999.

24 Kratochwil 2000; Tannenwald 2007; and Hurd 2007.

of "normative structure" in world politics,[25] and examines how such law influences the use of force by states and whether a perceived sense of legal obligation helps us understand this influence.

Recent research is more theoretically developed than the older IL literature.[26] However, although such research presumably aims to be *international* in scope and to say something more broadly about how international law affects *different states* when they use force, it nonetheless continues to focus primarily on the actions and views of a single country: the United States.[27] Related to this trend, the breadth of empirical work – particularly comparative work – pursued by recent research is still limited and developing.[28] For instance, in a 1993 book, Robert Beck analyses the role of international law in the US invasion of Grenada.[29] But he does not compare different states or conflicts. Likewise, in a study of NATO's 1999 intervention in Kosovo, Nicholas Wheeler focuses on American targeting policy and one use of force.[30] Similarly, in their book on US legal advisers, Michael Scharf and Paul Williams concentrate on American foreign policy and assess only one case study.[31] Building on this work, Laura Dickinson has noted the lack of qualitative studies in contemporary empirical research, and addressed this by interviewing US military lawyers about their role in armed conflict.[32] Finally, two theoretically innovative books by Janina Dill and Travers McLeod have assessed the impact of international law in, respectively, America's bombing practices[33] and its recent counterinsurgency operations abroad.[34]

Granted, focusing on the US is justifiable insofar as its material power makes it a strong test for studying the normative impact of international law. And conducting single case studies helps us to better understand how law affected

---

25 The term "normative structure" is based on Byers 1999: 8. See also Reus-Smit 2004: 38 (referring to international law as a "normative order"). Broadly, or ontologically speaking, I conceive of international law as a normative structure. Specifically, or theoretically speaking, I define it in the text below, and in the next chapter, as a distinct set of binding rules that are generally determinate.

26 On the theoretical progress and improved debate in the literature on international law and international relations, see Raustiala and Slaughter 2002: 538; Reus-Smit 2004: 16–18; and Hafner-Burton, et al. 2012: 97.

27 See e.g. Beck 1993; Dunlap 2001 and 2008; Roth 2003; Boyle 2004; Wheeler 2004; Carvin 2010; Scharf and Williams 2010; Dickinson 2010; Shue 2011; Warren and Bode 2014; Dill 2015; and McLeod 2015.

28 For scholars who have complained more generally about the lack of adequate empirical research examining how international law affects state conduct, see Keohane 1997: 493–494; Raustiala and Slaughter 2002: 548–549; Hathaway and Koh 2005: 14; and Dickinson 2010: 2.

29 Beck 1993.

30 Wheeler 2004.

31 Scharf and Williams 2010.

32 Dickinson 2010: 2.

33 Dill 2015.

34 McLeod 2015.

a specific case. However, inasmuch as our accounts are being based disproportionately on US practice and single cases, and insofar as America's power makes it different from most other contemporary states, then examining less studied and less anomalous countries, such as Britain and Canada, can help make our theories of international law more comprehensive and, perhaps, accurate.[35] Finally, comparing different wars can strengthen the empirical basis against which our hypotheses are derived and evaluated.

Alongside its US emphasis, recent research has often disproportionately examined how one particular rule – the prohibition on the targeting of civilians – has affected states when they use force.[36] Contemporary studies, such as this book, can learn much from this work. But this focus on the civilian immunity norm has also left analytical and empirical gaps in the literature that I seek to help address. For example, in Wheeler's study of the Kosovo intervention noted above, he usefully observes that one does not have to *quantify* the influence that a legal, political, or military factor had to establish such influence.[37] However, this study posits that, where possible, one should acknowledge which factors were more relevant. This is because current research should aim to learn more about how law affects and *fails* to affect the use of force, rather than assume it has a uniform or consistent impact. And recognizing that law's influence may vary is important because, otherwise, one risks eroding the distinct and independent role that law potentially plays, and supporting the critical view[38] that questions whether one can really show the impact of legal norms in world politics because proponents tend to see the effect of norms wherever they look.

Further, although studies like Wheeler's demonstrate that the civilian immunity norm can affect the use of force by states, this may show the influence of moral and political factors more than international law. For instance, insofar as enemy civilians are seen as innocent non-parties to a war, the civilian immunity norm is arguably morally easy for members of the public to support and politically rewarding for states to respect in war.[39] By contrast, inasmuch as enemy

---

35 I thank Michael Byers for this observation. Similarly, Anthony Clark Arend notes that recent research on the role of law in foreign policy decision-making has "tended to focus on United States foreign policy decision-making." Clearly, he argues, "for any comprehensive theory to be developed, scholars must examine the behaviour of a wide range of states and a variety of issue areas" (Arend 1996: 306).

36 See e.g. Dunlap 2001; Canestaro 2004; Wheeler 2004; Kahl 2007; Petrova 2008; and Dill 2015.

37 Wheeler 2004: 199, 201.

38 See e.g. Sinclair 2010: 160.

39 For a study whose premises resonate with this observation, see Petrova 2008. In it, Petrova stresses the moral equality of enemy civilians, and the role of public opinion and NGOs, in limiting the use of cluster bombs in war. Similarly, in her study of US air targeting, Janina Dill notes that this "comprehensively legalized" issue area is "the easiest specific case for showing" the ability of *jus in bello* rules to effectively regulate armed conflict (Dill 2015: 7).

fighters are viewed as guilty parties to an armed conflict, the international legal rules governing the treatment of POWs and detainees[40] are arguably more difficult for members of the public to support and less politically rewarding for states to respect in war. To this extent, examining these latter rules, as this study in part seeks to do, provides a harder case for assessing whether international law receives low priority in war or whether, alternatively, states adhere to such law in part *because* it is law and less because of moral or political factors.

As a final thought, I should note that although recent research has focused on America and contemporary conflicts, there are some relevant exceptions that this book draws on and seeks to advance. Charlotte Peevers has studied the role of the media in shaping public debate over the international legality of Britain's military actions in the 1956 Suez Crisis and 2003 Iraq War.[41] While this work offers much needed historical insight, it still ultimately focuses on whether international law *constrains* states. I suggest in the next chapter that this limited view fails to adequately recognize the other productive roles that law can play. Prior to Peevers's book, Nigel White studied a number of UK military deployments since 1945 to examine how international law impacts domestic politics in Britain.[42] Although White uses parliamentary debates to assess law's relevance in executive decisions, this study will, as elaborated below, look at additional sources of evidence (e.g., the private views of leaders and officials) and employ further research tools (e.g., interviews) to analyse such decision-making more comprehensively, and strengthen the empirical basis against which the relevance of law is assessed. Finally, while the two studies above indicate that recent research is expanding to consider other countries like Britain, this expansion has not yet included Canada. Thus, by analysing the influence and interpretation of international law in Canada's two most significant uses of force since 1945, this book addresses an important gap in the literature, and broadens the evidentiary scope of existing research.

Research Design, Method, and Premises

In addressing the question of how international law influences state practice regarding the use of force, scholars encounter at least three analytical and methodological challenges. First, despite the important theoretical advances in recent research noted earlier above, current IR scholars are still formulating and assessing our nascent understanding of international law's role in international

---

40 The term "detainee" is controversial because it can suggest a captured individual is not legally a POW. I use the term in this study mainly because Britain and Canada often employ it when referring to such persons.

41 Peevers 2013.

42 White 2009: v, 1–5.

politics, particularly in war.[43] Consequently, the availability of agreed-upon, testable hypotheses is growing but still somewhat limited. To this extent, therefore, developing theory in this area of study is arguably as important as evaluating the analytical propositions that are available. Second, as Michael Byers comments, the "legitimizing and constraining effects of the international legal system are less noticeable than power derived from military strength, wealth or even moral authority, although they are perhaps equally important."[44] Thus, studying the role of international law in the use of force by states requires conceptual tools and research methods that can theorize and detect the influence of this "less noticeable" phenomenon. Such tools and methods, Laura Dickinson agrees, should allow us to better see and tease out the "*subtle* ... psychological, sociological and institutional factors that make obeying the law habitual, legitimate, socially acceptable, convenient, normal, and so on" [emphasis added].[45]

Finally, insofar as international law is, as suggested earlier, a normative structure, and inasmuch as such social facts are not "out there" in the world like physical phenomena such as tanks,[46] then studying international law can only be done indirectly and by proxy. To this extent, then, an issue for researchers examining the impact of law in international politics and the use of force by states is how close they can or should get to their subject.

Some IR studies respond to the above challenges by examining the influence of international law in world affairs and armed conflict over long periods of time, and by focusing on proxy concepts such as institutions or treaties.[47] In

---

43 Within the small but growing body of recent IR work that seeks to explicitly address international law (i.e., as opposed to earlier concepts such as "regimes" or "institutions"), much of the analysis fails to address the use of force by states (e.g., Goldstein et al. 2000; Goldsmith and Posner 2005). And of the work that does in part address this issue, one of the leading studies emphasizes that it does not aim to provide a theory of international law (Reus-Smit 2004: 4).

44 Byers 1999: 6. More generally, Richard Price has similarly noted that, contrary to traditional positivist approaches in IR scholarship that might prioritize only "brute behaviour (compliance or not)," more "*subtle* indicators are needed for a nuanced appreciation of the phenomena of norms" [emphasis added] (Price 2008: 258).

45 Dickinson 2010: 2. In light of the relevance of such factors in explaining compliance with international law, Dickinson wonders why scholars have spent so little time trying to untangle and study them.

46 Jackson 2000: 49.

47 For instance, Stephen Krasner studies the impact of the legal concept of sovereignty over a period of 350 years, and acknowledges that the effects of this concept have been felt over time because it has been embodied in institutions (1993: 238). Further, in his examination of the moral and legal norm proscribing the use of chemical weapons, Richard Price analyses the evolution of the norm over a long period of time, and focuses in part on how the codification of this norm in international agreements helps explain the non-use of chemical weapons in the twentieth century (1995 and 1997). Finally, Beth Simmons studies the impact of international human rights law in world politics over the past sixty years, and considers how the domestic ratification of such treaties has affected the realization of human rights (2009).

contrast to these approaches, this book investigates the influence of international law in the use of force by states over shorter periods of time, and – as elaborated in the next chapter – by theorizing that law plays four observable roles in such situations. In addition to studying the impact of international law, I also analyse whether leaders and officials see this law as a distinct and binding set of legal rules, and whether the legal status of these rules affects their decision-making. In doing so, I seek to take up a conceptually important but methodologically difficult challenge noted by Andrew Hurrell: If we want to understand whether and how states feel bound by international law, then we need to look in far more detail at how this sense of obligation plays out within the policy-making process and among the individual policymakers who are capable of feeling a sense of obligation.[48] Such detailed qualitative analysis, Dickinson has observed separately, will also provide contextual richness that is currently missing in the blunt quantitative approaches of much existing research on international law.[49]

Thus, in examining Britain and Canada's involvement in Korea and Afghanistan, I focus on each state's policy and practice regarding whether and how to be involved in the two wars; the major international legal issues related to each conflict; and the treatment of captured individuals. I centre my analysis on the discourse and conduct of Britain and Canada's main political and military leaders during each war, and the views and actions of important officials.

In conducting this study, five major methodological and analytical premises guide my investigation. First, I use a method of historical reconstruction[50] and process tracing.[51] By this I mean that my primary goal is to better understand how international law influenced Britain and Canada's involvement in the two conflicts, and how key leaders and officials viewed this law. I do not seek to explain this involvement or the wars in their entirety.[52] With this aim in mind, I accept that structures – both material and ideational – as well as human agency will have affected Britain and Canada's participation in the two conflicts.[53] The

---

48 Hurrell 1996: 221.

49 As Dickinson remarks, although recent scholarship has taken a more empirical turn, this "has been largely quantitative, relying on relatively blunt numerical measures that lack contextual richness or detailed analysis" of how and why compliance occurs (Dickinson 2010: 2). See e.g. Ku and Nzelibe 2006; and Hathaway 2002.

50 I use the term "historical reconstruction" with reference to the methodological insights of Hurrell 1996 and Trachtenberg 2006.

51 I use the term "process tracing" with regard to the methodological observations of George and Bennett 2005 and Bennett 2008.

52 On the distinction between understanding and explaining, see Hollis and Smith 1992; and Trachtenberg 2006.

53 Trachtenberg 2006: 6.

roles that I theorize international law can play in the use of force reflect this assumption. On a more practical level, the use of historical reconstruction and process tracing means that I critically examine the evidentiary sources listed earlier with reference to the hypotheses and questions posited in this and the following chapter.[54] Focusing on a micro-level of analysis of the decision-making processes within each of my cases, I look for the observable implications – described more below and in the next chapter – of the impact that I theorize international law has, and the way that I hypothesize it is interpreted.[55] Finally, by comparing the results of this analysis across my cases, I seek to strengthen the inferences that I make, and assess whether the influence and understanding of law varies temporally and by state.

Second, although disagreement exists as to what will constitute evidence of the influence of international law in world politics and the use of force by states,[56] I investigate this influence by theorizing that law can play four observable roles in such situations. I employ this approach, rather than assessing whether there was compliance with international law, because the fact of compliance is not, in and of itself, sufficiently compelling evidence for the influence of law. This is because one could find – through rigorous legal inquiry, for example[57] – that a state is complying with international law without necessarily knowing what role that law played or did not play in this compliance. For instance, a state might be complying for reasons unrelated to international law. And, conversely, one could find that another state is not complying, but fail to see that international law was nonetheless important in the state's decisions in this regard.[58]

In addition, because I am concerned mainly with *how* international law influences the use of force, as opposed to the more pessimistic and less salient

---

54 Trachtenberg 2006: 16, 79.

55 Bennett 2008: 705.

56 This disagreement stems from differing ontological, theoretical and epistemological views on what the threshold is for inferring that law affected a particular outcome, and how observable that threshold should be. Further, as Beth Simmons usefully notes, basic divisions exist over who has the burden of proof: those who believe that international law compliance is pervasive and thus think that it falls to the sceptics to prove otherwise, versus those who view international law as inherently weak and epiphenomenal and require firm causal evidence of its impact (2009: 4).

57 The legal method generally involves (1) defining the legal question that arises from the facts at issue; (2) determining the law relevant to this question; (3) applying the facts to this law; and (4) concluding whether the act or omission at issue was or will be consistent with this law.

58 This is arguably because, as Benedict Kingsbury remarks, "[T]he concept of 'compliance' with law does not have … any meaning except as a function of prior theories of the nature and operation of the law to which it pertains" (Kingsbury 1998: 346). For a survey of the literature on compliance, see Bradford 2005. For a critical assessment of this literature, see Brunnée and Toope 2010: chapter 3.

question of *whether* it does so,[59] I do not focus on disproving what I call "Clausewitz's null hypothesis."[60] The extreme version of this view would assume that, insofar as war is hell and thus incapable of being seriously limited by law, then we should expect to see states use any and all force necessary to meet their political and military objectives in such matters, and treat captured enemy fighters in any way that they believe furthers their goals. Thus, to show that British and Canadian leaders were influenced by international law in Korea and Afghanistan, one would need to find evidence that they did not in fact use any and all force required to meet their political and military objectives in these wars, and did not simply torture or kill any and all enemy fighters that they deemed hostile to their interests. While such an approach may seem extreme, its utility is endorsed by some leading constructivist scholars.[61] Alternatively, a less extreme version of the null hypothesis could suggest that, inasmuch as security concerns and political factors overwhelmingly dominate state relations, then British and Canadian participation in the Korean War and Afghan Conflict can be entirely understood with reference to non-legal considerations.

As noted earlier, this book seeks in part to respond to realist and rational choice ideas about the relative unimportance of international law in world politics and the use of force. To this extent, it will offer evidence against the extreme and less extreme versions of the null hypothesis above. However, I do not focus on disproving this null. Again, although doing so could address *whether* international law influenced Britain and Canada's participation in the two wars, it would inadequately illuminate *how* this law affected such participation. With this latter aim in mind, I thus analyse whether and how key aspects of British and Canadian involvement reflect the four roles that I theorize international law can play in the use of force.

Third, I focus on the major political and military *leaders* of Britain and Canada because, from a legal and theoretical perspective, it is not "states" that decide to use force but "the decision-making elites in states" who act on their behalf.[62] Regarding the decisions of whether and how to use force in Korea and Afghanistan, the analysis of these choices focuses on the prime ministers of

---

59 As Hafner-Burton et al. note, after decades of debate, most IR scholars now acknowledge "that international law, along with other international institutions, plays a substantial role in ordering relations between states." Therefore, they continue, most research now focuses on *how* law influences outcomes (Hafner-Burton et al. 2012: 97).

60 This null-hypothesis is based in part on the following quote from German war theorist Carl von Clausewitz: "Attached to force are certain self-imposed, imperceptible limitations hardly worth mentioning, known as international law and custom, but they scarcely weaken it ... To introduce the principle of moderation into the theory of war itself would always lead to logical absurdity" (quoted in Thomas 2001: 1).

61 See Price 2008: 258–259; and, more generally, Thomas 2001.

62 Arend 1999: 43.

Britain and Canada who were in power leading up to and during these wars, as well as relevant foreign and defence ministers. This is because, in both countries, the decision to use military force rests primarily with the prime minister,[63] and the foreign secretary and defence minister often contribute to these decisions.[64] Focusing on the views and actions of such high-level political leaders is also important because existing qualitative research on international law, war, and foreign policy has insufficiently examined these important actors.[65]

In addition to these political leaders, I also examine the opinions and conduct of some key government officials, because these individuals often advise the above leaders, and their perspective helps contextualize the policy background behind the decisions to use force. Finally, where possible, I assess the input of relevant government legal advisers, because these individuals often provide advice on the international legality of such decisions.[66] Regarding Britain and Canada's policy and practice with respect to individuals captured in the two wars, insofar as these decisions involved strategic considerations, the analysis again focuses on the relevant political leaders in power at the time. However, inasmuch as these decisions also involved operational considerations of military conduct in the field, I also briefly examine the views and actions of some key military leaders and officials in the armed forces and defence departments.

Fourth, I seek in part to understand whether British and Canadian leaders *felt bound* by international law in the Korean War and the Afghanistan Conflict because most interdisciplinary scholars, particularly IL scholars, interested in such topics assume that the binding, obligatory nature of international law – like all law – helps it play a distinct[67] and important[68] role in world affairs. However, despite the significance and prevalence of this fundamental conceptual premise, there is surprisingly little empirical research that assesses its accuracy,

---

63 Heyman 2005: 9.

64 For instance, Janice Gross Stein and Eugene Lang note that Canada's foreign secretary and defence minister are "most responsible for Canada's role in the world" (Stein and Lang 2007: 37).

65 See e.g. Scharf and Williams 2010 (who interview US legal advisers); Dickinson 2010 (who interviews US military lawyers); Dill 2015 (who interviews members of the US armed forces); and McLeod 2015 (who interviews members of the US armed forces, policymakers, and advisers).

66 Wood 2008: 1–2.

67 For scholars who stress the distinctness of international law and the relevance of legal obligation for understanding this specificity, see e.g. Hurrell 1996: 214; Byers 1999: 6; Simmons 2009: 7; and Brunnée and Toope 2010: 9–13.

68 As Travers McLeod notes, while IR scholars have started *empirically* studying how and why international law maters, IL scholars have instead generally *assumed* it is "increasingly independent, central to state decision-making and routinely followed" (McLeod 2015: 6).

particularly regarding war.[69] If international law does influence states when they use force, for instance, we do not really know how political leaders understand this law, or whether a felt sense of legal obligation helps explain this influence. By shedding light on these admittedly difficult questions, this book therefore aims to help break new empirical and conceptual ground in the IR and IL literature, and advance related theoretical debates in these fields.

Regarding these debates, there are good reasons to theorize a priori that – despite the lack of adequate empirical confirmation noted above – the binding nature of international law is what distinguishes it from other phenomena in international relations, such as political, military and moral factors, which are not binding. For example, from a policy perspective, the specificity of international law is significant because, as Jutta Brunnée and Stephen Toope note, in international society "some distinction between legal obligations and broader social norms is crucial in upholding an admittedly weak rule-of-law tradition."[70] As we saw earlier, some realists argue that international law is not really law but a "body of ethical distillation."[71] To address such pessimistic views of international law (i.e., that it does not exist or is not really law), and to help build the rule of law in international society based on public and universal principles, international law, however nascent it may be, should be thought of as distinct from other social phenomena, such as the private moral views of individuals or the political and military considerations of states.

Moreover, from a theoretical viewpoint, the distinctness of international law is analytically important because, as will be discussed in the next chapter, IR scholars of different perspectives have all struggled to articulate what *difference* law makes in international relations, and how that difference should be conceived.[72] Drawing on the thinking of Brunnée, Toope, and other legal theorists, this study believes that legal obligation is what constitutes law's "added value."[73]

Finally, from an empirical perspective, the idea that international law is distinct and binding is supported by the observation that many states and international actors *appear* to act and speak as if it has these traits and should be thought of as law. For example, the constitutions of many countries explicitly incorporate international law into their provisions, the national laws of numerous states refer to international law, and domestic courts often apply international law to decide cases.[74] Similarly,

---

69 For an important exception to this general lack of empirical work on the distinct effects of international law's binding nature and the related concept of legal obligation, see Brunnée and Toope 2010.

70 Brunnée and Toope 2010: 27.

71 Acheson 1996: 107.

72 See e.g. Morgenthau 2006; Goldstein et al. 2000; and Finnemore 2000.

73 Brunnée and Toope 2010: 55. See also Fuller 1958: 630 and 1969: 39–41; and Waldron 1994: 282.

74 Arend 1999: 34.

the leaders of international organizations, from the United Nations to the European Union, frequently refer to international law, and most actors in the international system seem to behave with the understanding that the international legal rules about which they speak are law and not, for instance, nonbinding moral norms or political "rules of the game."[75]

Fifth, as evidence of whether British and Canadian leaders and officials in the Korean War and the Afghanistan Conflict felt bound by international law, I analyse the sources described earlier for "law talk"[76] and employ the concept of legal obligation. If leaders and officials felt bound by law, then we should see them (a) recognize that the use of military force and the treatment of captured individuals were in part legal issues, in that they were governed by a pre-existing set of international legal rules; (b) discuss the extent to which they were legally obligated to consider these rules when deciding whether and how to use force in Korea and Afghanistan, and what policy to adopt for captured individuals; and (c) acknowledge that, due to their legal nature, these rules should be applied reciprocally and equally.[77]

Further, if leaders and officials felt bound by law, they should recognize that breaching relevant international legal rules could lead to civil litigation or criminal prosecution at the domestic or international level,[78] and would require legal justification at the domestic and international level.[79] An example of such recognition is the analysis present in the so-called Torture Memos that circulated among American political and military leaders following the al-Qaeda attacks of 11 September 2001.[80] Finally, leaders and officials should

---

75 Arend 1999: 34. As Hedley Bull notes, that international legal rules are believed to have the status of law "makes possible" an important corpus of international activity that supports the working of international society (2002: 136).

76 Similarly, in Nina Tannewald's study of the impact of the "nuclear taboo" on US military policy and behaviour since World War II, she analyses her evidentiary sources for "taboo talk" (Tannenwald 2007: 69).

77 These observable implications are based in part on Reus-Smit 2004: 38–39.

78 This assumes that, in addition to their obligatory character, international law and legal norms are different from non-legal institutions and norms because violation of the former can lead to formal sanctioning (Simmons 2009: 7).

79 As some constructivists argue, to study the impact of norms, one can assess the justifications that states provide when they violate a norm, and the reactions of other states (Finnemore and Sikkink 1998: 892; and Percy 2007a: 36–37). Expanding on these arguments, one can posit that if a state contemplates that a formal legal justification for its action will be required at the domestic and international level, then it is reasonable to infer that some leaders and officials of the state likely felt bound to consider the international legal rule(s) most relevant to said action.

80 See Greenberg and Dratel 2005. The legal analysis in the memos was highly contorted. However, the documents paid a lot of attention to the domestic and international legal aspects of the US response to the al-Qaeda attacks, and recognized that American officials involved in this response could be held criminally liable.

express concern that decisions regarding the use of force should follow, not precede, any legally significant events related to such force. An example of such concern, or lack thereof, is former US President Ronald Reagan's decision to invade Grenada in 1983 prior to receiving two invitations for assistance from the Governor-General of Grenada and the Organization of Eastern Caribbean States.[81]

Case Selection

With the above key research premises in mind, I now want to elaborate on why this book examines Britain and Canada's involvement in the Korean War and the Afghanistan Conflict, and highlight the benefits and trade-offs of comparing these two countries and these two wars. I do so in part because, although IR scholars are generally expected to justify their case selection, IL researchers examining how international law matters often provide comparatively less explanation of such selection.[82] Thus, by being reflective and transparent about its choice of case studies, this book also aims to help advance the methodological debate between the fields of IR and IL.

Why Focus on Britain and Canada?

I focus on Britain and Canada for four main reasons. First, insofar as existing research disproportionately focuses on the US and single case studies, comparing other less examined states can help make our theories of international law more comprehensive, and strengthen the empirical basis against which our hypotheses are evaluated. Moreover, insofar as we would expect America's closest allies to be motivated primarily by their alliance with the US, and inasmuch as their conduct is thus tied to a hegemonic power that is not seriously constrained by international law, Britain and Canada are harder cases than other Western countries for assessing the influence of international law on the use of force.[83]

Even if one accepts these arguments, one might respond that Canada is a weak case and thus less revealing about the potential impact of international law. Insofar as Canada is perceived as a law-abiding country that pursues its

---

81 Beck 1993: 207.

82 See e.g. Peevers 2013, which provides limited justification for why it examines Britain (as opposed to other states) and the 1956 Suez Crisis and 2003 Iraq War (as opposed to Britain's many other uses of force since 1945). For a more thorough discussion of case selection by an IL scholar examining the effects of invoking the law in armed conflict, see Marxsen 2018: 11–15.

83 I thank Andrew Hurrell for this observation.

interests mainly through multilateral institutions,[84] and if one believes that to show law's relevance one must find examples where international law constrains powerful states that are perceived as less law-abiding, Canada is admittedly a weaker case than – depending on one's legal and historical view – Russia or the US. On the other hand, in the Afghanistan Conflict, Britain and Canada have had fewer financial, technological, and human resources per geographic area of responsibility than the US. As well, during some of the most violent periods of the war, Canada[85] and Britain[86] have suffered more casualties as a proportion of total force size than the US or any other NATO country. In light of these considerations, one could argue that complying with the *jus in bello* is relatively costly for Britain and Canada – i.e., we might expect states with (a) fewer resources per area and per capita of the Afghan population, and (b) more casualties relative to their allies, to be more likely to use disproportionate force and less likely to be tolerant of enemy fighters who have killed their soldiers.[87] To this extent, then, Canada is a stronger case for assessing law's impact in the use of force than one might initially assume.

The second reason I focus on the UK and Canada is because these countries are similar in domestic political composition yet different in external power capabilities, and these traits are analytically and methodologically relevant to this study. For example, Britain and Canada are both parliamentary democracies led by a prime minister who,[88] with the Cabinet, is primarily responsible for conducting foreign relations, entering into treaties, and deciding whether to use

---

84 I thank Jennifer Welsh for this observation. As she has written, Canada's active role in the development of the United Nations following World War II "solidified Canada's reputation as a good multilateralist and upstanding member of a new class of 'middle powers.'" Since then, she continues, Canada's international vocation has "evolved into a more general support for multilateral institutions and the rule of law" (Welsh 2010: 363).

85 In a September 2006 report, the Canadian Centre for Policy Alternatives estimated that, after the US, Canada had sustained the highest number of military deaths as a result of hostile actions in Afghanistan since the original invasion in 2001 (27 of 244 coalition military deaths). Further, since February 2006, when Canadian ground troops were re-deployed to combat operations in Kandahar, Canada had sustained 43 per cent of all military deaths among US allies in the coalition (20 of 47 non-US deaths). Finally, when adjusted for the relative size of troop commitments, a Canadian soldier in Kandahar during this period was nearly three times more likely to be killed in hostile action than a British soldier, and four and a half times more likely to be killed than an American soldier. See CCPA, "Canada's Fallen: Understanding Canadian Military Deaths in Afghanistan" (Ottawa, Sept. 2006).

86 Research from Cambridge University has found that, from around 2008 to 2010, the rate at which UK troops were killed in Afghanistan was almost four times that of US soldiers, and double the rate which is defined as "major combat" ("British Dead and Wounded in Afghanistan," *The Guardian* newspaper website, updated June 2013).

87 I thank David Blagden for this idea.

88 Savoie 2010: 172.

military force. Both states share common history and profess a commitment to the rule of law in their domestic and international affairs.[89] These similarities help this study control the number of domestic variables it must consider in order to understand why and how Britain and Canada used force in Korea and Afghanistan, and to focus on the international political and legal factors involved. Moreover, although similar in the above respects, Britain and Canada are also different in their relative power capabilities, in that the UK possesses nuclear weapons while Canada does not;[90] Britain is a permanent member of the UN Security Council; and it has a larger population,[91] economy,[92] and military.[93] Such differences in power allow this study to assess whether the influence of international law on state conduct regarding the use of force varies with the relative capabilities of a country. And this, in turn, helps me critically assess the idea that powerful states are not seriously constrained by international law when they use force, and the possibility that law plays a different role for less powerful states in such matters.

Third, Britain and Canada's participation in the Korean War and the Afghanistan Conflict is empirically puzzling and politically relevant, and offers potential insights for developing and assessing our theoretical understanding of the role of international law in world politics and armed conflict. As I elaborate in chapters four and five, both countries thought Korea was not strategically important, and their Labour and Liberal governments (respectively) were focused on socio-economic issues following the Second World War. Most

---

89 For instance, regarding the UK, then Foreign Secretary William Hague, in a speech given on 15 Sept. 2010, stressed the need "to strengthen a rules-based international system based on our values," and that the government saw human rights and upholding international law "as essential to and indivisible from our foreign policy objectives."

90 Britain tested an atomic bomb in 1952, and a hydrogen bomb in 1957. By 2001, at the start of the Afghan Conflict, Britain's nuclear deterrent consisted of the Trident II system (Phythian 2007: 30; and Self 2010: 195).

91 Britain's population was about 50 million people in 1950, and 59 million in 2001. Canada's population was about 13.7 million people in 1950, and 31 million in 2001. See www.statistics.gov.uk and www.statcan.gc.ca

92 Following World War II, Britain was insolvent, and its economy was in bad shape relative to the US, Australia, Canada, Sweden, and Switzerland. Relative to the rest of Europe and Japan, however, the UK economy was doing better, and it recovered more quickly. By contrast, Canada emerged from World War II in better economic shape than the UK. In absolute terms, though, Canada's economy was still smaller, and this economic inequality between the two states still existed in 2001.

93 Following World War II, Britain and Canada both demobilized much of their armed forces and decreased their defence spending. However, in absolute and relative terms, Canada did so much more extensively than the UK. See Wood 1966: 17–18; Warner 1993: 99–100; and Self 2010: 39. The military inequality between Britain and Canada, in absolute and relative terms, still existed in 2001.

importantly, the alliance with the US and fear of the USSR do not adequately explain why and how these states decided to use force in Korea, and to support UN activity regarding the crisis. Canada's actions, for instance, are difficult to explain considering that, relative to its small population size,[94] the costs Canada bore by participating were significant,[95] while the domestic benefits that Canadian leaders gained were limited.[96] Canada and Britain's participation in the Korean War, I suggest, cannot be fully understood without reference to normative considerations such as the obligations and rights that leaders believed their countries had under international law.

Similarly, as I elaborate in chapters six and seven, the extensive and costly involvement of Britain and Canada in the Afghanistan Conflict is also not immediately easy to explain in strict national interest terms, narrowly conceived. The US alliance and the perceived threat of al-Qaeda may help explain why the UK and Canada initially used force in Afghanistan. However, it is less clear why these states kept troops in the country for so long, and why they agreed to contribute to the difficult nation-building and counterinsurgency efforts there. As with the Korean War, I contend that Britain and Canada's involvement in the Afghan Conflict cannot be fully understood without reference to normative considerations, such as the rights and obligations that leaders and officials thought their countries had under international law.

Furthermore, because the conduct of states in war became subject to increased legal restrictions in the Geneva Conventions of 1949, and insofar as the influence of international law would be expected to increase over time,[97] one might anticipate that the international legal rules on the treatment of captured individuals should play a greater role in Britain and Canada's involvement in the Afghanistan Conflict (which began in 2001) than in the Korean War

---

94 Canada's population in 1950 was about 13.7 million people. By comparison, the population of the US was about 150.7 million, and the population of the UK was about 50 million.

95 Canada suffered 1,588 casualties in the Korean War, with 516 killed in action or dead on active service (Bercuson 2004). Moreover, after the US and Britain (and not including South Korea's forces), Canada committed the third largest overall contribution of troops, ships, and aircraft to the UN operation in Korea. This contribution was particularly costly considering that following World War II, Canada had demobilized much of its armed forces and decreased its defence spending in absolute and relative terms. Additionally, the Liberal government in power at the time had hoped to focus on socio-economic issues following World War II, and "was profoundly unhappy over the necessity of once again debating warlike moves" and rearmament (Wood 1966: 21).

96 In contrast to World War II, the Korean War generated vastly less public and media interest in Canada (Granatstein and Oliver 2011: 240). This casts doubt on the potential argument that Canada's leaders decided to participate in the war to please their domestic constituencies or the media.

97 For views that the role of international law in armed conflict is more significant today than in the past, see Kennedy 2006 and 2012: 158–162; and Dill 2015: 6–7.

(which began in 1950). As we will see, however, British and Canadian forces in Afghanistan reportedly transferred captured suspected Taliban and al-Qaeda fighters to US and Afghan authorities knowing they could be mistreated or tortured.[98] If this study finds that the role of international law has now changed when the UK and Canada use military force, such a conclusion will be relevant to policymakers and citizens in these countries and abroad. As Commonwealth states that have done much to develop and promote international law, Britain and Canada tend to pride themselves on their normative commitment and perceived historical fidelity to this institution.

The final reason for focusing on Britain and Canada's participation in Korea and Afghanistan is that there is extensive data available about the policies and actions of these states in the first and, to a lesser extent, second war.[99] Because the Korean War occurred in 1950–53, government documents and private papers about this conflict are available in edited collections and the archives of the UK and Canada. Memoirs and diaries of leaders and officials also refer to the conflict.[100] Good secondary literature on the war exists, although this work often focuses on the US.[101] A valuable study of Canada's diplomacy in the crisis is available, and it refers to extensive interviews with former leaders and officials.[102] There is also a helpful two-volume official history of Britain's part in the crisis.[103]

Regarding the Afghanistan Conflict, because adequate archival material is not yet available, the data is drawn in part from the elite interviews described earlier with key leaders and officials from Britain and Canada. In these interviews, I aimed to understand which factors influenced Britain and Canada's participation in the Afghan war, and to assess the hypotheses described in this and the following chapter. I also "triangulated" the findings from my review of relevant news articles, parliamentary statements, UN documents, public speeches, and the memoirs and diaries of important political figures and government officials.[104] In addition, there

---

98 See "Afghanistan – Detainees Transferred to Torture: ISAF Complicity?" (Amnesty International, 2007); "All Afghan Detainees Likely Tortured: Diplomat," CBC news (18 Nov. 2009); "Military Told to Heed Abuse Claims," *Toronto Star* (25 Feb. 2010); and "Afghan Torture Allegations Erupt in UK," CBC news (21 April 2010).

99 Selecting data rich cases is important because we learn more from case studies that let us answer more questions about the case, and the more data we have the more questions we can answer, and the more assessments we can make of our hypotheses and theories (Van Evera 1997: 79).

100 See e.g. Attlee 1954; Truman 1956; Pearson 1973; and Pickersgill 1975.

101 See e.g. Rees 1964; Foot 1987; MacDonald 1986 and 1990; Cotton and Neary 1989; and Kaufman 1997.

102 Stairs 1974.

103 Farrar-Hockley 1990 and 1995.

104 See e.g. Meyer 2005; Goldenberg 2006; Campbell 2008; Chrétien 2008; Martin 2009; Blair 2010; and Graham 2016.

are formal investigations,[105] official reports,[106] parliamentary proceedings,[107] and court cases[108] in Britain and Canada that refer to oral evidence, witness statements, and government documents related to the Afghanistan Conflict. Finally, although the secondary literature on Britain and Canada's involvement in the conflict is still developing, this also means that this book helps contribute to this growing body of research.

Why Focus on the Korean War and the Afghanistan Conflict?

Insofar as there are good theoretical and empirical reasons for focusing on British and Canadian uses of force in the post World War II period, the next issue is which uses of force should be studied. Since 1945, the UK and Canada have allied to use military force in five armed conflicts: the Korean War of 1950–53; the Gulf War of 1991; the Kosovo Intervention of 1999; the Afghanistan Conflict of 2001–14; and the Libya Intervention of 2011.[109] Focusing on the Korean War and the Afghanistan Conflict has three advantages.

First, examining these two wars allows me to focus in part on the international law regarding the treatment of POWs, and examining such law is relevant to this study's overall aim. For example, while Canada did not employ regular ground forces in the Gulf War, the Kosovo Intervention, or the conflict in Libya, and the UK did not send regular ground forces to the latter two wars, both states did send regular troops to Korea and Afghanistan. Moreover, in both wars, Canadian and British troops captured enemy fighters, and the leaders of both states had to make decisions on the POW policies that their country should adopt. These empirical details are theoretically relevant. As suggested earlier, in contrast to examining the civilian immunity norm in armed conflict, studying the impact of the international legal rules on captured prisoners

---

105 See e.g. Canada's Military Police Complaints Commission 580-page report of 27 June 2012 (which examined whether certain MPs failed to investigate the detainee transfer orders of commanders in Afghanistan from May 2007 to June 2008), and Britain's Iraq Inquiry (which makes some helpful reference to the Afghan Conflict).

106 See e.g. the report entitled *Independent Panel on Canada's Future Role in Afghanistan* (January 2008), and the UK House of Commons Defence Committee, *Operations in Afghanistan*, HC 554, 17 July 2011.

107 See e.g. Canada's Special Committee on the Canadian Mission in Afghanistan.

108 See e.g. the main Afghan detainee cases in Canada (the three Federal Court decisions *Amnesty International Canada et al v. Attorney General of Canada et al*, 2008 FC 162, 2008 FC 336, and 2008 FCA 401); and in the UK (*R (Evans) v SS Defence*, [2010] EWHC 1445 (Admin); *Hussein v. Secretary of State for Defence*, [2014] EWCA Civ 1087; and *Mohammed v. Ministry of Defence*, [2014] EWHC 1369 (QB)).

109 This list does not include cases where Britain has used force without Canadian participation, or the peacekeeping operations to which the UK and Canada have contributed since 1945.

may provide a harder case for assessing whether international law receives low priority in war or whether, alternatively, states adhere to such law in part *because* it is law and less because of moral or political factors. Furthermore, POWs are an issue in international politics that has seen the greatest efforts at legal codification and regulation over the years, and yet their treatment is far from being a success story.[110] To this extent, therefore, studying the impact of the rules on POWs and captured individuals is a strong test for assessing the success and progress of the *jus in bello* regime more generally,[111] and for analysing whether and how normative structures influence state behaviour in world politics and war.

Second, because I seek to examine how international law influences the use of force by states in the post World War II period, focusing on the Korean War and the Afghanistan Conflict allows me to investigate a wide chronological spectrum of this period. Moreover, because these two wars represent opposite ends of this time period, focusing on these conflicts helps me assess whether the impact of international law in the use of force increases over time.

Finally, insofar as the Korean War was a conventional "industrial" armed conflict involving large numbers of soldiers and mechanized fighting,[112] while the Afghanistan Conflict represents a less conventional counterinsurgency war involving a smaller number of soldiers fighting lightly armed Taliban and al-Qaeda fighters,[113] then studying these two wars allows me to examine whether international law impacts state practice across different types of armed conflict. And this, in turn, will help make our theories of the role of international law in the use of force more comprehensive, and broaden the empirical basis upon which our conclusions are derived.

Notwithstanding such advantages, the trade-offs of focusing on Britain and Canada's involvement in these two conflicts should also be acknowledged. Foremost among them is the observation that, by examining the behaviour of only two states in two wars, this study is limited in its ability to generalize its findings broadly to other states or conflicts.[114] Further, insofar as the UK and Canada are members of a particular Western group of liberal-democratic states,[115] the conclusions I derive are likely limited to countries within and across this group. On the other hand, the in-depth analysis that this book conducts offers important insights into the nature and impact of the relevant international legal rules on

---

110 Scheipers 2010: 1–2.

111 Ibid.

112 Johnston 2003; and Granatstein and Oliver 2011.

113 Egnell 2011; and Griffin 2011.

114 Bennett 2008: 719.

115 Armstrong, Farrell and Lambert 2009: 139.

the two states and two wars that are studied. And this in turn offers rich material for analytical development and refinement.[116]

It should also be acknowledged that, in both the Korean War and the Afghanistan Conflict, the dominant Western actor was the United States,[117] not the UK or Canada. Further, the key factors determining British and Canadian policy in these wars were often non-legal in nature, such as the perceived security threat of the USSR (in Korea) and al-Qaeda (in Afghanistan), as well as Britain and Canada's political and economic relationship with America. Nonetheless, this study takes the view that, for all the reasons described thus far, it is still theoretically and empirically fruitful to analyse how, *despite* an environment of US dominance and perceived security threats, international law influenced Britain and Canada's use of force in Korea and Afghanistan.

---

116 Ragin 2004: 135.

117 As noted by the leading study of Canada's diplomacy in the Korean War, Canadian leaders knew that, in the end, the parameters of the crisis in Korea would be determined by the US (Stairs 1974: 39). And, as observed by the official account of Britain's participation in the war, the US "features frequently in [this] account due to the scale of American influence and participation" (Farrar-Hockley 1990: viii).

3 Theoretical Framework

With the analytical observations of the previous chapters in mind, the following further develops my theoretical framework for examining the influence and understanding of international law during Britain and Canada's participation in the Korean War and the Afghanistan Conflict. In essence, readers who are less familiar with the specialized debates about international law in the fields of International Relations (IR) and International Law (IL) will note that IR scholars tend to focus on the *effect* – or lack thereof – of law in world politics, while IL researchers often care more about law's *nature*. Readers who are aware of these debates will appreciate this book's genuine interdisciplinary approach, and the innovative suggestion that, although theorists often focus narrowly on its constraining influence, international law can actually play four broad and understudied roles in world affairs and the use of force. Moreover, this book helps advance existing research by assessing the conceptually fundamental but methodologically challenging idea that law plays these roles in part because leaders and officials feel bound by its distinct rules.

How Should We Conceive of International Law – as Rules or as Process?

In theorizing how to conceive of international law, some IL and IR scholars argue that it is best understood as process,[1] and that it is indeterminate.[2] For instance, Rosalyn Higgins argues that law refers to "specialized social processes" that include many things besides rules, and that international law is "a continuing process of authoritative decisions" directed towards the attainment

---

1 McDougal 1953, Reisman 1992, Higgins 1994, and Wheeler 2004.
2 Wheeler 2004, and Sinclair 2010.

of certain declared values.[3] Moreover, in his study of the 1999 Kosovo Intervention, Nicholas Wheeler relies on Higgins's theory and argues that international law is not a fixed category: there is not a "single correct way of applying the law in particular cases because it is open to different interpretations, each of which is plausible in its own terms."[4] In contrast to these perspectives, this book takes the view that – although international law is not *only* a set of rules, and non-legal factors are a part of law as practiced in the real world – international law is better thought of as a distinct set of binding rules that are generally determinate.

This view is adopted for three reasons. First, if one defines international law as process, and then studies how it influences the decision-making process of states regarding the use of force, confusion could arise about what, in the words of political scientists, the "independent variable"[5] is, and how it can be distinguished from the decision-making process itself. As Higgins acknowledges, one of the reasons "traditionalists" define international law as rules is that, if it is regarded as more than rules, international law can become "confused with other phenomena, such as power or social or humanitarian factors."[6]

Second, if one defines international law, as Higgins does, as the "entire" authoritative decision-making process,[7] this risks turning international law into everything and nothing, thus making it difficult to define theoretically and observe empirically. This also risks supporting the critical view that international law is whatever powerful states say it is. For example, while the law as process view is influenced by legal scholars Harold Lasswell and Myres McDougal and the New Haven school of policy science of the 1950s and 1960s, Friedrich Kratochwil notes that this policy-oriented approach to international law is "in constant danger of becoming just an apology for the policies and preferences of the most powerful."[8]

Finally, if one does not believe that international legal rules are, at some level, determinate and independent of individual interpretations of them, it is difficult for one to objectively assess state behaviour against these rules because

---

3 1994: 2, 4–6.

4 2004: 191.

5 Here, the independent variable would be interntional law, and the dependent variable would be the decision-making process or policy outcome.

6 1994: 3.

7 1994: 2.

8 2000: 42. In a 1955 article, McDougal found – without even considering the views or actions of other states – that the US could legally engage in atmospheric nuclear tests "in preparation for the defence of itself and its allies and of all the values of a free world society" (1955: 361). Commenting on this view, Michael Byers notes that, despite its usefulness as a justification for US foreign policy, the policy-oriented approach accords no independent influence to international law. And, by expanding the ambit of analysis to include a plethora of non-legal factors, this approach leaves "the *specificity* of international law behind" [emphasis in original] (2010: 614).

every assessment will, in Wheeler's words, be "plausible" and thus consistent with almost any argument one seeks to advance. For instance, Wheeler himself begins his study of the Kosovo Intervention by stating that "NATO's compliance with the laws of war represents an important case for exploring how far law influences the conduct of military operations."[9] The issue of compliance, however, is in part a *legal* issue that presupposes one can determine whether NATO *is* complying with the laws of war. And this presupposes that, at least at some minimal level, international law is determinate and exists independent from individual interpretations of it.[10]

International Law in the Study of International Relations

While the above considered the specific issue of how international law should be conceived, the following addresses the more general question of how it has been theorized by three major IR approaches, namely realism, neo-liberal institutionalism, and constructivism. In explaining each theory, I draw out their shortcomings for understanding how law impacts the use of force. And this, in turn, sets the stage for outlining the key insights of an interactional lens.

1. Realist Approaches

While neo-realism tends to ignore international law,[11] and contemporary realist thought has had less to say on the topic when compared to other IR theories,[12] it is important to note that early or classical realism explicitly addresses international

---

9 2004: 189.

10 From an IL perspective, the issue of compliance presupposes that one can (1) define the legal issue most relevant to NATO's targeting activities (e.g., the question of whether "dual-use" civilian-military targets can be bombed); (2) determine the *jus in bello* rule most relevant to NATO's targeting activities; (3) apply the relevant facts to this rule; and (4) conclude whether NATO did or did not comply with the *jus in bello*. These steps essentially comprise the legal method, and Wheeler uses this method in his study. What helps make this method systematic is the fact that it is not random or idiosyncratic. It does not rely, for instance, on Higgins's view that individuals will each "know" which legal claims are intellectually supportable and which are not (1994: 7), based, presumably, on a sense of professional duty. Instead, the legal method relies on a commitment to the four steps above, and an awareness that one's reasoning is potentially subject to external review.

11 For instance, neo-realist Kenneth Waltz does not discuss international law in his often-quoted *Theory of International Politics*. The only references Waltz makes to "laws," notes Martti Koskenniemi, are to the laws of logical relation and scientific explanation (2000: 28).

12 As Casper Sylvest observes, although the continued growth of interdependence and the proliferation of international institutions and international law have fostered an interest in re-integrating IL and IR scholarship, so far "realism has had little to contribute to this interdisciplinary development" (2010: 410).

law.[13] Despite this engagement, however, classical realism is generally dismissive of the significance of international law in world politics and the use of force by states. This is because, from a realist perspective, states are engaged in a continuous and self-interested struggle for material power. They are portrayed as homogenous actors principally concerned with survival in an anarchic system, as having fixed and conflicting goals, and as focusing primarily on the distribution of military capabilities.[14] And international law, as will be seen below, is thought of as political and primitive when compared to domestic law, and as weak and ineffective in constraining the struggle for power and the use of military force.

For example, E.H. Carr argues that international law differs from domestic law in that it is the law of an undeveloped community, as it lacks a judiciary, an executive, and a legislature.[15] Similarly, Hans Morgenthau contends that international law is "primitive" because, unlike domestic law, it has no central law-enforcing authority.[16] Despite these shortcomings, both scholars still think international law exists and should be considered law. For Carr, this is because law's relation to politics is the same in the international and domestic sphere.[17] As in the domestic sphere, where law is a function of political society, Carr argues international law "is a function of the political community of nations."[18] However, due to the embryonic character of this community and the tiny number of its members, international law is "weaker" than domestic law, and its rules, however general in form, will always "be aimed at a particular state or group of states." For this reason, Carr notes, power is "more predominant" in international than in domestic law, and international law is "more frankly political" than other branches of law.[19]

Because Carr emphasizes the weakness of international law and the importance of power, one might conclude, as Chris Reus-Smit does, that realists believe international law is not really binding.[20] Such a conclusion reflects some

---

13 Early realist thinkers, such as Hans Morgenthau, Carl Schmitt, and E.H. Carr engaged with the topic of international law in part because of a perception among some scholars in the 1930s and 1940s that the study of international relations focused too much on legal and moral considerations, and not enough on power and political factors. Indeed, because many early realists (e.g., Morgenthau and Schmitt) had been trained in law but were nonetheless sceptical of the empirical and political relevance of international law, some contemporary scholars argue that the discipline of IR emerged out of an intellectual split between two groups of German, British, and American lawyers during this period (Byers 2010: 613, and Koskenniemi 2000 and 2002).

14 Legro and Moravcsik 1999.

15 2001: 159.

16 2006: 285.

17 2001: 160.

18 2001: 165.

19 2001: 165.

20 2004: 16.

realist views, such as former US Secretary of State Dean Acheson's remarks that international law is not really law but a "body of ethical distillation."[21] Yet other realists express more subtle positions. Morgenthau, for instance, refers to international law as "a system of binding legal rules."[22] And Carr argues that international law exists to the extent that there is an international community which recognizes it as binding, and notes that, by some "process," international law has come into being.[23]

On the other hand, while Morgenthau and Carr may think of international law as binding, their interest in the concept of obligation is limited. For example, Carr believes an explanation of *why* international law is regarded as binding "cannot be obtained from the law itself."[24] This book disagrees, and argues later below that law has distinct internal traits that help explain its "felt sense" of obligation. Instead, Carr thinks law is regarded as binding "because, if it were not, political society could not exist and there could be no law."[25] An explanation of *how* or by what process international law is regarded as binding, Carr says, is the job of "the social psychologist."[26] Thus, insofar as researchers are interested in whether states feel bound by international law, and how this sense of obligation plays out in the policy-making process regarding the use of force, then realism provides limited insight into these analytical concerns.

Consistent with their belief that international law is primitive and weak, realists emphasize that it is also ineffective. As Morgenthau stresses, to recognize that international law exists is not to assert "that it is as effective a legal system as the national legal systems are and that, more particularly, it is effective in regulating and restraining the struggle for power on the international scene."[27] This limitation of international law, Morgenthau thinks, is particularly obvious with respect to the use of force by states. As he argues, unlike the numerous "typical" treaties that regulate issues such as postal services, the "spectacular instruments" of international law such as the UN Charter "are indeed of doubtful efficacy (that is, they are frequently violated) and sometimes even of doubtful validity (that is, they are often not enforced in case of violation)."[28]

Realist approaches usefully draw our attention to the possibility that the content and objectives of international law can reflect the unequal distribution of power in the international system, and the interests of strong states. However,

---

21 1996: 107.
22 2006: 285.
23 2001: 160, 165.
24 2001: 160.
25 2001: 164.
26 2001: 160.
27 2006: 285.
28 Ibid.

there are at least four problems with how realism conceives of international law and its role in the use of force. First, realism does not offer an adequate account of how law can come to constrain strong states.[29] As shown by the studies of international law and the United States noted earlier,[30] contrary to what realism might predict, international law can help restrain the behaviour of powerful states. Moreover, as Chris Reus-Smit notes, strong states do not invariably ignore international law, and when they choose to deliberatively violate it they do so knowing this will incur political costs.[31]

Second, insofar as realism emphasizes that international law simply reflects the distribution of power and the interests of strong states, it cannot adequately explain how weaker states use law to influence strong states and shape outcomes in world politics.[32] For example, during the Kosovo Intervention, France used its interpretation of the relevant *jus in bello* targeting rules to influence the administration of US President Bill Clinton. In France's view, NATO planes should not be allowed to bomb bridges on the Danube River due to the disproportionate risk this would cause to civilians. Some key US Air Force Generals disagreed. Nonetheless, in the end, Clinton decided not to allow American pilots to bomb the Danube bridges.[33]

Third, realism does not offer an adequate account of how legal rules that are originally institutionalized for reasons of power and interest can, over time, influence events in ways that may conflict with such power and interest. For instance, in his study of the historical impact of the concept of sovereignty, Stephen Krasner finds, consistent with realist predictions, that the view that the 1648 treaties of Westphalia were a turning point in history is "wrong," and the forces behind the elimination of universal institutions and the primacy of the sovereign state "were material."[34] However, he also acknowledges that the "impact of ideas about the sovereign state system has been felt over time because they have been embodied in institutions."[35] In other words, Krasner's study indicates that a legal rule that is institutionalized for reasons of power and interest can nonetheless have independent subsequent impact, by "precluding a range of alternative political practices."[36]

---

29 Reus-Smit 2004: 17.

30 See e.g. Chayes 1974, Beck 1993, Dickinson 2010, Scharf and Williams 2010, Dill 2015, and McLeod 2015.

31 2004: 17.

32 Reus-Smit 2004: 17–18.

33 This example is drawn from Wheeler 2004, and Richmond 2016b.

34 1993: 235, and 261.

35 1993: 238.

36 Goldstein and Keohane 1993: 22.

Finally, by arguing that international law is primitive because it lacks domestic institutions such as a legislature, judiciary, and centralized enforcement, realism articulates assumptions that potentially misrepresent what it is that makes international law "law," and what explains its "felt sense" of obligation. As Brunnée and Toope argue, when we assume that the defining features of domestic law, and by extension of all law, are formal enactment by a superior authority, application by courts, and centralized enforcement, we are bound to see international law as a poor cousin.[37] We also risk misjudging how law operates in international society and obscuring its potential power. As will be discussed later below, what distinguishes law from other types of social ordering is not form, but adherence to specific criteria of legality.[38]

2. Neo-liberal Institutionalism

Like realists, neo-liberal institutionalists tend to emphasize material factors and the agency of states. Nonetheless, they are less dismissive of the significance of international law in world politics.[39] This is because they tend to see states as rational egoists who recognize that their long-term interests are often best achieved through co-operation, and that – because of problems such as cheating, insufficient information, and high transaction costs – co-operating often requires regimes or institutions, including formal ones such as international law.[40] Neo-liberal institutionalism helps us to better understand why states co-operate under conditions of anarchy, particularly regarding "secondary" issues such as trade.[41] However, its assumption that states are rational actors who use international law instrumentally fails to adequately explain why states feel obliged to obey this particular "institution," and how international law can help

---

37 2010: 6.

38 Brunnée and Toope 2010: 6.

39 Indeed, neo-liberal scholars have often called for greater collaboration between the fields of IR and IL, and have written on the challenges and opportunities of such interdisciplinary cooperation. See Abbott 1989; Slaughter Burley 1993; Keohane 1997; and Slaughter, Tulumello and Wood 1998.

40 Robert Keohane defines institutions as "persistent and connected sets of rules (formal and informal) that prescribe behavioural roles, constrain activity, and shape expectations" (1989: 3).

41 In "Legalization and World Politics," a leading neo-liberal account of international law described in the text below, six of the seven case studies address secondary issues such as third-party dispute resolution, the European Union's legal system, international monetary affairs, and world trade. Regarding trade, Frederick Abbott's study of the North American Free Trade Agreement is indicative of the neo-liberal view more generally (2000: 519–547). In it,

constitute states' identities and influence their conduct, particularly regarding the use of military force.

A leading neo-liberal account by Judith Goldstein et al. argues that "legalization" is a particular form of institutionalization characterized by three criteria: obligation; precision; and delegation.[42] By offering these criteria, these scholars are seeking to clarify why institutions that are legalized are different from those that are not, and how such legalized institutions can be identified in IR and IL research. As such, they are responding to a gap in the literature of both disciplines, namely the fact that scholars, including constructivists, have not yet adequately explained the "distinctiveness" of international law. However, the articulation by Goldstein et al. of obligation, precision and delegation – and the concept of legalization more generally – also have limits, particularly with respect to conceptualizing how international law influences the use of force by states.

For example, regarding obligation, Goldstein et al. argue that "fully legalized institutions bind states through law: their behaviour is subject to scrutiny under general rules, procedures, and discourses of international law."[43] With respect to this study, insofar as Canada and Britain are bound to obey the international law on the use of force (*jus ad bellum*) and the international law of armed conflict (*jus in bello*), these two "institutions" meet the obligation criterion. However, to draw this conclusion, and to note that the use of force by Canada and Britain and the conduct of these states in war are thus "subject to scrutiny" under the above institutions, is only to describe the legal nature of these institutions. We would not, for instance, be saying anything about why or how Canada and Britain may feel obliged to obey them.

Martha Finnemore and Stephen Toope have expanded on this observation. They argue that, while the issue of obligation and how norms affect state behaviour is arguably the central concern of lawyers and political scientists, neo-liberal institutionalists offer no theory of obligation and seem remarkably incurious about this concept.[44] To be fair, neo-liberals do try to show how the principle of *pacta sunt servanda*[45] and the degree to which states consent to

---

Abbott examines the trend of states using "hard" law (precise, binding obligations with third-party delegation) in international trade governance, and explains this trend in the context of NAFTA. Consistent with the summary of neo-liberal institutionalism in the text above, he finds that law reduces intergovernmental transaction costs and private risk premiums; promotes transparency and provides corollary participation benefits; and restrains strategic political conduct.

42 Goldstein et al. 2000.

43 2000: 387.

44 2001: 748.

45 Neo-liberal institutionalists define *pacta sunt servanda* as "the principle that rules and commitments contained in international legal agreements are regarded as obligatory, subject to

treaties yield differing levels of obligation.[46] However, it is true that this explanation is very formal and contractual,[47] and prioritizes the agency of states. Moreover, to say states feel bound by international law because they have consented to it only begs the question of why states see consent as obligation-inducing.[48] While neo-liberals tend to respond to this issue by arguing that the binding nature of legalized regimes stems from the legitimacy of the background institution of the international legal system, they have limited analytical resources to explain why states attach legitimacy to this system.[49]

Because the neo-liberal institutionalist account of obligation is formal and contractual, and relies on state consent, it cannot adequately explain how customary international law, which does not operate on the basis of explicit state consent or formal agreements, arises or helps influence state behaviour.[50] And, to the extent that the use of force by states and the conduct of states in war are regulated by treaties *and* custom, then the neo-liberal account is ill equipped to theorize how international law influences state practice in these issue areas.[51]

Regarding the second criterion of legalization, precision, Goldstein et al. argue that legalized institutions "demonstrate a high degree of precision, meaning that their rules unambiguously define the conduct they require, authorize, or proscribe."[52] This study agrees that the idea of precision helps us in part to understand why a rule or institution should be thought of as distinctly legal in nature. Indeed, many IL scholars, such as Jutta Brunnée, Stephen Toope, and Thomas Franck, argue that concepts similar to precision – for instance clarity or, as noted earlier, determinacy – are key traits of international law that help explain its ability to promote adherence and its perception of legitimacy among international actors.[53]

---

various defences or exceptions, and not to be disregarded as preferences change" (Abbott et al. 2000: 409). A more simple definition is that "promises are binding."

46   Abbott et al. 2000: 408–412.

47   Finnemore and Toope 2001: 748–749.

48   Hart 1994: 224.

49   Reus-Smit 2004: 20.

50   Finnemore and Toope 2001: 748–749.

51   In light of the significance of customary law on the topic of the use of force, Finnemore and Toope argue it is not surprising that the Legalization collection contains but the briefest discussion of security issues, for they simply cannot fit within a narrow judicial and treaty-based perspective on law's influence in world affairs (2001: 747).

52   2000: 387.

53   Brunnée and Toope argue that one of the eight internal features of law is "clarity": citizens must be able to understand what is permitted, prohibited or required by law – the law must be clear (2010: 26). Similarly, Franck contends that one of the four "objective factors" that can assist in the identification of legitimate rules of international law is "determinacy": the ability of a rule to convey a clear message (1990: 25, 32, 35–36; and 1998: 713).

Where this book disagrees with Goldstein et al., however, is with their application of the precision criterion to the *jus ad bellum*, and the implication that this branch of international law is not a fully "legalized" institution. As an example of precision, Goldstein et al. argue that the 1999 Kosovo Intervention is an instance "of a decline in the precision of rules governing armed interventions, as challenges to the old norms of territorial sovereignty have mounted."[54] This view, however, fails to recognize the extra-legal justifications that all but one NATO member offered for the intervention,[55] and the clear criticisms that many states made of the unilateral bombing campaign.[56] These actions suggest that most states believe the key *jus ad bellum* rules – i.e., the general ban on the use of force and the two limited exceptions to this ban, self-defence and authorization from the UN Security Council – are not ambiguous and not declining in precision.

And yet, while the Kosovo Intervention may not suggest that the key *jus ad bellum* rules are declining in precision, it cannot be ignored that, regardless of the extent to which these rules are viewed as unambiguous by most states, NATO members still chose to use military force against the Federal Republic of Yugoslavia (FRY) in perceived violation of these rules. This indicates that the intervention is less an instance of a decline in the precision of the key *jus ad bellum* rules, and more an example of a decline in the fidelity of NATO member states to these rules, and in the degree to which these states feel bound to limit their actions to conform with the views of other states about these rules. And this, in turn, suggests two points relevant to this inquiry. First, while the precision of a rule helps us in part to understand why the rule should be thought of as legal in nature, this precision alone does not predict whether the rule will inspire fidelity among those to whom it is addressed. Second, the precision of a rule and the impact of the rule may not be correlated.

In terms of the third criterion of legalization, delegation, Goldstein et al. argue that "legal agreements delegate broad authority to a neutral entity for

---

54 2000: 386.

55 Contrary to the idea that the key *jus ad bellum* rules – i.e., the general ban on the use of force and the two exceptions to this ban, self-defence and Security Council authorization – were perceived as ambiguous at the time of the Kosovo Intervention, most NATO members agreed on the nature and scope of these rules, and were worried about acting in contravention of them. Only one member, Belgium, justified NATO's action as lawful humanitarian intervention. Generally speaking, the other members did not justify the intervention on legal grounds, and were satisfied that their action was illegal but legitimate for moral and political reasons. See Richmond 2016b.

56 In response to the Kosovo Intervention, China, Russia, India, Namibia, Belarus, Ukraine, Iran, Thailand, Indonesia, South Africa, and the 133 developing states of the G77 all reaffirmed that unilateral humanitarian intervention was illegal and unacceptable, and the UN General Assembly in September 1999 voted 107 to seven (with 48 abstentions) in favour of a resolution rejecting "unilateral coercive measures." See Byers and Chesterman 2003: 184.

implementation of the agreed rules, including their interpretation, dispute settlement, and (possibly) further rule making."[57] Regarding this study, the UN Charter arguably delegates primary authority to the Security Council to implement two of the three key *jus ad bellum* rules (i.e., the general ban on the use of force and one of its exceptions, Council authorization).[58] Moreover, the International Court of Justice (ICJ) has interpreted and pronounced on *jus ad bellum* rules in some of its case law.[59] However, insofar as the Security Council is a political entity whose decisions are often made on non-legal grounds, it is not a "neutral entity" in the way a court is.[60] And, while the ICJ is arguably neutral, states have generally consented to the Court interpreting and pronouncing on *jus ad bellum* rules on a case by case basis, and have not delegated "broad authority" to it for implementing these rules. Finally, to the extent that the second exception to the ban on the use of force, self-defence, is primarily interpreted by states,[61] this also suggests that the key *jus ad bellum* rules do not meet the delegation criterion.

Similarly, regarding the *jus in bello*, states party to the Geneva Conventions have delegated some monitoring duties to the International Committee of the Red Cross,[62] and the ICRC is neutral in that it does not take sides in a war.[63] Moreover,

---

57 2000: 387.

58 See e.g. Article 2(4) (which prohibits the threat or use of force); Article 24(1) (which states that UN members confer on the Security Council primary responsibility for maintaining international peace and security); and Article 39 (which states that the Council shall determine breaches of the peace, and how to restore international peace and security).

59 Among others, see *Case Concerning Military and Paramilitary Activities in and against Nicaragua (Nicaragua v. United States of America), Merits*, [1986] I.C.J. Rep. 14; and *Legality of the Threat or Use of Nuclear Weapons, Advisory Opinion*, [1996] I.C.J. Rep. 226. For a study of the role and record of the ICJ in the settlement of disputes which are likely to affect international peace, see Akande 2003.

60 The political nature of the Security Council is suggested by: (1) the existence of the veto power outlined in Article 27 of the Charter, which ensures that the five permanent members of the Council cannot have action mandated by that body used against them or their allies; and (2) the fact that Article 39, which assigns to the Council the duty of determining threats to international peace, grants the Council significant discretion regarding the types of situation with which it deals, and the measures it can take. See Lowe et al. 2010: 13–14.

61 Article 51 of the Charter states that nothing in that treaty shall impair the inherent right of self-defence if an armed attack occurs against a UN member, until the Security Council has taken measures to maintain international peace.

62 Article 9 of the 1949 Geneva Convention on Prisoners of War states that the provisions of the treaty "constitute no obstacle to the humanitarian activities which the [ICRC] … may, subject to the consent of the Parties to the conflict concerned, undertake for the protection of [POWs]."

63 See *Statutes of the International Red Cross and Red Crescent Movement*, adopted at the 25th International Conference, Geneva, 1986. As the *Statutes* note, "to enjoy the confidence of all, the Movement may not take sides in hostilities or engage at any time in controversies of a political, racial, religious or ideological nature."

various ad hoc international criminal tribunals[64] and the now permanent International Criminal Court (ICC) have interpreted and pronounced on the international criminal law aspects of some *jus in bello* rules. However, the ICRC is not a court, and any monitoring it conducts is generally subject to the consent of the states at issue. Moreover, while ad hoc tribunals and the ICC have interpreted and pronounced on the individual criminal responsibility of violating certain *jus in bello* rules, states arguably believe that the primary authority to implement the *jus in bello* still lies with them.[65] To this extent, therefore, it is questionable whether this area of law meets the criterion of delegation.

In sum, while the *jus ad bellum* and *jus in bello* arguably meet the obligation criterion of the concept of legalization, and the *jus ad bellum* meets the precision component, this assessment tells us very little about why or how these branches of international law may or may not influence state practice regarding the use of force. Moreover, both areas of law arguably fail to meet the delegation criterion. Consequently, these three criteria, and the concept of legalization more generally, offer limited theoretical guidance for this inquiry. In contrast, constructivist scholars offer more promising ideas, as will be seen below.

3. Constructivist Perspectives

A third major IR theory that engages with the topic of international law is constructivism. While constructivists have much to say on the social nature of international relations, four claims should be highlighted for present purposes. First, insofar as structures shape the behaviour of states and other actors, normative and ideational structures are as important as material structures.[66] As Alexander Wendt argues, shared knowledge embedded in normative and ideational structures affects how actors respond to their material environment, and inter-subjective beliefs shape actors' identities and, in turn, their interests.[67] Second, if one wants to understand the behaviour of states and other actors, one needs to understand how their social identities condition their interests and actions.[68] Such identities must be seen as social, Chris Reus-Smit notes, because they are *learned* – i.e., actors are in a constant dialogue with the prevailing

---

64 Following World War II, International Military Tribunals were established in Germany and the Far East. Moreover, in the 1990s, the UN Security Council created the International Criminal Tribunal for the Former Yugoslavia, and the International Criminal Tribunal for Rwanda. See Kittichaisaree 2005: 17–27.

65 The Rome Statute of the ICC emphasizes that the Court's jurisdiction shall be "complementary" – i.e., not concurrent or primary – to national criminal jurisdictions. See Kittichaisaree 2005: 281.

66 Reus-Smit 2004: 21.

67 1995: 73, 1999: 92–138.

68 Reus-Smit 2004: 22.

norms of legitimate agency that constitute role identities to define their senses of self.[69] Third, although constructivists grant relevance to the constitutive power of normative and ideational structures, they stress that these structures only exist because of the "routinized practices" of knowledgeable social agents, which makes them human artifacts amenable to change.[70] Finally, constructivists emphasize the significance of "reasons for action."[71] From this perspective, a reason is both an individual or collective motive (e.g., the reason why NATO bombed the FRY), and a justificatory claim (e.g., the reason NATO gave for bombing the FRY).[72] Thus, reasons have internal (or private) and external (or public) aspects. Importantly, normative and ideational structures are constitutive of actors' reasons in both senses.[73]

Because constructivists see normative structures as important to understanding international relations, and as constitutive of actors' reasons for action, they tend to portray international law as one such normative structure, and a site for "communicative" struggles over legitimate identity and rightful behaviour. By prioritizing normative structures, and granting international law with "productive" power, constructivists thus take us beyond the materialist and state-centred focus of realism and neo-liberal institutionalism, and the weak or functional roles that these theories allocate to law. Furthermore, by demonstrating that in addition to its productive force, international law can also constrain state behaviour, including the behaviour of powerful states in war,[74] constructivists show that international law can play an important role in world politics.

Notwithstanding its insights, however, constructivism's engagement with international law suffers from at least two limitations. First, although constructivists frequently cite international law and draw on legal philosophy, they are unclear about what exactly distinguishes international law from other phenomena in world politics, and how legal norms differ from political and moral norms. For example, some constructivists ponder whether any valid distinctions exist between legal and non-legal norms;[75] some think that categorical differences do not exist but that legal argument is a particular kind of "practical reasoning";[76] while still others believe legal norms are indeed distinct.[77] Reflecting these

---

69 Ibid.

70 Wendt 1987, and Reus-Smit 2004: 22.

71 Kratochwil 1989.

72 Reus-Smit 2004: 22.

73 Through processes of socialization, Reus-Smit argues, reasons shape actors' definitions of who they are and what they want, and through processes of public justification they frame logics of argument (2004: 22).

74 Wheeler 2004.

75 Finnemore 2000.

76 Kratochwil 1989 and 2000.

77 Katzenstein 1996, and Arend 1996 and 1999.

disagreements, constructivists have tended to distinguish among norms based on *function* rather than substance – e.g., between regulative norms, which order and constrain behaviour, and constitutive norms, which create new actors, interests, or categories of action[78] – and have said much on the *effects* of norms in the use of force by states, particularly the effects of moral norms.[79] However, constructivists have had less to say about the particular *nature* of legal norms and international law, and the distinct impact these phenomena may have in the use of force.[80]

The second limitation of constructivism's treatment of international law is that, like neo-liberal institutionalism, it has not adequately explored the concept of legal obligation.[81] And yet if the binding nature of international law is what distinguishes it from other phenomena in international relations, then a fuller account of obligation is critical for understanding how law operates. Constructivism's inadequate engagement with obligation is unfortunate because, as a social theory of international relations, it can increase our understanding of the concept.[82] For instance, by showing how international law can help socialize actors and shape their interests and choices, constructivism supports the view that law's obligatory effect results from a commitment to law that is generated by, as will be discussed below, adherence to specific criteria of legality.[83] In turn, by engaging with such "interactional" legal theory, constructivism will be better able to discern the distinct impact of international law.

The "Interactional" Approach

In their book *Legitimacy and Legality in International Law*, Brunnée and Toope draw together the legal theory of Lon Fuller and the ideas of constructivism to advance a pragmatic view of how international legal obligation is created and maintained. In doing so, they help us to better understand the distinct role that law can play in international society. In sum, they make three main arguments relevant to this study. First, legal norms can only arise in the context of social norms based on shared understandings. Second, internal features of law are crucial to law's ability to promote adherence, to inspire "fidelity." Third,

---

78 Finnemore 2000.

79 Price 1997, Thomas 2001, Tannenwald 2007, and Percy 2007.

80 While some constructivists have written on the nature of legal norms and legal reasoning (Onuf 1989, and Kratochwil 1989), these scholars have not focused on the distinct impact these phenomena may have in the use of force by states.

81 While some constructivists have discussed the concept of legal obligation (Reus-Smit 2003 and 2004: 41–43), this work has not focused on the concept in the context of the use of force by states.

82 Brunnée and Toope 2010: 12.

83 Ibid.

legal norms are built, maintained or destroyed through a continuing practice of legality. These three elements, Brunnée and Toope argue, produce a distinctive legal legitimacy and a sense of commitment among those to whom law is addressed.

First, legal norms can only arise in the context of pre-existing social norms based on shared understandings. Drawing in part on two of the constructivist propositions noted earlier – i.e., that normative structures shape the behaviour of actors, but that structures only exist because of social agents – Brunnée and Toope argue that shared understandings are collectively held background knowledge, norms or practices which are generated and maintained through social interaction.[84] On the one hand, they note, agents generate and promote particular understandings, while on the other, once in existence, shared understandings become "structures" that shape how actors perceive themselves, form interests, and argue.[85] Social norms, Brunnée and Toope contend, emerge when societies generate shared understandings of the need for norms, and deeper shared understandings of the need for specific norms to guide behaviour.[86] Such understandings may include merely a basic acceptance of the need for law in a society, or they may be more substantive and value-laden.[87] However, *interactional* law only emerges when shared understandings become fused with a "practice of legality," rooted in Fuller's eight criteria described below, and embraced by a "community of practice" that adheres to those criteria in day-to-day decision-making.[88] Importantly, these criteria are not simply a list for checking whether a particular legal form – e.g., a treaty – is law. Instead, Brunnée and Toope argue, the criteria "come alive" when actors reason with rules in continuing processes of mutual engagement, creating a "community of legal practice."[89]

Second, internal features of law are crucial to understanding its ability to promote adherence. As was noted earlier, some IR perspectives assume that the defining features of law are found in its form – for example, in enactment by legislature, application by courts, and central enforcement. In contrast, Brunnée and Toope argue that what distinguishes law from other types of social ordering is not form, but adherence to eight specific criteria of legality: generality, promulgation, non-retroactivity, clarity, non-contradiction, not asking the impossible, constancy, and congruence between rules and official action.[90] First, legal norms

---

84 2010: 64.
85 2010: 65.
86 2010: 86.
87 Ibid.
88 Ibid.
89 Ibid.
90 2010: 6.

must be general, meaning that they prohibit, require, or permit certain conduct. Second, they must be promulgated, and thus accessible to the public, enabling citizens to know what the law requires. Third, law should not be retroactive, but prospective, enabling citizens to take it into account in their decision-making. Fourth, the law must be clear – that is, citizens must be able to understand what is permitted, prohibited or required by law. Fifth, law should avoid contradiction, not requiring or permitting and prohibiting at the same time. Sixth, law must be realistic and not demand the impossible. Seventh, law's requirements of citizens must remain relatively constant. Finally, there should be congruence between legal norms and the actions of officials operating under law.[91] When these eight criteria are met, law will tend to attract its own adherence.[92] Fidelity is generated and obligation felt, Brunnée and Toope argue, because adherence to the eight criteria of legality produces law that is legitimate in the eyes of the persons to whom it is addressed.[93]

Finally, legal norms are built, maintained or destroyed through a continuing practice of legality. In other words, international law is created and maintained through interaction. The idea of continuous practice is not new to IL scholars, as it is central to customary international law and is also involved in the evolution of treaties. However, Brunnée and Toope argue that a very particular kind of practice is required to make and sustain international legal norms, namely "inclusive practice" that adheres to the criteria of legality.[94] Importantly, and perhaps counter-intuitively, this perspective reveals the weakness of some customary and treaty rules.[95] However, by appreciating law's grounding in social interaction, interactional theory also identifies the locus of law's power to shape human behaviour, through the generation of fidelity, rather than through reciprocal advantage, as rationalists might posit, or through coercion, as realists might argue.[96]

---

91 2010: 26.

92 Fuller called this effect "fidelity to law" (1958: 630, and 1969: 39–41). Others refer to it as law's "loyalty-advantages" (Waldron 1994: 282), or the "self-bindingness" of law. Brunnée and Toope call it law's "obligatory quality," and argue that legal obligation is thus best viewed as an "internalized commitment" and not an externally imposed duty matched with a sanction for non-performance (2010: 27).

93 2010: 27.

94 2010: 54.

95 This weakness, Brunnée and Toope contend, "lies not in the absence of enforcement or other attributes of 'hard' law, but in a legitimacy deficit resulting from limited participation in norm building and insufficient attention to the requirements of legality" (2010: 54). An example of this, they argue, is the anti-torture norm, as there is inadequate congruence between the norm as codified and the actions of officials operating under the norm (2010: 220–270).

96 An example where such fidelity has been generated, Brunnée and Toope contend, is the prohibition on the use of force and its exceptions (2010: 271–349).

Positing the Four Roles of International Law

Drawing on the analytical insights of constructivism and interactional theory described above, and employing additional philosophical reflections and historical examples I have derived from the IR and IL literature, I theorize that international law can play four main roles in world politics and the use of force. I elaborate on each role below.

1. International Law Helps Constitute the Identities of Actors

International law helps constitute the identities of the actors at issue, whether these are states, at the macro level of analysis, or individual leaders and soldiers at the micro level of study.[97] As we saw earlier, constructivists often emphasize the "productive" power of normative structures such as international law, and argue that normative structures can help shape actors' identities and interests, and act as a site for "communicative" struggles over legitimate identity and rightful behaviour. Thus, insofar as the *jus ad bellum* and *jus in bello* are normative structures, we would expect them to have productive influence on the actors bound by their rules, and to help shape the identities and interests of these actors. For instance, regarding the *jus in bello*, Chris Reus-Smit notes that when states negotiated the laws of war, "they were not just formulating and enshrining a set of rules, they were enacting and proclaiming a particular conception of legitimate statehood and rightful state action."[98] Thus, regarding this inquiry, to the extent that Canada and Britain were involved in negotiating the Geneva Conventions following World War II,[99] we would expect them to believe that, as well as formulating and enshrining a set of legal rules, they were also enacting and proclaiming a particular conception of legitimate statehood and rightful state conduct.

2. International Law Helps Regulate the Political and Military Practice of Actors

In addition to its constitutive role, international law helps regulate the political and military practice of actors leading up to and during the use of force. By regulate, I mean that international law helps govern or control such political and military practice by law – i.e., by a felt sense of legal obligation – and less by material self-interest, as rationalists might suggest, or by coercion, as realists

---

97   I thank Jennifer Welsh for the thoughtful discussions on whether and how law shapes state identity, particularly Canada's domestic and international outlook.

98   2004: 20. For illuminating new research on the construction of compliance in the drafting of the 1949 Geneva Conventions, see Rapp 2021.

99   See Best 2002.

might argue. As noted above, constructivists often stress the productive power of normative structures such as international law. This is in part a reaction to neo-liberal institutionalists, who tend to argue that, inasmuch as norms and ideas affect state behaviour at all, this influence is best conceived as a constraint on such behaviour.[100] However, as we saw earlier, constructivists also argue that international law can constrain state action regarding the use of force, including the conduct of strong states.[101] Further, even constructivists who stress the constitutive nature of most international legal norms acknowledge that *jus ad bellum* and *jus in bello* norms *regulate* the use of force.[102] Thus, if we accept that these branches of international law help regulate the use of force, then the question becomes how we should define the concept of "regulate."

The primary definitions of "regulate" are (1) to govern or control by law, or (2) subject to, especially, legal restrictions.[103] The first definition is more active and socio-political, in that the words "govern" and "control" suggest that, if international law regulates the use of force by states or the conduct of states in war, then international law *does* something to these activities. The second definition is more descriptive and legal, in that stating that the use of force by states and the conduct of states in war are regulated by international law because said uses of force and conduct are "subject to legal restrictions" only restates a description about the legal nature of these activities.[104] Thus, for purposes of studying the impact of international law in the use of force, the active definition of regulate is more useful.

There are three elements to this definition: to govern; or control; by law. I assume that govern means to control or influence (a person, a function, the course of events, etc.), and control means the power of restraining.[105] Most importantly, I posit that in the active definition of regulate, it is crucial that a person, function, or course of events is being governed or controlled in part by *law* – i.e., by a felt sense of legal obligation – and less by material self-interest, as rationalists might suggest, or by coercion, as realists might argue. By employing the active definition of regulate, and the interactional concept of obligation, I

---

100 See e.g. Goldstein and Keohane 1993: 20, and Simmons 2009: 5, 8.

101 As discussed earlier, constructivists such as Chris Reus-Smit argue that realists cannot adequately explain why and how international law can constrain state action regarding the use of force.

102 Kratochwil 2000: 48.

103 *Canadian Oxford Dictionary.*

104 Similarly, recall that neo-liberals argue that one of the three criteria of legalization is obligation, and define obligation by noting that "fully legalized institutions bind states through law: their behaviour is *subject to scrutiny* under ... international law" [emphasis added] (Goldstein et. al. 2000: 387). In other words, the neo-liberal definition of obligation is more descriptive than active.

105 *Canadian Oxford Dictionary.*

am theorizing that Canada and Britain's participation in the Korean War and the Afghanistan Conflict was governed or controlled, at least in part, by *jus ad bellum* and *jus in bello* rules; and it is a felt sense of legal obligation among at least some policymakers that did this governing or controlling.

3. International Law Permits and Legitimates Certain Conduct

International law can play a third role in that it permits and legitimates certain conduct that otherwise might not be allowed. As Nina Tannenwald argues, in addition to constitutive and regulative influence, norms also have permissive effect.[106] "This refers," Tannenwald notes, "to the way norms ... by serving as focal points, selectively divert our normative gaze."[107] For instance, she argues that the "nuclear taboo," the norm she studies, labels some weapons as "weapons of mass destruction" and others as "conventional" and thus legitimate.[108] Similarly, because much of what the *jus ad bellum* and *jus in bello* do is prohibit certain conduct (such as the unilateral use of non-defensive force, or the inhumane treatment of captured enemy fighters), it can be easy to forget that these branches of international law also permit certain conduct (such as the use of force in self-defence or when authorized by the Security Council, and the intentional killing of combatants in war or the unintentional killing of civilians in war if this is militarily necessary and proportional).

However, by permitting this conduct, it is important to remember that the *jus ad bellum* and *jus in bello* are also helping to legitimate the use of armed force and the killing of human beings in certain circumstances.[109] And there is something about international law that makes it especially appealing to leaders when justifying and explaining why and how their countries have gone to war. As David Kennedy notes, when states use force, law has become the mark of legitimacy, and legitimacy has become the currency of power.[110]

4. International Law Helps Structure the Development of New Rules and Legitimate Behaviour

International law helps structure the development of new international legal rules and new legitimate behaviour for states, international institutions, and

---

106 2007: 46.

107 Ibid.

108 In this case, Tannenwald argues, the nuclear taboo draws our attention to one particular "normative injunction" (i.e., weapons of mass destruction), while obscuring other "facts" about the world and shielding other practices from attention (i.e., the continued use of conventional weapons) (ibid).

109 For a critical elaboration of this argument, see Jochnick and Normand 1994: 49–95.

110 Kennedy 2005 and 2006.

other international actors. As previously noted in the analysis of constructivism and of interactional theory, shared understandings are collectively held background knowledge, norms, or practices that are generated and maintained through social interaction. Moreover, while agents generate and promote particular shared understandings, once in existence, shared understandings become normative and ideational structures that can create new categories of action and act as a site for communicative struggles over legitimate identity and behaviour.

Therefore, to the extent that the *jus ad bellum* and *jus in bello* represent particular shared understandings among a "community of legal practice" (to use Brunnée and Toope's term), then we would expect these branches of international law to help structure the process by which agents within this community seek to generate and promote new legal norms or new legitimate practices. For example, when state leaders and officials negotiated the collective security provisions of the UN Charter and the mandate of the Security Council during and following World War II, the nature and scope of these negotiations were shaped in part by shared understandings of pre-existing treaties such as the Covenant of the League of Nations and the Kellogg-Briand Pact of 1928.[111]

---

111 This theoretical idea is based on empirical observations in Lowe et al. 2010: 9–13.

4 Britain and the Korean War

Drawing on the theoretical insights outlined in the previous chapters, I now turn to the empirical component of this book. The following chapter examines the United Kingdom's participation in the Korean War. As we will see, in essence this early Cold War crisis highlighted the tension between Britain's traditional perception of itself as an independent world power, and the emerging recognition of its reliance on the United States and on the international institutions that the two allies helped create following the Second World War. Balancing this tension by becoming extensively involved in a bloody civil war in a strategically unimportant and distant Asian country, I will suggest, is not immediately easy to explain. And equally intriguing is that throughout this involvement, international law helped define and shape Britain's possible course of action, and the justifications that could be made for its conduct. Before we explore that story, though, let me briefly outline the origins of the conflict, and how the United Nations got involved.

Brief Background to the Korean War

Following the Second World War, Korea was occupied by the United States south of the 38th parallel and by the USSR north of this line.[1] After bilateral independence talks proved fruitless, America asked the United Nations to become involved. A UN-supervised election was held in South Korea in May 1948,[2] and the General Assembly recognized the Republic of Korea (ROK). A separate election was held in the north, and the Democratic People's Republic of Korea (DPRK) was recognized by the USSR and its allies. The last Soviet and

---

1 Farrar-Hockley 1990: 4–6.
2 MacDonald 1990: 10–11.

American troops were withdrawn in December 1948 and June 1949, respectively.[3] Six months later, in January 1950, US Secretary of State Dean Acheson remarked in a speech that America's defence perimeter in the Pacific did not extend to Korea, and that such areas would have to depend for their defence upon themselves and the United Nations.[4]

On 25 June 1950, DPRK forces crossed the 38th parallel to unify the peninsula by force. ROK forces virtually collapsed and retreated south. In response, US President Harry Truman announced on 27 June that America would provide military support to South Korea, and deploy the Seventh Fleet to protect Formosa (Taiwan) from potential Chinese Communist attack.[5] Truman also sought UN support for an international military operation to restore peace in the area. To this end, the US secured three key resolutions from the Security Council. The first, entitled *Complaint of Aggression upon the Republic of Korea*, was passed on 25 June. It determined that North Korea's attack constituted "a breach of the peace," and called for the cessation of hostilities and withdrawal of DPRK forces to the 38th parallel.[6] The second resolution of 27 June noted that North Korea had not withdrawn, and recommended that UN members furnish such assistance "as may be necessary" to repel the attack and restore peace in the area.[7] The third resolution of 7 July recommended that UN members providing help do so under a unified US command.[8] America was able to pass these resolutions because the USSR was boycotting the Security Council at the time for refusing to recognize Communist China.[9]

Truman named US General Douglas MacArthur as UN commander. American forces arrived in Korea in July, and 39 other countries – including Britain and Canada – contributed to the effort.[10] Following initial military setbacks, UN forces recaptured South Korea in September.[11] By late October, they had reached China's border. This occurred under a "rollback" doctrine, whereby US leaders decided that, rather than restoring the status quo, UN forces would cross the 38th parallel and unify Korea by force. As will be seen later below, the

---

3 Farrar-Hockley 1990: 25–26.

4 Rees 1964: 18.

5 Truman 1956: 357–358.

6 UNSC Resolution 82 (25 June 1950), [S/1501].

7 UNSC Resolution 83 (27 June 1950), [S/1511].

8 UNSC Resolution 84 (7 July 1950), [S/1588].

9 The USSR had been boycotting the Security Council since January 1950 for its refusal to recognize Communist China's representative in the place of Nationalist China's representative following the 1949 military victory of the Communist Party of China over the Chinese Nationalist Party (Kuomintang) in the Chinese civil war of 1948–52.

10 For details of these offers of assistance – which ranged from naval, air and ground forces, to food and medical supplies – see the 1950 *Yearbook of the United Nations* at 226–228.

11 Farrar-Hockley 1990: 143–158.

UK helped draft a General Assembly resolution which sought to provide UN support for this crossing.

In response to these developments, China intervened in the war. Over the coming months, hundreds of thousands of Chinese soldiers (described as "volunteers" by China's leaders) entered Korea and helped push back the UN force. Seoul was captured in January 1951, and retaken by UN troops in March. Truman dismissed MacArthur in April, because the general had publicly criticized the president and obstructed peace negotiations. Opposing forces became divided along the 38th parallel, and engaged in trench fighting for two more years.[12] Difficult peace talks continued during this time, due to disagreement over the future demarcation line, and the ideologically charged issue of whether communist prisoners who did not want to return home should nonetheless be repatriated. An armistice was finally signed on 27 July 1953, after Joseph Stalin's death in March led to a slight relaxing of Cold War tensions.[13] Almost seventy years later, the war continues today through a "cold peace," with thousands of US soldiers stationed in South Korea, and approximately one million North and South Korean troops confronting each other along the demilitarized zone.[14]

Why Britain Participated in the Korean War

In the language of political scientists, the puzzle to be explained is why Britain participated so extensively in the Korean War when a number of factors suggested it would not do so. For instance, many UK officials initially believed that the Korean crisis should be solved by other states,[15] and throughout the war political and military leaders thought Korea was not strategically important.[16] Further, Britain was encumbered with other imperial concerns at the time, such as an anti-colonial uprising in Malaya,[17] and the Labour government of Prime Minister Clement Attlee was focused on improving the social and economic

---

12 Young and Kent 2004: 151; and Farrar-Hockley 1990: vii.

13 MacDonald 1990: 87.

14 Cumings 2001: 474–475; "N Korea under Scrutiny as Obama Visits Border," Al Jazeera, 25 March 2012; and Clint Work, "How to Constructively and Safely Reduce and Realign US Forces on the Korean Peninsula," 38 North, 25 Aug. 2020.

15 Farrar-Hockley 1990: 1.

16 See e.g. *Extract from the Conclusions of a Meeting of the Cabinet*, 29 Nov. 1950, [CAB 128/18], doc. 79 in Yasamee and Hamilton 1991: 215–221, where Prime Minister Attlee said "it was of the first importance that the [UN] should not be trapped into diverting a disproportionate effort to the Far East," and while UN "operations in Korea had been important as a symbol of their resistance to aggression … Korea was not in itself of any strategic importance to the democracies and it must not … draw more of their military resources away from Europe and the Middle East."

17 Farrar-Hockley 1990: 1.

conditions of a country still impoverished and in debt from World War II. Despite these considerations, Britain ultimately participated, at great financial and human cost,[18] in a divisive and bloody civil war located on the other side of the world.[19] Scholars generally cite three reasons: (1) the perceived security threat of the USSR and the assumption that it was ultimately responsible for North Korea's attack; (2) a belief that strengthening the UK's relationship with the US was the best way to address the Soviet threat, and that fighting in Korea would further this goal; and (3) the view that, because of Britain's prior experience with Germany, aggression must not be appeased.[20]

Britain, like the US, was surprised by North Korea's attack on South Korea,[21] and viewed it as primarily a Soviet initiative.[22] This view was influenced by the development of Britain's foreign and defence policy following World War II. Since 1945, Attlee's government had feared Soviet expansion and believed that a close alliance with the US was vital to Britain's security and to maintaining its position as a great power.[23] To meet the Soviet threat, Foreign Secretary Ernest Bevin[24] aimed to harness US power towards British interests and commit America to the containment of communism.[25]

By 1947, Bevin's approach was paying off. The president had declared the "Truman Doctrine" – i.e., that the US would support all free peoples resisting communism; and the US had agreed to help finance Europe's recovery through the Marshal Aid Program.[26] And still, Bevin was so keen to ensure that the

---

18 Regarding the financial cost of the Korean War, Britain's defence spending rose from £700m in 1948 to £1,112m in 1951–52, increasing its share of the budget from six per cent to ten per cent and committing the UK to a higher expenditure per head on defence than even in the US (Self 2010: 39). In terms of the human cost of the war, British casualties were 1,078 killed in action, 2,674 wounded, and 1,060 missing or taken prisoner (Hickey, 21 March 2011).

19 On the violent nature of the conflict, Bruce Cumings notes, "Eventually the Korean War will be understood as one of the most destructive and … important wars of the twentieth century. Perhaps as many as 4 million Koreans died, three-quarters of them civilians" (Cumings 2001: 475).

20 These factors are emphasized, to varying degrees, by Lowe 1989; MacDonald 1990; Yasamee and Hamilton 1991; Farrar-Hockley 1990; and Self 2010. For a historical overview of Britain's foreign and domestic concerns during the early Cold War, see Deighton 2012.

21 MacDonald 1990: 19.

22 As Sir Pierson Dixon, Deputy Under Secretary of State, observed on 26 June 1950, Soviet involvement was "virtually certain." Moreover, as the UK Ambassador in Moscow remarked in a 30 June telegram to Kenneth Younger, deputy Foreign Secretary, the "attack was certainly launched with Soviet knowledge and almost certainly Soviet instigation." See FK 1015/62, calendar to doc. 2; and NS 1029/4, doc. 8, both in Yasamee and Hamilton 1991: 4, 18–20. Privately, ministers and officials generally agreed with these views (Yasamee and Hamilton 1991: vi).

23 MacDonald 1990: 1; and Self 2010: 77–82.

24 Bevin was Foreign Secretary from 27 July 1945 to 9 March 1951. He was ill for much of his tenure during the Korean War, and Kenneth Younger, his deputy, often acted in his place.

25 Edmonds 1986: 21; and Self 2010: 80.

26 Morgan 1989: 270; and Self 2010: 81.

US did not fall back to an isolationist policy that, during the Berlin crisis of 1948–49,[27] he allowed American bombers to be based on UK soil without any formal guarantee of consultation before their use.[28] Bevin regarded the NATO alliance of 1949 as a great achievement, and evidence of America's commitment to Europe.[29]

In sum, by 1950, the Labour government had moved "into the economic, political and military orbit" of the US.[30] As such, Callum MacDonald, a leading authority on Britain and the Korean War, argues that when Truman drew the line against communist aggression in this conflict, the UK participated to consolidate the Anglo-American alliance and resist such aggression.[31]

Britain's desire to strengthen the US alliance is indeed crucial to understanding its response to the Korean War. However, scholars like MacDonald sometimes prioritize this objective to such a degree that they portray the UK's reaction as "inevitable."[32] This deterministic and teleological view is inaccurate. As we will see, Britain's decisions to send military forces to Korea were not inevitable, particularly its decisions to send ground troops. More generally, to understand the UK's response to the crisis, one must recall that four other goals were important to Britain at the time. As a government paper noted in April 1950, these objectives included (1) maintaining Britain's position as a world power; (2) maintaining the Commonwealth structure; (3) consolidating the Western democratic system; and (4) ensuring that the Middle East and Asia were stable and friendly.[33] Indeed, because this paper listed the first two goals *ahead* of maintaining the UK's special relationship with the US and resisting Soviet Communism, some scholars argue that Britain was more concerned with prestige and status than with security.[34] To this extent, non-material considerations and Britain's self-identity are thus also relevant to understanding its response to the Korean conflict.

Further, Britain's pursuit of these four other goals during the conflict sometimes led it to adopt policies that clearly ran *against* the perceived wishes of the US. The UK's support for India's diplomacy regarding the conflict often

---

27 For a description of the Berlin crisis, see Young and Kent 2004: 92–93.

28 MacDonald 1990: 3.

29 Young and Kent 2004: 128–130.

30 MacDonald 1990: 4.

31 MacDonald 1990: 5. For another study that resonates with MacDonald's argument, see Truscott 1985.

32 MacDonald 1990: 4.

33 These objectives are listed in *British Overseas Obligations*, 27 April 1950, Prime Minister's Office (PREM) 8/1202, PUSC (79), cited in Phythian 2007: 38.

34 Jong-yil 1984: 304. Similarly, Anne Deighton notes that from 1945 to 1955, the defining bipartisan trait of UK foreign policy was "to sustain the image and the reality of great powerdom" (2012: 113).

frustrated US officials.[35] Moreover, Britain's legal recognition of Mao's Communist China, its trade interest in that country,[36] and London's financial interest in Hong Kong often put UK and US leaders at odds with each other. In addition, public opinion – both in Britain and internationally – as well as emerging understandings of the relevant tenets of international law and Britain's relationship to that law, affected the discourse and actions of the Attlee and Churchill governments during the conflict. Finally, as we will see, a perception of obligation under the UN Charter and Geneva Conventions shaped the thinking and decisions of these governments regarding the war, and the justifications that could be made for the UK's actions.

Following its decision to fight in Korea, Britain had three objectives in the conflict.[37] First, it aimed to contribute to the UN's military effort. Second, it sought to prevent the conflict from spreading elsewhere. And third, absent a clear military victory, Britain wanted to end the fighting with a negotiated settlement. The main military problem for the UK, as we shall see, was how to support the UN's goals without diverting scarce resources from areas seen to be more vital to Britain's strategic interests, such as Western Europe, the Middle East, and Hong Kong.[38]

The Four Roles of International Law in Britain's Use of Force in Korea

Britain's involvement in the Korean War illustrates the four roles that international law can play when states use force: (1) it helps constitute the identity of actors; (2) it helps regulate their conduct; (3) it permits and legitimates certain actions; and (4) it helps structure the development of new legal rules and legitimate behaviour.

---

35 See *Indian views on China, UN and Korea*, 4–6 July 1950, [UP 123/116, 120, 121], calendar ii to doc. 7; and *Sir D. Kelly to Mr. Younger*, 18 July 1950, [FK 1022/152], doc. 22; in Yasamee and Hamilton 1991: 17–18, 71. In sum, Britain wanted to build up India and have it take a lead in Asia, to bolster the non-communist countries in the area.

36 See *Mr. Bevin to Mr. Hutchison (Peking)*, 22 July 1950, [FC 1021/2], doc. 24; and *Record by Mr. Dening of a Meeting with the China Association*, 26 August 1950, [FC 1106/206], doc. 41, both in Yasamee and Hamilton 1991: 75, and 116. Established in London in 1889, the China Association aimed to advance British trade with China.

37 Yasamee and Hamilton 1991: v.

38 In a report on global strategy circulated among British policymakers just prior to the Korean War, the Defence Chiefs of Staff listed Western Europe as the top priority, followed by the Middle East, and noted that the gap in British defence lay in the Far East. See *Report by the Chiefs of Staff*, 7 June 1950, [CAB 131/9], Appendix I in Yasamee and Hamilton 1991: 411–431.

1. International Law Helped Constitute the Identities of Key UK Leaders

The fact that Britain decided to support the Security Council resolutions on the Korean crisis, and contribute significant naval, air, and ground forces to the UN mission there even though political and military leaders thought the country was not strategically important, suggests that international law can help constitute a state's identity and be used to reorient its political and military objectives. As will be seen below, Prime Minister Attlee felt a strong sense of obligation to the United Nations and the conflict in Korea, and there is evidence that this perception of obligation was partly based on and affected by Britain's formal membership in the UN, as well as Attlee's belief in the international rule of law. While other UK leaders, such as the Defence Chiefs of Staff, did not feel the same responsibility regarding the UN and the Korean crisis, Attlee sought to reorient their thinking and explain Britain's actions by reaffirming the importance of responding to aggression; making the new world organization effective; and upholding the rule of law in international affairs.

For example, Attlee instructed Britain's UN delegation to vote for the first Security Council resolution on the crisis, and this was endorsed by the Cabinet on 27 June.[39] At this meeting, the Cabinet Secretary remarked that "Korea is rather a distant obligation, Prime Minister." To this Attlee replied, "Distant – yes, but nonetheless an obligation."[40] Accordingly, the government also supported the Council's second resolution, provided its scope was limited to Korea, as well as the third resolution.[41]

While Britain's support for the Council resolutions was relatively forthcoming, its decisions to send naval, air, and ground forces to Korea were less so. In response to the second resolution, the Defence Chiefs and Cabinet agreed that Britain's naval forces in Japan[42] should be placed under US command "to operate on behalf of the Security Council in support of South Korea."[43] However, the Chiefs stressed, no land or air forces should be sent, as this would divert resources from more important areas like Europe and Hong Kong. Likewise, acting Foreign Secretary Kenneth Younger[44] and his advisers thought that

---

39   Farrar-Hockley 1990: 31–33; and Yasamee and Hamilton 1991: vi.

40   Farrar-Hockley 1990: 31–33.

41   Yasamee and Hamilton 1991: vi.

42   These forces consisted of one light fleet carrier, two cruisers, and five destroyers and frigates. See telegram of instructions (COS (W) 814 of 28 June 1950), in Yasamee and Hamilton 1991: 9, footnote 5.

43   D.O. (50)48, cited in *Minutes of a Meeting of the Defence Committee of the Cabinet*, 28 June 1950, D.O. (50) 11th Meeting [FK 1015/139], doc. 4 in Yasamee and Hamilton 1991: 7.

44   From February 1950 until the Labour government's defeat in the general election of October 1951, Kenneth Younger was the second-ranking minister in the Foreign Office under Ernest

sending troops would seriously jeopardize Britain's existing defence commitments in the Far East.[45] Expressing similar hesitation, albeit for reasons different than those of Younger and the Chiefs, two left-leaning Cabinet ministers, Chancellor of the Exchequer Stafford Cripps and Health Minister Aneurin Bevan, articulated significant dissent at the time. This was due to the lack of American consultation regarding the war, and because contributing to the conflict – and rearmament more generally – would further delay Britain's socio-economic recovery following World War II.[46]

As the UN's military position in Korea deteriorated in July, the US asked the UN Secretary General to appeal for further contributions, and pressured Britain to send troops.[47] The Cabinet thus faced a policy dilemma, in that the government's purported commitment to the UN, described below, its need to show its continued relevance to America, and its ongoing belief in Britain's world role were pitted against the realities of an already stretched military commitment, the implications of increased defence spending on domestic socio-economic programs, and the clear warning of military leaders.[48]

In response to this dilemma, Attlee convinced his Cabinet on 25 July to send the 29th Infantry Brigade from Britain.[49] A month later, in response to renewed American requests and advice that the threat to Hong Kong had decreased, Attlee and Foreign Secretary Bevin also agreed to send the 27th Infantry Brigade from that island.[50] These contributions indicate the seriousness with which the situation was viewed, and the costs that Attlee and Bevin were prepared to incur, as they stripped Britain's remaining military capacity and forced the recall of reservists from the Second World War.[51]

Bevin (Foreign Secretary from 27 July 1945 to 9 March 1951) and Herbert Morrison (Foreign Secretary from 9 March 1951 to 26 October 1951). Because Bevin was ill for much of his tenure during the Korean War, Younger often acted in his place.

45 *Minister of State Meeting*, 15 July 1950, doc. 21 in Yasamee and Hamilton 1991: 70.

46 Pearce 1991: 189; and *Cabinet Conclusions*, 1 Aug. 1950, [CAB 128/18], cited in Morgan 1989: 424.

47 MacDonald 1990: 21–22.

48 Phythian 2007: 42–43.

49 See Morgan 1989: 423; and *Extract from the Conclusions of a Meeting of the Cabinet*, 25 July 1950, [CAB 128/18], doc. 27 in Yasamee and Hamilton 1991: 81. The formation and transport of the 29th Brigade was a slow process. The first troops did not arrive at Pusan, Korea, until 3 November 1950 (Farrar-Hockley 1990: 447–450).

50 *Minute by Mr. Attlee of 17 August*, in Yasamee and Hamilton 1991: 111, footnote 6. The forces arrived in Pusan on 29 August 1950. It was hoped they could leave after the 29th Brigade arrived. However, because of China's intervention in the war, the 27th Brigade stayed until April 1951 (Yasamee and Hamilton 1991: 128, footnote 3).

51 Many of these reservists had just established themselves in peacetime occupations. See MacDonald 1990: 21.

Britain supported the Security Council resolutions on Korea and contributed to the UN force there in part because the government thought a clear act of aggression had occurred. As Deputy Prime Minister Herbert Morrison told a Labour party rally one week after North Korea's attack, free democracies needed to act in Korea to demonstrate that "aggression does not pay."[52] Similarly, Prime Minister Attlee said at another rally on 30 July that if the UN was not to go the way of the League of Nations, "it is absolutely ... necessary that a halt should be called to aggression."[53] Picking up on this theme in a public broadcast the next day, he emphasized:

> The attack by the armed forces of North Korea on South Korea has been denounced as an act of aggression by the United Nations ... If the aggressor gets away with it, aggressors all over the world will be encouraged. The same results which led to the Second World War will follow; and another world war may result. This is why what is happening in Korea is of such importance to you. The fire that has been started in distant Korea may burn down your own house.[54]

In these remarks, note that Attlee stresses that North Korea's attack has been labelled as aggression – i.e., an international crime – by the UN; implies the significance of upholding the authority of the world organization; and links the war in faraway Korea to Britain's immediate security interests.

There is evidence that Attlee's support for the United Nations during the Korean War, and his perception of obligation regarding the conflict, were sincere and shaped by Britain's formal membership in the UN and by Attlee's belief in the international rule of law. However, this evidence also suggests that Attlee prioritized these factors more than most other British leaders. For example, prior to World War II, Attlee had been committed to the principles underpinning the League of Nations.[55] Emphasizing this commitment to Parliament in 1935, he stated that Britain can only truly defend itself "by moving forward to a new world – *a world of law*, the abolition of national armaments with a world force" [emphasis added].[56] After the war, the Labour government actively contributed to the establishment of the UN, and Attlee transferred his support for the League to the new world organization.[57] For

---

52 Quoted in Donoughue and Jones 1973: 463.
53 Quoted in Harris 1982: 455–456.
54 Ibid.
55 Phythian 2007: 22.
56 HC Debates, Hansard, 11 March 1935, col. 46.
57 Phythian 2007: 6, 22. On Labour's support for the League and UN more generally, see Vickers 2004 and 2011.

example, during the Potsdam Conference of July 1945, Attlee noted in diplomatic correspondence:

> The concept of the special interest of Great Britain in the strategic areas and the acceptance of responsibility for them involves us in a continuing heavy burden of defence expenditure … If we really believe and intend to operate a world organisation for peace we ought, I think, to get away from old conceptions. In my view the only realistic policy is that of placing all these strategic areas under international control, not the control of one or two powers, but of the United Nations.[58]

Attlee's outlook was criticized by some members of the UK Foreign Office (FO). For instance, Gladwyn Jebb, the head of reconstruction at the FO, questioned Attlee's concern about "power politics," and argued that until the countries of the world are willing to renounce their sovereignty and create a World State, "international politics can only be an expression of power."[59]

Nonetheless, Attlee continued to prioritize the UN, and its role in Britain's foreign policy. In September 1945, he argued the following in a memorandum to Cabinet and military leaders:

> The British Empire can only be defended by its membership of the United Nations Organisation. If we do not accept this, we had better say so. If we do accept this we should seek to make it effective and not at the same time act on outworn conceptions. If the new organisation is a reality, it does not matter who holds Cyrenaica [Libya] or Somalia or controls the Suez Canal.[60]

The Defence Chiefs tended to disagree with this view. Admiral Andrew Cunningham, the First Sea Lord, noted in his diary at the time that "[t]he PM misreads the lessons of the war – practically preaches unilateral disarmament and advocates not putting in our claim for trusteeship of Cyrenaica and … Somalia."[61] Similarly, Field Marshall Alan Brooke, the Chief of the Imperial General Staff, wrote in his diary that "[w]e were … shaken by Attlee's new Cabinet paper in which apparently the security of the Middle East must rest in the power of the United Nations!!"[62]

---

58 *Minute from Mr Attlee to Mr Eden (Berlin)*, 18 July 1945, doc. 179 in Butler, Pelly and Yasamee 1984: 363–364.

59 *Memorandum by Mr Jebb (Berlin)*, 29 July 1945, doc. 459 in Butler, Pelly and Yasamee 1984: 990–994.

60 *Memorandum by Attlee*, 1 Sept. 1945, doc. 18 in Bullen and Pelly 1985: 42–43.

61 Cunningham diary, British Library, entry for 3 Sept. 1945, in Smith and Zametica 1985: 243.

62 Alan Brooke diary, 5/11, Liddell Hart Centre for Military Archives, King's College, London, entry for 3 Sept. 1945, in Smith and Zametica 1985: 243.

Again, however, Attlee continued to support the UN. He also stressed the importance of the rule of law in world affairs. Speaking in January 1946 at the opening session of the General Assembly in London, the prime minister stated that the United Nations

> must become the overriding factor in foreign policy. After the First World War there was a tendency to regard the League of Nations as something outside the ordinary range of foreign policy. Governments continued on the old lines, pursuing individual aims and following the path of power politics, not understanding that the world has passed into a new epoch. In just such a spirit in times past in these islands, great nobles and their retainers used to practise private war in disregard of the authority of the central government. The time came when private armies were abolished, when the rule of law was established throughout ... this island. What has been done in Britain and in other countries on a small stage has now to be effected throughout the whole world.[63]

Moreover, at a Labour party meeting in November 1946, in response to party members who thought the government was moving too close to the US in the emerging Cold War, Attlee re-emphasized the centrality of the UN to the party's international outlook. At this meeting, Dick Crossman, a critic of Attlee's foreign policy, stressed that the party had fought the 1945 election on a claim that only a Labour government could prevent the division of the Western world into two ideological blocs, and that Attlee's government had created the impression that British foreign policy was now governed by "an exclusive Anglo-American tie-up."[64] In response, Attlee said it was remarkable that Crossman had got through a speech on foreign affairs without once mentioning the UN. "[T]he Government," he added, "does not believe in the forming of groups and opposes groups East, West or centre. We stand for the United Nations."[65]

Again, the above indicates that Attlee's support for the UN during the Korean War and his perception of obligation regarding the conflict were sincere and shaped in part by Britain's formal membership in the organization

---

63 Attlee 1954: 198–199.

64 Quoted in Harris 1982: 302.

65 Ibid. The debate between Attlee and Crossman reflected a broader foreign policy division between the right and left wings of the Labour party following World War II, and this division resurfaced during the Korean War. During this period, those on the right wing of the Labour party tended to prioritize the UK-US alliance; downplay the possibility of cooperating with the USSR; and accept the realpolitik logic of the Cold War. By contrast, those on the left tended to question whether aligning with the US might ultimately erode Britain's sovereignty; believe that cooperating with the USSR was not impossible; and advocate a "third way" socialist internationalism that included a restrictive view of the legitimate use of military force abroad. See Phythian 2007: 35–37.

and by Attlee's belief in the international rule of law. However, it is important to acknowledge the political context of this support and perception. At the time of the Korean War, the majority of states comprising the UN Security Council and General Assembly were generally considered sympathetic to the US and its allies.[66] As such, some scholars, such as Callum MacDonald, argue that leaders like Attlee and President Truman "found no difficulty in regarding [the UN] as an important tool in the Cold War, lending moral authority to the policy of containment."[67] However, while MacDonald is correct to point out the political circumstances under which the US and UK were able to respond to the Korean crisis through the UN, he underestimates the extent to which acting through the world organization imposed legal limitations on their behaviour in the war.[68] We will see such limitations at work in the next section.

MacDonald also underappreciates the degree to which some British leaders understood UN involvement as providing more than just "moral authority" for the policy of containment. As we will also see, acting Foreign Secretary Younger believed that in any action the Security Council took regarding the Korean crisis, it was important that the *legal* authority for such action was correct and made clear, and that the perception that the Western powers were simply making use of UN machinery for their own ends was avoided.

2. International Law Helped Regulate Britain's Conduct

Alongside its constitutive effect, international law also had a regulative influence in the Korean War. Two examples of this are Britain's non-participation in the US naval blockade of Taiwan, and the UK's use of the Security Council resolutions and other relevant international legal instruments to help constrain America's response to the crisis.

---

66 At the outbreak of the Korean War, seven of the Security Council's eleven members were generally considered sympathetic to the Western bloc of states in the emerging Cold War (the US, UK, France, Norway, Nationalist China, Cuba, and Ecuador), while the remaining four were generally viewed as loyal to the Communist bloc (the USSR and Yugoslavia) or as relatively neutral (Egypt and India). Moreover, when the General Assembly voted to create its first Commission on Korea in November 1947, the vote was adopted by 43 votes to zero with six abstentions. These abstentions came from members of the Communist bloc (the USSR, Byelorussia, Czechoslovakia, Poland, the Ukraine and Yugoslavia). See Higgins 1970: 156–157, 162.

67 MacDonald 1990: 5.

68 Regarding these limitations, see Truman 1956; Hoyt 1961; Ridgway 1967; Stairs 1974; and Stueck 1995. As William Stueck notes, President Truman and Secretary of State Acheson's decision to address the Korean crisis through the UN led to legal agreements that restricted America's freedom of action regarding the war, and sparked criticism of this decision from some US military professionals, legislators, and members of the public (Stueck 2010: 275).

First, recall that when the Attlee government supported the Council's second resolution, it did so provided the instrument's scope was limited to Korea. Accordingly, when the Cabinet and Defence Chiefs sent UK naval forces to the UN mission, these forces were to operate on behalf of the Security Council to support South Korea. In the debate behind this decision, First Sea Lord Fraser said, "It was important that any operations … undertaken by British Naval Forces should be in support of South Korea and not in protection of [Taiwan] or in any way against the Communist Government in China."[69] The Cabinet Defence Committee, which was chaired by Attlee, agreed.[70] As such, during the next three years of the Korean War, Britain's naval assets did not participate in the Taiwan blockade, and were "strictly limited to resisting aggression in Korea."[71]

In addition to its understanding of the second Council resolution, there is further evidence that international legal considerations helped shape Britain's non-involvement in the Taiwan blockade. It was agreed in a meeting on 30 June between Younger and some other ministers that, in any public statement, Britain would "welcome" America's action around Taiwan because the island was a "ward of the allied powers and it was in our interest that orderly government should be maintained there until a peace treaty was signed."[72] However, leaders would also emphasize that British "forces were not involved in the [Taiwan] action and while we approve of that action we did not participate in it *because* of the special *legal* position we were in" [emphasis added].[73]

Younger and the other ministers did not specify what they meant by the "special legal position" that Britain was in regarding Taiwan. However, they were likely referring to the fact that the Attlee government (a) had recognized Mao's Communist regime as the de jure government of China on 6 January 1950 while the US had not;[74] (b) would continue this recognition during the Korean War;[75] and (c) thought that, following an appropriate treaty, China should regain authority over Taiwan. To this extent, these leaders likely thought that

---

69 *Minutes of a Defence Committee Meeting*, 28 June 1950, [FK1015/139], doc. 4 in Yasamee and Hamilton 1991: 8.

70 Ibid: 9–10.

71 MacDonald 1990: 26.

72 *Minutes of a Meeting held in the Minister of State's Room*, 30 June 1950, [FK 1022/59], doc. 9 in Yasamee and Hamilton 1991: 21.

73 Ibid.

74 Wolf 1983: 299.

75 Foreign Secretary Bevin told the UK Ambassador in the US that "our attitude is that the Peking Government is without any shadow of doubt the Government of China and that the Nationalist representatives in the United Nations represent nothing but a small clique in [Taiwan] which in itself represents nothing." See *Mr. Bevin to Sir O. Franks (Washington)*, 11 Aug. 1950, [UP 123/143], doc. 35 in Yasamee and Hamilton 1991: 100.

the international legal position Britain had previously articulated prevented it from participating in any coercive military action that – while "welcome" and consistent with its interest in order – nonetheless conflicted with this legal position and risked a broader war with China.

Note that the government refused to allow UK forces to participate in the Taiwan blockade even though some British officials thought such participation might prove necessary if China attacked the disputed island. In a draft paper dated 24 July 1950, R.H. Scott of the Foreign Office gave a joint FO-Commonwealth Relations Office view "on behalf of implicit British involvement in [Taiwan] in the event of a Communist attack."[76] In response, Foreign Secretary Bevin strongly dissented, and argued that "any of [Scott's] recommendations means a general war."[77]

This empirical observation is relevant for two reasons. First, it suggests that contrary to what a deterministic account might suggest, Britain's policy on Korea was neither inevitable nor dictated solely by the US. Second, this observation resonates with other studies that have found international law helped regulate a state's use of force.[78] Consistent with this investigation, these studies assume that – as noted in chapter two – one way to show law helped govern or control a state's use of force is to find evidence that some leaders or advisers considered implementing military responses that were broader or more severe than the force that was actually employed, and these responses were avoided in part because other leaders thought this would be more consistent with international law. Finding such evidence regarding Britain's participation in the Korean conflict therefore helps suggest that international law influenced the UK in this war.

Another related example of law's regulative impact is Britain's use of the Security Council resolutions and other relevant legal instruments to help constrain America's response to the Korean crisis.[79] During negotiations on the second resolution, for instance, the US suggested that other Communist Asian "encroachments" be mentioned, and the invasion be attributed to "centrally directed Communist Imperialism."[80] Drafts of Truman's announcement on 27 June, noted earlier, expressed similarly expansive and accusatory language.[81] Concerned, Bevin (who was ill in hospital) told the Americans that the

---

76 *Draft paper by R.H. Scott of the Foreign Office,* 24 July 1950 (FO 371/83298), in Morgan 1989:
    424.
77 Ibid.
78 See e.g. Chayes 1974; Wheeler 2004; and Scharf and Williams 2010.
79 For first-hand accounts of this constraint, see Truman 1956 and Ridgway 1967. For scholarly
    elaboration, see Hoyt 1961; Stairs 1974; and Stueck 1995.
80 Farrar-Hockley 1990: 32–33.
81 Yasamee and Hamilton 1991: vi.

resolution should be confined strictly to Korea, and omit threats which had not yet been brought before the Council. Similarly, Younger asked that Truman's speech be modified.[82] In the end, the US agreed to both requests.[83] Accordingly, references to Communist "encroachments" and "centrally directed Communist Imperialism" were deleted from the second resolution, and the latter term was removed from Truman's speech.

When negotiating the third resolution, Britain was again able to influence these talks and America's position, and its interpretation of the international legal considerations at issue played a role in this regard. An early US draft of the resolution noted the Council's initial "decision" to assist South Korea, and suggested that an enforcement committee be created to act as a link between the Security Council and General MacArthur.[84] It also implied that Yugoslavia and Egypt be excluded from any such committee, even though these states were often considered relatively neutral by members of both the Western and Communist blocs.

In response, Younger told Britain's UN delegation that calling the initial action a "decision" was erroneous, and an enforcement committee was similarly inappropriate. This was because, he noted, enforcement means action under Article 42 of the UN Charter, "whereas we are all agreed" that action is instead being taken under a "recommendation" in Article 39, and this should be kept clear.[85] Further, Younger remarked, if a committee is created that excludes Yugoslavia and/or Egypt, this "might lend some weight to the criticism that the Powers opposed to the Soviet bloc are simply making use of United Nations machinery for their own ends."[86] Summing up the situation, Younger stated:

> Assistance to Korea is now being given as a result of a recommendation of the Security Council and it therefore seems reasonable that the Council should wish

---

82 Bevin and Younger made these suggestions because there was no hard evidence yet that the USSR or China *was* responsible for North Korea's attack; Britain wished to contain the Korean crisis by giving Stalin and Mao face-saving room to retreat should the opportunity arise; and the UK did not want to appear to support Chiang Kai-shek, the Nationalist Chinese leader in Taiwan, because this could lead to Chinese Communist actions against British-controlled Hong Kong. See Yasamee and Hamilton 1991: vi; and Farrar-Hockley 1990: 32.

83 Truman 1956: 357.

84 *Mr. Younger to Sir G. Jebb*, 2 July 1950, [UP 2113/4], doc. 10 in Yasamee and Hamilton 1991: 24–26. The US proposed creating an enforcement committee in part because it wanted to avoid involving the Military Staff Committee envisaged by the Charter. Article 47(iii) of the Charter gave the MSC responsibility for the strategic direction of any armed forces placed at the disposal of the Security Council. If the MSC became involved, however, the US and its allies worried that the USSR could demand to see the Committee's plans for the UN force in Korea.

85 Ibid.

86 Ibid.

to be as actively associated with the progress of operations as is possible in the circumstances. Moreover, it is important from the *legal* and political standpoint and from the point of view of world opinion that the necessary action should be taken under the United Nations "umbrella" [emphasis added]. On the other hand ... it [is] imperative that the actual conduct of military operations should remain squarely in the hands of General MacArthur with the minimum possible interference from outside.[87]

Reflecting this view, British diplomats helped steer their American counterparts away from the idea of an enforcement committee, and towards a solution that emphasized the UN character of operations, while also giving freedom for their conduct to MacArthur.[88] On 7 July, a final agreement was reached for a UK-France sponsored resolution on a unified command in Korea.[89]

To appreciate the legal relevance of the above events, recall that Article 39 of the Charter provides that the Security Council shall determine any threats to the peace, and "make recommendations, or decide what measures shall be taken" under the non-forceful provisions of Article 41, or the forceful measures of Article 42, to restore peace.[90] The word "decide" matters because, under Article 25, UN members "agree to accept and carry out" Council decisions in accordance with the Charter. Because the second Council resolution *recommended* that UN members help South Korea, UK leaders thought that UN forces were acting under the first half of Article 39, and this should be kept clear in the third resolution. Leaders also thought that a UN enforcement committee was thus inappropriate because, as Younger noted, enforcement action means action under Article 42 (and not, by implication, under Article 39). We will see the significance of this interpretation arise again later below.

The foregoing events illustrate how a legal provision – in this case, the term "recommend" in the second Council resolution – that may have been selected for reasons of power or expediency can nonetheless have independent subsequent

---

87 Ibid.

88 See *Minutes of a Meeting held in the Minister of State's Room to discuss Korea*, 30 June 1950, [FK 1022/59], doc. 9; *Mr. Younger to Sir G. Jebb*, 2 July 1950, [UP 2113/4], doc. 10; and C.M. (50) 43rd Conclusions on CAB 128/18, 6 July 1950, all in Yasamee and Hamilton 1991: 21, 24, and 41 (at footnote 11). For the US perspective on these negotiations, see US Department of State, *Foreign Relations of the United States, 1950. Korea, v. VII*, at 300–301.

89 Yasamee and Hamilton 1991: 26, footnote 8. The final agreement was reached after it was decided to defer action on the creation of a coordinating committee, and after the language of a new draft resolution was amended in response to constitutional problems raised by the UK over the use of the UN flag.

90 Charter of the United Nations, signed 26 June 1945, 1 U.N.T.S. XVI (entered into force 24 Oct. 1945).

impact by "precluding a range of alternative political practices"[91] – in this case, by limiting the institutional responses that the US delegation at the UN could convincingly propose. These events also suggest the particular impact that the term "recommend" had on the thinking and actions of UK leaders. In light of Prime Minister Attlee's support for the UN leading up to and during the Korean War, and his desire to strengthen the organization and make it effective, one might expect Britain to have agreed with the US proposal to create an enforcement committee that would link the Security Council with General MacArthur. However, the UK opposed such institutional development, and explained its opposition with reference to the Council's prior resolutions on the crisis.

Importantly, Britain also used its understanding of the Security Council resolutions and other relevant legal instruments to help constrain America's behaviour regarding Taiwan. Attlee's government and Foreign Office officials were worried that the Taiwan blockade could expand hostilities in the area.[92] They also, recall, viewed the Council resolutions as limited to Korea. Accordingly, Bevin warned his US counterpart on 8 July that America could not rely on wholehearted UK support for a policy based on denying territory to Mao's government that had been promised to China under the Cairo Declaration of December 1943 and the Potsdam Conference of July 1945.[93] As a short-term response, Bevin successfully pressed for President Truman to tell Congress on 19 July 1950 that all questions affecting Taiwan would be settled peacefully as envisaged in the UN Charter.[94] Thus, after MacArthur nonetheless went on to visit Taiwan later that summer and to publicly stress its strategic value, Truman made him withdraw his statement and approved a military directive limiting US action in defence of the disputed island.[95]

In sum, Britain's non-participation in the Taiwan blockade, and its use of the Security Council resolutions to help constrain America's response to the crisis, support the observation that when states use force, international law helps regulate their political and military practice.

3. International Law Helped Permit and Legitimate Britain's Conduct

When Britain reacted to the Korean crisis, international law also helped permit and legitimate behaviour that otherwise might not have been allowed. Two

---

91 Goldstein and Keohane 1993: 22.

92 Yasamee and Hamilton 1991: xi.

93 *Mr. Younger to Sir O. Franks*, 8 July 1950, [FK 1022/56], doc. 15 in Yasamee and Hamilton 1991: 42.

94 *US Department of State Bulletin*, XXIII, 578, 31 July 1950, 166.

95 Rees 1964: 73; and Truman 1956: 354.

examples illustrate this. First, the UK intervened militarily in what was in many respects an ideologically divisive and extremely violent internal, *civil* war, and justified this publicly and privately with reference to the Security Council resolutions on the conflict and the UN Charter's provisions on self-defence. Second, the UK ultimately supported America's decision to cross the 38th parallel in Korea in October 1950, and it helped draft a General Assembly resolution aimed at providing UN support for this policy of rollback.

Regarding the first example, due to the majority interpretation of the Council resolutions, the US and UK thought they were allowed to intervene militarily in what was in many ways an ideologically divisive and tremendously destructive civil war. The question of how British leaders and officials understood the complex legal situation in Korea, and whether it was seen as a traditional war or novel police action, will be elaborated later below. For now, note that consistent with the above description, Britain's attorney general observed that the rules of war would likely apply in Korea because such rules "have been applied in civil wars" in the past.[96] UK military action in this conflict, we saw Prime Minister Attlee and Deputy Prime Minister Morrison stress earlier in public, was justified because North Korea's attack was denounced as aggression by the Security Council, and Britain was acting pursuant to this body's resolutions. In addition to these statements, there is further evidence that international legal considerations were relevant to explaining Britain's use of force to the UK public and British officials, and to securing the support of the international community.

In response to concerns from the public and left-wing Labour party members regarding the international legality of Britain's military reaction,[97] a sophisticated legal defence was developed and articulated by the Attlee government, and prolonged and careful legal analysis of the situation was ordered. One concern was that, although South Korea was recognized by the General Assembly in 1948, it was not yet a UN member. Article 51 of the Charter, however, states that nothing in that treaty "shall impair the inherent right of individual or collective self-defence if an armed attack occurs against a member of the [UN]." At a meeting on 4 July 1950, the Cabinet observed that, although South Korea was not a UN member, "the action taken on her behalf was clearly in accordance with the principle embedded in [Article 51]."[98] As Attlee explained in Parliament the following day, the purpose of this provision was "not to create a new

---

96 *Letter from the Attorney General to the Lord Chancellor*, 4 Sept. 1950, Annex to *Legal Implications of the Korean Conflict*, 14 Sept. 1950, C.P.(50)207.

97 For commentary on these concerns, see the two-part article by Keeston entitled "International Law and Korea," in the *Manchester Guardian*, 29 and 31 July 1950.

98 *Extract from the Conclusions of a Meeting of the Cabinet*, 4 July 1950, [CAB 128/18], doc. 11 in Yasamee and Hamilton 1991: 28.

right but merely to make it clear that an inherent right vested in every State is not prejudiced."[99]

Elaborating on this position, the Foreign Office's UN department sent an update to Britain's diplomats stationed abroad on 7 July. It stated that under international law,

> any state which is attacked has a right to defend itself and any other state has a right to assist the state which is the subject of aggression. The Charter does not take away or limit this common law right, which is, indeed, specifically preserved in Article 51. No valid objection can be made on the grounds that Article 51 refers specifically to the event of "an armed attack … against a member of the United Nations." The Republic of Korea, although not a member of the United Nations is not thereby disqualified from receiving assistance from a member when subject to an attack … [E]ven if that [Security Council] resolution were not valid (as claimed by the Soviet Union), all that is now being done to assist the Republic of Korea remains justified by the right of collective self-defence recognised by the Charter … His Majesty's Government are not at present at war. They are engaged in a collective international police operation under the authority of the Security Council to repel aggression and to restore international peace and security in Korea.[100]

In sum, the statements above suggest that Attlee's Cabinet believed that the action taken on South Korea's behalf was consistent with the customary international law on self-defence, and that FO officials thought that Britain was using force in Korea under the authority of the Security Council or, insofar as this basis was invalid, under the doctrine of collective self-defence.

Cognizant of these arguments, the Cabinet decided that while Attlee "should not ignore the constitutional points which were being made, [he] should argue that the action … in South Korea was fully in accordance with the spirit of the … Charter and was in fact the first significant demonstration of the principle of collective security against aggression."[101] Moreover, the Cabinet held, "it was the duty of peace-loving nations to make the machinery of the [UN] work effectively, despite legal quibbles, and not to allow it to be frustrated by the abstentions of a single member."[102] To this end, such nations "were entitled to take advantage of procedures which, though they might appear to conflict with the strict letter of the Charter, had been accepted as reasonable by member

---

99 HC Debates, Hansard, 5 July 1950, col. 494.

100 Intel No. 143 of 7 July 1950, [UP 2113/53], in Yasamee and Hamilton 1991: 22, footnote 8.

101 *Extract from the Conclusions of a Meeting of the Cabinet*, 4 July 1950, [CAB 128/18], doc. 11 in Yasamee and Hamilton 1991: 28.

102 Ibid.

States."[103] As Attlee stated the next day, he hoped that Parliament would not focus on these "legal subtleties," and instead concentrate on the central reality: If the UN "is not to go the way of the League of Nations, the members must be prepared to act when the need arises. If the peoples wish to avoid another world war they must support their Governments in asserting the rule of law."[104]

In Attlee's arguments, note that he articulates a slight contradiction – namely, that Parliament should not focus on the international legal nuances of America and Britain's use of force in Korea, but governments and their constituents should be upholding the rule of law there. This suggests that the broad substantive aims of the collective security regime were likely relevant to Attlee's thinking on the Korean conflict, but he was less concerned about implementing this regime according to the "black letter" procedural details of the Charter's text. That said, the legal concerns that were raised about these details appear to have shaped the public justification that Attlee could give in Parliament regarding Britain's use of force, and the private explanation that Foreign Office officials provided to British diplomats abroad.

Perhaps because the military response to North Korea's attack might, as noted above, "appear to conflict with the strict letter of the Charter," further legal analysis of the situation was ordered in the fall of 1950 and winter of 1951. The role of this analysis in Britain's effort to create new collective security law will be discussed in the next section. For now, note that, like the Cabinet ministers they advised, UK Attorney General H.W. Shawcross and Lord Chancellor Viscount Jowitt also recognized how international law could help legitimate Britain's use of force. As Shawcross remarked to Jowitt on 4 September 1950:

> [F]rom one point of view it does not much matter what the law is: we are committed to a certain course of action and we must pursue it without any unduly nice argument about the legal position. But for the purpose of *rallying world opinion* it is ... important to show that the steps we take are firmly based on the rule of law and for our own domestic purposes ... it is essential to know on what view of the law we take our stand [emphasis added].[105]

In these remarks, note that Shawcross believed that, from one perspective, Britain's response must be pursued without excessive legal debate. However, he also thought that, to secure international support, Britain should show that its actions are based firmly on the rule of law.

---

103 Ibid.

104 HC Debates, Hansard, 5 July 1950, col. 495.

105 *Copy of Letter from the Attorney General to the Lord Chancellor*, 4 Sept. 1950, Annex to *Legal Implications of the Korean Conflict*, 14 Sept. 1950, C.P. (50)207.

A second example of international law's role in permitting and legitimating behaviour can be seen in Britain's decision to ultimately support the US-led crossing of the 38th parallel, and its efforts to draft a General Assembly resolution aimed at providing UN support for this crossing. These British actions must be understood in light of the military and diplomatic context at the time. Recall that by late September 1950, UN forces in Korea had managed to push back North Korea's army and recapture Seoul. As such, Prime Minister Attlee and Foreign Secretary Bevin knew that the US would soon be deciding whether UN forces would remain near the 38th parallel and thus simply restore the status quo broken by North Korea's original attack, or cross the parallel and seek to unify Korea by force.[106] Consequently, the government had to determine what its policy on this issue would be. Additionally, like the military situation in Korea, the diplomatic landscape had also changed. In August, the USSR had returned to the UN Security Council. To avoid the Soviet veto there, the US and its allies shifted much of their diplomatic efforts on Korea to the General Assembly, and explained this shift in part by referring to changing state practice on the issue of peace and security.[107]

In debating how the UK should respond to the altered military situation in Korea, Bevin dismissed warnings from Communist China[108] and stressed to his Cabinet colleagues the need to move into North Korea. Otherwise, Bevin argued, "If [UN forces] stop at the 38th Parallel and leave North Korea as an entity Russia will virtually have triumphed and the whole [UN] effort will have been in vain."[109] While more cautious, Attlee also thought it might be necessary for UN forces to enter North Korea to restore peace in the country as a whole, and establish a democratic government for all Korea.[110] By contrast, the UK Defence Chiefs were worried that crossing the parallel could lead to China intervening in the war.[111]

---

106   Yasamee and Hamilton 1991: xvii.

107   The shift arguably contradicted Article 12 of the UN Charter, which states that while "the Security Council is exercising in respect of any dispute or situation the functions assigned to it … the General Assembly shall not make any recommendations with regard to that dispute or situation unless the Security Council so requests." However, prior to the Korean crisis, the Assembly had addressed the long-term political aspects of the Palestine dispute while the Council had dealt with the short-term pacification of that dispute. Further, the Assembly was tasked to consider a UN committee report which involved the independence and unification of Korea. This gave the US an opportunity to suggest informally that the Assembly consider additional issues related to the crisis. See Stairs 1974: 118.

108   FC 1022/489, 26 Sept. 1950, in Yasamee and Hamilton 1991: 150, footnote 9.

109   *Sir G. Jebb (New York) to Mr. Attlee*, 25 Sept. 1950, [FK 1022/344], doc. 54 in Yasamee and Hamilton 1991: 152.

110   *Extract from the Conclusions of a Meeting of the Cabinet*, 26 Sept. 1950, [CAB 128/19], doc. 55 in Yasamee and Hamilton 1991: 153.

111   CAB 21/1985, 25 Sept. 1950, in Yasamee and Hamilton 1991: 148, footnote 4.

In the end, the Cabinet agreed with Bevin and Attlee's views, although they stressed that any continuing British commitment should be as small as possible.[112] Accordingly, Bevin asked the US for assurances that operations would be limited to Korea, and that – reflecting an observable implication posited in chapter two – there would be a gap between the passing of the Assembly resolution and the move across the parallel. While the US readily gave assurances of a delay, its troops crossed the parallel on 7 October 1950, the same day the resolution was passed by the General Assembly.

One of the reasons Bevin, Attlee, and the other Cabinet members were prepared to accept the potential crossing of the 38th parallel by UN forces is because Britain had helped draft the Assembly resolution, and they thought it provided UN support for the crossing. In brief, the instrument came about as follows. In response to a suggestion made by India, Bevin prepared a plan for a statement of UN aims in Korea, including the establishment of a unified, independent, and democratic government in accordance with the Cairo Declaration of 1943.[113] This plan was approved by the UK Cabinet on 4 September, and by officials at the UN in talks leading up to the meeting of the General Assembly. By 22 September, the draft resolution recommended in part: "(a) that all necessary steps be taken to promote conditions of stability and security throughout the whole of Korea, (b) that when such conditions have been created new elections be held throughout the whole of Korea with a view to the establishment of a unified, independent and democratic government of all Korea."[114]

Commenting on this draft, Bevin said to Attlee that the "really tricky thing is whether the United Nations forces are to go north of the 38th Parallel. Clearly they must do so if the unification of Korea is to be achieved. Our resolution seeks to cover this contingency, though admittedly in veiled terms in the first recommendation."[115] The "veiled terms" that Bevin was likely citing were the provisions that "all necessary steps" be taken to promote conditions of stability and security throughout Korea. When the final resolution was passed, however, the language had been changed in negotiations so as to recommend that "all appropriate steps" be taken to ensure stability throughout Korea, and "all

---

112 *Extract from the Conclusions of a Meeting of the Cabinet*, 26 Sept. 1950, [CAB 128/19], doc. 55 in Yasamee and Hamilton 1991: 155.

113 Yasamee and Hamilton 1991: xvi–xvii. The Cairo Declaration was a product of US, UK, and Chinese discussions about post-war Asia. Among other things, it aimed to affirm (Nationalist) China as an allied power, and agreed that territories taken from China by Japan, including Taiwan, would be returned after the conflict.

114 FK 1022/329, in Yasamee and Hamilton 1991: 147, footnote 2.

115 *Sir G. Jebb (New York) to Mr. Attlee*, 22 Sept. 1950, [FK 1022/328], doc. 52 in Yasamee and Hamilton 1991: 147.

constituent acts" be taken, under the auspices of the UN, for the establishment of a unified, independent and democratic government.[116]

In drafting and supporting this resolution, it is clear that Bevin and his colleagues aimed to provide UN support for the potential crossing of the 38th parallel. However, it is less clear whether they aimed to provide formal legal authorization for this action. On the one hand, in separate negotiations on the US-led "Uniting for Peace" resolution that was passed by the General Assembly on 3 November 1950, the government expressed *concern* about strengthening the Assembly at the expense of the Security Council, and relaxing Britain's veto power there.[117] Further, at a Cabinet meeting in late September, Attorney General Shawcross noted that "in strict law, the General Assembly was probably not entitled to make recommendations about Korea while the matter was still in the hands of the Security Council."[118]

On the other hand, in a private discussion with Sir Roger Makins, Deputy Under-Secretary of State, on 5 October, Bevin remarked that "[o]n legal grounds the view was ... that General MacArthur would be justified in crossing the 38th Parallel."[119] Moreover, at the above Cabinet meeting, Shawcross also "recognized ... that this was an occasion on which the action of the Assembly should be guided by the wishes of the great majority of the Member States."[120] Whether or not the 46 other states who voted for the resolution thought that UN forces would cross the 38th parallel, it remains the case that the Attlee Cabinet believed that Bevin's resolution "was designed to meet that situation."[121]

4. International Law Helped Structure the Development of New Rules and Legitimate Practice

Britain's reaction to the Korean crisis suggests that international law can help structure the process by which agents seek to develop and promote new legal

---

116 The resolution was passed by a vote of 47 to five (Soviet bloc countries), with seven abstentions (India, Yugoslavia, and several Arab states). See Stairs 1974: 121–123.

117 Yasamee and Hamilton 1991: xv.

118 *Extract from the Conclusions of a Meeting of the Cabinet*, 26 Sept. 1950, [CAB 128/19], doc. 55 in Yasamee and Hamilton 1991: 153–154.

119 Yasamee and Hamilton 1991: 171, footnote 7. Bevin did not specify whether this legal justification would stem from the upcoming General Assembly resolution, or the original Security Council resolutions on the crisis.

120 *Extract from the Conclusions of a Meeting of the Cabinet*, 26 Sept. 1950, [CAB 128/19], doc. 55 in Yasamee and Hamilton 1991: 153–154.

121 Ibid. While the resolution did not authorize the use of force to achieve the UN's goals in Korea, MacDonald argues that it nevertheless "gave tacit approval to the crossing of the [38th] parallel, since its provisions could only be enforced in the north at the point of a bayonet" (MacDonald 1990: 30–31).

rules and legitimate practice for states and other international actors. An important example of this phenomenon is the Security Council's novel response to North Korea's attack, and the efforts of UK leaders to justify and study this response, and to create new collective security law.

When the Security Council authorized UN members to restore peace in Korea, it did so in a manner not anticipated by the drafters of the UN Charter in 1945. At that time, it was expected that members would provide permanent military forces to the Council under Article 43 of the Charter.[122] By June 1950, however, no such forces had been granted. Thus, following North Korea's attack, the Council authorized an ad hoc response that saw UN members provide their own forces towards a collective cause. As Britain's Foreign Office noted, the USSR said this action was invalid,[123] due mainly to the absence of the Soviet representative at the Council meetings when the Korean resolutions were passed.[124] In response to the Soviets' concern, UK leaders argued that the Council's actions were a necessary reinterpretation of the Charter's text, and consistent with altered state practice on the issue.

As the Cabinet noted on 4 July, under Article 27 of the Charter, Security Council decisions on non-procedural matters required the affirmative votes of seven members, including the concurring votes of permanent members; and the USSR had argued that the Council's second resolution was invalid because the Soviet representative was absent.[125] On the other hand, the Cabinet observed, the Council had previously taken decisions despite the abstention of a permanent member; "the Soviet Government had at least acquiesced in that procedure; and it was arguable that the written constitution of the Council was in process of modification by practice."[126] Moreover, they reasoned, it was relevant to this argument that forty UN members had subsequently supported the resolution.[127] Prime Minister Attlee drew on this thinking the next day when he updated Parliament on Britain's response to the Korean conflict. As he argued, "If a member of the Security Council, and in particular a permanent member, chooses to refrain from exercising its right of voting, not by failing to vote when present, but by refraining from attending the meeting at all, that member must be regarded as having deliberately abstained from voting."[128]

---

122 Franck 2002: 24–25.

123 Intel No. 143, 7 July 1950, [UP2113/53], in Yasamee and Hamilton 1991: 22, footnote 8.

124 Concerns were also raised over the absence of Communist China from the Security Council at the time and, as noted above, whether South Korea could rely on the self-defence provisions of the UN Charter.

125 *Extract from the Conclusions of a Meeting of the Cabinet*, 4 July 1950, [CAB 128/18], doc. 11 in Yasamee and Hamilton 1991: 27–28.

126 Ibid.

127 Ibid.

128 HC Debates, Hansard, 5 July 1950, col. 491.

In sum, the above suggests that during the Korean War, British leaders sought to alter existing understandings of (a) Article 27 of the Charter and (b) Security Council voting procedures in order to help develop and promote a new legal rule – i.e., that refraining from attending a Council vote is equivalent to abstaining from that vote – and new legitimate practice for the organization. Further, leaders aimed to strengthen their efforts by citing the Council's continuing practice, and the supporting views of forty states.

As the crisis in Korea progressed, UK leaders also, as we will see, ordered extensive and sophisticated legal analysis of the conflict. Further, they consulted with other Commonwealth states and the US about using the situation to create new collective security law. Finally, leaders believed that, depending on how the conflict ultimately came to be understood by Britain and the international community, the UK might need to pass new legislation to address the domestic legal effects of such situations.

Reflecting on whether the Korean conflict constituted a traditional war or novel police action, Attorney General Shawcross advised the Cabinet on 14 September 1950 that because the situation was so unprecedented, Britain would to some extent be "able to make new law about it and the position we take up must have significant political and legal consequences."[129] Elaborating on this view with Lord Chancellor Jowitt earlier that month, Shawcross expressed ideas that resonated with Attlee's speech to the UN General Assembly in 1946:

> We have in effect the law-making function of declaring what the law is, [and] it may be that the present is ... a proper ... opportunity of distinguishing between war as a private, and now illegal, contention between States ... and collective action for restraining the aggressor and enforcing the law. Just as in the field of domestic law action which would, as between private citizens constitute an illegal assault may, when taken by the State, constitute a legal use of force, so we must elevate collective action on behalf of the [UN] to the dignity of a legal institution higher than war ...[130]

Perhaps because this argument was without clear precedent, Shawcross advised the Cabinet along more traditional lines. He and Jowitt agreed that "English laws apply to the present conflict as if it were a war in the ordinary sense," and Jowitt further thought "the conflict is a war in the ordinary sense, both under municipal law and internationally."[131] This view, Shawcross noted, contrasted with the position of US President Truman and Canadian Prime

---

129 *Copy of Letter from the Attorney-General to the Lord Chancellor,* 4 Sept. 1950, Annex to *Legal Implications of the Korean Conflict,* 14 Sept. 1950, C.P. (50)207.
130 Ibid.
131 Ibid.

Minister Louis St. Laurent, who had both declared that their countries were not at war but engaged in a police operation under the UN.[132] In light of these declarations, Shawcross said he had enunciated the following tentative proposition:

> International law does now recognise a kind of twilight condition [i.e., between war and peace] in which collective enforcement action taken under the aegis of the United Nations does not constitute a war in the old sense, which was the settlement by force of arms of a contention between individual States. There is here no contention between individual States and North Korea; the contention is between the United Nations collectively and North Korea.[133]

Notwithstanding this proposition, Shawcross also warned the Cabinet that "[a]ll this is … frankly new law and we have to decide whether to create new law in this sense."[134] As such, he recommended that the government determine what position to adopt, and arrange for high-level consultation and potential agreement with other Commonwealth countries and the US.

After discussing this legal advice, the Cabinet decided that the practical aspects of the international status of the Korean conflict would be further examined by the departments concerned, and that relevant ministers and officials would discuss the legal and practical issues involved with their American and Commonwealth counterparts.[135] Summarizing the results of these efforts, Foreign Minister Bevin noted on 11 December 1950 that the "strong political arguments" for avoiding saying that Britain is technically at war with North Korea were reinforced by China's intervention that fall.[136] Moreover, he said, the balance of practical advantage lay in treating the situation as an international police operation.[137] Commenting on this summary at a Cabinet meeting on 2 January 1951, Shawcross noted that the position of people in Britain who traded with China continued to present "many legal difficulties," and that further investigation of the domestic implications of regarding such conflicts as UN police operations might reveal the need for legislation empowering the King to declare that "the consequences of being at war should [also] follow the undertaking" of

---

132 *Legal Implications of the Korean Conflict*, 14 Sept. 1950, C.P. (50)207. While Shawcross did not say so in his memo, Jowitt's view also contrasted with the opinion from the UK Foreign Office on 7 July, noted earlier in the text.

133 Ibid.

134 Ibid.

135 *Conclusions of a Meeting of the Cabinet*, 18 Sept. 1950, C.M. (50) 60th Conclusions.

136 *C.P. (50)307 on international status of Korean conflict*, 11 Dec. 1950, [CAB129/43], calendar i to doc. 100, in Yasamee and Hamilton 1991: 281.

137 Ibid.

such operations.[138] Accordingly, the Cabinet ordered further study of the issue, and asked for a report to be written on the required legislation.[139]

In sum, the legal analysis and Cabinet decisions above indicate that during the Korean crisis Britain took the international legal status of the conflict very seriously, and consulted with its allies about the possibility and desirability of using the situation to create new collective security law. Further, UK leaders believed that, depending on how the conflict ultimately came to be seen by Britain and the international community, new domestic law might also be needed.

One final point should be made. Britain's actions outlined above were of course part of a larger US-led effort to use the United Nations to help respond to North Korea's attack, and to create new collective security law. As will be seen in the next chapter, Canada also took a lead in this regard. In the language of International Relations theorists, these efforts were in many ways an "agent" story, in that key leaders such as Truman, Attlee and Canadian Foreign Minister Lester Pearson sought to develop and promote new legal rules and legitimate conduct. However, the "structure" of international law was also important.

Commenting on the historical and legal significance of the Security Council's response to the Korean crisis, Thomas Franck argues that the Council's authorization of action in its name by ad hoc national contingents represented a "creative adaption" of the Charter's text.[140] Far from being paralyzed by the failure to realize the potential of Article 43, Franck points out that "the *system*, in actual practice … developed new ways to deploy force to secure peace and resist aggression" [emphasis added].[141] More than seventy years later, as the 1991 Gulf War suggests, the Security Council continues to authorize ad hoc coalitions to restore international peace.[142] This generally accepted practice, with its origins in the Korean War, supports the idea that when military force is used, international law helps structure the process by which agents seek to develop and promote new legal rules and legitimate behaviour for states and other international actors.

The Understanding of International Law in Britain's Use of Force in Korea

While the above suggests that international law helped influence Britain's involvement in the Korean War, it is less clear the extent to which UK leaders understood

---

138 *Conclusions of a Cabinet Meeting*, 2 Jan. 1951, [CAB128/19], doc. 100 in Yasamee and Hamilton 1991: 280–281.

139 Ibid. An inter-departmental committee on the domestic aspects of the Korean conflict was constituted in February 1951, and a preliminary report was submitted to Cabinet on 20 March of that year.

140 Franck 2002: 24–25.

141 Ibid.

142 Ibid.

this law as a distinct and binding set of legal rules, and whether the legal status of these rules impacted their decision-making. As will be seen below, leaders and officials tended to interpret the Security Council resolutions on Korea more in political and moral, rather than distinctly legal, terms. Moreover, while a key repatriation rule in the Third Geneva Convention on Prisoners of War (POWs) was seen in binding terms, the perceived requirements of this rule conflicted with other political and moral considerations at the time. And these considerations appear to have ultimately exerted a greater impact on the government than the law at issue.

1. Britain's Interpretation of the Security Council Resolutions on the Korean Crisis

As previously mentioned, the main substantive provisions of the UN Charter animating Britain's understanding of the Security Council resolutions on the Korean crisis were Articles 39, 41 and 42. Under Article 39, the Council "shall make recommendations, or decide what measures shall be taken in accordance with Articles 41 and 42" to restore peace. And under Article 25, UN members "agree to accept and carry out" Council decisions. During the vote for the second Council resolution on 27 June 1950, the Egyptian delegate, Mahmoud Fawzi, refused to participate because of the Council's "previous laxities and delays" on several other aggressions, particularly the conflict in Palestine.[143] In response, Gladwyn Jebb, Britain's UN delegate, expressed disappointment at Egypt's decision. However, Jebb conceded that because the resolution "was only a recommendation, Egypt was free to make this decision if she so chose."[144]

By noting that the resolution "was only a recommendation," Jebb was implying it was not a decision. Consistent with this view, Jebb received advice from the Foreign Office beforehand that, for legal and expediency reasons, the resolution should be viewed "as a recommendation under Article 39 and not action under Article 42."[145] This position also reflected acting Foreign Secretary Younger's subsequent comments to Jebb – noted earlier – that "we are all agreed" that we are acting under the first half of Article 39, and this should be kept clear.

The view that the Security Council's resolutions on the Korean conflict stemmed from a recommendation would recur in the government's analysis of the crisis. It suggests that, had the Council responded to the conflict by "deciding" to authorize measures under Articles 41 or 42, UK leaders and advisers

---

143 Following Egypt's position at the vote of the Security Council on 27 June, other Arab states also declined to participate in the UN action in Korea, giving as the reason the failure of the Council to check "the aggression of Zionism." Quoted in Higgins 1970: 162–163.

144 Quoted in Higgins 1970: 162–163.

145 The FO telegrams, dated 26–30 June, were entitled *Possible course of action under U.N. Charter in Korea*, [FK 1015/19, and FK 1022/42], doc. 10, calendar i, in Yasamee and Hamilton 1991: 26.

would likely have believed that this imposed legally binding obligations on UN members. However, because the Council had "recommended" action under Article 39, this constituted more a political or moral request that members were technically free to ignore. As Attorney General Shawcross noted on 4 September 1950, the operations in Korea "are not the result of any direction by the United Nations."[146] This was because, he reasoned, "[t]he Security Council refrained from action under Articles 41 and 42, which would have given rise to obligations on the part of member Nations, and contented itself with making recommendations under Article 39."[147]

Again, this suggests that – consistent with Jebb and Younger's position – Shawcross believed that had the Security Council responded with a decision, this would have imposed a binding obligation on UN members. However, because he thought the Council had only made a recommendation, one could infer that, like Jebb, Shawcross also thought the first half of Article 39 does not give rise to obligations in the way that Articles 41 and 42 do. Further, because Britain ultimately argued that UN forces in Korea were acting on a recommendation under Article 39,[148] this suggests that Shawcross might have contended that Britain contributed to these forces less because it was legally obligated to do so and more because of the political and moral considerations at issue.

2. Britain's Interpretation of Article 118 of the Geneva Convention on POWs

The provisions of the UN Charter described above are part of the *jus ad bellum*. Again, this body of international law governs the use of force by states, while the *jus in bello* – the international law of armed conflict – governs the conduct of states in war. As we will see, in contrast to their *jus ad bellum* views above, some British leaders saw a key *jus in bello* rule regarding POWs in distinctly binding terms.

At the outbreak of the Korean War in June 1950, the US and North Korea both said they would abide by the Geneva Conventions of 1949.[149] Interestingly, this commitment was made even though the treaties did not come into force

---

146 *Copy of Letter from the Attorney-General to the Lord Chancellor*, 4 Sept. 1950, Annex to *Legal Implications of the Korean Conflict*, 14 Sept. 1950, C.P. (50)207.

147 Ibid.

148 Yasamee and Hamilton 1991: viii.

149 The US was an original signatory to the four Geneva Conventions in 1949. While America did not ratify the treaties until 1955, it announced at the beginning of the Korean War that it would apply these rules. Moreover, although neither North Korea nor China were signatories to the Geneva Conventions at the time of the Korean conflict, Pyongyang declared its intention to observe their rules in June 1950, and Beijing in July 1952. See US Department of the Army, *The United States Army in the Korean War*, v. 3; and Hermes 1966: 135–136.

until October 1950; the US had signed but not yet ratified the agreements; and North Korea had neither signed nor ratified them. Like the US and Canada, Britain was an original signatory when the treaties were successfully negotiated in 1949.[150] Although the UK did not ratify them until 1957, we saw Attorney General Shawcross observe earlier that the rules of war would likely apply in Korea because such rules have been applied in past civil wars, and the Geneva Conventions reflect this accepted practice.[151] Accordingly, he advised, Britain and the UN should perhaps declare that they are prepared "on the basis of reciprocity" to apply the accepted rules of warfare.[152]

A rule that became highly relevant during the Korean conflict was Article 118 of the Third Geneva Convention on POWs. As noted in the introduction chapter, this rule requires that "[p]risoners of war shall be released and repatriated without delay after the cessation of active hostilities."[153] The language of the article is explicit because, following World War II, the USSR held on to many of its POWs as forced labour.[154] As such, in arguing for Article 118, the US and its allies aimed to shed light on Moscow's behaviour and prevent such non-repatriation from occurring in future wars.[155] However, the rule that was agreed to in 1949 had unintended effects less than one year later in the Korean conflict.

During the negotiations aimed at ending the fighting, it became known that some of the North Korean and Chinese soldiers who had been captured by the UN force did not want to be repatriated. In response to this development, the Communist delegation at the truce talks invoked Article 118, while the US proposed an alternative principle, "voluntary repatriation," which would allow

---

150 See "Treaties, States Parties and Commentaries," on the website of the International Committee of the Red Cross, at https://ihl-databases.icrc.org/applic/ihl/ihl.nsf/vwTreatiesByCountry Selected.xsp?xp_countrySelected=GB.

151 *Copy of Letter from the Attorney General to the Lord Chancellor*, 4 Sept. 1950, Annex to *Legal Implications of the Korean Conflict*, 14 Sept. 1950, C.P. (50)207. Law scholars may note a potential inconsistency in the legal reasoning of Shawcross and other UK leaders at the time: if the 1949 Geneva Conventions applied to the hostilities in Korea, then the situation presumably had to be categorized first as an international armed conflict. Alternatively, if the situation was categorized as a civil war, then Common Article 3 (which requires minimum humane treatment in non-international conflicts) of the treaties would presumably apply, and the more detailed POW rules would not. I thank one of the anonymous reviewers of this book for this insightful observation.

152 Ibid.

153 See Article 118 of the 1949 Third Geneva Convention Relative to the Treatment of POWs. Earlier treaties stated that prisoners should or shall be repatriated after an armistice or peace treaty was legally concluded, rather than after the factual cessation of hostilities. This left a loophole open for some states to keep prisoners following WWI and WWII. See Pictet et al. 1960: 540–541.

154 Hermes 1966: 135.

155 MacDonald 1989: 135–136.

POWs to be interviewed and choose where they would be sent.[156] In deciding how to respond to the American position, British leaders faced a policy dilemma. Under the political circumstances of the nascent Cold War, with President Truman under domestic pressure to look strong in the fight against communism, it seemed unwise and unrealistic to forcefully send anti-communist POWs back to communist countries.

Further, leaders believed it would be morally wrong for them to send men back to face possible punishment or death by what the West perceived to be oppressive regimes.[157] For instance, UK Foreign Secretary Anthony Eden remarked in February 1952 that while the legal grounds for voluntary repatriation might be poor, this "doesn't make me like the idea of sending these poor devils back to death or worse."[158] Going further than Eden, recently elected Prime Minister Winston Churchill stressed one month later that the fate of the POWs in Korea involved considerations of "honour and humanity," and they could not be turned over for execution or imprisonment.[159]

And yet, notwithstanding such political and moral concerns, Article 118 clearly stated that POWs shall be released and repatriated without delay after the cessation of active hostilities. To disregard this rule would have been inconsistent with Britain's former position in 1949 and, leaders worried, could have threatened the safety of British and Commonwealth POWs, and set a dangerous precedent for future wars. Resonating with these concerns, the UK Foreign Office (FO) expressed considerable scepticism about America's motives. As one official noted in January 1952, while there was an element of humanitarianism in the US approach, it was also strongly influenced by political and ideological factors.[160] On 23 April, a paper was drafted for the Cabinet on the POW issue. In it, J.M. Addis of the FO's Korea department argued that "if it should clearly come to the breaking-point our right course would be to accept an armistice at the cost of agreeing to the forcible repatriation of a number of Chinese and anti-Communist prisoners ... I also feel that the humanitarian argument, that we could not have it on our conscience to force prisoners to return to death or slavery, has been given too much importance."[161]

---

156 Ibid.

157 MacDonald 1990: 73.

158 *Minute by Eden*: FK 1071/151, FO 371/99568, in MacDonald 1989: 145.

159 *Minute by Churchill*, 25 March 1952: FK 1551/33, in MacDonald 1989: 145. As MacDonald notes, Churchill and Eden were likely influenced by their experience of the 1945 Yalta agreement. Under that treaty, Britain and the US agreed to repatriate all Soviet citizens in Western Europe at the end of the war. Rather than accept forced repatriation, many Russians committed suicide, and the people who were returned faced reprisals by the Soviet government.

160 Cited in MacDonald 1990: 72.

161 *Paper on POWs prepared for Ministers*, by J.M. Addis, 23 April 1952, FO 371/99632, in Dockrill 1989: 106.

The above suggest that, in deciding how to respond to America's position on POWs during the Korean truce negotiations, UK leaders faced a situation where political and moral factors pointed in one direction – i.e., support the principle of voluntary repatriation – and international law pointed in another – i.e., implement Article 118. If theorizing and observing a distinct nature and effect of international law is possible in the fields of International Relations and International Law, then this is arguably one such situation.[162] Indeed, while Churchill rejected the Foreign Office's view, Eden sympathized with it.[163] Nonetheless, in the end, the government did not adopt the FO's position and instead decided to support the American stand on POWs. Explaining the decision in a letter to Clement Attlee on 1 May 1952, Eden wrote that "it would in my view be repugnant to the sense of values of the free world to send these men home by force."[164]

Key Findings

The aspects of Britain's participation in the Korean War assessed above support the argument that, when states use force, international law helps define and shape their possible course of action, and the justifications that can be made for their behaviour. More specifically, these aspects help illustrate the four roles that I theorize international law can play in such situations.

First, the fact that Britain decided to support the Security Council resolutions on the Korean crisis and contribute significant naval, air, and ground forces to the UN mission in Korea, even though political and military leaders thought the country was not strategically important, suggests that international law can help constitute a state's identity and be used to reorient its political and military objectives. As we saw, Prime Minister Attlee felt a strong sense of obligation to the United Nations and the conflict in Korea, and there is evidence that this perception of obligation was partly based on and affected by Britain's formal membership in the UN as well as Attlee's belief in the international rule of law. While other UK leaders, such as the Defence Chiefs of Staff, may not have felt the same responsibility regarding the UN and the Korean crisis, Attlee sought to reorient their thinking and explain the government's actions by reaffirming the importance of responding to aggression; making the new world organization effective; and upholding the rule of law in international politics.

Second, international law also had a regulative impact in the Korean War. The first example of this influence was Britain's non-participation in the US

---

162 I thank Duncan Snidal for a spirited discussion regarding this observation.
163 Dockrill 1989: 106; and MacDonald 1990: 73.
164 *Eden to Attlee*, 1 May 1952, FO 371/99572, in Dockrill 1989: 107.

naval blockade of Taiwan. As we saw, there is evidence that this non-participation was shaped in part by the UK's understanding of the scope of the Security Council's resolutions on the Korean crisis, and by the "special legal position," as acting Foreign Secretary Younger put it, that Britain was in regarding Taiwan and China. Again, it is important to note that the UK refused to allow its forces to participate in the Taiwan blockade even though some British officials thought that such participation might prove necessary if China attacked the disputed island. The second example of law's regulative role was Britain's use of the Security Council resolutions and other relevant international legal instruments to help constrain America's response to the crisis. As we saw, in the discussions leading up to the second and third Council resolutions, the UK was able to influence the US negotiating position and shape the outcome of the talks, and Britain's interpretation of the international legal factors at issue played a role in this regard. Britain also used its understanding of the Council resolutions, as well as other related instruments such as the Cairo Declaration of 1943, to help constrain America's behaviour regarding Taiwan.

Third, when the UK responded to the Korean crisis, international law helped permit and legitimate certain political and military practices that otherwise might not have been permitted. The first example of this role was the fact that Britain intervened militarily in a violent *civil* war, and justified this publicly and privately with reference to the Security Council resolutions on the crisis and the UN Charter's provisions on self-defence. The second example was the fact that the UK ultimately supported the controversial US decision to cross the 38th parallel in October 1950, and it helped draft a General Assembly resolution aimed at providing UN support for this crossing.

Finally, Britain's reaction to the Korean crisis suggests that, when states use force, international law helps structure the process by which agents seek to develop and promote new legal rules and legitimate conduct. An important example of this phenomenon, we saw, was the Security Council's novel response to North Korea's attack, and the efforts of UK leaders to justify and study this response, and to create new collective security law.

Although the preceding analysis suggests that international law helped influence Britain's involvement in the Korean War, it is less clear the extent to which UK leaders understood this law as a distinct and binding set of legal rules, and whether the legal status of these rules impacted their decision-making. On the one hand, we saw that leaders and officials recognized that the use of force in Korea and the treatment of prisoners were in part legal issues, in that they were governed by pre-existing rules in the UN Charter and Geneva Conventions. Moreover, leaders and officials discussed the extent to which Britain was legally obligated to consider these rules when deciding whether and how to use force in Korea, and what policy to adopt regarding the repatriation of enemy POWs. Further, Attorney General Shawcross acknowledged that the accepted rules of war should apply reciprocally in the conflict, even though the 1949 Geneva Conventions came into force after the fighting began, and Britain had only signed but not yet ratified the treaties. Finally, leaders and officials recognized that Britain's involvement in the US-led intervention in Korea was subject to international legal critique, and required legal justification at the domestic and international level. The foregoing details resonate with most of the observable implications posited in chapter two, and suggest that many important UK leaders and officials, but particularly Prime Minister Attlee and Foreign Secretary Eden, felt bound in part by international law.

On the other hand, because the Security Council *recommended* that help be provided to South Korea, leaders and officials tended to interpret the Council's resolutions on the Korean crisis more in political and moral, rather than expressly binding, terms. By contrast, a key repatriation rule in the Third Geneva Convention on POWs, Article 118, was seen in distinctly legal terms. However, the perceived requirements of this rule conflicted with other political and moral considerations at the time, and these factors appear to have ultimately exerted a greater impact on Britain than the law at issue.

We will see similar outcomes about the influence and interpretation of international law in Canada's participation in the Korean War, which the next chapter will address.

5 Canada and the Korean War

As an Allied nation still recovering from the sacrifice and horrors of the Second World War, Canada and its leaders were caught off guard by the conflict in Korea. In essence, this early Cold War crisis pitted the old isolationist views of former Prime Minister W.L. Mackenzie King against the new internationalism of younger leaders like Louis St. Laurent, Lester Pearson, and Brooke Claxton. That the latter view ultimately prevailed had significant effects for Canadian foreign policy at the time, and for Canada's relationship to the United Nations and international law. As we will see, before and during the war, international law helped define and shape Canada's possible course of action, and the justifications that could be advanced for its conduct. However, it is less clear the extent to which leaders understood this law as a binding and distinct set of legal rules, and whether the legal status of these rules impacted their decision-making.

Why Canada Participated in the Korean War

As with Britain's participation in the Korean War, Canada's extensive involvement in the conflict is also not immediately easy to explain. Before and during the war, political and military leaders thought that Korea fell outside of Canada's direct national interest.[1] In addition, many leaders were concerned about other potential theatres of conflict in the emerging Cold War – such as Europe and North America – and other related international commitments – such as the recently created North Atlantic Treaty Organization (NATO).[2] Domestically, in light of the fact that earlier wars in 1899, 1914, and 1939 had divided English and French Canadians, leaders worried that sending troops to Korea in 1950 could do the same, particularly if such forces fought in a Commonwealth unit

---

1 Wood 1966: 12.
2 Wood 1966: ix.

under British command.[3] Moreover, as noted in chapter two, following World War II Canada had demobilized much of its military and decreased its defence spending significantly in absolute and relative terms. By 1950, the Liberal government of Prime Minister Louis St. Laurent had hoped to continue focusing on socio-economic issues, and "was profoundly unhappy" about having to once again debate war policy and rearmament.[4]

Despite these considerations, Canada ultimately participated, at great cost,[5] in the divisive and bloody conflict in faraway Korea. By the time of the armistice in July 1953, nearly 27,000 Canadians – out of a country of 13.7 million people – had served in or contributed to the war.[6] This was the third largest foreign contribution to the UN force, after the US and Britain.

In explaining why Canada participated in the Korean War, a number of scholars emphasize the perceived threat of international communism, the belief that the USSR was ultimately behind North Korea's attack, and the view that Canada had to support the United States in its response to this attack.[7] Other observers suggest that Canadian leaders saw the conflict as an exercise in collective security, in which it was essential to constrain US decisions by acting multilaterally through the United Nations.[8] These differing accounts likely reflect the fact that, in the years leading up to the Korean War, three different views of Canadian foreign policy had developed among government leaders and high-level civil servants.

First, influenced by the trauma and loss of World War I, and the perceived failures of the League of Nations, "isolationists" such as Prime Minister W.L. Mackenzie King were concerned more with domestic harmony than with world affairs, and believed that problems were best solved by people and not by formal international organizations.[9] From this perspective, therefore, the task of Canadian foreign policy was three-fold:

> to gain and maintain Canada's recognition as an independent unified nation bound to the Commonwealth only by ties of loyalty to the Crown; to support Great Britain and the Empire in bad days as well as in good, but to do so because it is

---

3 Bothwell 2007: 86.

4 Wood 1966: 21.

5 Canada suffered 1,588 casualties in the Korean War, with 516 killed in action or dead on active service (Bercuson 2004).

6 Bercuson 2004.

7 These factors are emphasized, to varying degrees, by Bercuson 2004, Bothwell 2007, and Teigrob 2009.

8 See e.g. Stairs 1974 and Donaghy 1995.

9 King's Under-Secretary of State for External Affairs from 1925–41, O.D. Skelton, was also quite isolationist in his outlook. See Chapnick 2005: 7–9. Chapnick's illuminating historical study refers to extensive archive materials which, due to space limitations, are not cited here in full.

in Canada's best interest; and finally to promote close friendship between Canada and the United States and thus a closer understanding between the United States and Great Britain.[10]

An example of such isolationist thinking is arguably Canada's refusal to participate in the Allied airlift response to the Berlin crisis of 1948–49,[11] which was noted briefly in the prior chapter.

"Continentalists," by comparison, expanded on the third foreign policy objective quoted above – i.e., promoting relations between Canada and the US. This view was particularly aware that, following World War II, the US had displaced Britain as the most powerful Western country. It also tended to assume that cooperating with the USSR was unlikely. From this perspective, Canada's foreign policy was thus best pursued through closer military, political, and economic cooperation with its southern neighbour. Examples of such thinking can arguably be found in Canada's support for the NATO defence pact of 1949, and its decision in 1950 to allow nuclear-armed American bombers to be stationed in Labrador.[12]

While not denying the significance of the United States, "internationalists" such as Foreign Minister Lester Pearson, Defence Minister Brooke Claxton, and diplomat Escott Reid believed that global institutions like the United Nations were also important to Canada's post-war future.[13] From this perspective, Canada could best leverage its middle-power status and pursue its interests by working multilaterally through the UN,[14] and by acting as a moderating influence in the Western alliance.[15] Examples of this internationalist outlook can be found in Canada's contributions to the founding of the UN – particularly from 1943 to 1945[16] – and its subsequent support for and participation in the organization leading up to and during the Korean War.[17]

These three perspectives arose in the debates and decisions behind Canada's response to the Korean crisis. However, as we will see, the internationalist view was most relevant, with Canadian leaders tending to see the conflict as an exercise in collective security against aggression, in which it was important to

---

10 Chapnick 2005: 7.

11 Teigrob 2009: 169.

12 Donaghy 1996: xvii.

13 See e.g. Pearson's memoirs, where he contrasts his international outlook with that of Mackenzie King (1972: 294).

14 Chapnick 2005: 4–6, 9.

15 Donaghy 1995.

16 Holmes 1982, and Chapnick 2005.

17 For instance, despite King's worries, Canada accepted a non-permanent seat on the Security Council in 1947, and sent a judge to sit on the UN Palestine Commission. For other examples of Canada supporting the UN in this period, see Thomson 1967: 217–221.

moderate the course of American decisions through multilateral diplomacy. Within this perspective, moreover, a perception of obligation under the UN Charter and Geneva Conventions affected the thinking and decisions of the government regarding the war, and the justifications that could be advanced for Canada's actions.

Following its decision to fight in Korea, Canada had two broad objectives in the war. First, Canada aimed to contribute to the UN response to the conflict. And second, it sought to limit the intensity, duration, and geographic scope of the hostilities.[18] "In concrete terms," notes Dennis Stairs, "this meant (a) limiting the conduct of the war to the Korean peninsula; (b) making every effort to prevent the allies of North Korea – notably Communist China – from being driven by strategic or other considerations to participate in the hostilities; (c) ensuring in particular that the question of Formosa [Taiwan] did not become linked to the outcome of the conflict in Korea; and (d) concluding at the earliest possible opportunity a satisfactory cease-fire in the theatre."[19]

The main military problem for Canada, like Britain at the time, was how to support the goals of the UN without diverting scarce resources from areas perceived to be more vital to the country's strategic interests, such as North America and Europe. The primary political challenge for Canada was how to support the United States while also maintaining an independent foreign policy and domestic approval of the government's decisions. As we will see in chapter seven, this challenge arose again in the Afghanistan Conflict, and it arguably continues today.

The Four Roles of International Law in Canada's Use of Force in Korea

As with Britain's involvement in the Korean War, Canada's participation further suggests that international law can play four main roles when states use force: (1) it helps constitute the identity of actors; (2) it helps regulate their conduct; (3) it permits and legitimates certain actions; and (4) it helps structure the development of new legal rules and legitimate behaviour.

1. International Law Helped Constitute the Identities of Key Canadian Leaders

The fact that Canada decided to (a) join the United Nations Temporary Commission on Korea (UNTCOK) in 1948; (b) support the Security Council

---

18 Thomson 1967: 294, Stairs 1974: 93, and Donaghy 1996: xv.
19 Stairs 1974: 93.

resolutions on the Korean crisis in 1950, and (c) contribute significant naval, air, and ground forces to the UN mission in Korea even though political and military leaders thought the country was not strategically important, suggests that international law can help constitute a state's identity and be used to redefine its political and military objectives. As will be seen below, Prime Minister Louis St. Laurent, Defence Minister Brooke Claxton, and Foreign Minister Lester Pearson believed that Canada's formal membership in the UN carried corresponding obligations, including the duty to defend – by force if need be, and even in situations where Canada's own interests were not directly at stake – the principles of the UN Charter, the effectiveness of the UN organization, and the concept of collective security.

While other leaders, such as former Prime Minister Mackenzie King, did not feel the same sense of responsibility regarding the UN and the Korean crisis, St. Laurent and Pearson sought to reorient his thinking through legal interpretation of a relevant UN resolution. And it is this interpretation that ultimately led King to allow Canada to join UNTCOK. Following the government's decision to contribute to the UN force in Korea two years later, St. Laurent, Pearson and Claxton continued to believe that Canada, as a middle power state that had helped create the UN, was now obligated to support the organization's collective "police action" against aggression.

The constitutive effect of international law can be seen first in the debate behind Canada's decision to join UNTCOK in 1948. As was noted in the previous chapter, after talks between the United States and the USSR proved fruitless, the former requested in September 1947 that the UN appoint a temporary commission on Korea to supervise an election in the area. Although protested by the USSR, the US request was passed by the General Assembly in November. In the committee debate prior to this passage, Canada's representative, J.A. Bradette, spoke briefly in support of the American proposal.[20] When then Prime Minister Mackenzie King learned of Bradette's comments, he became irritated and told an aide, "This United Nations is going to destroy us yet. Just imagine, *Bradette* making speeches about Korea!"[21] Unknown to King at the time, this initial irritation would turn into a full-blown Cabinet crisis.

In its proposal to the UN, the US had listed Canada among its nominations for UNTCOK. Surprised by the request, the leader of Canada's delegation, Justice Minister J.L. Ilsley, reluctantly agreed on the advice of Lester Pearson, then Deputy Foreign Minister. In the absence of Mackenzie King, who was in Britain, Foreign Minister Louis St. Laurent approved Ilsley's decision. During a Cabinet meeting on 18 December 1947, St. Laurent then sought to appoint

---

20 United Nations, GAOR (First Committee), A/C.1/SR.116, 258, 284, cited in Stairs 1974: 7.
21 Quoted in Stairs 1974: 7. Bradette was not regarded as an authority on foreign affairs.

Canada's delegate to UNTCOK. In response, King "blew a gasket," and said he could not support the appointment.[22] It was a grave error, he warned, to embroil Canada in Asian affairs of which members of the government had no knowledge, and which involved the conflicting interests of great powers. War, he stressed, might well break out between the US and the USSR, and Canada could be drawn into such a conflict if it interfered with Soviet-American relations.[23]

St. Laurent, who was restraining "himself with noticeable difficulty,"[24] stated that so long as Canada was a member of the United Nations, the government was obligated to accept such responsibilities. King replied that, except as a vehicle for Russian propaganda, the UN "counted for nothing so far as any help in the world was concerned."[25] The proper role of Canada, he added, "was not that of Sir Galahad to save the whole world unless we were in a position to do it."[26] Another meeting on 22 December failed to settle the issue, but highlighted the stark isolationist-internationalist divide in the Cabinet's outlook.[27] Commenting on this divide in his private papers, Defence Minister Brooke Claxton later wrote "that an organization for international cooperation in every part of the world could only function if the disinterested countries ... were willing to act as mediators ... and even judges regarding points in issue involving other countries."[28]

The divergent views of the Cabinet members regarding the UNTCOK issue were so deeply held that King, Ilsley, St. Laurent, and Claxton all threatened or considered resigning if their positions were not accepted.[29] Ultimately, the situation was resolved by St. Laurent's legal interpretation of the General Assembly resolution that had created the commission. This instrument stated that, to observe that representatives chosen in Korea's election "are in fact duly elected by the Korean people," UNTCOK would "be present in Korea, with right to travel, observe and consult throughout Korea."[30] In St. Laurent's view, the resolution

22 Notes, Brooke Claxton papers, VI, 1126, cited in Stairs 1974: 9.
23 Pickersgill and Foster 1970: 134. There is a (bizarre) theory that the prime minister's angry reaction was attributable at least in part to an encounter he had with a London spiritualist while abroad, and a warning she gave from the late US President F.D. Roosevelt about an impending war in Asia. See Stairs 1974: 10.
24 Claxton notes, 1127, in Stairs 1974: 10.
25 Pickersgill and Foster 1970: 134–135.
26 Ibid.
27 King's view was supported by Labour Minister Humphrey Mitchell, Agriculture Minister James Gardiner, and Senate leader Wishart Robertson. Other Cabinet leaders supported St. Laurent's position.
28 Claxton notes, 1130–1131, in Stairs 1974: 12.
29 Thomson 1967: 223–224, and Claxton notes, 1131–1135, in Stairs 1974: 13.
30 UN General Assembly Resolution 112 (II), of 14 Nov. 1947, in Farrar-Hockley 1990: 403–404.

thus authorized the commission to supervise elections in the occupation zones of both the north and the south, or none at all.[31] And, since the USSR would likely refuse to cooperate, there was little risk that UNTCOK would have to take sides. When King noted that the US had implied that the commission might act in the south alone, St. Laurent assured him that his understanding of the resolution was that UNTCOK would act only if it could do so throughout Korea and with the consent of both occupation powers. On this basis, King agreed to Canada's participation.[32]

In sum, leaders took the wording of the UNTCOK resolution very seriously, and believed that a future event – in this case, the supervision of an election only in South Korea – was precluded by its terms. Further, Canada's foreign policy was altered on this view of the resolution's terms. Finally, in the debates behind this policy change, Canada's perceived obligations to the UN were a site for a "communicative" struggle over the country's legitimate identity and rightful behaviour.

The constitutive influence of international law can also be seen in Canada's decision to support the Security Council resolutions on the Korean crisis in 1950, and to contribute significant naval, air, and ground forces to the UN operation there even though Korea was not seen as strategically important.[33] Like their US and British counterparts, Canadian leaders were surprised by North Korea's invasion of South Korea.[34] They were also not immediately sure the Americans would actively intervene.[35] After hearing news of the attack, St. Laurent – who was now prime minister – and Foreign Minister Pearson consulted together and agreed that the UN should be brought into the picture to restore order.[36] However, they worried, since Canada's earlier plea for an international police force had fallen on deaf ears, "it was not immediately clear how the world organization could act effectively."[37] While the US was the only country capable of providing effective military aid to South Korea, they were

---

31 Stairs 1974: 16.

32 Ibid.

33 As Pearson noted in an update to Canada's embassies abroad, "the strategic consequences of the loss of Korea would not be serious," as it "would not result in any substantial weakening of the forces now available to the anti-Communist world." See *Telegram*, 28 June 1950, [DEA/50069-A-40], doc. 16 in Donaghy 1996: 31.

34 Stairs 1974: 33.

35 See Stairs 1974: 39; and comments made by Hume Wrong, Canada's Ambassador to the US, to Lester Pearson on 27 June 1950 (*Telegram WA-1417*, 27 June 1950, [DEA/50069-A-40], doc. 13 in Donaghy 1996: 27).

36 See *Extract from Memorandum from Secretary of State for External Affairs to Prime Minister*, 27 June and 4 July 1950, [PCO/Vol. 167], doc. 11 in Donaghy 1996: 22; Thomson 1967: 292; and Stairs 1974: 43.

37 Thomson 1967: 292.

further concerned that if America acted unilaterally, the war might turn into a global struggle between the Communists and the non-Communists.[38]

Accordingly, St. Laurent and Pearson were pleased when the Security Council was called into emergency session on 25 June.[39] Speaking in Parliament the next day, Pearson expressed his hope "that as a result of the intervention of the United Nations some effective action may be possible ... to restore peace."[40] North Korea's attack, he said, constituted "a breach of the peace" and "an action of unprovoked aggression."[41] As such, he urged support of the Council's resolution on the matter, which determined that North Korea's attack constituted "a breach of the peace," called for a cessation of the hostilities, and the withdrawal of North Korean forces to the 38th parallel. Further, it asked all member states to help the UN in the execution of the resolution. In the following days, Canada also expressed its support for the Council's second resolution,[42] which recommended that UN members "furnish such assistance ... as may be necessary to repel the armed attack and to restore international peace and security in the area."

Canada's support for the Council's third resolution, by contrast, was more qualified. This instrument recommended that all UN members providing assistance make such provisions available to a unified command under the US. In the negotiations prior to the resolution, Pearson argued that references to "the United *States*" appeared too often in light of the UN character of the Korean operation [emphasis in original].[43] He also protested the repetition of the phrase "in the area," worrying that it gave inadequate definition to the scope of UN operations, and that it could be misinterpreted as including the US blockade of Taiwan.[44] Despite these private concerns, though, Canada did not publicly criticize the resolution, and explicitly linked its military actions in Korea to the Security Council's recommendations on the issue.

As was the case with Britain, although Canada's backing of the Security Council resolutions was relatively forthcoming, its decision to send ground forces to Korea was less so. In response to the Council's first two resolutions, the

---

38 See ibid, and the reflections of John Holmes, Canada's acting UN delegate during the Korean War, in Stairs 1974: 53.

39 Thomson 1967: 292.

40 HC Debs., Hansard, 26 June 1950, 4116–4117.

41 Ibid.

42 HC Debs., 28 June 1950, 4251; and *Extract from a Memorandum from Secretary of State for External Affairs to Prime Minister*, 27 June and 4 July 1950, [PCO/Vol.167], doc. 31 in Donaghy 1996: 49.

43 See Pearson's comments to Canada's Ambassador in the US in *Telegram EX-1068*, 5 July 1950, [DEA/50069-A-40], doc. 33 in Donaghy 1996: 52.

44 See the comments made by Pearson's deputy, A.D.P. Heeney, on his behalf, to John Holmes in *Telegram 327*, 5 July 1950, [DEA/50069-A-40], doc. 36 in Donaghy 1996: 55.

Cabinet initially agreed to send two Canadian military officers to the UN Commission on Korea.[45] Following diplomatic inquiries from the US,[46] and further debate, the Cabinet also agreed to send five long-range air transport planes[47] and three naval destroyers.[48] These vessels, the government told the UN Secretary General, are "made available to the United Nations and appropriate action is being taken by the Canadian Government to place them at once under the operational control of the Commander-in-Chief of the forces made available by members of the United Nations for the defence of the Republic of Korea against the aggression committed by North Korean forces."[49]

As noted in the prior chapter, the military position of the UN force in Korea deteriorated during the summer of 1950, and concern grew in the US that it was the only Western state sacrificing its soldiers there. Consequently, US officials asked the UN Secretary General in mid-July to appeal for ground forces, and pressured Canada to send troops.[50] Like Britain at the time, Canada thus also faced a policy dilemma, in that the government's public commitment to the UN, its relationship with the US, and its belief in its world role as a middle power conflicted with the realities of a demobilized military, a concern for domestic political harmony and socio-economic development, and a worry that other international commitments and theatres of potential conflict should not be forgotten.

The government's initial reaction to this dilemma appears to have prioritized these latter concerns. As A.D.P. Heeney, Deputy Foreign Minister, argued in a memo on 18 July, "Serious as is the Korean situation, and important as it is that we should not fail in our responsibility as a member of the United Nations … Western Europe is … still the main theatre … It is suggested therefore that any Canadian contribution should not be at the expense of our capacity to fulfill our responsibilities for the direct defence of Canada and under the North Atlantic Treaty."[51] Consistent with this logic, the Defence Chiefs advised that Canada was not in a position to contribute ground forces in Korea.[52] In light of

---

45 *Extract from Cabinet Conclusions*, 28 June 1950, [PCO], doc. 17 in Donaghy 1996: 33.

46 See the update provided by Canada's Ambassador in the US to Pearson, *Telegram WA-1422*, 28 June 1950, [DEA/50069-A-40], doc. 19 in Donaghy 1996: 35.

47 *Secretary of State for External Affairs to Acting Permanent Delegate to United Nations, Telegram 360*, 21 July 1950, [DEA/50059-A-40], doc. 52 in Donaghy 1996: 89.

48 *Secretary of State for External Affairs to Permanent Delegate to United Nations, Telegram 343*, 12 July 1950, [DEA/50069-A-40], doc. 40 in Donaghy 1996: 60.

49 Ibid: 60–61.

50 See Pearson's comments in *Extract from Cabinet Conclusions*, 19 July 1950, [PCO], doc. 80 in Donaghy 1996: 82; and the reflections of various former leaders and advisers in Stairs 1974: 74.

51 *Memorandum from Under-Secretary of State for External Affairs to Secretary of State for External Affairs*, 18 July 1950, [DEA/50069-A-40], doc. 45 in Donaghy 1996: 67.

52 *Extract from Cabinet Conclusions*, 19 July 1950, [PCO], doc. 49 in Donaghy 1996: 81.

these concerns, St. Laurent announced on 19 July that, although Canada would increase its defence efforts, it would not send troops to Korea.[53] However, he added, if the Security Council recruited a voluntary force for service there – an idea that had been floated at the UN and endorsed by Pearson[54] – Canada would immediately consider participating.

Following St. Laurent's statement, no such international brigade was created. But a combination of internal and external factors ultimately led the government to alter its position and send soldiers to Korea. Domestically, most English language newspapers were critical of the government's announcement, and even the left-wing Cooperative Commonwealth Federation Party pressed for the dispatch of troops.[55] Externally, a number of other states – including fellow Commonwealth countries Britain and Australia – decided to send ground forces, and the US and UK continued to ask Canada to do the same.[56] Importantly, Dennis Stairs notes that "all of the Canadian officials" he interviewed for his leading study on Canada and the Korean War "were agreed that American pressure was not a major consideration for Canadian decision makers on this issue," and that it was the appeal from the UN, not Washington, that had the most significant impact on leaders at the time.[57] While it is possible that these men under-reported the impact of the US, there is documentary evidence from that period to support their account.[58]

In any event, the net result of these inputs was that the Cabinet decided in August to recruit and train an additional army brigade of about 10,000 men "for use in discharging Canadian obligations under United Nations or North Atlantic Treaty commitments."[59] In the months following this decision, the military position of the UN force in Korea improved. As such, Canada sent only one battalion from its brigade to the peninsula in late November.[60] It was initially thought that the rest of the force might then serve in Europe.[61] After China

---

53 Department of External Affairs, *Statements and Speeches*, no. 50/28.

54 *Extract from Cabinet Conclusions*, 19 July 1950, [PCO], doc. 49 in Donaghy 1996: 84.

55 Stairs 1974: 83.

56 See *Memorandum from Secretary of State for External Affairs to Prime Minister*, 26 July 1950, [L.B.P/Vol.35], doc. 55 in Donaghy 1996: 92; and Wood 1966: 22–23.

57 This point, Stairs notes, was stressed especially by John Holmes, Lester Pearson, and A.D.P. Heeney (1974: 75).

58 As Pearson wrote to Canada's Ambassador in Washington on 20 July 1950, US officials have, "I suspect, been instructed by the State Department to make every effort to impress on us that we should send land forces to Korea, but they have not had much success. I do not need to tell you that we tend to react vigorously to pressure of this kind" (*Secretary of State for External Affairs to Ambassador in United States*, 20 July 1950, [L.B.P/Vol.35], doc. 50 in Donaghy 1996: 85).

59 *Extract from Cabinet Conclusions*, 2, 3 and 7 Aug. 1950, [PCO], doc. 62 in Donaghy 1996: 101.

60 *Extract from Cabinet Conclusions*, 15 Nov. 1950, [PCO], doc. 91 in Donaghy 1996: 147.

61 See Brooke Claxton's update to Parliament, in HC Debs., 5 Feb. 1951, 92.

intervened in the war, however, and the military situation changed again, fresh requests were made for more troops. This led to a decision in February 1951 to send the whole brigade to Korea.[62]

Canada supported the Security Council resolutions on the Korean conflict and contributed to the UN force there because it valued its relationship with the US[63] and Britain,[64] and feared Soviet expansion.[65] However, Canada was also concerned with its perceived obligations under the UN Charter and the Council resolutions. As Pearson stressed in a memo to St. Laurent, since the outbreak of fighting in Korea, "We have made it abundantly clear in Washington that if Canada is to help, it must be help to the UN, fulfilling our obligations under the Charter, and *not* help to the United States" [emphasis in original].[66] Consistent with this private description, St. Laurent announced to Parliament early in the crisis that Canadian "responsibility in this matter arises entirely from our membership in the United Nations and from our support of the [second] resolution of the Security Council."[67] Continuing, he added:

> Any participation by Canada in carrying out the foregoing resolution ... would not be participation in war against any state. It would be our part in collective police action under the control and authority of the [UN] for the purpose of restoring peace to an area where an aggression has occurred as determined under the Charter of the United Nations by the Security Council, which decision has been accepted by us. It is only in such circumstances that this country would be involved in action of this kind.[68]

The above comments suggest that, like their British counterparts, Canada's highest political leaders believed that North Korea's attack constituted a formal act of aggression, and emphasized the importance of responding to this breach of the peace collectively through the United Nations. Unlike Britain, though, Canada went further and immediately portrayed the situation not as a war but as a "police action" authorized by the Security Council.

---

62 HC Debs., 21 Feb. 1951, 563. The brigade arrived in Korea in April 1951.

63 See the comments of the Minister of Fisheries in *Extract from Cabinet Conclusions*, 27 July 1950, [PCO], doc. 56 in Donaghy 1996: 93.

64 See the comments of the Trade and Commerce Minister, C.D. Howe, in ibid.

65 See Pearson's description of the "menace which faces us" in Korea, and "the necessity of defeating it there by United Nations action," in *Memorandum from Secretary of State for External Affairs to Prime Minister*, 3 Aug. 1950, [L.B.P./Vol.35], doc. 63 in Donaghy 1996: 105.

66 *Extract from Memorandum from Secretary of State for External Affairs to Prime Minister*, 27 June and 4 July 1950, [PCO/Vol.167], doc. 31 in Donaghy 1996: 49–50.

67 HC Debs., 30 June 1950, 4459.

68 Ibid.

There is evidence that the support of St. Laurent, Pearson, and Claxton for the UN prior to and during the Korean War, and their perception of obligation under the UN Charter and Security Council resolutions, were sincere and shaped in part by Canada's formal membership in and contributions to the organization. However, this evidence also indicates that these men perhaps valued this membership and these contributions more than other important Canadian leaders. Significantly for history, though, it was the former and not the latter who occupied Canada's highest positions of political leadership when the conflict in Korea broke out.

Prior to World War II and the founding of the UN in 1945, Canada had become familiar with the idea of an institutional structure to support international order as a member of the League of Nations.[69] During the war, the US and UK led the post-conflict planning effort,[70] and the government of Mackenzie King did not get seriously involved until 1943.[71] An obstacle at the time was that Deputy Foreign Minister O.D. Skelton shared King's "isolationist" outlook, and argued that Canada would not survive entrance into another European war.[72] By implication, there was no reason to think comprehensively about the peace that might follow.[73]

In response to this perceived lack of international leadership, organizations like the League of Nations Society and the Canadian Institute of International Affairs (CIIA) aimed to promote a greater awareness of global problems and the need for collective security.[74] One of the Society's affiliates and a CIIA leader was Brooke Claxton, who would later become Canada's defence minister during the Korean War. In the early 1940s, Claxton actively sought to redefine Canada's world role, and to link this re-conception to the soon-to-be created UN organization.[75] He also directed a campaign to assert Canada's independence from Britain.[76] During this period, other voices in Canada, such as key Conservative politicians, disagreed with Claxton's views, especially those on the Commonwealth.[77]

While Canada was becoming more vocal about its independence and world role, it was also getting more formally involved in post-war planning. In this regard, Canada helped create two early UN bodies: the UN Relief and

---

69 Keating 2013: 20. Membership in the League of Nations, it should be noted, was not universal. For instance, neither the US nor the USSR joined the organization.

70 The US and Britain were later joined by the USSR and China.

71 Chapnick 2005: 3, and Keating 2013: 20.

72 Chapnick 2005: 9.

73 Stacey 1981: 269, and Granatstein 1982: 28–44.

74 Chapknick 2005: 8.

75 For a description of Claxton's efforts, see ibid: 9, 13, 18, 52–54.

76 Ibid: 53–54.

77 Howard Green, in HC Debs., 9 July 1943, vol. 238, 4564; and John Diefenbaker, in ibid: 4593.

Rehabilitation Administration (UNRRA), and the Food and Agriculture Organization (FAO). One of the main Canadian diplomats involved in the creation of these organizations was Lester Pearson. Pearson, who was posted in Washington at the time, was more "idealist" in his approach to the UN negotiations than some other Canadian officials, such as Deputy Foreign Minister Norman Robertson (who had replaced Skelton) and his assistant, Hume Wrong.[78] Whereas Robertson and Wrong tended to accept the domination of the great powers in the talks, Pearson saw these powers as part of the problem.[79] And he also saw a need for an effective collective security system. As he wrote to Robertson in February 1944, "we now know … that there is no safety in a League of Nations which does not make adequate provision for peaceful change and police action against the aggressor."[80]

When the final draft of the UN Charter was negotiated in San Francisco in June 1945, Pearson attended the historic conference. Another Canadian who attended was then Justice Minister Louis St. Laurent. Following the signing of the Charter, St. Laurent asked Parliament to approve the document in October. He conceded that the Charter was a product of "compromise," and that it included a great power veto at the Security Council.[81] Nonetheless, he stressed, it was a significant improvement from earlier versions, and Canada helped bring about some of these changes. After warning that no organization could succeed without the will of its members, St. Laurent concluded: "The Charter of the United Nations is a first step in the direction of that co-operation between nations which appears to be essential to the survival of civilization."[82]

Importantly, St. Laurent's commitment to the United Nations continued after he became Foreign Minister. For instance, in an important speech from January 1947 that outlined the principles that should guide Canadian foreign policy in the post-war period, St. Laurent affirmed the significance of the rule of law, the "acceptance of international responsibility in keeping with our conception of our role in world affairs," and support for international institutions.[83] As he stated, "If there is one conclusion that our common experience has led us to accept, it is that security for this country lies in the development of a firm structure of international organization."[84]

Again, the above suggests that the support of St. Laurent, Pearson, and Claxton for the United Nations leading up to and during the Korean War, and their

---

78 Keating 2013: 22–24.
79 Eayrs 1972: 154.
80 Cited in Keating 2013: 28.
81 St. Laurent, HC Debs., 16 Oct. 1945, vol. 246, 1185–1202.
82 Ibid.
83 The speech was made at the University of Toronto. See Mackenzie 1995: 149.
84 This quote is from Keating 2013: 20, and appears to be part of the same speech.

perception of obligation under the UN Charter and the Security Council resolutions on Korea, were sincere and shaped in part by Canada's formal membership in, and contributions to, the world organization. As acknowledged in the previous chapter, such support and perception by Western leaders were possible because a majority of UN member states were considered sympathetic to the US and its allies, and because the USSR was absent when the Council resolutions were passed. Consequently, one might be tempted to conclude that leaders like Prime Minister St. Laurent and President Truman were only using the UN as a convenient tool in the Cold War, lending cover to the policy of containment.

However, while it is important to recognize the political conditions under which the US and its allies were able to respond to the Korean crisis through the UN, one should not underestimate the degree to which key leaders saw UN involvement as providing more than just "cover" for the policy of containment. As Pearson noted in a letter to Hume Wrong, now Canada's Ambassador to the US, in July 1950: "I think Washington has been sincere and praiseworthy in its efforts to work through and with the United Nations, but … I [also] think that they should be very careful … not to play into the hands of those communists and their friends who claim that the UN is merely a cover for US policy in regard to Korea. No doubt they appreciate this in the State Department."[85]

2. International Law Helped Regulate Canada's Conduct

International law also had a regulative influence during Canada's involvement in the Korean crisis. Two examples of this impact can be seen in Canada's non-participation in the US naval blockade of Taiwan, and in Canada's use of the General Assembly's 1948 UNTCOK resolution and the Security Council's resolutions on Korea to help constrain America's response to the crisis.

Regarding the first example, we saw that in the negotiations leading up to the Security Council's third resolution on Korea, Lester Pearson protested the inclusion of the phrase "to restore international peace and security *in the area*" [emphasis added], and worried that it could be misinterpreted as including the US blockade of Taiwan. Further, when Canada later reported its naval contribution to the UN secretary general, it said that the vessels are "made available to the UN" under the operational control of the Commander-in-Chief "for the defence of the Republic of Korea." There is evidence that these concerns about the geographic scope of the third Council resolution, as well as the formal authority of the UN force in Korea, were deeply felt by key leaders and helped define and shape Canada's non-participation in the Taiwan blockade.

---

85 *Secretary of State for External Affairs to Ambassador in United States*, 20 July 1950, [L.B.P./ Vol.35], doc. 50 in Donaghy 1996: 86.

For instance, commenting on a US draft of the third resolution, Deputy Foreign Minister A.D.P. Heeney wrote to John Holmes, Canada's acting UN representative, on 5 July 1950:

> We are nervous about the phrase "in the area of Korea" and feel strongly that it should be replaced simply by "Korea." You will be aware that on previous occasions the [US] Government has given a very broad interpretation to similar phrases which have included the formula, "in the area of." We would not wish the resolution to contain anything which would suggest that we are in any way involved in the decision of the [US] Government to defend [Taiwan]. We regard the order of President Truman to the Seventh Fleet to prevent any attack on [Taiwan] as a decision taken by the [US] Government alone and on its own authority. It does not flow in any way from a decision by the United Nations. As a member of the [UN] we have a responsibility, pursuant to the resolutions of the Security Council of the 25th and 27th of June, to assist, so far as we are able, in the defence of Korea. We have no (repeat no) such responsibility to assist in the defence of [Taiwan].[86]

In expressing this view, Heeney and Pearson had two fears in mind: that General MacArthur might use non-US naval forces meant for Korean operations instead for the Taiwan blockade; and that a US vessel flying both the UN and American flags could be fired on by Communist China, thus leading to allegations that all UN members had been attacked.[87]

Although Pearson and Heeney had these fears, they and other officials later recalled in interviews that – like their UK counterparts – they also thought the Taiwan blockade "was well calculated to limit the scope of the hostilities, not only because it would place constraints upon the behaviour of the regime in Peking, but also because it would inhibit Chiang Kai-shek, who might otherwise be tempted to take advantage of the situation in order to renew active operations against the Chinese Communist forces."[88] Despite seeing the blockade in this positive strategic light, however, these leaders nonetheless refused to let Canadian forces participate, and explained this non-participation with reference to the international legal considerations they deemed relevant at the time. Speaking to Parliament on 31 August, Pearson said the government was "concerned solely with carrying out our United Nations obligations in Korea or elsewhere," and these did not include anything that could be "interpreted as the

---

86 *Secretary of State for External Affairs to Acting Permanent Delegate to United Nations*, 5 July 1950, [DEA/50069-A-40], doc. 36 in Donaghy 1996: 55.
87 Ibid.
88 Stairs 1974: 52.

restoration of the nationalist Chinese government to the mainland of China, or an intervention in [Taiwan]."[89] Accordingly, Pearson's only specific injunction to Captain J.V. Brock, the commander of Canada's naval contribution to Korea, was that he "be sure to avoid embroilment in any action involving [Taiwan]."[90] As such, during the next three years of the Korean War, Canada's naval forces did not participate in the Taiwan blockade, and were limited to operations in Korea.[91]

Importantly, Canada's concerns about Taiwan arose not just in its decision to send naval forces to Korea but also in its later decision to contribute ground troops. For instance, during meetings with US and UN officials in Washington and New York on 29 July, Pearson discussed the conditions under which the government would be willing to send soldiers to Korea.[92] Among other things, he wanted guarantees that under no circumstances would the troops be involved in any way in the defence of Taiwan.[93] These assurances were given, and for the remainder of the war Canadian soldiers did not participate in the Taiwan blockade.

In addition to Canada's non-participation in the neutralization of Taiwan, another example of international law's regulative impact is Canada's use of the General Assembly's UNTCOK resolution and the Security Council's resolutions on Korea to help constrain America's response to the crisis. As noted earlier, Canada agreed to participate in UNTCOK based on the view that, under the General Assembly's resolution on the matter, the commission would act only if it could do so throughout Korea. As St. Laurent predicted, however, during the winter of 1948, Soviet authorities in North Korea refused to allow UNTCOK to operate there. In response, US officials argued for a new resolution that would allow the commission to "implement its programme … in such parts of Korea as are accessible."[94] Demonstrating independence we might not see today, Canada and Australia were the only two countries that maintained their opposition to this US proposal.[95] Part of Canada's concern, Pearson argued, was that supervising elections in the South alone would involve changes in the commission's terms of reference which were beyond the power of the Interim Committee of the General Assembly – the body overseeing UNTCOK – to decide.[96] Doing

---

89 HC Debs., 31 Aug. 1950, 90–97.

90 Stairs 1974: 70.

91 Thorgrimsson and Russell 1965.

92 See Pearson's update to Parliament, HC Debs., 4 Sept. 1950, 221–222.

93 See HC Debs., 4 Sept. 1950, 221–222; and Wood 1965: 46–47. Pearson also wanted to ensure that the troops would not be used in combat before they were adequately trained.

94 Cited in Spencer 1967: 106.

95 Gordenker 1959: 70–71. The final vote on the resolution, which occurred on 26 February 1948, was 31 to 2 in favour, with 11 abstentions.

96 Stairs 1974: 21.

so, he stressed, would be "unconstitutional."[97] As Stairs usefully notes, these arguments implied that UNTCOK "was subject solely to the resolutions of the United Nations as a whole, and was completely independent of the American authorities."[98]

When UNTCOK was instructed to supervise elections in South Korea, Canada's delegate, George Patterson, protested this instruction and withdrew from the commission's proceedings.[99] These actions "infuriated" the American diplomats involved.[100] By 23 March 1948, Patterson had been told to cooperate in the election observations.[101] Publicly, though, Canadian leaders continued to express concern that the international legal authority for the elections be clearly understood, and that the independence of the UN in this matter be maintained. As St. Laurent stressed at the time, "the responsibility for running the elections [now] rests with the [US] military government authorities and any action towards the establishment of a government in Korea following the elections will not be on the strength of the resolution of the General Assembly but on the legal position of [these] ... authorities."[102]

In addition to the General Assembly's UNTCOK resolution, Canada also drew upon the Security Council's resolutions on Korea to help constrain America's response to the crisis. Unlike Britain, Canada was not a member of the Security Council at the time of the conflict. As such, John Holmes, Canada's acting UN representative, attended but did not participate in the Council meetings on Korea. Nonetheless, in the informal discussions surrounding these meetings, Holmes consulted with UN officials and other state delegates.[103] Canada's ambassador in Washington, Hume Wrong, also conveyed the government's views on these issues.

There is evidence that US officials took these concerns seriously, and that US policy was modified in part to better reflect the views of America's allies. For instance, we saw in chapter four that a draft of US President Truman's speech on 27 June stated that North Korea's attack had been launched by "centrally directed Communist Imperialism." Like his UK counterpart at the time, Pearson was unhappy with Truman's draft statement,[104] and he told Wrong that the reference to "Communist imperialism" was "unnecessary."[105] Wrong passed on Pearson's

---

97 Stairs 1974: 21.

98 Ibid: 28.

99 Ibid: 22–23.

100 Ibid: 23.

101 Ibid: 24.

102 St. Laurent in HC Debs., 22 March 1948, 2453.

103 *Extract from Memorandum from Secretary of State for External Affairs to Prime Minister*, 27 June and 4 July 1950, [PCO/Vol. 167], doc. 31 in Donaghy 1996: 49.

104 *Extract from Memorandum from Secretary of State for External Affairs to Prime Minister*, 27 June and 4 July 1950, [PCO/Vol. 167], doc. 11 in Donaghy 1996: 23.

105 Ibid: 22–23.

observations to US Counselor George Kennan. Kennan "was impressed by them and thought that the text should be modified accordingly."[106] Reflecting such concerns, the reference to "centrally directed Communist Imperialism" was removed from Truman's final statement.[107]

In addition to Truman's statement, Canada also sought to influence the wording of the third Security Council resolution on Korea. Again, this instrument recommended that UN members assisting South Korea make such provisions available to a unified command under the US. In the negotiations leading up to the resolution, recall, Pearson and Heeney expressed worries about the formal authority of the UN force in Korea, and the geographic scope of the initiative. These two concerns dominated Canada's diplomatic activity regarding the resolution.

For instance, following the Council's first two resolutions, Truman approved a draft third proposal that would create a unified command in Korea and ask the US to name a commander.[108] Worried that the proposal insufficiently linked the Korean operation to the UN organization, UN Secretary General Trygve Lie suggested that military operations be supervised by a "Committee on Coordination of Assistance for Korea."[109] St. Laurent and Pearson, for their part, shared Lie's desire to "make it clear that the operations being conducted in Korea are under the authority of the [UN], exercised through a commander appointed by the [UN]."[110] Accordingly, in their respective discussions with US and UK officials on the matter, Wrong and Holmes stressed the importance of "giving full and ostensible United Nations aegis to the operations against the North Koreans."[111] Although the US and Britain were "bending as far as possible" to do so,[112] strategic and US domestic legal considerations were pulling in the opposite direction.[113]

---

106 Ibid: 23.

107 Although Canada had expressed a similar concern, Wrong said the rewording was "to accord with the wishes expressed by the [UK] Government" (*Ambassador in United States to Secretary of State for External Affairs*, 27 June 1950, [DEA/50069-A-40], doc. 12 in Donaghy 1996: 24).

108 Truman 1956: 394–395.

109 Lie 1954: 336, and Stairs 1974: 67.

110 *Extract from Memorandum from Secretary of State for External Affairs to Prime Minister*, 27 June and 4 July 1950, [PCO/Vol. 167], doc. 31 in Donaghy 1996: 49.

111 *Acting Permanent Delegate to United Nations to Secretary of State for External Affairs*, 30 June 1950, [DEA/50069-A-40], doc. 23 in Donaghy 1996: 39.

112 Ibid.

113 Strategically, the idea of using the Military Staff Committee envisioned in the UN Charter was rejected because of potential interference by the USSR, and the option of a Security Council sub-committee was abandoned as ineffective. Legally, the Act covering US military participation in the UN only authorized forces made available under Article 43 of the Charter to operate as UN forces outside the authority of Congress. See ibid; and *Ambassador in United States to Secretary of State for External Affairs*, 30 June 1950, [DEA/50069-A-40], doc. 24 in Donaghy 1996: 41.

In response to this dilemma, Pearson and Heeney tried their hand at drafting the resolution in a way that they thought balanced the competing factors at issue.[114] The operative parts of their draft read as follows: "The Security Council requests the United States to designate a commander … of the forces made available by members of the [UN] *under the Security Council resolutions*; and, Recommends that all members providing forces under the said resolution place such forces under the [UN] commander" [emphasis added].[115] Such wording, Pearson and Heeney believed, "would give to the Korean operations a genuine United Nations character," while also not impinging "upon the rights of Congress or the freedom of action of MacArthur."[116] The US and UK replied in detail to Canada's suggestion, but disagreed with much of its wording.[117]

In addition to the formal authority of the UN force in Korea, recall that Pearson and Heeney also expressed reservations about the geographic scope of the Security Council's third resolution. Reflecting this concern, they proposed that the instrument include "a territorial demarcation of the area around Korea in which [US] forces and the forces of other members of the [UN] will be acting."[118] Such a demarcation, they noted, would "exclude the whole of Communist China from the area in which operations under the [UN] would be undertaken."[119] And this, in turn, would lessen the danger of UN members "becoming involved in incidents with Chinese forces outside Korea," and establish "a framework in which the conflict in Korea might be localized."[120] In response, Wrong emphasized that the US considered the Taiwan blockade to be an American operation, and said it was too late in the negotiations to secure such an important change.[121]

Alongside its attempts to alter the US negotiating position on the Korean conflict, Canada also used its understanding of the Security Council resolutions to help constrain America's conduct with respect to Taiwan and China. Regarding Taiwan, Canadian leaders thought that the US blockade of the disputed island could lead to an expansion of hostilities in the area, and argued that the

---

114 *Secretary of State for External Affairs*, 1 July 1950, [DEA/50069-A-40], doc. 29 in Donaghy 1996: 46.

115 *Secretary of State for External Affairs to Ambassador in United States*, 1 July 1950, [DEA/50069-A-40], doc. 28 in Donaghy 1996: 45.

116 Ibid.

117 *Memo by Secretary of State for External Affairs*, 3 July 1950, [DEA/50069-A-40], doc. 30 in Donaghy 1996: 47.

118 *Secretary of State for External Affairs to Ambassador in United States*, 6 July 1950, [DEA/50069-A-40], doc. 37 in Donaghy 1996: 57.

119 Ibid.

120 Ibid.

121 *Ambassador in United States to Secretary of State for External Affairs*, 6 July 1950, [DEA/50069-A-40], doc. 38 in Donaghy 1996: 58.

scope of the Council resolutions was limited to Korea. Reflecting these views, Hume Wrong repeatedly asked the US State Department in the summer of 1950 to make the separation of the Korean and Taiwan issues more explicit.[122] Acting on instructions from Ottawa, Wrong went so far as to suggest that a separate command be established for the Taiwan blockade.[123] As we saw in the previous chapter, Britain expressed similar worries to the US at the time, and based these concerns in part on its view of the Council resolutions and the Cairo Declaration of 1943.

Following these expressions of concern from America's allies, recall that President Truman made a second declaration on 19 July 1950. In this address to Congress, he affirmed his desire to ensure that Taiwan did "not become embroiled in hostilities disturbing to the peace of the Pacific and that all questions affecting [the island] be settled by peaceful means as envisaged in the [UN] Charter."[124] In light of this assurance, MacArthur's subsequent visit to Taiwan on 31 July worried Lester Pearson, and he conveyed his concerns to Secretary of State Dean Acheson, Assistant Secretary for UN Affairs John Hickerson, and the US ambassador in Ottawa.[125] In these latter talks, Pearson stressed the "great danger" of linking UN policy in Korea with US policy on China, and the ambassador said Truman and Acheson "were as worried about this matter as [Pearson] was."[126]

Reflecting this shared concern, Truman sent an official to discuss the matter with MacArthur on 3 August. The official cited the worries of America's allies regarding Taiwan, and stressed the "importance of maintaining UN unity among the friendly countries."[127] Following this meeting, Truman approved a military directive to MacArthur limiting US action in the defence of Taiwan.[128] When MacArthur nonetheless went on to publicly stress the strategic importance of the island later that month, he was, as noted in the prior chapter, forced to withdraw his statement by Truman.

Finally, in addition to US conduct regarding Taiwan, Canada also used its understanding of the Security Council resolutions to help constrain American bombing policy with respect to China. Following China's intervention in the Korean conflict in the autumn of 1950, an issue arose as to whether the UN force could engage aircraft and troops that were physically located above China's border with North Korea but were nonetheless thought to be contributing

---

122 Stairs 1974: 97.

123 Ibid.

124 US Department of State, *Department of State Bulletin*, XXIII, 578, 31 July 1950, 166.

125 *Memorandum from Secretary of State for External Affairs to Prime Minister*, 14 August 1950, [L.S.L./Vol.234], doc. 65 in Donaghy 1996: 110.

126 Ibid.

127 Truman 1956: 352.

128 Ibid: 354.

to the war below. Initially, MacArthur reported to the UN that "our present mission is limited to the destruction of those forces now arrayed against us in North Korea."[129] Unconvinced by this assurance, Pearson and his deputy worried that MacArthur was perhaps "setting the stage for action against the Chinese bases of troops and supply in Manchuria."[130] Regarding such "retaliatory strikes against Chinese bases in the rear," they told Canada's UN delegation that "we should insist that such action is not covered by the present [Security Council] resolution, and would require further authorization from the [UN]."[131]

Consistent with this view, a new US-led resolution was proposed in the Security Council on 10 November. Although it sought to portray China as an aggressor, France insisted that the draft affirm that "the Chinese frontier with Korea is inviolate."[132] In response, the US and UK sought to include a warning that if China's action continued, the "Yalu River [border] would be crossed, by aircraft at least, to break up Chinese concentrations and supply bases in Manchuria."[133] Without this warning, they worried, the UN "commander might have been *prevented* by [the] resolution from taking necessary military action beyond the Yalu River" [emphasis added].[134]

Ultimately, a different version of the resolution was passed by the General Assembly in February 1951, and the diplomatic debate over UN bombing policy regarding China unfolded mainly in private exchanges between the US and its allies. For instance, despite MacArthur's report to the UN, and consistent with Pearson and Heeney's doubts, the General had requested permission in early November 1950 to bomb air bases in China and to engage in "hot pursuit" of aircraft fleeing to this "privileged sanctuary" from Korea. In response, the US State Department and the Joint Chiefs of Staff agreed that it would be desirable to have UN approval for such a policy and, therefore, inquiries were made of all UN countries that had forces in Korea. Without exception, Truman recalls in his memoirs, they indicated strong opposition.[135]

Canada was one such country that expressed this opposition.[136] Although Canada's Chief of the General Staff, Charles Foulkes, strongly disagreed,[137]

---

129 Quoted in *Secretary of State for External Affairs to Chairman, Delegation to UN General Assembly*, 7 Nov. 1950, [DEA/50069-A-40], doc. 150 in Donaghy 1996: 223.

130 Ibid.

131 Ibid.

132 *Chairman, Delegation to UN General Assembly, to Secretary of State for External Affairs*, 11 Nov. 1950, [DEA/50069-A-40], doc. 152 in Donaghy 1996: 227.

133 *Chairman, Delegation to UN General Assembly, to Secretary of State for External Affairs*, 13 Nov. 1950, [DEA/50069-A-40], doc. 155 in Donaghy 1996: 231.

134 Ibid.

135 Truman 1956: 382.

136 Reid 1967–68: 584, and Stairs 1974: 137.

137 Stairs 1974: 137.

Heeney told US officials that his government considered it important to wait until China had been warned that hot pursuit might be taken if hostile aircraft continued to use Chinese airspace.[138] Elaborating on Canada's earlier position at the UN, and reflecting its view during the UNTCOK debate that UN action in Korea was subject only to the legal authority of that organization, Heeney said that while a case "could be made under international law that the [UN] Commander ... has the right to authorize [UN] aircraft to pursue attacking aircraft into Manchurian air space, [we] consider it most important that no military operations take place outside Korean borders without specific authority from the [UN]."[139]

The anger with which MacArthur recalls this issue in his memoirs suggests that allied protests such as Canada's were effective in helping to restrain UN bombing policy regarding China, at least initially.[140] By June 1952, though, with peace negotiations stalled over the Prisoner of War issue, the US had authorized the bombing of power installations on the Yalu River, and Canada was neither consulted nor informed in advance.[141] Furthermore, there is evidence that the rules against hot pursuit were often violated by US pilots and mid-level officers in the field.[142]

As the latter points suggest, the role that Canada and its understanding of international law played in constraining the US prior to and during the Korean War should not be overstated. Indeed, insofar as the US was restrained, the impetus for this likely came more from domestic inputs, such as the acute policy disagreements that arose between Truman and MacArthur. Nonetheless, although Canada may have had less influence than Britain in this regard, it remains the case that Canada expressed its concerns to the US about American policy in the Far East, and based its worries in part on the international legal considerations it deemed relevant at the time. The US took such concerns seriously, and US policy was modified in part to better reflect the views of America's allies.

As Stueck notes, during the crisis the UN "provided the setting for allied and neutral pressure on the [US], an institutional framework within which weaker nations could coordinate their efforts to influence the world's greatest power."[143]

---

138 *Aide Memoire*, 16 Nov. 1950, [DEA/11073–40], doc. 158 in Donaghy 1996: 234–35.

139 Ibid: 235. Pearson repeated this view while speaking in Parliament on 26 April 1951.

140 See MacArthur's complaint that "step-by-step my weapons were being taken away from me" (1965: 415).

141 See draft "Memo for the UN Division, Korea-Collective Security," 28 April 1953, by Chester Ronning, Far Eastern Division (in Lee 1995: 219); and docs. 71–76 in Barry 1990: 78–85.

142 See the informal reporting of such violations in *Charge d'Affaires in Japan to Under-Secretary of State for External Affairs*, 22 May 1952, [DEA/50069-A-40], doc. 54 in Barry 1990: 59. Some of the US pilots and officers went so far as to destroy combat films to hide the fact that action had occurred north of China's border (Mahurin 1962: 68–72, 83–89).

143 Stueck 1995: 4.

Similarly, Bloomfield argues that the cost to the US of involving the UN in its response to the conflict was that it gave countries like Canada a licence to intervene in the decision-making process, and thus "to impose constraints on American policy-making, some of which seemed at the time irksome."[144] Whatever perceived drawbacks such constraints had during the war, General Ridgway – the man who replaced MacArthur after Truman relieved him of his post – conceded later that they "also laid a restraining hand on military adventures that might have drawn us into deeper and deeper involvement in Asia."[145]

3. International Law Helped Permit and Legitimate Canada's Conduct

When Canada responded to the Korean crisis, international law also helped permit and legitimate certain conduct that otherwise might not have been permitted. Two examples illustrate this role. First, like Britain, Canada intervened militarily in what was in many respects a divisive *civil* war, and it justified this publicly and privately with reference to the Security Council resolutions on the crisis and the UN Charter's provisions on collective security. Second, although Canada was more worried than the UK about the issue of crossing the 38th parallel in October 1950, it ultimately supported the American decision to do so, and voted for the General Assembly resolution that aimed to provide UN support for this crossing.

Regarding the first example, due to the majority interpretation of the Council resolutions on the Korean conflict, Canada thought it was allowed to intervene militarily in what was in many ways a civil war.[146] Canadian military action in this conflict, as we saw Prime Minister St. Laurent and Foreign Minister Pearson emphasize earlier in public, was justified insofar as North Korea's original attack was denounced as aggression by the UN Security Council, and because Canada was acting pursuant to the Council's resolutions on the crisis. In addition to these statements, there is further evidence that international legal considerations were relevant to explaining Canada's use of force to the Canadian public.

---

144 Bloomfield 1960: 61. For this reason, some US officials, such as George Kennan, thought that responding to the Korean crisis through the United Nations was a mistake (Kennan 1967: 490).

145 Ridgway 1967: 230.

146 On the internal aspect of the conflict, see Lester Pearson's observation early in the crisis that, although he thought South Korea was "an independent State with a government created by action of the [UN]," it "may be argued that the fighting now taking place is really a form of civil war, since the bulk of the combatants on both sides are undoubtedly Koreans" (*Secretary of State for External Affairs to All Missions Abroad*, 28 June 1950, [DEA/50069-A-40], doc. 16 in Donaghy 1996: 32); and the description by *La Presse*, a Quebec newspaper, of the crisis as "a local affair, a civil war" (in Stairs 1974: 58).

For instance, Canada's involvement in previous wars had divided English and French Canadians, and members of the St. Laurent government worried that sending troops to Korea could do the same, particularly if such forces fought under British command. In light of this concern, St. Laurent and Pearson thought that the formal UN nature of the mission in Korea would help the government secure public support for Canada's participation in a conflict that otherwise might not be tolerated, particularly by French Canada. As Pearson remarked to Hume Wrong on 13 July 1950, "[A]s the situation deteriorates in the field, with Americans alone fighting, they will become somewhat impatient with formal insistence on the United Nations character of the operations. However, *if we are to keep this country united*, and if we are to limit our intervention to Korea alone, which is our only obligation in the present circumstances, we must continue to emphasize ... that we are participating solely in a United Nations operation and that that operation is solely for the defence of Korea" [emphasis added].[147]

In addition to the opinion of French Canada, members of the government were also worried about the international legal criticisms that might be made of America and Canada's reaction to the conflict.[148] In response to these potential criticisms, a legal defence was articulated by the government that emphasized the substantive validity of the Security Council's actions, and explained the procedural shortcomings of these actions in light of the political realities of the nascent Cold War. One concern was that the second Council resolution of 27 June was passed almost 11 hours after President Truman made his statement to the press, and 24 hours after he committed US forces to the defence of South Korea.[149] Anticipating this concern, and resonating with an observable implication posited in chapter two,[150] Pearson told Wrong early in the crisis that a US intervention "should be done *after* the matter had been discussed at the Security Council and appropriate action had been taken there through a resolution, which would bring such intervention within the terms of the [UN] Charter" [emphasis added].[151]

---

147 *Secretary of State for External Affairs to Ambassador in United States, Telegram EX-1118*, 13 July 1950, [DEA/50069-A-40], doc. 41 in Donaghy 1996: 62.

148 For a discussion of some of these criticisms, see Warner 1951: 104.

149 Ibid. Regarding this concern, although Canada's three main federal political parties generally endorsed the Security Council's response to the Korean crisis, some supporters of the left-wing CCF party were critical of the US acting in advance of the UN. See Stairs 1974: 60.

150 As elaborated in chapter two, if leaders and officials felt bound by international law, they should express concern that decisions regarding the use of force should follow, not precede, any legally significant events related to such force.

151 *Extract from Memorandum from Secretary of State for External Affairs to Prime Minister*, 27 June and 4 July 1950, [PCO/Vol. 167], doc. 11 in Donaghy 1996: 22.

Perhaps because the commitment of US forces preceded the Security Council's second resolution, Pearson highlighted the first resolution in his initial formal justification of this commitment. Speaking to Parliament on 28 June, he observed that the North Koreans had ignored the Council's first resolution, and that the Council itself had been unable to take direct military action because the UN forces envisioned under Article 43 of the Charter had never been established.[152] As a result, he said, if any steps were to be taken to deal with the crisis, they would have to be taken by individual Council members "acting within the terms of the Charter, but on their own initiative." In the Korean case, he noted, the US had recognized a special responsibility which it discharged with admirable decisiveness. Although the US government had taken this step on its own authority, Pearson continued, "it is acting not only in accordance with the spirit and letter of the UN Charter," but also in pursuance of the first Council resolution, which called on all UN members to render every assistance in regard to its execution.[153] If further international authorization were required, he added, it had been provided by the second Council resolution, which recommended that UN members furnish such assistance to the Republic of Korea as may be necessary to repel the armed attack and to restore international peace in the area.[154]

Although Pearson's explanation was well received by the politicians in Parliament, his senior advisers knew that its legal reasoning was somewhat tenuous.[155] The account skirted the fact that the first Council resolution had called only for a cease-fire and for the withdrawal of North Korean forces; the second resolution had been passed a day after the American decision to intervene had been made; and the USSR was absent when these resolutions were passed.[156] Despite these potential criticisms, Stairs notes that Pearson's arguments were necessary "if the response to the North Korean invasion was to be *viewed* as having been collectively rather than unilaterally derived, and if American policy was to be brought within the United Nations arena" [emphasis added].[157]

Resonating with his initial explanation to Parliament, Pearson continued to defend the Security Council's actions regarding Korea, and to justify Canada's

---

152 HC Debs., 28 June 1950, 4251–4252.

153 Ibid.

154 Ibid.

155 Stairs 1974: 48.

156 On the other hand, as Stairs notes, "it could also be argued that the Americans knew in advance from their diplomatic consultations with other Security Council members that the [second] 27 June resolution would be approved, and that accordingly they could proceed with their military deployments without worrying unduly about matters of form" (1974: 50). Warner, for instance, observes that the US delegation had assurances of support for a resolution specifically calling on UN members to give military assistance in repelling North Korea (1951: 104).

157 Stairs 1974: 48.

response in light of these actions. Speaking to a group of Canadian and American engineers in Toronto in mid-July, he stressed that the Council's response had been supported by 53 states.[158] These included "many countries, and Canada is one of them, who resent … the charge that in doing our duty to the international community, and to peace, we are merely following the orders of a single member of the [UN] which has particular interests to safeguard in Korea. This is not the case. The people of Canada know that it is not the case."[159] Canada's position, Pearson explained, was dictated by the necessity of supporting UN action. That was, he stressed, "our only obligation."[160]

Like Pearson, St. Laurent also referred to Canada's international legal commitments to help legitimize the country's military action in Korea to the Canadian public. Repeating the observations he made in Parliament on 30 June, the prime minister said in a national radio address on 7 August that the Korean operation was not a war but a "police action intended to prevent war by discouraging aggression."[161] Before this aggression, he explained, no definite plans existed for an international UN force, and Canada had not planned on maintaining an expeditionary force available for such operations. As such, he said, the current action in Korea was the UN's first effective attempt to organize an international force to stop aggression. Canada, he noted, had provided three destroyers and a transport squadron to this effort, and was recruiting a special brigade to send if required. This brigade, St. Laurent stressed, was being recruited "for use in carrying out Canada's obligations under the UN Charter or the North Atlantic Pact."[162]

Again, the foregoing statements indicate that international legal considerations were relevant to key members of the St. Laurent government when they explained Canada's use of force in Korea to the Canadian public. And these explanations, it should be noted, appear to have helped secure public support for the UN action in Korea, at least among English Canadians.[163]

A second example that suggests that international law helped permit and legitimate certain actions that otherwise might not have been allowed is the fact that Canada – while more reluctant than Britain about the issue – publicly

---

158 Fraser, "Backstage at Ottawa," *Maclean's*, 1 Sept. 1950 at 4. For the text of Pearson's address, see Department of External Affairs, *Statements and Speeches*, no. 50/26.

159 Ibid.

160 Ibid.

161 Department of External Affairs, *Canada and the Korean Crisis*, 31–35.

162 Ibid.

163 Canada's three main federal political parties and most English newspapers endorsed the UN intervention in Korea, and supported the government's response or called on it to do more. Further, in a poll of public views on the Korean War released on 3 August 1950, 75 per cent of respondents supported the US decision to send equipment and troops to Korea, 59 per cent thought Canada should provide equipment, and 34 per cent favoured sending troops (Stairs 1974: 87).

supported the US decision to cross the 38th parallel in October 1950, and voted for the General Assembly resolution that aimed to provide UN support for this crossing. By late September 1950, UN forces in Korea had managed to push back North Korea's army and recapture Seoul. As such, Canadian leaders knew that the US would soon be deciding whether UN forces would remain near the 38th parallel, and thus simply restore the status quo, or cross the parallel and seek to unify Korea by force. As a result, the Cabinet had to determine what its policy on this issue would be. Like the military situation in Korea, the diplomatic landscape had also changed. In August, the USSR had returned to the UN Security Council. To avoid the Soviet veto there, the US and its allies shifted much of their diplomatic efforts on Korea to the General Assembly.

One challenge to developing a response to the altered military situation in Korea was that Canada's prior policy on the 38th parallel had never been precisely defined. US official George Kennan had told Canada's NATO ambassador on 27 June that America's goal in Korea was to restore the status quo,[164] and the government initially assumed this to be true.[165] Privately, however, Lester Pearson had doubts, and he conveyed these in a memo to the prime minister early in the crisis. Foreshadowing future events with remarkable accuracy, Pearson noted that one of the dangers of the hostilities in Korea was that the US action

> may prove decisive, and … public opinion in that country will then insist that [UN] forces move beyond the 38th parallel and clean up the whole of the Korean situation. In that case, there may be an unhappy conflict between [US] and [UN] policy. The latter is pledged merely to defeat an aggression and not, as I understand it, to change the political situation in Korea. Of course, some such change is bound to take place, as a result of developments of the last week. I do not see how there can be a return to the status quo. Either the communists make good their claim to all of Korea, or the United Nations will have to do something to strengthen the position of democratic forces under a better government than that of Syngman Rhee.[166]

Despite these worries, Pearson continued to publicly explain as late as 31 August that Canada was helping the UN to defeat aggression.[167] But he did not specify what that meant exactly in Korea.

---

164 *Ambassador in United States to Secretary of State for External Affairs*, 27 June 1950, [DEA/50069-A-40], doc. 12 in Donaghy 1996: 24.

165 Stairs 1974: 116.

166 *Extract from a Memorandum from Secretary of State for External Affairs to Prime Minister*, 27 June and 4 July 1950, [PCO/Vol.167], doc. 31 in Donaghy 1996: 50.

167 See e.g. Pearson's speech to Parliament on 31 August (HC Debs., 31 Aug. 1950, 95–96).

Pearson's memo to St. Laurent implied that, although returning to the status quo in Korea was unlikely, additional authorization was needed if the political situation was to be changed. By contrast, the US initially responded to their military gains in Korea by arguing that crossing the 38th parallel would be covered by the Security Council's existing resolutions.[168] These had recommended the restoration of "peace and security *in the area*." Canada had protested this term, and worried that it inadequately defined the scope of UN operations in Korea. But if the existing resolutions provided ambiguous authority to cross the 38th parallel, senior officials at the Department of External Affairs also recognized that it would be desirable to have some UN decision on the issue in advance of this possibility.[169] Accordingly, it was decided that an effort should be made to have the General Assembly pass a resolution restating its short-run and long-run objectives for Korea.[170] The UN's immediate goals, Escott Reid noted, were the cessation of hostilities and withdrawal of North Korean forces to the 38th parallel, and the restoration of international peace in the Korean area.[171] The long-run goals, moreover, were the achievement of Korean independence and unity by the procedures outlined in earlier General Assembly resolutions.

While Canadian leaders and officials generally agreed on these goals, they were worried about pursuing them by force. As St. Laurent noted at a Cabinet meeting on 4 October, while the "British and Americans seemed convinced that, if the [UN] did not authorize General MacArthur to proceed beyond the 38th parallel, action taken so far by the [organization] might prove to have been futile," they "apparently did not consider too seriously the possibility that Communist China and Soviet Russia might intervene directly."[172] After discussing the issue with Cabinet Secretary Norman Robertson and Arthur Menzies, head of the Far-Eastern Division at External Affairs, Reid told Pearson that the three of them had similar concerns.[173]

In light of these worries, it was decided that the upcoming General Assembly resolution should "leave it open to the [UN] to take military action north of the 38th parallel if the North Koreans refused to sign an agreement pledging cessation of hostilities."[174] Consistent with this policy, Reid rewrote the initial UK draft of the resolution. Essentially, he told Pearson, this rewrite limits the UN to

---

168 Stairs 1974: 119.

169 See Escott Reid's comments in *Secretary of State for External Affairs to Chairman, Delegation to UN General Assembly*, 26 Sept. 1950, [DEA/50069-A-40], doc. 103 in Donaghy 1996: 165.

170 Ibid.

171 Ibid.

172 *Extract from Cabinet Conclusions*, 4 Oct. 1950, [PCO], doc. 106 in Donaghy 1996: 170.

173 *Secretary of State for External Affairs to Chairman, Delegation to UN General Assembly*, 28 Sept. 1950, [DEA/50069-A-40], doc. 105 in Donaghy 1996: 168.

174 Ibid.

fulfilling the Security Council resolutions.[175] However, he added, the "reference to the restoration of international peace and security in the Korea area would *permit* the [UN] Commander to order punitive action against North Korea if the latter continued aggressive action against South Korea" [emphasis added].[176]

Both Canada and Britain wanted the Assembly resolution to cover the possibility of UN forces crossing the 38th parallel. Accordingly, although the UK's initial draft was revised in negotiations at the UN, the final resolution recommended that "all appropriate steps" be taken to ensure stability throughout Korea, and "all constituent acts" be taken, under the UN, for establishing a unified, independent and democratic government. Contrary to Canada's wishes, however, the resolution did not link the crossing of the 38th parallel to North Korea's failure to stop fighting. This worried Canadian leaders, as well as their counterparts in India.

As St. Laurent stated at the Cabinet meeting noted above, the Indian delegation at the UN had indicated that "they could not support the Eight-Power resolution on the ground that it contemplated, or at least *permitted*, the penetration of UN forces beyond the 38th parallel and that this might in itself involve the risk of intervention by Communist China and Soviet Russia" [emphasis added].[177] In light of such concerns, St. Laurent suggested that the resolution be modified to address India's position, and to require less than the "destruction or the unconditional surrender of North Korean forces."[178] Pearson, though, was unable to secure such changes due to the quick pace of events at the UN.[179] Similarly, when he asked Dean Acheson to delay the resolution vote until contact was made with North Korea, Acheson was sympathetic but was ultimately overruled by Truman and the US military.[180]

Despite the private reservations of its leaders, Canada ultimately voted for the Assembly resolution,[181] and publicly acknowledged that the 38th parallel might have to be crossed. Outlining Canada's position at the UN on 27 September, Pearson said the general objective of the organization in Korea "should be to fulfill now the purposes which have repeatedly been stated at previous Assemblies – a united Korea, a free Korea."[182] And this, he added, should be achieved by UN action.[183] While Pearson sought to reassure China and reaffirm

---

175 Ibid: 169.

176 Ibid.

177 *Extract from Cabinet Conclusions*, 4 Oct. 1950, [PCO], doc. 106 in Donaghy 1996: 169.

178 The Cabinet approved St. Laurent's suggestion. See ibid: 170.

179 Stairs 1974: 123.

180 Pearson, comments to seminar on Canadian external relations, Carleton University, 16 Oct. 1972 (Stairs 1974: 124).

181 Stairs 1974: 121–123.

182 Department of External Affairs, *Statements and Speeches*, 50/34.

183 Ibid.

India's diplomatic role, he also said the UN "must assist the people of Korea to establish peace and order throughout their territory."[184] As such, he noted, "This is the time for the aggressors to cease fire ... If they do, it may not be necessary for [UN] forces in Korea ... to advance far beyond their present positions.[185]

In debating what their country's position on the Assembly resolution should be, it is clear that Canadian leaders and officials saw a need for additional UN authorization if the political situation in Korea was to be changed, and were aware that the resolution that was passed could be seen as permitting the crossing of the 38th parallel. However, it is less clear whether leaders and officials thought the resolution provided formal legal authorization for this action.

On the one hand, during talks with US officials, Hume Wrong argued that the adoption of the resolution "would create a new position which in effect merged from the Assembly resolutions dealing with the unification of Korea adopted in 1947, 1948, and 1949 with the Security Council resolutions of June 25th and 27th, 1950, under which alone military action to repel the North Korean attack had been taken. This created *a new constitutional position* which the North Korean authorities ... should have a chance to consider before [UN] troops moved into their territory" [emphasis added].[186] On the other hand, we saw that Canada's suggestion that North Korea be warned fell on deaf ears, and that Canadian leaders and officials, as Wrong's comments indicate, granted formal priority to the prior Security Council resolutions on Korea. In any event, whether or not the 46 other states who voted for the Assembly resolution believed that UN forces would cross the 38th parallel, Canada's government thought that the instrument could be seen as permitting this behaviour.

4. International Law Helped Structure the Development of New Rules and Legitimate Behaviour

Finally, Canada's reaction to the Korean crisis offers further evidence that, when states use force, international law can help structure the process by which agents seek to develop and promote new legal rules and legitimate conduct for states and other international actors. As noted in the previous chapter, a key example of this phenomenon is the Security Council's novel response to North Korea's attack. Like their UK counterparts, Canadian leaders sought to justify this response, and to use the situation to help create new collective security law.

Recall that when the Security Council authorized UN member states to restore peace in Korea, it did so in a manner not anticipated by the drafters

---

184 Ibid.
185 Ibid.
186 *Ambassador in United States to Secretary of State for External Affairs*, 5 Oct. 1950, [DEA/50069-A-40], doc. 110 in Donaghy 1996: 174.

of the UN Charter in 1945. At that time, it was expected that member states would provide permanent military forces to the Council under Article 43 of the Charter. By June 1950, though, no such forces had been granted. Thus, following North Korea's attack that month, the Council authorized an ad hoc response that saw UN members provide their own forces towards a collective cause. We saw that Foreign Minister Pearson often emphasized this view in his public speeches on the Korean crisis.

For instance, in his update to Parliament on 28 June, Pearson stated that North Korea had ignored the first Security Council resolution, and the Council itself had been unable to take direct military action because the UN forces envisioned under Article 43 had never been established. As a result, he said, if any steps were to be taken to deal with the crisis, they would have to be taken by individual Council members "acting within the terms of the Charter, but on their own initiative." Further, recall that during his address to a group of engineers in July, Pearson linked this individual state "initiative" to a collective view by emphasizing that the Council's novel response had been supported by 53 states.

Notwithstanding such justifications by America's allies, we saw that the USSR argued that the UN action in Korea was invalid due to the absence of the Soviet delegate at the Security Council when the initial resolutions on the Korean conflict were passed. In response to this concern, Canadian officials and leaders argued that the Council's actions were a necessary reinterpretation of the Charter's text, and were consistent with altered state practice on the issue. For example, commenting on the Council's first resolution following North Korea's attack, Douglas LePan, a diplomat in the UN division of the External Affairs Department, remarked:

> The [US] resolution was presented under Article 39 of the [UN] Charter ... [and] it was likely that the Soviets would protest [it] alleging that it is illegal under Article 27, which requires the affirmative vote of seven [Council] members, including the concurring votes of the permanent members. The Soviet Delegation absented itself from the meeting of June 25. Although in the past an *abstention* by a permanent member has not affected the capacity of the Security Council to take decisions on substantive questions, the Soviet Union may claim that its own *absence* on June 25 invalidates the resolution ... [emphasis in original].[187]

Pearson responded to this concern in an update to Canada's embassies abroad. He noted: "It will probably be argued by Soviet apologists that the resolution

---

187 *Extract from Minutes of Meeting of Heads of Division,* 26 June 1950, [DEA/8508–40], doc. 10 in Donaghy 1996: 21.

passed by the Security Council on the 25th of June is illegal because it was not passed with the concurring votes of all permanent members. In rebuttal, it could be urged that the practice by which an *abstention* of one of the permanent members has been construed to be equivalent to assent could be extended to cover as well the *absence* of a permanent member" [emphasis added].[188]

In sum, the above suggests that, during the early stages of the Korean War, Canada – like Britain – also sought to alter existing understandings of Article 27 of the UN Charter, and Security Council voting procedures, in order to help develop and promote a new legal rule – i.e., that refraining from attending a Council vote is equivalent to abstaining from that vote – and new legitimate conduct for that international body. Further, Canada aimed to strengthen its position by citing the continuing practice of the Council and the supporting views of 52 other states.

In addition to the foregoing efforts, Canadian leaders also used the Korean crisis to try to create a permanent volunteer UN brigade that would continue long after the conflict had been resolved.[189] This might, they hoped, address the fact that the forces envisioned under Article 43 of the UN Charter had never been made available. Although Canada was ultimately unsuccessful in establishing this brigade, the diplomatic discussions it had and the proposals it made were shaped by its interpretation of the relevant Charter provisions and state practice on the issue.

For example, following the signing of the Charter in 1945, Canadian military leaders were asked to prepare for the possibility of Canada contributing forces to the UN under Article 43. By 1947, however, the St. Laurent government became frustrated with the USSR's use of its veto at the Council, and thought this continued behaviour would render the collective security provisions of the Charter meaningless.[190] Faced with this situation, St. Laurent and his advisers thought that an alternative was needed, either by revising the Charter or by using its articles which could not be vetoed. This desire to develop new legal rules and state practice helped lead to the creation of the NATO treaty in 1949,[191] but it also animated Canada's reaction to the Korean crisis one year later.

Following the Security Council's response to the outbreak of hostilities in Korea, the office of the UN Secretary General received numerous offers of voluntary service by citizens of different countries.[192] In response, the office

---

188 *Secretary of State for External Affairs to All Missions Abroad*, 28 June 1950, [DEA/50069-A-40], doc. 16 in Donaghy 1996: 32.

189 Donaghy 1995.

190 Mackenzie 1995: 150.

191 Ibid.

192 *Memorandum from Head, UN Division, to Secretary of State for External Affairs*, 28 July 1950, [L.B.P./Vol.35], doc. 57 in Donaghy 1996: 94.

proposed the idea of creating a UN "Foreign Legion" comprised of individual volunteers or a UN "Division of organized national units."[193] According to Gerald Riddell, a Canadian official at the UN, the proposal initially received little encouragement in either form.[194] Lester Pearson, though, mentioned the idea to St. Laurent. And, as we saw earlier, when the Prime Minister announced on 19 July that Canada would not send troops to Korea, he qualified this by adding that if the Security Council recruited a voluntary force for service there, Canada would immediately consider participating. St. Laurent's statement, Riddell noted, brought the idea back to light.[195] Further, he said, because the proposal lacked any real sponsorship, there was a tendency at the UN "to suggest it is a Canadian idea."[196]

In advocating for this proposal, Pearson's analysis reflected the challenges and opportunities the Foreign Secretary saw in the relevant provisions of the UN Charter, and in the related practice of states. In a memo Pearson sent to the Prime Minister in early August, he noted that the "brigade would … be the kind of help we would presumably have organized if we had been able to make a military agreement with the Security Council under Article 43."[197] In effect, Pearson wrote, this would mean that the Canadian army would include a brigade "specially trained for UN operations, as a contingent with other UN formations."[198] Apparently willing to sacrifice some of Canada's sovereignty over the conditions under which it would use force, Pearson said the brigade

> underlines the fact that from now on we fight only as a result of UN decisions, and with other UN members as a Police Force to make such decisions effective and to restore peace. If Canada emphasized this principle in announcing its decision [to contribute to the brigade], *we might be initiating something new* in the way of backing up the United Nations which could have important consequences [emphasis added]. At the same time we would be basing one part of our small army on the Charter of the UN.[199]

Again, due to insufficient support from other states, Canada and the office of the UN Secretary General were ultimately unsuccessful in establishing a permanent voluntary UN brigade. Nonetheless, Pearson and St. Laurent's efforts

---

193 Ibid.
194 Ibid.
195 Ibid.
196 Ibid.
197 *Memorandum from Secretary of State for External Affairs to Prime Minister*, 3 Aug. 1950, [L.B.P./Vol.35], doc. 63 in Donaghy 1996: 106.
198 Ibid.
199 Ibid.

in this regard, along with the government's related attempt to alter the understanding of Article 27 of the Charter, provide further evidence that when states use force, international law can help structure the process by which agents seek to develop and promote new legal rules and legitimate behaviour.

The Understanding of International Law in Canada's Use of Force in Korea

While the prior discussion suggests that international law helped influence Canada's involvement in the Korean War, it is less clear the extent to which Canadian leaders understood this law as a distinct and binding set of legal rules, and whether the legal status of these rules impacted their decision-making. Like their British counterparts, some Canadian leaders saw the Security Council resolutions on Korea more in political and moral, rather than distinctly legal, terms. Further, while Article 118 of the Third Geneva Convention on POWs – the important repatriation rule described earlier – was interpreted as binding, the perceived requirements of this rule conflicted with other political and moral considerations at the time. And these considerations appear to have ultimately exerted a greater impact on the government than the law at issue.

1. Canada's Interpretation of the Security Council Resolutions on the Korean Crisis

As discussed in the previous chapter, during the Korean crisis UK leaders emphasized that the Security Council had "recommended" under Article 39 of the UN Charter – not "decided" under Articles 41 or 42 – that action be taken to assist South Korea. By contrast, Canadian leaders appear to have been less concerned about this issue.[200] Nonetheless, like their UK counterparts, some Canadian leaders also saw the Council resolutions more in political and moral, rather than binding, terms.

For instance, in the update he sent to Canada's embassies abroad on 28 June 1950, Pearson remarked that the legal disputes that could arise over the Security Council's first resolution on Korea "are perhaps immaterial when set beside the plain fact that the [US] has secured a condemnation of this Communist attack by all those members of the Security Council which were present (with the

---

200 See e.g. the government documents in Donaghy 1996. Consistent with the conclusion that Canadian leaders appeared less aware of, or concerned about, whether the Security Council had "recommended" or "decided" that help be provided to South Korea, Lester Pearson (erroneously) referred to the Council's "decision" regarding Korea in a telegram in July 1950; he did not use the term "recommend."

single exception of Yugoslavia, which abstained) and has thus obtained strong *moral* support for whatever military measures it feels able to take in Korea" [emphasis added].[201]

In addition to Pearson's private comments, his public remarks indicate a similar understanding of the Security Council's resolutions on Korea. For example, in his address to the group of engineers in July, noted earlier, Pearson stated that Canada's position on Korea was "dictated by the necessity of supporting United Nations action."[202] That was Canada's only obligation, he said, and it was being discharged "from considerations both of *national honour* and *national safety*" [emphasis added].[203] We will see similar reflections from Prime Minister Paul Martin sixty years later regarding Canada's involvement in the Afghanistan Conflict.

2. Canada's Interpretation of Article 118 of the Geneva Convention on POWs

At the outbreak of the Korean War in June 1950, the US and North Korea both said they would abide by the Geneva Conventions of 1949.[204] Again, it is interesting to note that this commitment was made even though the treaties did not come into force until October 1950; the US had signed but not yet ratified the agreements; and North Korea had neither signed nor ratified them. Like America and Britain, Canada was an original signatory when the treaties were successfully negotiated in 1949.[205] Although Canada did not ratify them until 1965, we will see that relevant Canadian leaders and officials appeared to believe that the rules in the agreements, at least regarding prisoners, applied to the hostilities in Korea.

A key rule that became relevant during the Korean conflict was Article 118 of the Third Geneva Convention on POWs. It states that "[p]risoners of war shall be released and repatriated without delay after the cessation of active

---

201   *Secretary of State for External Affairs to All Missions Abroad*, 28 June 1950, [DEA/50069-A-40], doc. 16 in Donaghy 1996: 32.

202   Cited in Stairs 1974: 73.

203   Fraser "Backstage at Ottawa," *Maclean's*, 1 Sept. 1950, at 4.

204   The US was an original signatory to the four Geneva Conventions in 1949. While America did not ratify the treaties until 1955, it announced at the beginning of the Korean War that it would apply these rules. Moreover, although neither North Korea nor China were signatories to the Geneva Conventions at the time of the Korean conflict, Pyongyang declared its intention to observe their rules in June 1950, and Beijing in July 1952. See US Department of the Army, *The United States Army in the Korean War*, v. 3; and Hermes 1966: 135–136.

205   See "Treaties, States Parties and Commentaries," on the website of the International Committee of the Red Cross, at https://ihl-databases.icrc.org/applic/ihl/ihl.nsf/vwTreatiesByCountry Selected.xsp?xp_countrySelected=CA.

hostilities."[206] During the negotiations aimed at ending the Korean War, however, it became known that some of the North Korean and Chinese soldiers who had been captured by the UN force did not want to be repatriated. In response to this development, we saw earlier, the communist delegation at the truce talks invoked Article 118, while the US proposed a new principle, "voluntary repatriation," which would allow POWs to be interviewed and choose where they would be sent.

In deciding how to respond to the US position, Canadian leaders faced the same dilemma as UK officials. Under the political circumstances of the nascent Cold War, it seemed unwise and unrealistic to forcefully send anti-communist POWs back to communist countries. Further, leaders understood the moral implications of sending men back to face possible punishment or death by what the West perceived to be oppressive regimes. For instance, in an update to Canada's ambassador in Washington on 7 February 1952, Under-Secretary for External Affairs Dana Wilgress said that he and Pearson "appreciate the very strong arguments in favour of the [UN] demand for the voluntary repatriation of prisoners."[207] There would, Wilgress noted, "be strong protests in this country against returning to the North Korean or Chinese authorities [POWs] whom we hold and who do not want to be returned because of their opposition to those communist regimes."[208] Voluntary repatriation, he added, was an effort to be "humane" to these prisoners.[209]

And yet, notwithstanding the above political and moral concerns, Article 118 clearly stated that POWs shall be released and repatriated without delay after the cessation of active hostilities. To disregard this rule would have been inconsistent with Canada's former position in 1949 and, leaders worried, could have threatened the safety of UN prisoners in North Korea.[210] It could also set a dangerous precedent for future wars. As Wilgress explained, the issue

> is further complicated ... by the question [of] whether it is in the interest of the Western World to establish in Korea the precedent that [POWs] have the right to waive their right to repatriation. If this precedent is established by the Korean Armistice, the Soviet Union might in the event of a general war contend that any

---

206 See Article 118 of the 1949 Third Geneva Convention Relative to the Treatment of POWs. Earlier treaties stated that prisoners should or shall be repatriated after an armistice or peace treaty was legally concluded, rather than after the factual cessation of hostilities. This left a loophole open for some states to keep prisoners following WWI and WWII. See Pictet et al. 1960: 540–541.

207 *Extract from Telegram from Secretary of State for External Affairs to Ambassador in United States*, 7 Feb. 1952, [DEA/50069-A-40], doc. 90 in Barry 1990: 100.

208 Ibid.

209 Ibid.

210 Ibid.

> [POW] whom they hold had the right at any time during hostilities to request release from prison camp in lieu of eventual repatriation, and, having been released from camp, to enlist in the armed forces of Russia.[211]

With such a precedent, Wilgress and Pearson worried, allied POWs in a future war would be in "a position where the Soviet Government could, with some outward show of *legality*, intimidate them into waiving their right to repatriation" [emphasis added].[212]

Citing Article 118 and Article 7,[213] Wilgress further noted that one of the principles of the Third Geneva Convention "is the unconditional release and repatriation of prisoners ... Presumably, the Western Powers had this principle embodied in the Convention because they considered that it would serve their interests in a general war. The [UN] proposal for the voluntary repatriation of [POWs] is, in the opinion of our Legal Division, *contrary* to these Articles" [emphasis added].[214]

Summing up the government's concern, Wilgress explained: "Most of the countries which have forces in Korea have not yet ratified this Convention, and the Communist forces in Korea have not lived up to it. Our countries have, however, devoted considerable efforts to trying to conclude the Geneva (Red Cross) Humanitarian Conventions with the Soviet Union in the hope that if these Conventions are in force during a general war, they will at least do something to render less likely harsh and arbitrary treatment by the Russians of our prisoners. Our countries, therefore, have an interest in [preserving] the principles of these conventions."[215]

The above suggests that, in deciding how to respond to America's position on POWs during the Korean armistice negotiations, Canadian leaders were faced with a situation where political and moral factors pointed in one direction – support the principle of voluntary repatriation – and international law pointed in another – implement Article 118. As noted earlier, if theorizing and observing a distinct nature and effect of international law is possible in the fields of International Relations and International Law, then this is arguably one such situation.

Indeed, in arguing that the acceptance of voluntary repatriation could lead to a dangerous precedent, Wilgress and Pearson explicitly cited the current and future legality of this principle. Nonetheless, in the end, the government did

---

211 Ibid.

212 Ibid.

213 Article 7 provides that POWs cannot renounce their rights.

214 *Extract from Telegram from Secretary of State for External Affairs to Ambassador in United States*, 7 Feb. 1952, [DEA/50069-A-40], doc. 90 in Barry 1990: 100.

215 Ibid.

not publicly ask the US to withdraw its demand for the voluntary repatriation of prisoners. Reflecting the difficulty of the issue, during the protracted peace negotiations that continued until July 1953, Pearson sought to bridge the American position – which emphasized voluntary repatriation – with that of India's – which was more consistent with the wording of Article 118.[216]

Key Findings

The aspects of Canada's participation in the Korean War assessed above support the argument that, when states use force, international law helps define and shape their possible course of action, and the justifications that can be made for their behaviour. More specifically, these aspects help illustrate the four roles that international law can play in such situations.

First, Canada decided to join UNTCOK in 1948, support the Security Council resolutions on the Korean crisis in 1950, and contribute significant naval, air, and ground forces to the UN mission in Korea even though the country was not seen as strategically important. These decisions suggest that international law can help constitute a state's identity and be used to redefine its political and military objectives. As we saw, Prime Minister St. Laurent, Defence Minister Claxton, and Foreign Minister Pearson believed that Canada's formal membership in the UN carried corresponding obligations, including the duty to defend – by force if need be, and even in situations where Canada's own interests were not directly at stake – the principles of the UN Charter, the effectiveness of the UN organization, and the concept of collective security.

While other leaders, such as former Prime Minister Mackenzie King, did not feel the same sense of responsibility regarding the UN and the Korean crisis, St. Laurent and Pearson sought to reorient his thinking through legal interpretation of a relevant UN resolution. And it is this interpretation that ultimately led King to allow Canada to join UNTCOK. Following the government's decision to contribute to the UN military force in Korea two years later, St. Laurent, Pearson and Claxton continued to believe that Canada, as a middle power state that had helped create the UN, was now obligated to support the organization's collective "police action" against aggression.

Second, international law also had a regulative impact on Canada's participation in the Korean War. The first example of this influence was Canada's non-participation in the US naval blockade of Taiwan. As we saw, this non-participation was shaped in part by Canada's understanding of the scope of

---

216 In December 1952, Canada supported India's resolution on Korea at the UN General Assembly. This instrument implicitly recognized Article 118. In April 1953, however, Canada also supported the US negotiating position, which was based in part on the principle of voluntary repatriation. See Lee 1995: 218. For a description of Canada's diplomatic response to protests by communist prisoners in the later stages of the war, see Stairs 1974: 249–258.

the Security Council's resolutions on the Korean crisis. The second example of law's regulative role was Canada's use of the General Assembly's 1948 UNTCOK resolution, and the Security Council's resolutions on Korea, to help constrain America's response to the crisis. As we saw, in the discussions behind the election in South Korea in 1948 and the adoption of the third Security Council resolution in 1950, Canada sought to influence the US negotiating position and shape the outcome of the talks. And Canada's interpretation of the international legal factors at issue played a role in this regard. In addition, Canada used its understanding of the Security Council resolutions to help constrain America's conduct with respect to Taiwan and China.

Third, when Canada responded to the Korean crisis, international law helped permit and legitimate certain actions that otherwise might not have been permitted. The first example of this role was the fact that Canada intervened militarily in what was in many ways an ideologically divisive and extremely violent *civil* war, and justified this publicly and privately with reference to the Security Council resolutions on the crisis and the UN Charter's provisions on collective security. The second example was that Canada – while more worried than Britain about the issue – ultimately supported the US decision to cross the 38th parallel in Korea in October 1950, and voted for the General Assembly resolution that aimed to provide UN support for this crossing.

Finally, Canada's reaction to the Korean crisis suggests that international law can help structure the process by which agents seek to develop and promote new legal rules and legitimate practice for states and other international actors. An important example of this was the Security Council's novel response to North Korea's attack, and the efforts of Canadian leaders to justify this response and to create new collective security law.

Although this analysis suggests that international law helped influence Canada's involvement in the Korean War, it is less clear the extent to which Canadian leaders understood this law as a distinct and binding set of legal rules, and whether the legal status of these rules impacted their decision-making. On the one hand, we saw that leaders recognized that the use of military force in Korea and the treatment of enemy POWs were in part legal issues, in that they were governed by pre-existing rules in the UN Charter and Geneva Conventions. Moreover, leaders discussed the extent to which Canada was legally obligated to consider these rules when deciding whether and how to use force in Korea, and what policy to adopt regarding the repatriation of enemy POWs. Finally, leaders recognized that Canada's involvement in the US-led intervention in Korea was subject to international legal critique, and required legal justification at the domestic and international level. The preceding details resonate with many of the relevant observable implications posited in chapter two, and suggest that Canadian leaders such as St. Laurent and Pearson felt bound in part by international law.

On the other hand, we also saw that some Canadian leaders interpreted the Security Council's resolutions on the Korean crisis more in political and moral, rather than expressly binding, terms. By contrast, a key POW obligation under the Third Geneva Convention, Article 118, was seen in distinctly legal terms. However, the perceived requirements of this rule conflicted with other political and moral considerations at the time, and these factors appear to have ultimately exerted a greater impact on Canada than the law at issue.

6 Britain and the Afghanistan Conflict

The Afghanistan Conflict is one of the most important wars that Britain has fought since 1945. The terrorist attacks against the United States on 11 September 2001 caught the world off guard, including Britain. At that time, most observers would not have predicted that the response to these attacks would lead to Britain's longest foreign military engagement ever, and the most difficult fighting its ground forces have faced since the Korean War. In essence, the decisions behind the Afghan Conflict highlighted the tension between the liberal internationalism and idealism that Britain helped support in the post-Cold War decade prior to 9/11, and the national security concerns and reality of the US-led war on terrorism that followed afterwards. As the UK sought to balance this tension and contribute to the effort in Afghanistan, international law helped define and shape its possible course of action, and the justifications that could be made for its conduct. Before turning to that story, let me briefly provide some background to the conflict, and why Britain got involved.

Brief Background to the Afghanistan Conflict

As is now infamously well known, on 11 September 2001, al-Qaeda terrorists hijacked four passenger jets and intentionally crashed two of the planes into the World Trade Center in New York City, and a third into the Pentagon in Washington, D.C.[1] Nearly 3,000 people died in the attacks, including nationals from 77 countries.[2] The overwhelming majority of the casualties were civilians.

---

1 The hijackers had directed the fourth plane toward Washington, D.C., aiming to target either the Capital Building or the White House. However, passengers aboard the aircraft attempted to retake control of the plane, and it crashed into a field in rural Pennsylvania. Everyone on board was killed.

2 For a list of these countries, see www.interpol.int/public/ICPO/speeches /20020911List77Countries.asp

In response to these events, and the perception that the Taliban in Afghanistan were allowing al-Qaeda to use their territory as a base of operation, US President George W. Bush declared that the attacks were an act of war and demanded in part that the Taliban deliver all al-Qaeda leaders in their territory to the US.[3] When the Taliban refused,[4] the US – aided by Britain, Canada, and other states – initiated military actions against Afghanistan on 7 October 2001.[5] These actions, which included air strikes and operations by special forces, were part of Operation Enduring Freedom (OEF), which itself was part of the broader US-led response to international terrorism that is global in scope and currently ongoing.[6]

On 13 November 2001, local Northern Alliance ground forces captured Kabul, effectively ending Taliban rule.[7] On 27 November, delegates from rival groups, excluding the Taliban, joined negotiations sponsored by the United Nations in Bonn, Germany, on the future of Afghanistan. These talks culminated in the Bonn Agreement of 5 December.[8] Hamid Karzai, a Pashtun tribal leader, was chosen to lead an interim power-sharing council, the Afghan Transitional Authority (ATA), which took office in Kabul on 22 December. Karzai was appointed President of the ATA by the UN on 13 June 2002.[9] He was formally elected President on 9 October 2004, and served until 2014. A second conference on Afghanistan was held in Bonn in December 2011.[10]

In addition to the US-led forces operating under OEF, an International Security Assistance Force (ISAF) was also present in Afghanistan from early 2002 to late 2014. In December 2001, following negotiations led in part by Britain,[11] the UN Security Council passed Resolution 1386.[12] Reflecting a request from the Bonn Agreement, this resolution created ISAF and authorized it to use "all

---

3 US President George W. Bush, "Address to Congress," 20 Sept. 2001.

4 From the late 1990s to the Fall of 2001, Taliban leader Mullah Omar consistently refused to hand over Osama Bin Laden to the US or Saudi Arabia. To do so, he argued, would be inconsistent with the Pashtun tribal code that forbade the betrayal of guests (Wright 2006: 267).

5 In total, 37 countries have contributed to the military mission in Afghanistan, and 60 countries have helped with development and reconstruction (Stein and Lang 2007: 285).

6 OEF officially ended in 2014. But US forces are to remain in Afghanistan until September 2021, and some of these troops conduct anti-terrorist operations with Afghan partners. See Max Boot, "US Troop Withdrawal from Afghanistan: What Are Biden's Options?," Council on Foreign Relations, 9 Feb. 2021.

7 Turner 2006: 81–82.

8 Agreement on Provisional Arrangements in Afghanistan pending the Re-establishment of Permanent Government Institutions (5 Dec. 2001), [UN Doc. S/2001/1154].

9 Karzai was appointed President after consultation with the Northern Alliance and a group of elected delegates known as the *Loya Jirga* (Turner 2006: 81–82).

10 Ahmed Rashid, "Afghan Peace at Stake in Bonn," BBC News online, 4 Dec. 2011.

11 Blair 2010: 361; and interview with Sir Nigel Sheinwald, London, 8 July 2013.

12 UNSC Resolution 1386 (20 Dec. 2001), [UN Doc. S/RES/1386], *On the Situation in Afghanistan.*

necessary measures," including force, to assist the ATA in providing security in and around Kabul.[13] ISAF's mandate was unanimously renewed by the Council in the years afterwards, and expanded to help provide security throughout Afghanistan.[14] NATO assumed leadership of ISAF in August 2003, in part as a result of lobbying efforts by Canada.[15] The mission expanded in four stages, from December 2003 to October 2006.[16]

The Three Phases of Britain's Military Participation in the Afghanistan Conflict

Britain's military participation in the Afghanistan Conflict can be divided into three main phases. The initial phase took place between October 2001 and late 2002. It involved an incremental buildup of forces operating first under OEF and then the ISAF mandate. On 7 October 2001, Prime Minister Tony Blair confirmed that UK forces were engaged in the initial US-led military actions against Afghanistan.[17] These included ground operations by special forces, missile strikes from Royal Navy submarines, and reconnaissance and refueling sorties by the Royal Air Force in support of the US.[18] In early 2002, Britain offered to lead the ISAF force in Kabul. It initially sent 1,800 troops to the mission.[19] The UK reduced this number to 400 after Turkey took command of ISAF in June 2002, but increased its contribution (at one point to 1,700 troops) to the ongoing US-led operations against the Taliban and al-Qaeda.[20]

Although somewhat overshadowed by Britain's participation in the Iraq War around the same time,[21] the country's second phase of military action in Afghanistan occurred between early 2003 and late 2005. It involved the UK leading a Provincial Reconstruction Team and contributing soldiers to ISAF after NATO took command of the operation in August 2003, and ISAF's mandate expanded to include the provision of security throughout Afghanistan.[22]

---

13 Ibid; and NATO website, "About ISAF."

14 Government of Canada, *Canada's Mission in Afghanistan* (February 2007) at 3. The Security Council expanded ISAF's mandate on 13 Oct. 2003, through Resolution 1510, [UN Doc. S/RES/1510].

15 The stated aim of having NATO take responsibility for the ISAF mission was to overcome the challenges of finding new countries to lead the mission, and to provide a more permanent headquarters for coordinated operations. See NATO website, "About ISAF."

16 Ibid.

17 HM Government website, "UK Forces: Operations in Afghanistan."

18 Hansard, House of Commons Debates ["HC Debs."], 16 Oct. 2001, vol. 372, col. 1132.

19 HC Debs., 19 Dec. 2001, vol. 377, cols. 304–5; and HC Written Answers, 14 Jan. 2002, vol. 378, col. 51w.

20 HC Debs., 29 April 2002, vol. 384, col. 649; and HC Debs., 20 June 2002, vol. 387, col. 409.

21 Clarke 2011: 14.

22 HC Written Answers, 22 Oct. 2003, vol. 411, col. 588w.

The third phase of Britain's military involvement started in early 2006 and ended in 2014. It included a significant number of UK forces being deployed to Helmand, a volatile province in southern Afghanistan, through a series of authorizations and extensions.[23] In January 2006, then Defence Minister John Reid announced that 3,300 soldiers were being sent to Helmand as part of ISAF, bringing the total number of UK troops in the country to over 5,000.[24] In response to escalating violence in Helmand, troop numbers there were increased to 4,500 six months later.[25] Further troop increases were announced in February 2007, bringing the total number of UK forces in Afghanistan to around 7,700,[26] and again in the spring of 2009, bringing the overall figure to over 8,000.[27] Despite indications by the Brown and Cameron governments that troop numbers would be maintained or decreased, levels actually peaked at over 10,000 by 2011.[28] Britain's active combat role ended in 2014, and troop levels remained relatively high until then.[29]

In total, the conflict in Afghanistan cost Britain £40 billion, thousands of UK personnel were wounded, and 446 soldiers lost their lives.[30] These deaths were much higher than those Britain incurred in the Iraq War and the Falklands War. They resulted from the most difficult fighting UK ground forces had faced since the conflict in Korea. Between 2008 and 2010, for example, the rate at which British soldiers were killed in Afghanistan was almost four times that of their American counterparts, and double the rate which is considered major combat.[31]

Following the end of Britain's combat role, some UK troops and personnel have remained in the country as advisers and trainers.[32] Peace talks between the Afghan government and the Taliban have continued, along with ongoing fighting and bombings. A withdrawal agreement was signed by the US and Taliban in February 2020, with remaining American troops scheduled to leave Afghanistan by September 2021. However, the future of the country remains uncertain.

---

23 For a description and analysis of the initial decisions behind this third phase, see Clarke 2011.

24 HC Debs., 26 Jan. 2006, vol. 441, cols. 1531–1533.

25 HC Debs., 10 July 2006, vol. 448, col. 1134.

26 HC Debs., 26 Feb. 2007, vol. 457, cols. 619–620.

27 HC Debs., 16 June 2008, vol. 477, col. 676.

28 See HM Government, *UK Policy in Afghanistan and Pakistan* (2009) at 18; and Clarke 2011: 7.

29 Clarke 2011: 7.

30 See "UK Troops in Afghanistan: Timeline of Key Events," BBC news website, 22 Dec. 2015.

31 See "British Dead and Wounded in Afghanistan, Month by Month," *The Guardian* website, June 2013.

32 See "The British Army in Afghanistan," at www.army.mod.uk.

Why Britain Participated in the Afghanistan Conflict

Like Britain's participation in the Korean War, the country's extensive and costly involvement in the Afghanistan Conflict is also not immediately easy to explain in strict national interest terms, narrowly conceived.[33] The two factors one might presume to be most relevant – i.e., Britain's alliance with the US and its security concern regarding al-Qaeda – may help explain why Britain initially used force in Afghanistan. But it is less clear why the UK military remained in the country for so long, and why Britain agreed to contribute to the difficult nation building and counterinsurgency efforts there.

Reflecting this empirical puzzle, much of the existing literature that addresses Britain's involvement in the Afghan Conflict has focused on analysing and criticizing the strategic coherence of this involvement,[34] or describing the experiences of UK forces on the ground.[35] Another body of related work has assessed Britain's adaptation to counterinsurgency operations in Helmand, and the implications of this process for the future of UK military doctrine.[36] In comparison to the foregoing accounts, however, there is less research available that comprehensively outlines and analyses the government decisions regarding the UK's three phases of participation in the Afghan Conflict, and the foreign and domestic factors that have shaped those decisions. John Kampfner's book, *Blair's Wars*, draws on interviews with more than 40 current and former senior ministers, advisers, and civil servants, and usefully engages in some description and assessment of the UK's first phase.[37] Kampfner's account suggests that Britain's military involvement in Afghanistan – as well as four other recent conflicts, including the Iraq War – should be understood in light of the bold personality of former Prime Minister Tony Blair, and his ethical view that evils such as mass terrorism must be addressed and that foreign intervention is sometimes necessary to do so.[38] It should also be understood, Kampfner suggests, in light of Blair's political belief that Britain must support the US.[39]

In addition, Michael Clarke's edited collection of essays, *The Afghan Papers*, also draws on interviews with former senior military, political and civil service personnel,

---

33 For an acknowledgment of this observation, see Kampfner 2004: ix. For a similar observation regarding Britain's difficult military campaign in Helmand since 2006, see Clarke 2011: 29.

34 See e.g. Fergusson 2008, Ledwidge 2011, Jermy 2011, Farrell 2011, and Bird and Marshall 2011.

35 See e.g. Bishop 2007, Terrill 2007, Tootal 2009, and Benitz 2011. See also BBC2, *Afghanistan: War Without End?*, 22 June 2011, and BBC2, *Afghanistan: The Battle for Helmand*, 29 June 2011.

36 See e.g. Farrell 2011, Griffin 2011, Egnell 2011, Catignani 2012, and Griffin 2013.

37 Kampfner 2004: 107–151.

38 Ibid: ix, 11, 110–111. For related observations, see Bower 2016: 234–236, 510–542 (who highlights Blair's ongoing self-belief and religious view in the face of criticism – including by defence leaders and journalists – over the wisdom of Britain's decade of wars abroad).

39 Kampfner 2004: ix, 11, 110–111.

and focuses on the initial decisions behind the third phase of the UK's involvement in the Afghan Conflict.[40] One way of understanding these decisions, Clarke contends, is as a result of the political view among the US and its allies that al-Qaeda and the Taliban must be denied any ungoverned space in Afghanistan from which future terrorist attacks could be launched, and of the international "momentum" created by the involvement of NATO and the UN in the country following 9/11.[41] "Having engaged with the need to 'do something' about Afghanistan in late 2001," Clarke notes, "the momentum of multinational action was very hard to escape. [By 2005, the] choice appeared to be to let the strategy fail, or engage more with it."[42]

In seeking to explain why Britain has participated in the Afghan Conflict, assessing whether primacy should ultimately be granted to internal factors, such as the particular psychology of Tony Blair, or external inputs, such as the international momentum associated with NATO's involvement in the war, will likely have to wait until more evidence becomes available. For instance, in contrast to Britain's participation in the Iraq War, the country's military involvement in Afghanistan has received significantly less official attention. Iraq has been the subject of five government inquiries, including the ambitious Chilcot Inquiry of 2009 to 2016. No comparable investigation has been completed on the Afghan Conflict, although some oral evidence given at the Chilcot Inquiry has addressed the topic.[43] Moreover, some reports have been released by government committees that discuss Britain's military involvement in Afghanistan,[44] and one of these reports has expressed concern about the way early decisions regarding this involvement appear to have been made.[45] Finally, there are some domestic court cases that address the issue of Britain's policy and practice regarding Afghan detainees, and these cases make helpful reference to witness statements and documentary evidence on the issue.[46]

In light of the current state of the literature on Britain and the Afghan Conflict, and the evidence that is available, this chapter draws on the work that exists and helps advance the growing body of knowledge on this topic. Consistent with what one might presume, there is evidence that Britain's alliance with America and its security concern regarding al-Qaeda are important to

---

40 Clarke 2011.

41 Ibid: 10–12.

42 Ibid: 12.

43 See e.g. the oral evidence given by Peter Ricketts (24 Nov. 2009), Jeremy Greenstock (27 Nov. 2009), and John Reid (3 Feb. 2010). Available online at http://www.iraqinquiry.org.uk/.

44 See e.g. HM Government, *UK Policy in Afghanistan and Pakistan* (2009); and Public Administration Select Committee, *Who Does UK National Security?*, HC 435, 18 Oct. 2011, and HC 713, 28 Jan. 2011.

45 House of Commons Defence Committee, *Operations in Afghanistan*, HC 554, 17 July 2011, at paras. 28, 67.

46 See e.g. *R (Evans) v SS Defence*, [2010] EWHC 1445 (Admin).

understanding the UK's military involvement in Afghanistan. However, *despite* this environment of US dominance and perceived security threats, Britain's understanding of its rights and duties under the UN Charter, and its obligations under relevant international human rights law, have also influenced the advice of officials and the decisions of leaders regarding the nature and scope of the UK's involvement, and the justifications that could be made for its actions.

The Four Roles of International Law in Britain's Use of Force in Afghanistan

Britain's military action in Afghanistan illustrates the four roles that international law can play when states use force: (1) it helps constitute the identity of actors; (2) it helps regulate their behaviour; (3) it permits and legitimates certain conduct; and (4) it helps structure the development of new legal rules and legitimate practice.

1. International Law Helped Constitute the Identities of Some UK Leaders and Officials

Like Clement Attlee during the Korean War, there is evidence that former Prime Minister Tony Blair felt a sense of obligation towards the conflict in Afghanistan that followed the events of 9/11. Unlike with Attlee, however, this perception of obligation appears to have been shaped less by Britain's formal membership in the United Nations and a belief in the international rule of law, and more by Blair's ethical views that mass terrorism must be addressed and that foreign intervention in Afghanistan was needed to do so. More generally, though, during the three phases of Britain's military participation in the Afghan Conflict, the UK's perceived commitments to the UN and NATO helped constitute the identities of some UK leaders and government officials, and helped shape the way in which Britain's interests were interpreted and pursued. Further, as the war became more challenging and US military policy in the region became more controversial, these perceived commitments acted as a site for a "communicative" struggle over Britain's legitimate identity and rightful behaviour with respect to these developments.

The decisions behind phase one of Britain's participation in the conflict appear to have occurred in three stages. The first stage involved the decisions that led to the various force deployments in the fall of 2001, described earlier. Stage two involved the decision in late 2001 to lead and send ground troops to the UN-authorized ISAF mission in Kabul. After Turkey took command of ISAF in June 2002, the third stage involved the decision to contribute soldiers to the ongoing US-led operations against the Taliban and al-Qaeda.

Regarding the first stage, Blair explains in his memoirs that he saw the events of 9/11 as a declaration of war on the US and "all of us who shared the same values."[47] President Bush also described 9/11 as an act of war. By contrast, we will see in the next chapter that Canadian leaders did not tend to describe 9/11 this way. To win the war against terrorism, Blair continues, "would not and does not require simply a military strategy to defeat an enemy that is fighting us. It requires a whole new geopolitical framework. It requires nation-building. It requires a myriad of interventions deep into the affairs of other nations. It requires above all a willingness to see the battle as existential and to see it through, to take the time, to spend the treasure, to shed the blood."[48]

These observations generally resonate with the security and alliance concerns that Alastair Campbell, who was Blair's Press Secretary and a trusted adviser, describes in his diary entries from the fall of 2001.[49] They are also consistent with the memoirs of Christopher Meyer, Britain's ambassador to the US at the time;[50] and the reflections of Peter Ricketts, a former Political Director of the Foreign and Commonwealth Office, UK representative to NATO, and National Security adviser to the prime minister.[51] Similarly, Nigel Sheinwald – a former UK representative to the EU, Foreign adviser to the prime minister, and ambassador to the US – says the core mission in Afghanistan has always been about security and "ensuring al-Qaeda can't operate [there]."[52]

Blair's observations above also reflect views he expressed in an important foreign policy speech in Chicago in April 1999, during NATO's bombing campaign in Kosovo. In that speech, Blair argued: "We are all internationalists now, whether we like it or not. ... We cannot turn our backs on conflicts and the violation of human rights within other countries if we still want to be secure."[53] He also set out criteria for determining when intervening in the internal affairs

---

47 Blair 2010: 345. Blair declined to be interviewed for this study.

48 Ibid: 349.

49 Campbell 2008: 559–596. At a meeting on the evening of 11 September 2001, Campbell noted that Blair stressed "the importance of a diplomatic strategy to support the US," and said "it was vital that we worked up an international agenda that went beyond the US just hitting Afghanistan."

50 Meyer 2005: 182–206.

51 Phone interview with Sir Peter Ricketts, 26 June 2013. The main reason Britain has fought in the Afghan Conflict, Ricketts says, is "a sense that we were all subject to the same terrorist threat of the al-Qaeda group ... and therefore we needed to have a collective reaction." This core reason, he thinks, has animated the thinking of the Blair, Brown and Cameron governments regarding Afghanistan, although different priorities have been emphasized at different times, such as development or counter-narcotics.

52 Interview with Sir Nigel Sheinwald, London, 8 July 2013. Unlike Blair, Sheinwald also says that, while Britain has pursued political and development goals in Afghanistan, "our aim was never grandiose nation-building."

53 Tony Blair, "Address to the Chicago Economic Club," 22 April 1999.

of sovereign states was appropriate.[54] Unlike similar criteria on such matters,[55] Blair did not stress the importance of having "right authorization" from the UN Security Council. Perhaps for this reason, members of the UK Foreign Office at the time, and particularly its legal team, were dismayed by Blair's speech.[56] Blair did, however, state that "[i]f we want a world ruled by law and by international cooperation then we have to support the UN as its central pillar," and argued for reforming the UN and its Security Council to make them work. Like his memoir reflections ten years later, Blair also stressed that intervening was only appropriate if the international community was "prepared for the long term ... [and would not] simply walk away once the fight was over."[57]

Consistent with this latter criterion, after 9/11, UK leaders recognized that Afghanistan would need to be secured and rebuilt, that the UN should play a role in this regard, and that Britain could take a lead in pursuing both objectives. For instance, in the lead-up to the initial military actions in Afghanistan in 2001, Blair and Foreign Secretary Jack Straw faced questions in Parliament from some Labour Party backbenchers who wanted confirmation that Britain was working with Secretary General Kofi Annan, and "that the UN's role in the programme on which we are embarked will not be limited simply to organising humanitarian aid."[58] These questions reflected the fact that, although members of the Labour Party supported George W. Bush immediately following 9/11, this support was challenged by his subsequent "gun-slinging 'wanted: dead or alive' declarations."[59]

This tension in the foreign policy outlook of the Labour Party, we saw earlier, was also present during the Korean War. Again, it reflects a larger disagreement between party members who think Britain's foreign and defence interests are best pursued by focusing on the country's alliance with the US, and those who believe the UK should support international institutions like the UN.[60] Following 9/11, Blair thought it was crucial that Britain stand "shoulder to shoulder" with the US.[61] But he also indicates that he would have supported a military

---

54 Professor Lawrence Freedman wrote much of the text on which Blair relied (Kampfner 2004: 52).

55 See e.g. the 2001 report by the International Commission on Intervention and State Sovereignty, *The Responsibility to Protect*.

56 Kampfner 2004: 53.

57 The other criteria were: "[A]re we sure of our case? ... [H]ave we exhausted all diplomatic options? ... [O]n the basis of a practical assessment of the situation, are there military operations we can sensibly and prudently undertake? ... And finally, do we have national interests involved?"

58 See Lynne Jones's statements in Parliament, in HC Debs., 4 Oct. 2001, col. 691.

59 Kampfner 2004: 122. Similarly, Chris Meyer notes that, following 9/11, "Some Labour Party backbenchers were getting restless about Blair's aligning himself so unreservedly with a Republican President" (2005: 198).

60 Phythian 2007.

61 Blair 2010: 341.

response in Afghanistan with or without the history of the Anglo-American relationship.[62]

One challenge members of the Blair government faced in supporting the US following 9/11 was that their American counterparts appeared to be more focused on the initial military actions in Afghanistan than on the difficult security work and nation-building that would have to occur there afterwards.[63] In contrast to this US approach, Blair told a Labour Party conference in early October 2001 that "[w]e will not walk away from Afghanistan, as the outside world has done so many times before."[64] In the weeks that followed, Blair asked Britain's permanent representative to the UN, Jeremy Greenstock, to put pressure on Lakhdar Brahimi, the UN special envoy tasked with finding a political solution for a post-Taliban Afghanistan. Blair wanted Brahimi to hold the UN meeting on the future of Afghanistan as soon as possible, although he later realized the diplomatic difficulty of this request.[65]

Elaborating on his thinking during this period, Blair notes: "The UN under Kofi Annan's guidance was being helpful and from the outset I was determined that they should help take the strain of the politics. Fortunately, in Lakhdar Brahimi they had a sensible interlocutor with the Afghans, one who was experienced and savvy."[66] Similarly, Peter Ricketts observes that the role of the UN was particularly significant at the beginning of the Afghan war.[67] And Nigel Sheinwald recalls that Britain supported the UN in this period, and was involved in the political settlement in Afghanistan as well as the UN-sponsored peace negotiations in Bonn.[68] Reflecting Blair's "determination" noted above, Robert Cooper, a UK diplomat, was appointed as Britain's special envoy on Afghanistan. Cooper was instructed to help Brahimi find a political solution in Afghanistan, and was even sent on a secret mission to meet the country's exiled former king.[69]

Following the Bonn conference, Britain took a lead in drafting and passing Security Council Resolution 1386 in December 2001.[70] This instrument, recall, created ISAF and authorized it to assist the Afghan Transitional Authority in providing security in and around Kabul. Initially, Blair wanted to commit 6,000 additional UK troops to support the continuing OEF operations to find Osama

---

62 Clarke 2011: 83.

63 Kampfner 2004: 146, and Clarke 2011: 12–13.

64 Cited in Kampfner 2004: 146.

65 Kampfner 2004: 142–144.

66 Blair 2010: 358.

67 Phone interview with Sir Peter Ricketts, 26 June 2013.

68 Interview with Sir Nigel Sheinwald, London, 8 July 2013.

69 Kampfner 2004: 142–145.

70 As Nigel Sheinwald notes, "we were closely involved in [the Security Council resolution that created ISAF] – the UK was very much in the lead" (interview, London, 8 July 2013).

Bin Laden.[71] When this offer was declined, however, it was decided that Britain would lead the ISAF force in Kabul and send 1,800 soldiers there. Commenting on the policy context at the time, Kampfner notes: "Some seventeen other countries also declared their willingness to participate [in ISAF], but Britain was very much in the lead. This was important to Blair, to … show off the peacekeeping role of the military, even after 9/11."[72] Blair's earlier wish was then partially fulfilled when, in April 2002, the UK announced that 1,700 troops would be sent to help the US flush out what was left of al-Qaeda.[73]

Throughout this period, Britain's commitment to rebuilding Afghanistan conflicted with America's broader war on terror, and international law acted as a site of debate over how to respond to this conflict of priorities. For instance, the UK Foreign Office had originally wanted ISAF's UN-mandate to extend beyond Kabul, but this was rejected by the Pentagon.[74] Clare Short, Britain's Minister of Development at the time, complained to her Cabinet colleagues that the US was not taking the aid situation in Afghanistan seriously enough.[75] This reflected the fact that US attention had already shifted, with talk in Washington now focusing on "phase two" in the war on terror – branching out to other states.[76]

This shift in attention could be seen when the US started transferring hundreds of alleged al-Qaeda members from Afghanistan to Guantánamo Bay in the winter of 2002. The Bush administration refused to call these individuals Prisoners of War (POWs), and argued that the Geneva Conventions did not apply to them.[77] The alleged mistreatment and harsh living conditions of these detainees came under extensive criticism, and the judicial basis for their indefinite internment was questioned.[78] Reflecting these concerns, many Labour Members of Parliament in Britain at the time expressed horror at the US

---

71 Kampfner 2004: 145.

72 Ibid: 146.

73 Defence Minister Geoff Hoon's statements in Parliament on 29 April 2002, in HC Debs., vol. 384, col. 649.

74 US commander General Franks feared the new ISAF force would "confuse the battlefield" (Kampfner 2004: 146).

75 Ibid.

76 Ibid: 146–147. Chris Meyer notes, "As to Iraq's possible complicity [in 9/11], there was no compelling evidence and strong skepticism on the British side. Blair urged Bush to focus to the exclusion of all else on the job in hand: Afghanistan, al-Qaeda and the Taliban" (2005: 191).

77 This initial position was challenged by, among other things, subsequent court proceedings in the US, including the Supreme Court's important 2006 decision in *Hamdan v. Rumsfeld*. In that case, it was held that the military commissions created by the Bush administration to try detainees at Guantánamo Bay violated the US Uniform Code of Military Justice and the four Geneva Conventions of 1949, specifically Common Article 3 of those treaties.

78 See e.g. Amnesty International, "United States of America: Guantánamo – An Icon of Lawlessness" (6 Jan. 2005).

detention facility.[79] Prime Minister Blair was embarrassed and frustrated by the issue, particularly because three UK citizens were among the individuals being held.[80] He urged the US to employ more humane conditions at Guantánamo, but also said that the detainees would provide valuable intelligence.[81]

In addition to the United Nations, Britain's membership in NATO was also relevant to the foreign policy outlook of some UK leaders and officials following 9/11. For instance, speaking to Parliament on 14 September 2001, Blair emphasized that "NATO has already, for the first time since it was founded in 1949, invoked [A]rticle 5 [of its treaty] and determined that this attack in America will be considered as an attack against the alliance as a whole."[82] Elaborating on this point, Foreign Secretary Jack Straw told his parliamentary colleagues that day:

> NATO has recognised the unprecedented nature of the threat. As we have heard, for the first time in the history of the alliance, it has invoked [A]rticle 5 of the Washington treaty, which states that an armed attack against one or more of the allies in Europe or North America shall be considered an attack against them all. There is no clearer signal that we could send to the perpetrators of these attacks than that they face a determined and united response by the international community.[83]

Resonating with Blair and Straw's comments, Peter Hain, Minister for Europe at the Foreign and Commonwealth Office, remarked in a television interview at the time: "We're a country, along with eighteen others, who are members of NATO. This is an attack on NATO, one of our members, we've taken a decision by invoking Article 5 of the NATO treaty, the first time that's happened since it was formed in 1949, to say we stand together in this."[84] And, responding to potential accusations that the government was overly prioritizing the Anglo-American relationship, Defence Secretary Geoffrey Hoon told Parliament on 4 October:

> I want to make it clear that there have been a range of ... contacts, not only with the United States, but with other allies. NATO defence ministers met in Brussels

---

79 Kampfner 2004: 149–150.

80 A Detainee Inquiry, described at the end of the next section below, was created in 2010 in part as a response to the controversy associated with the UK citizens who were detained at Guantánamo. It was never formally launched.

81 Kampfner 2004: 149–150.

82 HC Debs., 14 Sept. 2001, vol. 372, col. 605. For Article 5 of the North Atlantic Treaty, see: www.nato.int

83 HC Debs., 14 Sept. 2001, vol. 372, col. 619.

84 Cited in Marston 2001: 679. Text provided by the FCO (Transcript 030/WfC/2001).

last week to discuss how we can work together in our response to the threat of international terrorism. NATO has taken the unprecedented step of invoking [A]rticle 5 for the first time in its history, in recognition that the attack on the United States was an attack on all of us. Other allies, therefore, also stand by to assist the United States.[85]

Finally, in addition to Parliament and television, the significance of Article 5 of the NATO treaty being invoked was emphasized in debates that occurred in the House of Lords.[86]

Summing up the importance of the above references, General Robert Fry, former Director of Operations in the Ministry of Defence, and Desmond Bowen, a retired civil servant who worked in the Cabinet Office and Defence Ministry, have written that "NATO's invocation of Article V of its founding treaty provided a broader context for the sense of collective threat and an *inalienable responsibility* to respond" [emphasis added].[87] I discuss the invocation of Article 5 more in the next chapter, as it was considered particularly important by Canadian leaders.

Britain's perceived commitments to the UN and NATO also arose during the second and third phases of its military activities in Afghanistan, and these commitments helped animate the foreign policy outlook of some leaders and officials in power during these phases. For instance, Britain's second phase of military action in Afghanistan occurred from 2003 to 2005. It involved the UK contributing to ISAF and leading a Provincial Reconstruction Team (PRT), a concept that Britain had helped to pioneer.[88] As Peter Ricketts notes, the UK "was always a strong supporter of the PRT model for civil-military coordinated stabilization work" in Afghanistan, and it "wanted to show that we're willing to take a lead."[89] That is why, Ricketts says, Britain went to Mazar-e Sharif and other northern locations in those early years and set up PRTs – i.e., "to show how stabilization could be done."[90]

Again, Britain's second phase of military involvement in Afghanistan was overshadowed by its separate decision to participate in the US-led invasion of Iraq,[91] and the international legal controversy associated with this

---

85 HC Debs., 4 Oct. 2001, vol. 372, col. 805.

86 See e.g. the comments made on 14 Sept. 2001 by Lord Williams of Mostyn, and Baroness Symons, Minister for Trade (HL Debs., vol. 627, cols. 4–5, 12, in Marston 2001: 679–680).

87 Fry and Bowen 2011: 68–67.

88 Clarke 2011: 11.

89 Phone interview with Sir Peter Ricketts, 26 June 2013.

90 Ibid.

91 As Clarke notes, because operations in Iraq dominated the minds of leaders at the time, key military policymakers, including military service chiefs, struggle to recall any occasions on which a genuine strategic discussion of Britain's military activity in Afghanistan occurred (2011: 14).

decision.[92] Some public discussion about this second phase, however, did occur. In response to questions by parliamentarians about the UK's future military plans in Afghanistan, the government wrote in October 2003 that "the UK-led [PRT] based in Mazar-e Sharif will [likely] increase slightly in size by the end of the year. This expansion is part of the planned evolution of the [PRT] and is *coincidental to UNSCR 1510*" [emphasis added].[93] Security Council Resolution 1510 was passed that month. It expanded ISAF's mandate whereby the international force would help provide security throughout Afghanistan.

Britain's third phase of military action in Afghanistan took place from 2006 to 2014, and involved a significant number of UK forces being deployed to Helmand. Contrasting the difficult fighting of this phase with Britain's earlier military activities in Afghanistan, a former Chief of the General Staff has expressed the view that Britain's "original intention" in the country was "to support the UN's ISAF mission."[94] Consistent with this view, Defence Secretary John Reid – who ultimately authorized the initial deployment to Helmand and believed it was the "right thing" to do[95] – told Parliament in January 2006 the following about this operation:

Just over four years ago, on 11 September 2001, we were given a brutal lesson in the consequences of leaving Afghanistan in the hands of the Taliban and the terrorists. Since then, we in this country have been at the forefront of the international effort, *under the auspices of the United Nations*, to defeat international terrorism, to free Afghanistan from the ruthless grip of the Taliban and to rid the country of the menace of the terrorists and the greed of the drug traffickers [emphasis added].[96]

To bring stability and security to Afghanistan, Reid continued:

[T]here is a clear role for the military: helping to create and to maintain a framework of security on which legitimate Afghan institutions can grow and thrive.

---

92 For the views of leaders and officials on Britain's participation in the Iraq War, and the international legal context of this participation, see the various oral and written evidence provided to the Chilcot Inquiry.

93 HC Written Answers, 22 Oct. 2003, col. 589W.

94 Cited in Clarke 2011: 81.

95 For Reid's reflections on the Helmand decision, see his oral evidence at the Chilcot Inquiry, 3 Feb. 2010, transcript at 55–59. For Reid's view that it was the "right thing" to do, see the paper by Nick Beadle, who was the Private Secretary to Reid and his successor, Des Browne, from mid-2005 to mid-2007 (Beadle 2011: 74). Beadle's recollection of this period "is that across Whitehall there was a sense of redemption to be found in the proposed Afghanistan deployment and a drift toward denial about Iraq" (2011: 79).

96 HC Debs., 26 Jan. 2006, col. 1529.

NATO, through its leadership of the international security assistance force, itself under the auspices of the UN, has a major role to play in making that happen. Thanks to NATO's leadership, ISAF has already expanded its activities to cover the north and west of Afghanistan, at the request of the democratically elected Afghan Government and with the authorisation of the United Nations.[97]

Consistent with Reid's emphasis of NATO's role, Peter Ricketts notes that Britain sent forces to Helmand "because the NATO strategic plan for Afghanistan envisaged gradually extending stabilization from province to province ... and we felt we should play our part in that."[98] More generally, Ricketts also says that one of the reasons UK forces remained in Afghanistan is due to "a sense of solidarity with NATO."[99] Similarly, Nigel Sheinwald observes that, although Britain's alliance with the US has affected its participation in the Afghan war, NATO has also been "an important factor."[100] Expressing views that can be linked back to Ernest Bevin's support for the creation of NATO prior to the Korean War, noted in chapter four, Sheinwald points out that "Britain is a big supporter of NATO and wants it to continue. We have questions about [its] long-term survivability ... but it is important to our foreign policy and defence policy. It has always been. We've always been team players as far as NATO is concerned."[101]

In response to escalating violence in Helmand, UK troop numbers there were increased to 4,500 in July 2006.[102] The government was accused of failing to anticipate the difficult resistance UK forces would meet in the province.[103] Sheinwald thinks this accusation has been overblown, and notes that "we knew we would take casualties in Helmand" and that "there were going to be ... real

---

97   Ibid, col. 1530.

98   Phone interview with Sir Peter Ricketts, 26 June 2013.

99   Ibid.

100   Interview with Sir Nigel Sheinwald, London, 8 July 2013. Contextualizing the relative importance of the Anglo-American relationship, Sheinwald emphasizes that "the main reason we're doing this is because we need a foreign policy and national security objective fulfilled in Afghanistan. We're not 'inventing' the Afghan war in order to satisfy some abstract requirement to be nice to the Americans."

101   Ibid.

102   For a military perspective on the initial UK operations in Helmand, and the tension between the reality of these operations and the political goals of the government, see Brigadier Ed Butler's evidence to the House of Commons Defence Committee, *Operations in Afghanistan*, HC 554, July 2011, Ev. 103.

103   Regarding this difficult resistance, a government minister at the time reportedly asked a fellow minister in exasperation: "How the hell did we get ourselves into this position? How did we go charging up the valley without it ever being put to cabinet?" (cited in Clarke 2011: 21). This "charge," it should be noted, refers less to the initial government decision to deploy troops to Helmand, and more to a subsequent military decision in Afghanistan to move UK forces into offensive positions in the province.

fights involving the Taliban."[104] There "was a very exhaustive effort in 2004–05," he says, to plan "our Helmand operation, leading to the decision by our Cabinet in January 2006 to go ahead [with it]."[105] Commenting on the criticism at the time, Des Browne – John Reid's successor, who believed in the Helmand mission "even more so" than Reid[106] – reaffirmed the distinct importance of the UN-authorized ISAF mission, and reiterated that Britain's ultimate goal was the rebuilding of Afghanistan:

> We have been accused of naivety by drawing a distinction between the ISAF – international security assistance force – mission to spread security and the US-led [OEF] mission focused on counter-terrorism. But that distinction is not naive at all. In both cases, soldiers will have to fight, but the nature of the ISAF mission reflects the fundamental fact that we will not reach a lasting peace by force alone; we will reach it when Afghanistan has changed and when the Government have been able to deliver such security, development and prosperity that the ordinary Afghans will no longer tolerate terrorists and criminals in their midst. That is why rebuilding is our mission.[107]

Endorsing Browne's strategic goals in Afghanistan, Liam Fox, who would later become defence minister under the Cameron government, emphasized that one of the reasons Britain must succeed in the country is because "the reputation and cohesion of NATO is on the line."[108]

Further troop increases were announced in February 2007 (bringing the number of UK forces in Afghanistan to around 7,700), and in the spring of 2009 (bringing the overall figure to over 8,000). Explaining the first increase, Des Browne told Parliament that "we should understand what is at risk if we do not continue to live up to the *collective commitment* we have made to Afghanistan and its people" [emphasis added].[109] Browne reaffirmed this commitment when explaining the second increase: "Our forces … are in Afghanistan *to fulfill a UN mandate*, to support the elected Government, to train and mentor the Afghan army and police, and to give the Afghan people hope for the future. I believe, as I think do the majority of this House, that Afghanistan is a noble cause" [emphasis added].[110]

---

104 This was explicitly stated and understood during a key meeting with the UK Chiefs of Staff. Interview with Sir Nigel Sheinwald, London, 8 July 2013.

105 Ibid.

106 Beadle 2011: 74.

107 HC Debs., 10 July 2006, vol. 448, col. 1132.

108 Ibid, col. 1136.

109 HC Debs., 26 Feb. 2007, vol. 457, col. 619.

110 HC Debs., 16 June 2008, vol. 477, col. 676.

In conclusion, the above review has indicated that, like Clement Attlee during the Korean War, Prime Minister Blair felt a sense of obligation towards the conflict in Afghanistan that followed the events of 9/11. Unlike with Attlee, however, this perception of obligation appears to have been shaped less by Britain's formal membership in the UN and a belief in the international rule of law, and more by Blair's ethical views that international terrorism must be addressed and that foreign intervention in Afghanistan was needed to do so. More generally, though, during the three phases of Britain's military participation in the Afghan Conflict, the UK's perceived commitments to the UN and NATO helped constitute the identities of some UK leaders and government officials, and helped shape the way in which Britain's interests were interpreted and pursued. Further, as the Afghan war became more challenging and US military policy in the region became more controversial, these perceived commitments acted as a site for a "communicative" struggle over Britain's legitimate identity and rightful behaviour with respect to these developments.

2. International Law Helped Regulate Britain's Conduct

In addition to its constitutive effect, international law has also had a regulative influence on Britain's political and military practice regarding the Afghanistan Conflict. A key example of this impact is Britain's policy and conduct regarding individuals captured in Afghanistan by UK forces and transferred to local authorities. The history of this issue is legally complex and still unfolding.[111] For present purposes, it suffices to note that Britain's policy and conduct regarding Afghan detainees have been governed and controlled in part by its interpretation of (a) Security Council Resolution 1386 of 20 December 2001, which created ISAF, and (b) relevant basic principles of international human rights law, including the right to life and the prohibition on torture. This interpretation, moreover, has had a significant effect even though other material considerations – such as Britain's interest in gathering intelligence, preventing attacks, and cooperating with Afghan security and intelligence agencies – have arguably conflicted with some of its perceived requirements.

To understand the above arguments, one must understand the circumstances that led to Britain signing a Memorandum of Understanding (MoU) in April 2006 with Afghanistan concerning the transfer by UK forces of captured individuals to Afghan authorities. According to submissions made by the UK government in an important 2010 court case on the issue, *R (Evans) v SS Defence*,

---

111 For a more detailed review, see *R (Evans) v. SS Defence*, [2010] EWHC 1445 (Admin); and
      Serdar Mohammed v Ministry of Defence and *Al Waheed v Ministry of Defence* [2017] UKSC
      2. For a comparative analysis of Australia's approach to Afghan detainees, see Richmond
      2016a.

British policy in Afghanistan prior to this MoU "was to avoid detaining individuals, wherever possible."[112] Following the deployment of 3,500 UK troops to Helmand in 2006, however, it was thought that some captured individuals would likely have to be detained for reasons of force protection, intelligence gathering, and criminal investigations.[113]

Three international legal obstacles stood in the way of expanding Britain's policy and practice regarding detainees. First, although UK forces in Afghanistan were seen as authorized to kill or capture insurgents provided such forces comply with the laws of armed conflict (the *jus in bello*), the power of detention that stems from this authorization was understood as only extending to temporary detention.[114] Second, and similarly, unlike comparable resolutions on Iraq at the time, Security Council Resolution 1386 on Afghanistan did not refer to detention. The instrument did authorize ISAF forces to use "all necessary measures" to fulfill their mandate. However, this was also interpreted as allowing only temporary detention. As the judges in the *Evans* case noted, "Legal advice [prior to the MoU] confirmed that there was no basis upon which UK forces could legitimately intern such individuals [and] they must be transferred to the Afghan authorities."[115] Consistent with this view, the office of the UK Defence Secretary maintained in *Evans* that "[i]n the absence of any express authorisation in the UN Security Council resolutions … the UK has *no power* of indefinite internment" [emphasis added].[116]

Finally, there was a realization that transferring individuals might engage Britain's obligations under the European Convention on Human Rights (ECHR).[117] Article 1 of the ECHR imposes an obligation to respect human rights, stating that "[p]arties shall secure to everyone within their jurisdiction the [treaty's] rights and freedoms." Article 2 protects the right to life, and Article 3 prohibits torture. In light of these provisions, UK officials involved in negotiating the MoU with Afghanistan have remarked "that it was structured to avoid the risk of a breach of the UK's Convention obligations which might be applicable: key points were to *prohibit* the death penalty, to *prevent* the transfer of detainees to a third party, and to enable UK access to detainees transferred to the Afghan authorities" [emphasis added].[118]

In light of these international legal considerations, and the perceived need for British forces in Helmand to detain and transfer captured individuals, UK

---

112 *Evans* at paras. 92–93.

113 Ibid.

114 *Evans* at para. 17.

115 *Evans* at para. 93.

116 *Evans* at para. 17.

117 The text of the ECHR is available online at http://human-rights-convention.org.

118 *Evans* at para. 94.

Defence Secretary John Reid and his Afghan counterpart signed the MoU in April 2006.[119] Reflecting the "key points" from the ECHR noted above, the Memorandum had two main aims. First, it established the responsibilities, principles and procedures in the event of the transfer by UK forces to Afghan authorities of persons detained in Afghanistan.[120] Second, it sought to "[e]nsure that Participants will observe the basic principles of international human rights law such as the right to life and the prohibition on torture and cruel, inhumane and degrading treatment pertaining to the treatment and transfer of persons by the UK [armed forces] to Afghan authorities."[121] By contrast, we will see in the next chapter that Canada's detainee agreement with Afghanistan sought to ensure that transferred individuals would be treated in accordance not with international human rights law but with the Third Geneva Convention of 1949.

When news broke out in Canada in April 2007 that detainees transferred by Canadian forces had been mistreated by Afghan authorities, the UK decided that additional measures were necessary to ensure that those transferred by British forces were being treated properly.[122] Reflecting this concern, an Exchange of Letters (EoL) occurred in September 2007 between Afghanistan, on the one hand, and Britain, the US, Canada, the Netherlands, Denmark, and Norway on the other. The EoL aimed to establish a common approach of those parties regarding access to individuals detained by their forces and transferred to Afghan authorities.[123] It improved Britain's MoU with Afghanistan by expressly allowing transferred detainees to be interviewed in private.[124]

In addition to the MoU and EoL, Britain's policy on Afghan detainees also reflected ISAF standard operating procedures. This is because, the judges in *Evans* noted, the vast majority of UK forces in Afghanistan operated under the command of ISAF, and they were the only British forces involved in the capture and transfer of detainees.[125] This implies that UK forces which did not operate under ISAF, such as those that may have been part of OEF, did not capture or transfer detainees. Under ISAF procedures, a person could only be detained for ISAF force protection, self-defence, or for accomplishing the ISAF mission.[126] Such persons were to be detained for no longer than 96 hours, although this could be extended in certain circumstances. After 96 hours, they had to be

---

119 *Evans* at paras. 92–93. Reid is not mentioned by name in this section of the case, but he was
    Defence Secretary from 6 May 2005 until 5 May 2006.
120 *Evans* at para. 95.
121 Ibid.
122 *Evans* at para. 107.
123 *Evans* at para. 108.
124 Ibid.
125 *Evans* at para. 14.
126 *Evans* at para. 19.

released or transferred to the Afghan authorities.[127] The preferred reception body for ISAF detainees was the National Directorate of Security (NDS), Afghanistan's intelligence agency.[128] In accordance with this instruction, between July 2006, when UK transfers began, and March 2010, the vast majority (410 of 418) of individuals detained by British forces were transferred to the NDS.[129]

Importantly, the ISAF procedures stated that "[c]onsistent with international law, persons should not be transferred under any circumstances in which there is a risk that they be subjected to torture or other forms of ill treatment."[130] Reflecting ISAF's rules, the UK developed detailed standard operating instructions on how to detain individuals, look after them in detention and, where appropriate, manage their onward transfer to the Afghan authorities.[131] As with ISAF's procedures, Britain's policy – which reportedly applied at all material times to UK operations in Afghanistan – stated that detainees are not to be transferred into Afghan custody if there is a real risk that they will suffer torture or serious mistreatment.[132] This was set out clearly in a March 2010 written policy statement from then UK Defence Secretary Bob Ainsworth:

1.2 This Policy Statement, which is to be observed whenever UK Armed Forces undertake detention in an operational theatre, reflects the importance which I attach to ensuring the humane treatment of those it is necessary to detain in the course of our operations … 2.1 This policy applies across the MOD and the Armed Forces and to all detention activities undertaken in military theatres of operation. It sets out the minimum standards which must be applied … 3.1 I require the Ministry of Defence and Armed Forces to: … (f) Ensure that Detained Persons are not transferred from UK custody to any nation where there is a real risk at the time of transfer that the Detained Person will suffer torture [or] serious mistreatment …[133]

If there were specific grounds to believe that a detainee may be mistreated by the Afghan authorities after transfer, Britain's standard operating instructions

---

127 Ibid. The procedures also noted that the Government of Afghanistan has overall responsibility for the maintenance of law and order within the country, and that when transferring a detainee ISAF cannot seek to constrain the freedom of action of the Afghan authorities.

128 *Evans* at para. 43. This was reportedly to ensure common processing and tracking of the transferred detainee.

129 *Evans* at para. 48.

130 *Evans* at para. 19.

131 *Evans* at paras. 20, 43–48. As part of the UK's operating instructions, the International Committee of the Red Cross was to be informed of detainee transfers as soon as practicable, and the Afghanistan Independent Human Rights Commission should be informed where possible. This was to ensure that there was additional scrutiny and oversight of the assurances contained in Britain's MoU with Afghanistan regarding detainees (para. 47).

132 *Evans* at paras. 20–21.

133 Ibid.

stated that "such concerns should be raised with the legal advisor to UK forces and the Force Provost Marshal."[134]

Despite the formal arrangements and policies noted above, critics have argued that transferees into Afghan custody were at real risk of torture or serious mistreatment and, therefore, that the practice of transfer was in breach of Britain's policy and unlawful.[135] As evidence for this view, reference is often made to specific allegations by UK transferees,[136] and relevant reports by UN agencies, the Afghanistan Independent Human Rights Commission, NGOs, and the UK's own Parliamentary Foreign Affairs Committee.[137] Among other things, these reports document numerous cases of torture and mistreatment of Afghan prisoners, and allege that the NDS has a particularly poor record in this regard.[138]

Although the UK government was aware of these reports, and accepted that some of the allegations may be credible, it argued in *Evans* that notwithstanding this general background, "the specific circumstances relating to UK transferees are such as to ensure adequate safeguards for them."[139] Detention operations, the government further contended, are of "vital importance" to UK forces operating in Afghanistan, because they help such forces gather intelligence, protect themselves and local civilians from insurgent attacks, and assist the Afghan government in providing security and stability.[140] If it were not possible to transfer detainees, there would be a "severe impact" on the counterinsurgency strategy, and the UK-Afghan relationship.[141]

In response to these two opposing positions, the court ultimately held in *Evans* that a moratorium on transfers to the NDS facility in Kabul imposed by UK officials should be maintained, and that transfers to the NDS facilities in Kandahar and in Lashkar Gah (the capital of Helmand) could continue if existing safeguards were strengthened by the observance of three additional conditions.[142]

---

134 *Evans* at para. 46. The staff of the Force Provost Marshal specialize in custody and detention.

135 See e.g. the claimant's allegations in *Evans* at para. 1.

136 *Evans* at paras. 187–226.

137 *Evans* at paras. 49–75.

138 *Evans* at paras. 49–75.

139 *Evans* at paras. 76, 310.

140 *Evans* at para. 23.

141 Ibid.

142 *Evans* at paras. 315–322. These conditions required that "(i) all transfers must be made on the express basis (spelling out the requirements of the MoU and EoL) that the UK monitoring team is to be given access to each transferee on a regular basis, with the opportunity for a private interview on each occasion; (ii) each transferee must in practice be visited and interviewed in private on a regular basis; and (iii) the UK must consider the immediate suspension of further transfers if full access is denied at any point without an obviously good reason (we have in mind circumstances such as a security alert) or if a transferee makes allegations of torture or serious mistreatment by NDS staff which cannot reasonably and rapidly be dismissed as unfounded" (para. 320).

The extent to which one concludes that UK forces in Afghanistan met their international legal obligations regarding the transfer of detainees will turn mainly on the degree to which one thinks transferees faced a risk of torture or serious mistreatment, and the evidence and threshold one believes was needed to establish this risk. It will also depend on whether one thinks the onus is on critics or the government to demonstrate or disprove this risk, and the efforts one thinks Britain needed to make to guard against it. One challenge to drawing such conclusions, critics usefully note, has been the absence of sufficient information on the conditions and treatment of detainees, and on the legal framework and actual practices of the NDS.[143]

Leaving these legal and factual issues aside, there is evidence that the UK employed safeguards regarding transferred detainees and changed its transfer practices in response to specific concerns. Further, as the discussion of the *Evans* case suggests, these safeguards and altered practices were shaped in part by a concern for Britain's perceived obligations under relevant basic principles of international human rights law.

For instance, the UK's approach to monitoring transferred detainees improved over time, with an "enhanced awareness" of the importance of being able to visit such individuals privately.[144] This awareness is suggested by the earlier observation that, when it was decided in 2007 that additional measures were necessary to ensure that persons transferred by British forces were being treated properly, the EoL signed in September that year advanced the UK's MoU with Afghanistan by expressly allowing transferred detainees to be interviewed in private.

In addition, Britain also responded to specific concerns by pressuring Afghan officials, investigating allegations of mistreatment, and stopping the transfer of individuals to some Afghan prisons. For example, in March 2007, the attorney general for England and Wales asked the head of the NDS about the state of an investigation into the disappearance of a detainee in Kandahar.[145] In September that year, a UK transferee at NDS Lashkar Gah alleged that he had been ill-treated while in detention there. The allegation was investigated by UK personnel and found to be unsubstantiated.[146] In December 2008, Britain imposed a moratorium on transfers to NDS Kabul, the facility which acts as the investigating branch of the NDS. This was a result of the NDS refusing access to that facility for purposes of visiting transferees.[147] When the NDS repeated its view in February 2009 that it had no direct obligation under the MoU, UK officials

---

143 *Evans* at para. 63.

144 *Evans* at para. 319.

145 *Evans* at para. 118. The attorney general also raised the issue of human rights, and the legal basis for NDS activity and detentions.

146 *Evans* at para. 30.

147 *Evans* at para. 32.

in Kabul advised challenging them at a senior level, and noted that the "NDS had to appreciate that UK cooperation with it was in danger, *because of legal pressures* in London" [emphasis added].[148]

In the spring of 2009, British personnel visited Pol-i-Charki prison, another facility in Kabul.[149] These visits were aimed at checking on UK transferees who had been transferred on by the NDS without prior notification to British officials.[150] A number of these transferees alleged that they had been ill-treated while in detention at NDS facilities in 2007–08. In response, Britain imposed an immediate moratorium on UK transfers to NDS Kandahar. (The moratorium on NDS Kabul was also still in place.) The moratorium on Kandahar was lifted in February 2010, but no further transfers were made in the following months.[151] The UK sought to establish a dedicated Detainee Oversight Team, which would be responsible for monitoring if transfers to NDS Kandahar resumed.[152] Between February and April 2010, the UK experienced substantial difficulties in gaining access to NDS Lashkar Gah in Helmand. Those difficulties were subsequently resolved, and transfers were resumed.[153]

In the summer of 2011, NATO ordered that detainee transfers to certain Afghan prisons be stopped due to fears that prisoners were at risk of systematic torture.[154] Following this order, however, UK defence officials said the warnings did not apply to Helmand province, where most UK troops were based.[155] I discuss NATO's orders in 2011 more in the next chapter, as they were relevant to Canada's detainee policy.

In November 2012, Defence Secretary Philip Hammond banned the transfer of detainees due to fears that they would be abused.[156] Following that decision, individuals captured by UK forces were reportedly held at a temporary facility at Camp Bastion, Britain's main base in Afghanistan.[157] This extended internment is noteworthy because it appears to challenge Britain's earlier position that UK forces were only authorized to detain people temporarily, and it resonates with the measures some critics suggest ISAF states had to take to protect detainees

---

148 *Evans* at para. 124.

149 In contrast to NDS Kabul, Pol-i-Charki reportedly comes under the authority of the Afghan Ministry of Justice.

150 *Evans* at para. 33.

151 *Evans* at para. 35.

152 *Evans* at para. 319.

153 *Evans* at para. 37.

154 Jeremy Kelly, "NATO Stops Sending Prisoners to Afghan Jails over Torture Fears," *The Guardian*, 6 Sept. 2011.

155 Ibid.

156 "Afghan detainees: UK to Restart Transfers This Month," BBC News website, 6 June 2013.

157 Hammond argued that releasing such individuals could endanger UK troops (ibid).

from torture.[158] In the winter of 2013, Britain then worked with Afghanistan to find a safe way to resume the transfer of detainees to the Afghan judicial system. The UK Ministry of Defence said in June that year that it was "satisfied it is safe" to restart the transfer of around 90 individuals.[159] These detainees were to be moved to the Afghan National Detention Facility in Parwan province, which, according to Hammond, had received "positive reports" from humanitarian organizations.[160]

In conclusion, it should be noted that, following the *Evans* case, there have been additional court challenges in Britain regarding the UK's policy and conduct with respect to Afghan detainees.[161] Moreover, a Detainee Inquiry was created by the Cameron government in 2010, although this initiative was never formally launched, and it was not meant to focus on Afghan detainees.[162] Some of the court challenges have involved the individuals who were held at Camp Bastion, and sought to have the lawfulness of their extended detainment assessed by British judges.[163] Interestingly, these habeus corpus proceedings suggest that international legal rules may sometimes conflict – i.e., anti-torture rules that may require ISAF states to detain individuals for extended periods can clash with due process rules that, among other things, generally require that alleged criminals cannot be held for extended periods without charge, access to counsel, and review by a judge. Reflecting an apparent awareness of this tension, UK forces gave some detainees telephone access to British lawyers.[164] Additional transfer bans were also ordered by the courts, and the Ministry of Defence sought to transfer detainees who consented to such movement. This ongoing dialogue between the government and the judiciary about prisoner transfer further suggests that, through both an internal concern among leaders and officials about Britain's international legal obligations, and an external review of government decisions by the courts,

---

158 See e.g. Byers 2007.

159 "Afghan detainees: UK to Restart Transfers This Month," BBC News website, 6 June 2013.

160 Ibid.

161 See e.g. *Serdar Mohammed v Ministry of Defence* and *Al Waheed v Ministry of Defence* [2017] UKSC 2.

162 The Inquiry was created in response to concerns over Britain's possible role in the transfer and mistreatment of detainees held by other countries post 9/11. It was criticized for being too narrow in its terms of reference. Nigel Sheinwald notes that the Inquiry was delayed because there were still pending police investigations into some of its cases. Most of these cases, he emphasizes, are not about what happened within Afghanistan involving UK forces, but residual issues associated with British citizens who were captured in 2001 and sent to Guantánamo Bay, as well as Libyan cases. Regarding the Guantánamo cases, all but one individual, a UK resident, have returned to Britain (interview, London, 8 July 2013).

163 "UK Forces Begin Transfer of Afghan Detainees," BBC News online, 28 June 2013.

164 Ibid.

international law can help regulate the political and military practice of a state when it uses force abroad.

3. International Law Helped Permit and Legitimate Britain's Conduct

Britain's military action in Afghanistan also illustrates how international law can permit and legitimate state behaviour that otherwise might not be allowed. In response to 9/11, the US and its allies, including the UK, attacked, invaded, and occupied a sovereign state – i.e., Afghanistan – that had not technically attacked them. This response was significantly broader than prior US reactions to earlier terrorist attacks, such as the missile strikes in Sudan and Afghanistan ordered by President Clinton after two American embassies were bombed in Africa in 1998.[165] The broad military response to 9/11 was also strategically different than the reaction some critics say the US and Britain should have focused on, such as addressing the threat posed by al-Qaeda through increased intelligence and law-enforcement activity, and political negotiations with the Taliban.[166] Tony Blair acknowledges the validity of such views in his memoirs, but still ultimately believes that a military response to 9/11 was appropriate.[167] As will be seen below, international legal considerations were relevant to justifying and explaining Britain's role in the extensive military reaction to 9/11 to the UK public and the international community.

For example, in response to legal concerns expressed in Parliament about Britain's anticipated military reaction to 9/11 and the US-led operation that was about to start in Afghanistan, Foreign Secretary Jack Straw stated on 4 October 2001:

> International law was mentioned by several Members who questioned … the Prime Minister. I cannot emphasise enough that the actions that the United States, we and other partners in the international coalition have in contemplation are entirely within the framework of international law. The founding text of the United

---

165 On 7 August 1998, US embassies in Kenya and Tanzania were bombed. Two hundred and twenty-four people were killed, and al-Qaeda terrorists were thought to be responsible. In response, the US launched missile strikes on Kabul, and a factory in Khartoum that was thought to be making nerve gas. It was later learned that the factory made pharmaceuticals, and the US was criticized for acting on questionable intelligence. See Kampfner 2004: 27–28.

166 See e.g. Ledwidge 2013, and UK General Nick Carter's comments in June 2013 that the West could have struck a deal with the Taliban after they were removed from power in November 2001 ("'We Should Have Talked to Taliban' Says Top British Officer in Afghanistan," *The Guardian* website, 28 June 2013).

167 Blair 2010: 349.

Nations, its charter, provides at [A]rticle 51 for the right of UN members to individual or collective self-defence when they come under armed attack.[168]

Continuing, Straw added:

The UN Security Council has passed two resolutions in the response to the crisis. The first, resolution 1368, states that those directly responsible for the attacks should be held to account, together with those who harbour them. The second, resolution 1373, focuses on two key areas: suppressing the financing of terrorists and denying them a safe haven from which to operate. That is the first time that a resolution has imposed an obligation on all states to respond to the global terrorist threat.[169]

Consistent with Straw's comments, Prime Minister Blair – who thought that shaping world opinion was critical following 9/11[170] – made the following statement outside 10 Downing Street on 7 October:

I also want to say very directly to the British people why this matters so much to Britain. First, let us not forget that the attacks of September 11 represented the worst terrorist outrage against British citizens in our history. The murder of British citizens, whether it happened overseas or not, is an attack upon Britain. But even if no British citizen had died, we would be right to act. This atrocity was an attack on us all, on people of all faiths and people of none. We know the al-Qaeda network threatens Europe, including Britain, and indeed any nation throughout the world that does not share their fanatical views. So we have a direct interest in *acting in our self-defence* to protect British lives [emphasis added].[171]

The next day in Parliament, Blair reaffirmed that "[w]e believe that such action [in Afghanistan] is entirely justified under [A]rticle 51 in self-defence … the UN Security Council has agreed that it is right that action should be taken, and Britain, the United States of America and the other allies are acting in accordance with the UN resolution and international law."[172]

In the above statements, note that Straw and Blair focused on the doctrine of self-defence. Although they also cited the two Security Council resolutions that immediately followed 9/11 – which are described below – I will suggest in the next section that this reference was employed more as evidence of the broad support for the US-led action in Afghanistan and less as the international legal basis

---

168 HC Debs., 4 Oct. 2001, vol. 372, col. 690.
169 HC Debs., 4 Oct. 2001, vol. 372, col. 690.
170 Kampfner 2004: 118; Meyer 2005: 191; and Campbell 2008: 574.
171 Cited in Marston 2001: 682 (text provided by the PMO).
172 HC Debs., 8 Oct. 2001, vol. 372, col. 821.

on which Britain claimed to be contributing to this action. Indeed, in a formal update to the Security Council on 7 October, UK diplomat Stewart Eldon stated:

> In accordance with Article 51 of the Charter of the United Nations, I wish on behalf of my Government to report that the United Kingdom of Great Britain and Northern Ireland has military assets engaged in operations against targets that we know to be involved in the operation of terror against the United States of America, the United Kingdom and other countries around the world, as part of a wider international effort. These forces have now been employed in exercise of the inherent right of individual and collective self-defence, recognized in Article 51, following the terrorist outrage of 11 September, to avert the continuing threat of attacks from the same source.[173]

Consistent with this formal update, Defence Secretary Geoff Hoon told Parliament the next day: "Under [A]rticle 51, any state is entitled to act in self-defence to protect its citizens and entitled to use proportionate force to achieve that. That is precisely the basis on which I have cited [A]rticle 51, and precisely the basis on which the [US] and the [UK] have acted."[174]

Again, in the above statements, note that UK leaders and officials focused on the doctrine of self-defence and did not formally claim that Britain was using force in Afghanistan under the authority of the Security Council. Advancing the latter position would arguably have been possible considering that, as noted in part by Straw and Blair earlier above, following 9/11 the Council passed two resolutions which condemned the terrorist attacks and regarded them as a threat to international peace and security; recognized the inherent right of individual or collective self-defence in accordance with the Charter; and reaffirmed the need to combat by all means, in accordance with the Charter, threats to international peace and security caused by terrorist acts.[175] Significantly, however, after 9/11, the US did not focus on these resolutions or seek explicit authorization from the Security Council, and instead justified its military actions in Afghanistan as self-defence against a terrorist attack.[176]

---

173 Letter from the Charge d'affaires a.i. of the Permanent Mission of the United Kingdom of Great Britain and Northern Ireland to the United Nations Addressed to the President of the Security Council (7 Oct. 2001), UN Doc. S/2001/947 (2001).

174 HC Debs., 8 Oct. 2001, vol. 372, col. 834–835.

175 See UNSC Resolution 1368 (12 Sept. 2001), [UN Doc. S/RES/1368], *Threats to International Peace and Security Caused by Terrorist Acts*; and UNSC Resolution 1373 (28 Sept. 2001), [UN Doc. S/RES/1373], *ibid.*

176 Letter Dated 7 Oct. 2001 from the Permanent Representative of the United States of America to the United Nations Addressed to the President of the Security Council, UN Doc. S/2001/946 (2001). For an analysis of the US legal justification for the initial military actions in Afghanistan, see Byers 2002: 401–409.

The extent to which this US position impacted Britain's justification is unknown. While one might reasonably assume American influence in this regard, there is limited available evidence that UK leaders and their advisers were aware of the US position and its implications for Britain's stance. For example, when asked about this issue, Peter Ricketts emphasized the legal importance of the UN Security Council's resolutions regarding ISAF, and downplayed the significance of Britain's initial self-defence justification.[177] We will see similar findings in the next chapter regarding the awareness of Canadian leaders about this issue. On the other hand, Nigel Sheinwald thinks Britain's initial justification makes sense because self-defence "was ultimately [the basis] all the way through ... the rationale was to prevent Afghanistan from once again being a base for international terrorism for which the UK and US would have been the target."[178]

In sum, the foregoing review suggests that international legal considerations were relevant to justifying and explaining the UK's role in the extensive military response to 9/11 to the UK public and the international community. And this, in turn, supports the observation that when states use force, international law helps permit and legitimate certain conduct that otherwise might not be permitted.

4. International Law Helped Structure the Development of New Rules and Legitimate Practice

Finally, Britain's involvement in the Afghan Conflict suggests that international law can help structure the process by which agents seek to develop and promote new legal rules and legitimate practice for states and other international actors. Two examples highlight this phenomenon. The first is Britain's argument that it was using force in Afghanistan under the doctrine of self-defence, and the related perceived change in the customary international law on this issue. The second example is the passing of Security Council Resolution 1373 in September 2001, which required states to adopt new domestic measures to address international terrorism.

We saw above that, following 9/11, UK leaders and diplomats stated that British forces had been deployed to Afghanistan in exercise of the inherent right of self-defence recognized in Article 51 of the UN Charter. Repeating this view, Foreign Secretary Jack Straw told Parliament on 4 October 2001 that the US-led action would be "entirely within the framework of international law." While this public statement may have been aimed at permitting

---

177 Phone interview with Sir Peter Ricketts, 26 June 2013.
178 Interview with Sir Nigel Sheinwald, London, 8 July 2013.

and legitimating Britain's use of force in Afghanistan, it skirted a more complex legal reality, which I describe below. The extent to which this complexity was addressed by Britain's Legal Advisers and conveyed privately to political leaders at the time is difficult to assess with the evidence that is currently available.[179] However, the public record does suggest that, during Britain's initial participation in the Afghan Conflict, UK officials and leaders were concerned about the existing views of states on the use of force in self-defence, and actively sought to ensure that these views recognized the international threat posed by non-state actors such as al-Qaeda, and state actors such as the Taliban who aid or harbour them.

The argument that British forces had been deployed to Afghanistan in exercise of the right to self-defence recognized in Article 51 of the Charter is noteworthy from an international legal perspective for the following reasons. First, Article 51 states that nothing in the Charter shall impair the inherent right of individual or collective self-defence if an armed attack occurs against a UN member, until the Security Council has taken measures necessary to maintain international peace and security.[180] Importantly, the concept of "armed attack" is not defined in Article 51, and the provision does not explicitly say whether the right of self-defence applies only to an armed attack by a state, or to armed attacks by states *and* non-state actors.

Following 9/11, the US legal argument essentially suggested that if a sufficient nexus exists between a non-state terrorist group and State A, an attack by the terrorist group on State B could constitute an armed attack for purposes of Article 51 of the Charter and/or the customary international law on self-defence, and State B could respond under that law.[181] Further, while variations of this position had been advanced in the past, for instance by Israel and the US, they had not been accepted by the majority of states. Following 9/11, however, most states appear to have accepted – or at least not publicly criticized – the US argument.[182]

---

179 Michael Wood, the Legal Adviser at the Foreign and Commonwealth Office in 2001, and Elizabeth Wilmshurst, a Deputy Legal Adviser there at the time, declined to be interviewed for this study. Moreover, legal advice provided to government is not normally made public.

180 Article 51, UN Charter.

181 Technically, prior to 9/11, the use of force in self-defence by State B in this scenario was not prohibited by international law provided that, in addition to adhering to the principles of necessity and proportionality, the traditional criteria associated with such situations were met – i.e., (1) the terrorist attack was sufficiently serious and thus beyond a *de minimus* threshold, (2) the attack was attributable to the terrorists at issue, and (3) there was substantial involvement from State A in this regard. The key unsettled issue, however, was how *much* involvement from State A was required.

182 By contrast, following NATO's military actions in Kosovo in 1999, a large number of states publicly criticized what they believed to be an illegal use of military force. See Richmond 2016b. For an analysis of the legal significance of the absence of such clear criticism to the US justification for its initial military response to 9/11, see White 2009: 192–194.

Consequently, Western legal scholars generally believe that customary law changed accordingly.[183]

Consistent with the above observations, Britain considered the events of 9/11 to constitute an armed attack. For instance, when discussing the upcoming US-led military action in Afghanistan, Foreign Secretary Straw stated in Parliament on 4 October 2001 that Article 51 of the UN Charter provides "for the right of UN members to ... self-defence when they come under *armed attack*" [emphasis added]. Following 9/11, Straw, Prime Minister Blair, and Defence Secretary Hoon all emphasized that NATO had invoked Article 5 of its treaty, which – as Straw paraphrased – provides that an "*armed attack* against one or more of the allies in Europe or North America shall be considered an attack against them all." Britain, like other NATO members, voted in favour of this invocation following 9/11.[184] And the UK's representative at NATO "was very closely involved" in Article 5 being declared.[185] Reflecting the above comments and actions, recall that in his statement outside 10 Downing Street on 7 October, Blair said: "The murder of British citizens, whether it happened overseas or not, is an *attack* upon Britain" [emphasis added].

Having claimed that 9/11 constituted an armed attack, Britain also saw a need to demonstrate that this attack was attributable to al-Qaeda. In the UK's formal update to the Security Council on 7 October, mentioned earlier, Stewart Eldon reported the following:

> My Government presented information to the United Kingdom Parliament on 4 October which showed that Usama Bin Laden and his al-Qaeda terrorist organization have the capability to execute major terrorist attacks, claimed credit for past attacks on United States targets, and have been engaged in a concerted campaign against the United States and its allies. One of their stated aims is the murder of United States citizens and attacks on the allies of the United States.[186]

Further resonating with the legal observations described earlier above, UK leaders and officials also felt a need to show that a sufficient nexus existed between the al-Qaeda terrorists thought to be responsible for 9/11, on the one hand, and the Taliban regime of Afghanistan on the other. A week after 9/11, Blair and two of his advisers, Foreign Policy Adviser David Manning and Chief of Staff

---

183 For scholars whose positions are generally consistent with this view, see: Byers 2002; Falk 2002; Dinstein 2005; Currie 2008; and Murphy 2009. For an argument that the use of force in Afghanistan in 2001 was lawful, but custom did not change, see Moir 2010. For critical perspectives on this use of force, see Boyle 2004 and Williamson 2009.

184 Interview with Sir Nigel Sheinwald, London, 8 July 2013.

185 Ibid.

186 Letter from the UK Charge d'affaires to the Security Council, 7 Oct. 2001.

Jonathan Powell, were privately concerned about whether the Taliban could be held responsible for al-Qaeda's actions.[187] Apparently anticipating this concern, Jeremy Greenstock, Britain's UN representative, helped draft Security Council Resolution 1368 of 12 September 2001.[188] In addition to the other key provisions described earlier, the instrument called "on all States to work together urgently to bring to justice the perpetrators, organizers and sponsors of these terrorist attacks and stresses that those responsible for aiding, supporting or harbouring the perpetrators, organizers and sponsors of these acts will be held accountable."[189]

Consistent with this wording, Tony Blair told a Labour Party conference a few weeks later that the Taliban "aid and abet" Bin Laden.[190] And, in Britain's update to the Security Council on 7 October, it was noted that the UK's contribution to the military action in Afghanistan "is directed against Usama Bin Laden's al-Qaeda terrorist organization *and the Taliban regime that is supporting it*" [emphasis added].[191]

Finally, British leaders and diplomats sought to emphasize that the majority of states supported the US-led action in Afghanistan following 9/11 and, by implication, the legal argument that justified this action. Further, apparently concerned that many states had often reacted negatively to prior US military actions, leaders such as Foreign Secretary Jack Straw stressed the legitimacy of the historically unprecedented response to 9/11. For instance, speaking in Brussels on 21 September 2001 at the end of an Extraordinary Meeting of the European Council, Straw stated in part:

> The meeting this evening of European Heads of Government and Foreign Ministers, and the conclusions which have been reached, are a further indication of the widening and deepening of the international coalition in support of the United States, and against the terrorism which we saw on 11 September. The conclusions make clear that not only are the European Union and Member States expressing their solidarity with the United States at its time of need, but there is *a clear recognition* in the conclusions about the *legitimacy* of any action – the word used is riposte – any military action which the United States takes in respect of the matters on 11 September and the action is needed to ensure that such threats do not take place again [emphasis added].[192]

Further stressing the support of the international community, we saw earlier that Straw reminded Parliament on 4 October 2001 that the Security Council

---

187 Kampfner 2004: 118–119.

188 Ibid: 115. Greenstock worked on the resolution with his French counterpart. He declined to be interviewed for this study.

189 See para. 3 of Resolution 1368.

190 Kampfner 2004: 122.

191 Letter from the UK Charge d'affaires to the Security Council, 7 Oct. 2001.

192 Cited in Marston 2001: 680–681 (text provided by the FCO).

had passed two resolutions in response to 9/11. Elaborating on this international support eight years later, Jeremy Greenstock told the Chilcot Inquiry in 2009:

> It was extraordinary to me, given the divisions in the United Nations at the beginning of September 2001 and given the … geopolitically natural resistance to the United States as the single superpower in some other parts of the world, given the United States's normally selective approach to the use of the United Nations for its own interests or for collective interests, that, once 9/11 had happened, there was virtually universal sympathy for the United States in the United Nations.[193]

The symbols of that sympathy, Greenstock says, were the initial Security Council resolutions adopted in response to 9/11 – i.e., Resolutions 1368 and 1373. The former instrument, recall, was drafted and passed in part as a result of Greenstock's efforts. It, Greenstock notes, gave

> express cover for the US to use military force in Afghanistan [while Resolution] 1373 set up a programme for all member states to take further measures to counter terrorism in their jurisdictions, with a sense of *creating international law* through a mandatory Security Council Resolution which was regarded by many UN member states as unprecedented up to that point. And yet not a single member of the Security Council argued about 1373 in any detail [emphasis added].[194]

In sum, Greenstock's comments and actions – along with those of Straw, Hoon, and Blair noted earlier – indicate that, during Britain's initial participation in the Afghan war, officials and leaders were concerned about the existing views of states on the use of force in self-defence, and actively sought to ensure that these views recognized the international threat posed by non-state actors such as al-Qaeda, and state actors such as the Taliban who aid or harbour them. Importantly, the above comments and actions resonate with the expanded conception of self-defence outlined in Britain's security policy following 9/11. The 2002 addendum to the Strategic Defence Review of 1998, for instance, "made clear that, in the British view, terrorism at home had to be addressed by forward defence in Central Asia or wherever the contingent threat emanated from."[195]

In hindsight, it may seem that the nature, scale, and target of the 9/11 attacks made the applicability of the right to individual and collective self-defence

---

193 Greenstock, Chilcot testimony, 27 Nov. 2009, transcript at 14–15.
194 Ibid.
195 Fry and Bowen 2011: 68.

recognized in Article 51 of the UN Charter logical and inevitable. However, it is important to remember that this provision was originally included in the Charter with the primary aim of addressing conventional attacks by a state against another state, and not a terrorist action by a non-state actor against the world's only superpower.[196] The fact that the right to self-defence recognized in Article 51 could be interpreted and applied to respond to the latter situation, and that most states appear to have accepted that the customary law on self-defence changed more generally, supports the idea that international law helps structure the process by which agents seek to develop and promote new legal rules and legitimate practice.

The Understanding of International Law in Britain's Use of Force in Afghanistan

While the above analysis suggests that international law helped influence Britain's involvement in the Afghanistan Conflict, it is less clear the extent to which UK leaders understood this law as a distinct and binding set of legal rules, and whether the legal status of these rules impacted their decision-making. As we will see, leaders and advisers tended to view Britain's obligations and rights under the UN Charter in legal terms, and the country's commitments under the NATO treaty more in political terms. Further, while the legal status of the UK's obligations and rights under the Charter appear to have impacted the thinking and decisions of policymakers regarding Afghanistan, the same cannot be said of Britain's commitments under the NATO treaty.

Finally, some leaders and advisers have understood Britain's international human rights obligations in binding terms. However, the country's criticized approach to Afghan detainees indicates that the legal status of these obligations has perhaps had an uneven impact on the thinking and decisions of some policymakers. It also suggests that state and non-state views of what the prohibition on transferring to possible torture requires in practice are less settled than related shared understandings of other fundamental prisoner protections in international law and armed conflict.

1. Britain's Understanding of the UN Charter and NATO Treaty

In response to concerns about Britain's expected reaction to 9/11 and the US-led operation that was about to start in Afghanistan, recall that Foreign Secretary Jack Straw told Parliament on 4 October 2001 that UN Security Council Resolution 1373 was "the first time that a resolution has *imposed an obligation*

---

196 See the commentary on Article 51 in Simma 2012.

on all states to respond to the global terrorist threat" [emphasis added]. "For the first time in the history of the United Nations," Straw continued, this resolution "*mandates* member states – *they are not given an option* – to take a variety of actions to fight terrorism of all kinds" [emphasis added].[197] This binding view of Resolution 1373 likely stemmed from the fact that its operative paragraphs stated that the Security Council, acting under Chapter VII of the Charter, "*[d]ecides* that all States shall" take the variety of actions noted by Straw above [emphasis in original].[198] In addition to the word "shall," the word "decides" in the resolution is relevant because Article 25 of the Charter provides that UN member "agree to accept and carry out the decisions of the Security Council in accordance with the ... Charter."[199]

If the binding view of Resolution 1373 stemmed from the inclusion of the term "decides," this would be consistent with the way UK leaders understood the main Security Council resolution on the Korean War fifty years earlier. This instrument, recall, had "recommended" but not "decided" that states assist South Korea to repel North Korea's attack. Consequently, leaders tended to see this as a non-binding request that UN member states were technically free to ignore. By contrast, Resolution 1373 employed the term "decides" and, again, this likely contributed to it being seen as binding. In response to this perceived obligation, Britain initiated a number of changes to its domestic anti-terrorism laws.[200] It also, as I suggested earlier, cited Resolution 1373 as evidence of the international community's support for the initial US-led military actions in Afghanistan and, by implication, the self-defence justification advanced for these actions.

In addition to Britain's obligations under the UN Charter, the country's rights under that treaty have also been interpreted in legal terms. We saw that in the fall of 2001, a number of UK leaders explained Britain's initial use of force in Afghanistan to the British public and the international community by referencing the right to self-defence recognized in Article 51 of the UN Charter. Consistent with the legal complexities associated with this position, leaders appear to have considered the events of 9/11 to constitute an armed attack for purposes of Article 51, and sought to demonstrate that this attack was attributable to al-Qaeda. Finally, leaders saw a need to show that a sufficient nexus existed between al-Qaeda and the Taliban, and they emphasized that most states supported the US-led military response to 9/11.

In contrast to the above interpretation of Britain's obligations and rights under the UN Charter, leaders and advisers may have understood the country's

---

197 HC Debs., 4 Oct. 2001, vol. 372, col. 692.
198 Security Council Resolution 1373.
199 Article 25, UN Charter.
200 See e.g. the *Anti-terrorism, Crime and Security Bill* introduced in Parliament on 12 Nov. 2001.

commitments under the NATO treaty more in political terms. On the one hand, John Kampfner reports that during a key phone conversation between Tony Blair and George W. Bush in the initial days following 9/11, the view was expressed that "[s]upport from NATO and the UN would provide *legal* and political weight for a military response" [emphasis added].[201] Similarly, Chris Meyer, Britain's former ambassador to the US, recalls that "Blair and Bush were agreed on the importance of rapidly getting the UN and NATO four-square behind the United States in condemnation of the attacks: this would provide a *legal* and political framework for military action" [emphasis added].[202]

On the other hand, when asked whether Britain's obligations under Article 5 of the NATO treaty mattered to the UK's participation in the Afghanistan Conflict, Peter Ricketts indicated that these were not legal duties in the formal sense but alliance commitments.[203] Stressing the legal relevance of the UN Security Council resolutions pertaining to ISAF, Ricketts explained:

The invocation of Article 5, requested by the Americans, hasn't ever been part of our legal basis for our actions [in Afghanistan] ... Article 5 doesn't in itself create a legal basis, it's an obligation to come to collective aid. And in fact the Americans never asked for any particular NATO assistance under Article 5, as far as I recall. So it has remained dormant ... If they had, we would have looked at what they asked [for], and tried to respond positively. But it's not part of our legal basis for being there. It is a reminder we have obligations in NATO, and one day they might be called on ... So [the invocation of Article 5] had a political value, but it didn't have a legal value, and it didn't actually affect the conduct of the operation.[204]

Similarly, Nigel Sheinwald observed:

It's not that we were negative about the Article 5 declaration; we very much supported it ... Our Ambassador [to NATO] was very closely involved in it [being invoked]. But it wasn't going to be critical for us because I think the feeling in the UK was we were going to be politically supportive, going to be helping, more or less whatever happened ... The Article 5 [invocation] was helpful in drawing *political* attention to the issue, in showing a high degree of NATO unity and determination [emphasis added]. But it wasn't critical in getting the UK "into the line." We were there anyway.[205]

---

201 Kampfner 2004: 116.
202 Meyer 2005: 191.
203 Phone interview with Sir Peter Ricketts, 26 June 2013.
204 Ibid.
205 Interview with Sir Nigel Sheinwald, London, 8 July 2013.

"Of course," Sheinwald added, Afghanistan "then *became* a NATO operation ... and the reason NATO could get involved was because there was a solid legal basis, and a solid political basis, for what we were doing [emphasis in original]. Which was not the case with Iraq."[206]

2. Britain's Interpretation of International Human Rights Law

Some of the key legal provisions described above can be seen as part of the *jus ad bellum*, the body of international law that governs when states can use force, while the *jus in bello* – the international law of armed conflict – governs their conduct in war. The relationship between *jus in bello* rules, which apply in armed conflict, and international human rights law, which has traditionally applied in times of peace, is legally complex.[207] It suffices to recall that during Britain's military presence in Afghanistan, officials thought that, in addition to relevant *jus in bello* rules that likely apply, Britain's commitments under the European Convention on Human Rights (ECHR) were potentially engaged by the country's policy and actions regarding Afghan detainees.

Importantly, these ECHR rules have been seen in binding terms. For instance, recall that UK officials involved in negotiating the 2006 Memorandum of Understanding with Afghanistan on detainees remarked "that it was structured to avoid the risk of a *breach* of the UK's Convention *obligations* which might be applicable: key points were to prohibit the death penalty, to prevent the transfer of detainees to a third party, and to enable UK access to detainees transferred to the Afghan authorities" [emphasis added].[208] Consistent with these remarks, we saw that one of the explicit aims of the MoU is to "ensure that Participants will observe the basic principles of international human rights law such as the right to life and the prohibition on torture and cruel, inhumane and degrading treatment pertaining to the treatment and transfer of persons by the UK [armed forces] to Afghan authorities." Accordingly, the MoU goes on to provide that individuals arrested and detained by UK forces "are to be treated in accordance with *applicable* provisions of *international human rights law*" [emphasis added].[209]

Despite the above, we also saw that critics have argued that individuals transferred into Afghan custody were at real risk of torture or serious mistreatment and, therefore, that the practice of transfer was in breach of Britain's policy and

---

206 Ibid. Another reason NATO could get involved in Afghanistan, Sheinwald says, is because Russia did not fundamentally oppose such involvement.

207 For further analysis of the issue, see e.g. Droege 2007; and *Legal Consequences of the Construction of a Wall in the Occupied Palestinian Territory, Advisory Opinion*, I.C.J., 9 July 2004.

208 *Evans* at para. 94.

209 *Evans* at para. 96.

unlawful. UK transferees and relevant reports, recall, have documented numerous cases of torture and mistreatment of Afghan prisoners, and alleged that the NDS has a particularly poor record in this regard. The British government, we saw, was aware of these allegations, and UK officials themselves were concerned by the NDS claim that the agency had no direct obligation under the MoU.

Depending on the efforts one thinks Britain had to take to protect against the risk that transferees may be tortured, these details leave open the possibility that the legal status of the ECHR rules prohibiting torture have had an uneven impact on the thinking and decisions of some policymakers. These details also suggest that state and non-state views of what the prohibition on transferring to possible torture requires in practice are less settled than related shared understandings of other fundamental prisoner protections in international law and armed conflict. Assessing these hypotheses will likely have to wait until more evidence becomes available.

For now, what is clear is that the UK improved its safeguards regarding transferred detainees over time, and responded to specific concerns by pressuring Afghan officials, investigating allegations of abuse, stopping transfers to some prisons, and detaining some individuals for an extended period at Camp Bastion. These altered practices have been shaped in part by a concern for Britain's perceived obligations under the ECHR, and it is equally possible that the legal status of these obligations has influenced the thinking and decisions of certain policymakers. As Nigel Sheinwald recalls, the issue of Afghan detainees was "exhaustively" reviewed "by our defence department and intelligence agencies. A huge amount of attention has been given to it. Whether the policy [we adopted] was right or wrong, it wasn't without [extensive] debate, care and involvement of our legal experts. The attorney general was personally involved in all of those decisions."[210]

Key Findings

The aspects of Britain's military involvement in Afghanistan assessed above support the argument that, when states use force, international law helps define and shape their possible course of action, and the justifications that can be advanced for their conduct. More specifically, these aspects help illustrate the four roles that I posit international law can play in such situations.

First, like Clement Attlee during the Korean War, Prime Minister Tony Blair felt a sense of obligation towards the conflict in Afghanistan that followed the events of 9/11. Unlike with Attlee, however, this perception of obligation appears to have been shaped less by Britain's formal membership in the UN and

---

210 Interview with Sir Nigel Sheinwald, London, 8 July 2013.

a belief in the international rule of law, and more by Blair's ethical views that mass terrorism must be addressed and that foreign intervention in Afghanistan was needed to do so. More generally, though, during the three phases of Britain's military participation in the Afghan Conflict, we saw that the UK's perceived commitments to the UN and NATO helped constitute the identities of some leaders and officials, and helped shape the way in which Britain's interests were interpreted and pursued. Further, as the war became more challenging and US military policy in the region became more controversial, these perceived commitments acted as a site for a "communicative" struggle over Britain's legitimate identity and rightful behaviour with respect to these developments.

In addition, international law also had a regulative influence on Britain's involvement in the Afghan Conflict. A key example of this is Britain's approach to individuals captured in Afghanistan by UK forces and transferred to local authorities. As we saw, Britain's policy and conduct regarding Afghan detainees were governed and controlled in part by its interpretation of Security Council Resolution 1386, which created ISAF, and relevant basic principles of international human rights law, including the right to life and the ban on torture. This interpretation, further, had a significant effect even though other material factors – such as the UK's interest in gathering intelligence, preventing attacks, and cooperating with Afghan security and intelligence agencies – arguably conflicted with some of its perceived requirements.

Third, Britain's military action in Afghanistan also indicates that international law helps permit and legitimate certain conduct that otherwise might not be permitted. In response to the terrorist events of 9/11, the US and its allies, including the UK, attacked, invaded and occupied Afghanistan, a sovereign state that had not technically attacked them. This response was significantly broader than prior US reactions to earlier terrorist attacks, and strategically different than the reaction some critics say the US and Britain should have employed. As we saw, international legal considerations were relevant to justifying and explaining Britain's role in this extensive military reaction to 9/11 to the UK public and the international community.

Finally, Britain's involvement in the Afghan Conflict suggests that international law helps structure the process by which agents seek to develop and promote new legal rules and legitimate practice for states and other international actors. Two examples, we saw, highlight this phenomenon. The first is Britain's argument that it was using force in Afghanistan under the doctrine of self-defence, and the related perceived change in the customary international law on this issue. The second example is the passing of Security Council Resolution 1373 in September 2001, which required states to adopt new domestic measures to address international terrorism.

Although the above suggests that international law helped influence Britain's involvement in the Afghan war, it is less clear the extent to which UK leaders understood this law as a distinct and binding set of legal rules, and whether the legal status of these rules impacted their decision-making. On the one hand, we saw that key leaders and advisers viewed Britain's obligations and rights under the UN Charter in distinctly legal terms. Moreover, they also recognized that the use of military force in Afghanistan and the treatment of captured enemy individuals were in part legal issues, in that they were governed by pre-existing rules in the UN Charter, NATO treaty, and the European Convention on Human Rights. It also appears that leaders and advisers discussed the extent to which Britain was legally obligated to consider these rules when deciding whether and how to use force in Afghanistan, and what policy and practices to adopt regarding Afghan detainees. Finally, Prime Minister Tony Blair, Foreign Secretary Jack Straw, Defence Minister Geoff Hoon, and Defence Minister Philip Hammond saw that Britain's actions in Afghanistan would require legal justification at the domestic and international level. The foregoing details resonate with many of the relevant observable implications posited in chapter two, and suggest that a number of important UK leaders and officials felt bound in part by international law.

On the other hand, we also saw that key leaders and advisers saw the country's commitments under the NATO treaty more in political terms. And, although the legal status of the UK's obligations and rights under the UN Charter appears to have impacted the thinking and decisions of policymakers regarding Afghanistan, the same cannot be said of Britain's commitments under the NATO treaty. Finally, while leaders and advisers understood Britain's international human rights obligations in binding terms, the country's criticized approach to Afghan detainees suggests that the legal status of these obligations may have had an uneven impact on the thinking and decisions of some policymakers.

7 Canada and the Afghanistan Conflict

The Afghanistan Conflict is the most significant war that Canada has fought since its effort in Korea. As with Britain, it is the longest foreign conflict in which Canada has ever participated, and it has involved the most difficult fighting its ground forces have faced since 1953. In essence, the decisions behind the Afghan Conflict revealed two very different visions of Canada's international identity in the post 9/11 world: one as peacekeeper and supporter of multilateralism, and another as warrior and steadfast ally of the United States. Navigating these two identities by becoming extensively involved in a costly and challenging nation-building and counterinsurgency effort in faraway central Asia, I will suggest, is not immediately easy to explain. And throughout the Afghan Conflict, we will see, international law helped define and shape Canada's possible course of action, and the justifications that could be made for its conduct.

The Three Phases of Canada's Military Participation in the Afghanistan Conflict

As with Britain, Canada's military participation in the Afghanistan Conflict can be divided into three main phases. The initial phase, which occurred under the US-led Operation Enduring Freedom (OEF), took place between September 2001 and the summer of 2002. It involved an incremental buildup of forces. First, on 28 September 2001, more than 100 members of Canada's military serving on exchange programs with the US and other allies were authorized to participate in any operations conducted by their host units in response to al-Qaeda's attacks on 9/11.[1] Next, on 8 October, Canada announced

---

1 This authorization was made by Defence Minister Art Eggleton. See "Speaking Notes" for Press conference, Ottawa, 8 Oct. 2001.

it would deploy six naval ships[2] and six planes[3] to the region. It also said that special forces would be sent to contribute to the overall effort.[4] Finally, in early 2002, Canada decided to contribute around 800 regular ground troops to Kandahar, a volatile province in the south of Afghanistan, to serve with the US military.[5] This deployment was Canada's first combat mission since the Korean War. The soldiers arrived in theatre on 22 February 2002, and stayed for six months.[6]

Canada's second phase of military action in Afghanistan occurred between August 2003 and December 2005, and involved Canada sending around 2,000 soldiers to Kabul and taking command of the International Security Assistance Force (ISAF) there in February 2004.[7] As part of the decisions behind this phase, it was agreed that Canada would lead ISAF for one year, and that in order to find a replacement for Canada afterwards, Defence Minister John McCallum would lobby for NATO to take over the mission. As will be discussed below, the dominant existing view is that the Cabinet of Liberal Prime Minister Jean Chrétien decided in favour of the ISAF operation mainly because it allowed Canada to support the US in its "War on Terror" without having to support its controversial war in Iraq.[8] However, this book challenges that view and suggests instead that Chrétien, McCallum, and Foreign Minister Bill Graham were motivated more by a belief that the UN-authorized ISAF mission was legitimate and more consistent with Canada's national identity as a peacekeeper, and that the integrity of NATO was at stake.

The third phase of Canada's military participation took place from February 2006 to July 2011, and involved a significant number of Canadian forces being redeployed to Kandahar through a series of authorizations and extensions.[9] This phase began when, in May 2005, Liberal Prime Minister Paul Martin and his Cabinet approved a five-point plan proposed by then Chief of the Defence

---

2 Ibid, and Stein and Lang 2007: 10–11.

3 Three Hercules, one Airbus, and two Aurora maritime patrol aircraft were deployed to conduct surveillance and airlift support in the region. See "Speaking Notes," footnote above.

4 These special forces, known as Joint Task Force 2 (JTF2), had been requested. While Eggleton did not say so at the time, about forty commandos were deployed to southern Afghanistan in December 2001. They helped US and British forces in the initial ground war against Taliban and al-Qaeda forces. See Daniel Leblanc, "Elite JTF2 Goes into Kandahar War Zone," *The Globe and Mail*, 20 Dec. 2001, at p. A1.

5 Stein and Lang 2007: 18, and Granatstein 2011: 420. Transport planes were also sent to support the soldiers.

6 For descriptions of this deployment from the perspective of a military historian, see Granatstein 2011: 420–421.

7 Stein and Lang 2007: 73. For a description of this second phase, see Granatstein 2011: 422–425.

8 Variations of this view are articulated by Stein and Lang 2007: 71–73; Nossal 2010: 123; Granatstein 2011: 422; and Hillier 2009: 263.

9 For a description of this third phase, see Granatstein 2011: 430–441.

Staff (CDS), Rick Hillier.[10] Among other things, this plan involved the deployment for one year, beginning in February 2006, of about 1,000 ground troops to conduct stabilization and combat operations in the province.[11] In May 2006, at the request of newly elected Conservative Prime Minister Stephen Harper, Parliament voted to extend Canada's combat mission in Kandahar by another two years, until 2009. Following an independent review of the issue in 2008,[12] Parliament then extended the mission again until 2011.[13] In the summer of that year, Canada ended its combat operation in Kandahar, and began a new non-combat role in Kabul. This involvement focused on development, diplomacy, humanitarian assistance, and the training of local police and security forces. It ended in 2014.

In total, around 40,000 Canadians served in Afghanistan (13,000 more than served in or contributed to the Korean War). The conflict cost Canada an estimated $18 billion, around 2,000 personnel were wounded, and 165 soldiers and civilians were killed.[14] Like Britain, Canada's involvement resulted in the most difficult fighting its forces had seen since Korea. During some of the most violent periods of the war, for example, Canada suffered more casualties as a proportion of total force size than the US or any other NATO country. Further, Canada's extensive participation in Afghanistan also resulted in opportunity costs, in that the country's strategic ability to contribute to other military or peacekeeping initiatives was seriously constrained.[15]

---

10 Hillier did not respond to an interview request for this study.

11 For the other elements of the plan, see Stein and Lang 2007: 182–184.

12 The review, entitled the *Independent Panel on Canada's Future Role in Afghanistan*, was released in January 2008.

13 Parliament voted in February 2008. See Government of Canada, "History of Canada's Engagement in Afghanistan 2001–2012."

14 About 6,700 of the people who served receive federal support for post-traumatic stress disorder. Dozens have died from suicide. Canada's involvement in Afghanistan also, as Bill Graham notes, entailed reconstruction and development spending of more than $2 billion that peaked at more than $200 million a year in the years 2009–11 – by far our largest contribution to any single country in our history (Graham 2015: 50). See also: "Over 2,000 Canadians Were Wounded in Afghan Mission: Report," *National Post*, 1 Feb. 2012; "In the Line of Duty: Canada's Casualties," CBC News website, 31 Oct. 2011; Canadian Centre for Policy Alternatives, "Canada's Fallen: Understanding Canadian Military Deaths in Afghanistan" (Ottawa, Sept. 2006); Government of Canada, "Cost of the Afghanistan Mission: 2001–2011"; "Afghan Mission Could Cost up to $18.1 Billion," CBC News, 9 Oct. 2008; "Moment in Time – March 12, 2014: Canadian Mission in Afghanistan Ends," *The Globe and Mail*, 12 March 2021; and "War in Afghanistan," *The Canadian Encyclopaedia*, edited 8 June 2017, at: www.thecanadianencyclopedia.ca

15 McDonough 2008: 649.

Why Canada Participated in the Afghanistan Conflict

Like Canada's participation in the Korean War, the country's significant and costly involvement in the Afghan Conflict is also not immediately easy to explain in strict national interest terms, narrowly conceived.[16] The two factors that one might presume to be most relevant – Canada's alliance with the US and its security concern regarding al-Qaeda – may help explain why Canada initially used force in Afghanistan. But it is less clear why the Canadian military remained in the country for so long, and why Canada agreed to contribute to the difficult nation-building and counterinsurgency efforts there.[17]

Reflecting this empirical puzzle, scholarly opinion on why Canada fought in Afghanistan is divided and evolving.[18] This is likely because the war is relatively recent and, in some ways, still ongoing. Differing views on the topic also reflect the fact that both Liberal and Conservative governments decided to use force in the conflict, and the justifications for these decisions changed over time.[19] In a leading account on the subject, Janice Gross Stein and Eugene Lang argue that the main reason Canada took military action in Afghanistan was to show support for the United States in its "War on Terror," and that "Canada's military missions [in Afghanistan] were largely, if not exclusively, determined on the basis of Ottawa's relationship with the United States."[20] Similarly, Duane Bratt argues that one of the two reasons Canada remained in Afghanistan was

---

16 As Bill Graham observes, "In 2002, nobody could have foreseen that Canada would make such a large commitment to a country little known by most Canadians and geographically so far removed from anywhere that could have been perceived as touching on Canada's vital interests" (Graham 2015: 51).

17 On Canada's approach to peacebuilding and counterinsurgency in Afghanistan, see Travers and Owen 2008.

18 For instance, see: Stein and Lang 2007: 261 (who emphasize the Canada-US relationship); Windsor, Charters and Wilson 2008: 10 (who stress the perceived need to rebuild Afghanistan and advance global security); Charbonneau and Parent 2010: 87–88 (who situate Canada's participation within a larger US-led hegemonic global order); Bratt 2011: 316–317, 326 (who cites the perception that 9/11 was an attack on the Western world; the support of the US, UN and NATO for the initial invasion; and the desire to improve US-Canada relations and rebuild Canada's military); and Granatstein 2011: 442 (who stresses the importance of nation-building in Afghanistan). For additional views, see Cunningham and Maley 2015 (a collection of twelve essays analysing Canada and Australia's contributions to the Afghan Conflict), and Saideman 2016: 114 (who argues one reason the mission unfolded as it did was because Canadian politicians were immature). For a study that contends much of Canada's involvement in Afghanistan was shaped by the vagaries of domestic politics, and the unwillingness of leaders to see it as a war, see Boucher and Nossal 2017.

19 As Jean-Christophe Boucher observes, the rationales for Canada's Afghan mission have undergone "notable shifts," and have cited various nationalist, altruistic and international motivations (2009: 718, 721).

20 Stein and Lang 2007: 20, 261.

to support the Canada-US relationship.[21] Underlying the argument of Stein, Lang, and Bratt are the implicit observations that, in the post 9/11 era, Canada's economic, security, and political links with America have been so important that leaders of different ideological orientation have all believed that Canada should contribute militarily to America's global fight against terrorism, and that Afghanistan is a key theatre of that fight.[22]

Canada's relationship with the US is undoubtedly crucial to understanding Canadian decision-making regarding the Afghanistan Conflict. However, other important domestic and international factors have also animated such decision-making, including considerations that clearly ran *against* the perceived wishes of the US during the war. For instance, public opinion in Canada[23] – including the public's interpretation of the relevant tenets of international law, and its view of the administration of US President George W. Bush – has affected the discourse and action of the governments in power during the conflict. This effect is suggested by Canada's non-participation in the US-led invasion of Iraq[24] and in America's Ballistic Missile Defence program, despite intense external and internal pressure to join both initiatives. Further, and most importantly for this book, Canada's perception of its rights under the UN Charter and its obligations under the NATO treaty and Geneva Conventions have influenced the decisions of leaders regarding Canada's involvement in the Afghanistan Conflict, and the justifications that could be made for its behaviour.

The Four Roles of International Law in Canada's Use of Force in Afghanistan

Canada's participation in the Afghanistan Conflict offers further evidence that international law can play four roles when states use force: (1) it helps constitute the identity of actors; (2) it helps regulate their conduct; (3) it permits and

---

21 As Bratt usefully notes, the 9/11 attacks may explain why Canada *initially* went to Afghanistan but they do not explain the subsequent decisions to *stay* in the country for over a decade, and the government's stated aims in Afghanistan do not adequately explain the extent of Canada's unprecedented military commitment there. "Afghanistan," Bratt argues, "was being used to advance two additional foreign policy goals: (1) supporting the Canada-US relationship; and (2) rebuilding the Canadian military" (2011: 318).

22 For example, economically, the US is Canada's largest trading partner. In terms of security, cooperation between America and Canada is demonstrated by NORAD (the bi-national aerospace defence arrangement established in 1958), the NATO alliance, and military exchange programs between the two countries. Politically, the two countries cooperate at both the national and the sub-national levels of government.

23 On the topic of public opinion and Canada's Afghan mission more generally, see Boucher and Nossal 2015: 59–78.

24 For further analysis of Canada and the Iraq War, see e.g. Cunningham and Thakur 2015.

legitimates certain actions; and (4) it helps structure the development of new legal rules and legitimate behaviour.

1. International Law Helped Constitute the Identities of Key Canadian Leaders

As was the case with Louis St. Laurent, Lester Pearson, and Brooke Claxton during the Korean War, in the debate and decisions behind the three phases of Canada's military operations in Afghanistan, international law helped constitute the identities of key leaders, and shaped the way in which Canada's interests were interpreted and pursued.

For example, the decisions behind phase one of Canada's participation in the Afghan war occurred in two stages. The first stage involved the decisions that led to the various force deployments in the fall of 2001. The second involved the decision in January 2002 to send regular ground troops to Kandahar. Regarding the first stage, Canada's perceived obligations under the NATO treaty and its rights under the UN Charter animated the thinking and values of Defence Minister Art Eggleton, Prime Minister Jean Chrétien, Chief of the Defence Staff (CDS) Ray Henault, and Foreign Minister Bill Graham. Such commitments meant that following 9/11 these leaders thought Canada was obligated to support the US and NATO in the global fight against terrorism, and to participate militarily in this fight. An unstated assumption behind this view is that Canada is the kind of state that honours its prior international commitments, and takes action in this regard when necessary.

Reflecting on why Canada originally decided to participate in the Afghanistan Conflict, Art Eggleton, Canada's defence minister from 1997 to early 2002, acknowledges the relevance of the Canada-US relationship but ultimately grants more importance to Canada's commitment under Article 5 of the NATO treaty.[25] Article 5, recall, provides that an armed attack on one NATO member is an attack on all and, thus, if an attack occurs, each member, in exercise of the right to self-defence recognized in Article 51 of the UN Charter, will assist the member attacked by taking action, including force, to restore the peace of the North Atlantic area.[26] And Article 51 states that nothing in the UN Charter shall

---

25 Interview with Art Eggleton, Toronto, 19 Sept. 2011. As Eggleton puts it, while "there's no doubt" that in the back of leaders' minds at the time was the importance of the Canada-US relationship, "it's a little more fundamental than that. Remember we're part of the NATO alliance."

26 In full, Article 5 provides: "The Parties agree that an armed attack against one or more of them in Europe or North America shall be considered an attack against them all and consequently they agree that, if such an armed attack occurs, each of them, in exercise of the right of individual or collective self-defence recognised by Article 51 of the Charter of the United Nations,

impair the inherent right of individual or collective self-defence if an armed attack occurs against a UN member, until the Security Council has taken measures necessary to maintain international peace and security.[27]

We saw in the previous chapter that following 9/11 the North Atlantic Council (NAC) decided to invoke Article 5 of the NATO treaty. And when this provision was declared, Eggleton notes, "we had an obligation. It could have worked the same if the attack was on ... any other member of the alliance."[28] The essence of what Canada did, he explains, "was to acquit ourselves of our obligations under the NATO treaty."[29]

Other Canadian leaders echo Eggleton's views. In his memoirs, Jean Chrétien, Canada's Prime Minister from 1993 to late 2003, observes proudly that following 9/11,

> Canada had been the first to talk about the use of NATO's Article 5 ... and in October 2001 we joined our NATO and Afghani allies in an operation led by the United States and Great Britain to go after al-Qaeda in Afghanistan. Not only was this a multilateral undertaking in keeping with our commitment to NATO, but it made sense, because the fundamentalist Taliban government was undoubtedly in league with Osama bin Laden and his terrorist training camps.[30]

Whether or not Canada was "the first" to discuss the use of Article 5 following 9/11, it is true that David Wright, Canada's Ambassador to NATO at the time, took a lead in this regard, and that he chaired the meeting of the NAC on 12 September 2001 where the likely applicability of Article 5 was first formally discussed.[31] Present at this meeting were Eggleton and General Ray Henault,

---

will assist the Party or Parties so attacked by taking forthwith, individually and in concert with the other Parties, such action as it deems necessary, including the use of armed force, to restore and maintain the security of the North Atlantic area. Any such armed attack and all measures taken as a result thereof shall immediately be reported to the Security Council. Such measures shall be terminated when the Security Council has taken the measures necessary to restore and maintain international peace and security." Importantly, Article 5 does not provide, contrary to the questionable legal interpretation of some Canadian political scientists (e.g., Bratt 2011: 317), that NATO members are obliged to provide assistance "by all means necessary."

27 Moreover, Article 51 goes on to state, "Measures taken by Members in the exercise of this right of self-defence shall be immediately reported to the Security Council and shall not in any way affect the authority and responsibility of the Security Council under the present Charter to take at any time such action as it deems necessary in order to maintain or restore international peace and security."

28 Interview with Art Eggleton, Toronto, 19 Sept. 2011.

29 Ibid.

30 Chrétien 2008: 304.

31 Interview with Art Eggleton, Toronto, 19 Sept. 2011; and interview with Ray Henault, London, 28 Nov. 2011. While there was a belief among NATO members that an attack had been

Canada's CDS at the time.[32] Reflecting on the values that animated Canada's thinking at the NAC meeting, and the country's subsequent military response to 9/11, Henault notes that these were

> the recognition that [9/11] had been an atrocity perpetrated on the international community. Not just on the US … [Canada's thinking] really did lean towards our relationship with our NATO partners, with our Asia-Pacific partners, because all had lost or potentially lost people in the attacks. So it was very much a Canada-US issue, but also a multinational issue. And it was important that Canada's response be seen as demonstrating that solidarity with the US, but also [that it was] a responsible international citizen. And that influenced the thinking of the Prime Minister, I can assure you. There was no hesitation on his part, in terms of building a capable, measured, and appropriate response.[33]

Other Canadian decision makers who were not at the NAC meeting were also concerned with Canada's NATO commitments. As Bill Graham, chair of the Parliamentary Foreign Affairs Committee in the fall of 2001 and Foreign Minister from January 2002 to July 2004, states: "The reason we went [to Afghanistan] in the first place is that it was an Article 5 of NATO obligation … this was the first time Article 5 had ever been invoked."[34] Pointing out that it would have been "inconceivable" for Canada not to have rallied to the US after 9/11 and Article 5 being declared, Graham adds that "a great deal of the discussions we had in the Foreign Affairs Department around Afghanistan dealt with the integrity of NATO, and our NATO obligations."[35]

Following Canada's initial military contributions in the fall of 2001, some leaders, such as Deputy Prime Minister John Manley,[36] felt that the country had to do more to support the US.[37] The interpretation and pursuit of this

---

   perpetrated on one of its members, the American Ambassador to the Alliance, Nick Burns, stressed that, before Article 5 was formally invoked, the US wanted to be sure that 9/11 was an external and not an internal incident.

32 On 11 Sept. 2001, Eggleton and Henault were in Bulgaria and Hungary, respectively. The following day, they flew to Brussels to attend the NAC meeting with Wright.

33 Interview with Ray Henault, London, 28 Nov. 2011.

34 Interview with Bill Graham, Toronto, 12 Sept. 2011.

35 Ibid.

36 Manley was Foreign Minister from October 2000 to January 2002, and Deputy Prime Minister from January 2002 to December 2003. He also led the 2008 Independent Panel on Afghanistan. Manley kindly agreed to be interviewed for this study, but due to the author's travel schedule this was not possible.

37 This was due to the following observations. In the mid-1990s, in an effort to reduce Canada's deficit, the Chrétien government made significant cuts to the country's defence budget. As a result, many US military leaders reportedly thought Canada was inadequately contributing to the security of the North American continent. Following 9/11, the government wanted to improve Canada's stature in the US regarding defence and security issues. Consequently, after

objective was shaped by the government's preference for the UN-authorized ISAF mission in Kabul over the US-led OEF operation in Kandahar. For instance, agreeing that one of Canada's concerns was how to show its support for the US, and for the implementation of the NATO treaty, Eggleton describes the policy context at the time as follows. On the one hand, US forces were moving into Kandahar, where the Taliban and al-Qaeda had a strong presence, while on the other, the European countries were considering a largely peace enforcement role in Kabul under ISAF. As a result, the question became: "Where did Canada, as the only other North American member of NATO, fit into all this?"[38]

Initially, the government appears to have thought that the best fit for Canada was a peace enforcement role in Kabul. For example, following Canada's initial military contributions in the Fall of 2001, Eggleton spoke with UK Defence Minister Geoff Hoon about Canada participating in ISAF.[39] This mission, Eggleton was quoted at the time as saying, was "not an offensive mission, not a front-line mission. This is a stabilization mission to assist in opening corridors for humanitarian assistance."[40] Further, he added, "These people are not intended to go in under a full-conflict situation. And if it ever came to full conflict, they'd probably be taken out."[41]

By emphasizing the anticipated humanitarian nature of ISAF, Eggleton was likely seeking to portray it as more consistent with the peacekeeping operations that Canadians had become familiar with in the latter half of the twentieth century.[42] And the reason Eggleton likely sought to portray ISAF this way is because, in addition to wanting to show Canada's solidarity with the US following 9/11, the Chrétien government also wanted to ensure that any such support was acceptable to the Canadian public,[43] and resonated with the public's

---

NATO invoked Article 5 of the Alliance treaty, members of the Cabinet, such as Manley, who were "continentalist" in their thinking felt that Canada had to do more to demonstrate its support for the US. See Stein and Lang 2007: 14.

38 Interview with Art Eggleton, Toronto, 19 Sept. 2011.

39 Ibid.

40 Art Eggleton, cited by Sheldon Alberts, "Six Months and Out for Our Troops: Ottawa: Analysts Warn of Losses," *National Post*, 16 Nov. 2001, at A1.

41 Art Eggleton, cited by Brian Laghi, "Eggleton Plays Down Combat Role for Troops," *The Globe and Mail*, 16 Nov. 2001, at A1.

42 Since 1948, over 120,000 Canadians have served in almost 50 different UN peacekeeping operations ranging from truce observance to the supervision of elections in the Middle East, Asia, Europe, Africa, and Central and South America. See Rudderham 2008; and UN Association in Canada, "The Canadian Contribution to UN Peacekeeping."

43 Stein and Lang label these two ambitions the "core political goals" of the government following 9/11. And the ISAF mission, they note, appealed to the Chrétien Cabinet because it allowed leaders to appear independent and somewhat distant from Washington, while at the same time demonstrating solidarity with the US (2007: 16).

understanding of Canada's role in international affairs.[44] In the end, though, Canada did not participate in the ISAF mission and, as noted earlier, instead contributed to the US-led operation in Kandahar.[45]

Canada's second phase of military action in Afghanistan occurred from 2003 to 2005, and involved Canada sending soldiers to Kabul and taking command of the ISAF mission there in early 2004. The decisions behind this phase took place in the winter and spring of 2003. As with the first phase, in the debate and decisions behind phase two, Canada's perceived commitments to the UN and NATO helped constitute the identities of key leaders at the time. Moreover, while the dominant scholarly view is that the government decided in favour of the ISAF operation mainly because it allowed Canada to support the US in its "War on Terror" without having to support its controversial war in Iraq,[46] political leaders in fact appear to have been motivated more by a belief that the UN-authorized ISAF mission was legitimate and more consistent with Canada's national identity as a peacekeeper, and that the integrity of NATO was at stake.

For instance, describing why his government decided that Canada would lead the ISAF operation in Kabul, Jean Chrétien notes the following in his memoirs:

> Towards the end of [2002], NATO began seeking someone willing and able to assume command of [ISAF] … In January 2003, while responsibility for ISAF was passing from the UN to NATO, I instructed John McCallum … to inform his US counterpart, Donald Rumsfeld, that we were willing to take over from the Germans and the Dutch at the conclusion of their term in August. Even though the commitment would require on our part many more troops and a lot more money, we were going to get our soldiers into a more secure place where their assignment was closer to traditional peacekeeping.[47]

Reflecting on his thinking at the time, John McCallum, who was defence minister from June 2002 to December 2003, explains:

> I thought it would be a good thing … for Canada to play a major role in Kabul, in ISAF. And I thought it would be a good thing for us to be the leader of it for a

---

44 As Claire Turenne-Sjolander and Kathryn Trevenen argue, in an effort to strengthen Canada's national identity and manage public opinion, the peacekeeping "frame" has often been used to explain Canada's military presence in Afghanistan (2011: 96–109).

45 There are differing accounts for this shift in policy. The main reasons appear to have been Britain's opposition to Canada participating in ISAF, and America's request for support in Kandahar (Stein and Lang 2007: 16–19; and interview with Art Eggleton, Toronto, 19 Sept. 2011).

46 Again, variations of this view are articulated by: Stein and Lang 2007: 71–73; Nossal 2010: 123; Granatstein 2011: 422; and Hillier 2009: 263.

47 Chrétien 2008: 305. In contrast to Chrétien's account, NATO states that the Alliance assumed leadership of ISAF in August, not January, 2003. See NATO's website, "About ISAF." For a detailed description of the ISAF decision, see Stein and Lang 2007: 41–49.

year, or two. So I just pushed for that. And we got it. I wasn't doing that to appease Rumsfeld. That might have been a positive side benefit. But I just thought that it was the right thing for Canada to do. And obviously the Americans agreed. But my motive was not to "make up" for saying no to Iraq. My motive was that I thought that this was the appropriate thing for the Canadian military to do.[48]

Similarly, then CDS Ray Henault recalls that while the key concern at the time was, in his view, how to support the US and the broader campaign against terrorism, the decision to lead the ISAF mission in Kabul was made not to "dodge a bullet" on the Iraq issue but because the mission was thought to be the best way to support this campaign.[49] Although the decision was obviously seen that way, he adds, the Iraq issue "wasn't the overriding [reason]."[50]

Like McCallum and Henault, Bill Graham, who was Foreign Minister at the time of Canada's decision to lead ISAF, also downplays the impact of the Iraq War on the thinking and choices of the government with respect to Afghanistan. As he explains, arguing "that the only reason that we went to Afghanistan was to satisfy the Americans because we didn't go to Iraq, I mean that is far too bold … life is not that simple, it never is."[51] Noting that "of course" a concern for not participating in the Iraq War was "a factor" behind Canada's second phase of military participation in the Afghanistan Conflict, Graham suggests that three other considerations were also relevant.[52] First, there was "the integrity of NATO."[53] Second, there was a desire to support the implementation of the Bonn accords.[54] These were the UN-sponsored agreements of December 2001 that aimed to chart Afghanistan's future and the international community's role in this regard.

Finally, there was a concern for Canada's international reputation, because it had supported the internationalization of the issues in Afghanistan, and the government wanted to show that it was "a team player" in this regard.[55] As Graham explains:

[T]his was an area where the UN had come around, and we were going to rebuild Afghanistan … One of the elements of that is that we had to have security. So, do

---

48 Interview with John McCallum, Ottawa, 20 Sept. 2011.

49 Interview with Ray Henault, London, 28 Nov. 2011.

50 Ibid.

51 Interview with Bill Graham, Toronto, 12 Sept. 2011.

52 Ibid.

53 Ibid. Contextualizing Canada's decision to lead the ISAF mission in Kabul, and participate in the Afghanistan Conflict more generally, within a broader concern for NATO, Graham notes that since the Cold War, the Alliance has been "a very important foreign policy instrument for Canada, and a really important part of our security structure." Further, he adds, "there is a tremendous recognition of the need to reinforce NATO and make sure it's working, and Canada's role in it."

54 Ibid.

55 Ibid.

we step up for part of this security? Yeah, we did. Did it help us with the Americans, because they were glad we did it? For sure. Were there all sorts of other reasons for doing it? There were. We might well have done it [i.e., lead ISAF] even if we had *had* troops in Iraq [emphasis in original]. So that would be my answer to the whole thing.[56]

Elaborating on the Cabinet discussions and thinking at the time, Graham has written that among the different factors at play, it was "important to the government that ISAF was a multilateral undertaking with a UN mandate, and soon to become a NATO responsibility. The UN mandate itself assumed greater importance as concerns about US intentions toward Iraq intensified."[57] Moreover, Graham notes, while the change in mission from combat to nation-building did not fit with the Pentagon's ideas about what American soldiers should be doing, "For us that change in the nature of the mission in Afghanistan was an argument for Canadian participation."[58]

Canada's third phase of military action in Afghanistan took place from 2006 to 2011, and involved a significant number of Canadian forces being redeployed to Kandahar. Again, the initial decision behind this phase occurred in May 2005, when the Cabinet of Liberal Prime Minister Paul Martin (who had replaced Jean Chrétien) approved a plan proposed by CDS Rick Hillier (who had replaced Ray Henault).

Like the first and second phases, during the initial decisions behind phase three, Canada's perceived commitments to NATO helped constitute the identities of leaders at the time, and shaped the way in which Canada's interests were interpreted and pursued. For instance, when asked why Canada has participated in the Afghanistan Conflict, Martin discounts the idea that the primary reason has been to show support for the US and its war against terrorism, and stresses the importance of helping Afghanistan as a "failing state," and ensuring that Canada had "a seat at the table" as the international community responded to a post 9/11 world.[59]

Elaborating on this latter concern, Martin notes in his memoirs that in contrast to the tragedy of the Iraq War, Canada was "in Afghanistan for the right reasons and, having been part of displacing the Taliban regime, we continued to have a duty to help construct something sturdy to replace it."[60] That duty, he stresses, was something shared by the NATO allies, and Canada's responsibility was to "play our part, not to shoulder any and all burdens that might come our

---

56 Interview with Bill Graham, Toronto, 12 Sept. 2011.
57 Graham 2015: 55.
58 Ibid.
59 Phone interview with Paul Martin, 16 Sept. 2011.
60 Martin 2009: 391.

way."[61] As Scott Reid, Martin's Director of Communications in 2005 and one of his most trusted advisers, observes, "The Prime Minister felt that Canada, as a member of NATO, had an obligation to stand with the alliance in Afghanistan, but his interest in Afghanistan ended there."[62] Consistent with Reid's observation, Martin explains:

> My view of the Afghanistan mission was that it needed to fit within our overall foreign and defence priorities. I understood that this was more a peacemaking than a peacekeeping mission, as were many others I expected us to be called upon to perform: in Haiti, and Darfur, and perhaps in the Middle East. That's why I sought and received General Hillier's assurance that our role in Afghanistan would not compromise what I felt could be an increasing role in other theatres, and most certainly in Darfur.[63]

In sum, the thinking and decisions behind Canada's three phases of participation in the Afghanistan Conflict outlined above support the proposition that, when states use force, international law can help constitute the identities of key leaders at issue, and shape the way in which a state's interests are interpreted and pursued. Further, the discourse and actions of leaders reviewed above also suggest that, consistent with the observations of constructivist theory,[64] a country's perceived relationship to international law can be a site for "communicative" struggles over legitimate state identity and rightful behaviour.

2. International Law Helped Regulate Canada's Conduct

In addition to its constitutive effect, international law also had a regulative influence on Canada's political and military practice regarding the Afghanistan

---

61 As Martin stresses in his memoirs and when queried on the issue, when he approved the Kandahar mission, he did so under the condition that it would be for one year. His earlier experience with NATO's secretary-general, whereby Canada was asked repeatedly to keep its troops in Kabul because a replacement could not be found, convinced Martin that a short-term time limit was needed if Canada was to retain flexibility for its forces and maximize its leverage with the Alliance (Martin 2009: 392, 395; and phone interview with Paul Martin, 16 Sept. 2011).

62 Cited in Stein and Lang 2007: 192.

63 Martin 2009: 392. Martin sought Hillier's assurance in part because he was very concerned about the crimes against humanity that were reportedly occurring in Darfur, and he thought that helping address the Darfur crisis was a better fit for Canada than fighting in Afghanistan. Reflecting Martin's concern for Darfur, Canada's Ambassador to the UN, Allan Rock, helped guide the passage of a resolution by the UN General Assembly on the "Responsibility to Protect." (Phone interview with Paul Martin, 16 Sept. 2011; Stein and Lang 2007: 180; and Bill Schiller, "The Road to Kandahar," *The Toronto Star*, 8 Sept. 2006.)

64 Reus-Smit 2004.

Conflict. Two examples demonstrate this influence. First, when the Chrétien government decided that Canada would lead a naval group, Task Force 151, as part of Operation Enduring Freedom (OEF), its understanding of the legal circumstances at issue helped constrain the nature and scope of the force deployed with this group. Second, Canada's policy and conduct regarding Afghan detainees has been governed and controlled in part by its interpretation of its obligations under the Third Geneva Convention on Prisoners of War (POWs). However, these perceived obligations appear to have had a stronger impact on members of the Liberal governments of Jean Chrétien and Paul Martin than on those of the Conservative government of Stephen Harper.

Regarding the first example, the decision to lead TF 151 came about as follows. In February 2003, CDS Ray Henault told Defence Minister John McCallum that Canada had a chance to lead a multinational naval force, which would include US ships as well as those of other states not yet committed to an invasion of Iraq.[65] The task force, known as TF 151, would support OEF. However, McCallum was advised, Canada's navy would travel farther up into the Persian Gulf, close to Iraq's territorial waters. Over the coming weeks, it became clear that TF 151 would be "double-hatted" – i.e., it would support OEF but would also likely provide some yet to be defined support to Operation Iraqi Freedom (OIF) once the Iraq invasion began.[66] By the end of February, it also became increasingly apparent that Jean Chrétien was likely going to decide against Canada participating in the invasion.[67]

In response to these seemingly contradictory developments, two different views on TF 151 evolved. On the one hand, senior officials in the Department of Foreign Affairs, Foreign Minister Bill Graham, and Deputy Prime Minister John Manley were generally in favour of Canada leading TF 151, and tended to justify this as a way of supporting the US and OEF. On the other hand, military leaders in the Defence Department, including Henault and deputy CDS Greg Maddison, were now generally against Canada leading TF 151 if it was not going to also participate in the Iraq War, as doing so would be unfeasible militarily and too confusing operationally.[68] Not wanting Canada to be seen to be leaving the Persian Gulf at a critical time, Chrétien ultimately favoured the

---

65 Reflecting on why he and his deputy, Greg Maddison, thought Canada should participate in TF 151, Henault says: "[W]e felt strongly that it was important that we remain in Task Force 151, without being engaged in or seen to be a part of the operation for Iraq. Because we still saw Task Force 151 as an important component of the campaign against terrorism. And whether it was preventing arms shipments to Iraq, countering terrorist activity, or [enforcing] arms embargoes, we felt that it was still important that we stay engaged in the Persian Gulf" (interview with Ray Henault, London, 28 Nov. 2011).

66 Stein and Lang 2007: 80.

67 Ibid: 82.

68 Ibid: 80–85.

first view.[69] As such, it was decided that Canada would remain the leader of TF 151 but only support OEF, and the navy was asked to implement this policy.[70]

The advice and debate behind the TF 151 decision suggest that leaders interpreted the international legal considerations at issue in ways that best fit with other political and military objectives at the time, such as supporting the US and the international campaign against terrorism. However, this advice and debate also indicate that the legal considerations at issue helped regulate the actions of leaders in Canada, and the decisions of the task force commander in the Persian Gulf. For instance, in the lead-up to the TF 151 decision, the Judge Advocate General (JAG), Jerry Pitzul, was of the view that if the task force protected ships involved in the invasion of Iraq, then Canada might legally become a belligerent or a party to the conflict.[71] Consequently, then Defence Minister John McCallum recalls:

[W]e worked very closely with the JAG, the legal people, to do everything we could to ensure that we were not belligerents. And I remember having long conversations with our counterpart in New Zealand, my counterpart in France ... both of whom had ships in the area, as we did. And both of whom did not want to be associated with the Iraq War. And so we had discussions to make sure that that was in fact the case.[72]

When asked what role, if any, Canada's legal advisers played in the decision-making process at the time, McCallum responds that "they helped us to do the right things, to ... maximize our ability to isolate ourselves [from the Iraq War]. The lawyers advised as to what particular things we had to do to do that."[73]

Bill Graham's account generally resonates with that of McCallum, except in one respect. While Jerry Pitzul, the JAG at Defence, believed that if TF 151 protected ships involved in the invasion of Iraq then Canada might legally become a party to the conflict, Graham is not sure that Colleen Swords, the Legal Adviser at Foreign Affairs, was of that opinion.[74] "Our view," Graham notes, "was the naval operation dated from the original mission to restrain the Taliban and control al-Qaeda, and that therefore this was a legitimate presence in the Gulf for a different purpose [than the Iraq campaign]."[75]

---

69 Ibid: 85.

70 Ibid.

71 Interview with Bill Graham, Toronto, 12 Sept. 2011; interview with John McCallum, Ottawa, 20 Sept. 2011; and Stein and Lang 2007: 82.

72 Interview with John McCallum, Ottawa, 20 Sept. 2011.

73 Ibid.

74 Interview with Bill Graham, Toronto, 12 Sept. 2011.

75 Quoted in Stein and Lang 2007: 80.

Emphasizing that the legal opinions on the TF 151 issue were part of the decision-making process, and that they mattered to his thinking at the time, Graham cites the following example whereby Canada's understanding of the legal circumstances constrained the nature and scope of the force deployed with TF 151. As part of the discussions surrounding the task force issue, a decision had to be made regarding whether, in addition to Canada's naval contribution, Canadian fighter aircraft would also be deployed to help with the interdiction work of TF 151.[76] As Graham explains:

> It was decided not to do that, because [the aircraft] would have been too closely … integrated into what was going on in Iraq itself. There was a distinct recognition that [the aircraft] might be drawn into the Iraq War, in a way that wasn't intended. But there was also a distinct order that [they] were to continue doing their job of interdiction in Afghanistan, and they were not to be part of Iraq.[77]

In addition to influencing political leaders in Canada, the legal considerations associated with the TF 151 issue also impacted the thinking and decisions of Canada's commander of the task force in the Persian Gulf, Commodore Roger Girouard. As indicated in part earlier above, following Chrétien's decision that Canada would remain the leader of TF 151 but only support OEF, Girouard was given the difficult job of implementing this policy on the water. The naval commanders of other countries which were also contributing to TF 151 – such as the Netherlands, New Zealand, and France – had been instructed not to operate their ships in the entrance to the Persian Gulf, or to engage Iraqi vessels.[78] By contrast, Girouard's interpretation of the legal constraints applicable to his command appeared to be less geographic and more related to particular tasks. As he explained in a newspaper article on 9 April 2003:

> I've been given a box by the chief of the defence staff. I've coloured an awful lot of that box and there's no doubt in my mind that there are times when I've come really, really, really close to the edge of the line, but I haven't gone over. It was explained to me very succinctly, as I represent Canada now, where I should not be going. That has had its challenges. I was asked to do something and I assessed what the situation was and I told them that I could not do that, that I felt it fell into the … Operation Iraqi Freedom rubric. They thought about that for a little bit and they agreed and at that point, an American asset took up a particular job.[79]

---

76 Interview with Bill Graham, Toronto, 12 Sept. 2011.

77 Ibid.

78 Stein and Lang 2007: 86.

79 Quoted in Allan Thompson, "Sailors Would Not Hand Over Iraqis," *Toronto Star*, 9 April 2003 at A12.

Girouard's comments suggest that, as the commander of TF 151 at the time, interpreting which tasks fell under OEF and which supported OIF was likely very difficult. As John McCallum notes, we will likely never know with certainty whether Canada's contribution to TF 151 engaged in activity related to the Iraq War.[80] Nonetheless, Girouard's comments also indicate that Canada's interpretation of the legal considerations related to TF 151 were relevant to Gerouard's thinking at the time, and that he did his best to align his decisions with these considerations.

In addition to TF 151, Canada's policy and conduct regarding individuals captured in Afghanistan by Canadian forces and transferred to US and local authorities further demonstrate the regulative, if imperfect, impact of international law. As with Britain, the history of this issue is complex and still unfolding.[81] For present purposes, it suffices to note that Canada's policy and actions regarding Afghan detainees have been governed and controlled in part by its interpretation of its obligations under the Geneva Convention on POWs. These perceived obligations, however, appear to have had a stronger impact on members of the Liberal governments of Jean Chrétien and Paul Martin than on those of the Conservative government of Stephen Harper.

To understand the above arguments, one must understand the circumstances that led to the signing of Canada's detainee transfer arrangements with Afghanistan in December 2005 and May 2007,[82] and with the US in November 2011.[83] Following the 2005 decision to redeploy troops to Kandahar, an issue arose with respect to Canada's policy and practice regarding captured individuals. Since the Canadian Forces (CF) had first arrived in Afghanistan, Canada's position was that it did not hold on to suspected Taliban and al-Qaeda fighters that it

---

80 Interview with John McCallum, Ottawa, 20 Sept. 2011.

81 For further discussion, see e.g. the five essays in "Is the Afghan Detainee Case Unfinished Business?," 14 June 2017, opencanada.org; Forcese 2010; Hendin 2007; Stein and Lang 2007; *Amnesty International Canada et al v. Attorney General of Canada et al*, 2008 FC 162; *Amnesty International Canada et al v. Attorney General of Canada et al*, 2008 FC 336; and the Military Police Complaints Commission's *Final Report* of June 2012. The court cases involved Amnesty International and the BC Civil Liberties Association challenging the government's policy and practice of transferring Afghan detainees to local authorities due to an alleged risk of torture. The MPCC report dealt with a related complaint by these NGOs that certain Military Police failed to investigate such transfers.

82 See Arrangement for the Transfer of Detainees between the Canadian Forces and the Ministry of Defence of the Islamic Republic of Afghanistan, 19 Dec. 2005 [2005 Detainee Arrangement]; and Arrangement for the Transfer of Detainees between the Government of Canada and the Government of the Islamic Republic of Afghanistan, 3 May 2007 [2007 Detainee Arrangement].

83 Arrangement between the Government of Canada and the Government of the United States of America concerning the transfer of persons between the Canadian Forces and the U.S. Forces in Afghanistan, 18 Nov. 2011 [2011 Detainee Arrangement].

captured.[84] This was because, military leaders had told the government since 2002, the CF had no expertise or capability to run prisons, and the cost of building them was prohibitive.[85]

In addition, as the government explained in a set of important 2008 court cases on the issue, *Amnesty International Canada et al v. Attorney General of Canada et al*, "Canada has no legal authority to establish or run a long-term detention facility in Afghanistan," and the CF "have not been authorized to detain [individuals] for the long term, either by the Government of Canada or by ISAF commanders … nor [by] the Government of Afghanistan."[86] This legal position is similar to Britain's view on the matter. Unlike the UK, however, the Canadian government did not specify in the *Amnesty* cases whether the perceived lack of authority for long-term detention ultimately stemmed from Canada's understanding of relevant *jus in bello* rules, or UN Security Council Resolution 1386 that created ISAF.

Consistent with Canada's position on this issue, individuals captured by the CF in the early years of the Afghan Conflict were transferred to US authorities or, in some cases, to the Afghans.[87] Once transferred to the US, however, many of these individuals were sent to Guantánamo Bay. Since 2002 a growing list of critics alleged that detainees at Guantánamo were subjected to cruel and inhumane treatment and interrogation techniques, and that some of these techniques amounted to torture.[88] The reporting of prisoner abuse at Abu Ghraib in Iraq in 2004 led to further concern over US practice regarding captured enemy fighters.[89]

In light of these developments, Bill Graham, who was defence minister from mid-2004 to early 2006 under the Martin government,[90] became concerned about the CF transferring detainees to US and Afghan authorities.[91] As Graham – an international lawyer with a strong interest in the *jus in bello* – explains in his memoirs:

> One problem that continued to preoccupy me as we prepared to send our battle group to Afghanistan was the proper treatment of captured prisoners. This was a classic issue in international humanitarian law and especially important since the creation of the International Criminal Court, of which we were a party and a principal advocate.

---

84 Stein and Lang 2007: 246.

85 Interview with Bill Graham, Toronto, 12 Sept. 2011; and Stein and Lang 2007: 246.

86 *Amnesty*, 2008 FC 336, at para. 85.

87 Government of Canada, "Canadian Forces Release Statistics on Afghanistan Detainees," Feb. 2013.

88 See e.g. the European Parliament's 2004 Resolution on Guantánamo; UN Commission on Human Rights, "2006 UN Report on Guantánamo"; and Amnesty International, "Cruel and Inhuman: Conditions of Isolation for Detainees at Guantánamo Bay" (5 April 2007).

89 Interview with Bill Graham, Toronto, 12 Sept. 2011.

90 Graham was moved from Foreign Affairs to the Ministry of Defence.

91 Interview with Bill Graham, Toronto, 12 Sept. 2011; and Stein and Lang 2007: 247.

[General] Rick Hillier often used to emphasize that Canadian soldiers operate within a concept of a rule of law, and his successor, General Walt Natynczyk, reiterated that the rule of law governs how Canadian troops behave as soldiers.[92]

Reflecting these concerns, Graham and Hillier, the new CDS, decided to negotiate a bilateral detainee transfer arrangement with Afghanistan in 2005. This arrangement aimed to establish the standards and procedures to be followed in the event that the CF transferred a captured individual to Afghan authorities.[93] And the reason it was decided that Canada should transfer prisoners to Afghan authorities, rather than US partners, is because Canada was operating in Afghanistan's sovereign territory, at the invitation of their government.[94] As Graham explains, although there were legal arguments from the Defence Department that Canada would still meet its legal obligations if we continued to transfer prisoners to the Americans, this was not his view, due to the "increasingly erratic" international legal interpretation and conduct by the US regarding detainees.[95] In other words, despite the advice of some government officials to maintain a certain transfer policy that reflected Canada's military cooperation with US forces, a different option was ultimately chosen, in large part because of international legal concerns among some leaders.

Officials in Canada's Defence Department took the lead in drafting an agreement, and Graham met on many occasions with two of the lawyers in the office of the Judge Advocate General (JAG).[96] "We wanted," Graham says, "to make sure that all detainees enjoyed the Geneva Convention protections; that none would be subject to the death penalty; that the Red Cross could visit them and assess their treatment, and would be notified when they were transferred to a third party and could visit them and assess their treatment; and that the Afghan Independent Human Rights Commission would have monitoring responsibility."[97] After reviewing Denmark's detainee agreement, Graham asked whether

---

92 Graham 2016: 392.

93 2005 Detainee Arrangement.

94 Graham 2016: 394. In talks he had with the leaders of Amnesty International Canada, they stressed "that the right approach was to transfer detainees to the Afghans." For an elaboration of Amnesty's concerns, and the view that Canada may need to operate its own detention facilities in Afghanistan, see the testimony at the Standing Committee on National Defence, 11 Dec. 2006.

95 Ibid. Graham was worried about US black sites, interrogation, and rendition, and felt it would be "morally abhorrent" and unacceptable to Canadians to transfer detainees to this legal black hole.

96 Graham 2016: 396.

97 Ibid. Consistent with these aims, the final agreement stated that the International Committee of the Red Cross had the right to visit detainees, and was to be notified if someone was transferred (2005 Detainee Arrangement, para. 10). Accurate records were to be maintained regarding detainees, and Canada and Afghanistan committed to cooperating with the Afghan Independent Human Rights Commission (paras. 7 and 11). The arrangement also prohibited the death penalty for Canadian-transferred detainees (para. 12).

a provision should be added giving Canada the right to inspect transferred prisoners. But the Defence lawyers, he explains, said it would not be appropriate, because the Danish agreement was "too paternalistic."[98] This exchange foreshadowed a perceived omission that Canada's second detainee arrangement would later seek to address.

The final agreement was signed on 18 December 2005, in the middle of an election campaign that would lead to a new minority Conservative government. While Britain's detainee agreement sought to ensure that transferees were treated in accordance with relevant international human rights law, Canada's arrangement aimed to ensure that they were treated "in accordance with the standards set out in the Third Geneva Convention [on POWs]."[99] If there is any doubt as to whether a detainee is a POW, Canada's arrangement continues, they were nonetheless to be treated "humanely, at all times and under all circumstances, in a manner consistent with the rights and protections of the Third Geneva Convention."[100]

The reference to the Geneva Convention in the agreement likely reflects a view among Canadian leaders and officials that the *jus in bello* is the most relevant body of international law that applies to Canada's policy and practice regarding Afghan detainees.[101] However, like the complex legal situation in Korea over fifty years earlier, note that the standards of the Geneva Conventions were seen to apply in Afghanistan even though the formal status of the conflict had arguably changed by 2005 from international (when the Geneva Conventions traditionally apply) to non-international in character[102] (when Common Article 3 of the Conventions, which requires minimum humane treatment, applies). Adding further legal context to the situation, the CF also acknowledged in the *Amnesty* cases that Canada's "international obligations" regarding detainees "include obligations under the Convention Against Torture," which is an international human rights treaty.[103]

Commenting on the impetus behind the 2005 transfer arrangement, Bill Graham says that the reason he argued strenuously for a coherent detainee strategy

---

98 Graham 2016: 396.

99 2005 Detainee Arrangement, at para. 3.

100 Ibid, at para. 8.

101 Consistent with this interpretation, in the *Amnesty* cases, the government did not argue that international human rights law was most relevant to Canada's policy and practice regarding Afghan detainees, and instead referred mainly to the Geneva Convention on POWs. It also argued that Canada's constitutional bill of human rights, the *Charter of Rights and Freedoms*, does not apply to the transfer of Afghan detainees by Canadian forces.

102 See e.g. Graham's earlier comments that Afghan authorities were seen as the proper recipients of detainees because Canada was operating in Afghanistan's sovereign territory, at the invitation of their government.

103 *Amnesty*, 2008 FC 162, at para. 115.

was because he saw the need to justify what Canada was doing in Afghanistan "on the highest grounds of behaviour," and "consistent with international legal standards."[104] From a political perspective, he could see that, if not managed properly, the issue was going to be a huge problem.[105]

By contrast, Stein and Lang argue that Graham's concerns at the time "were not widely shared among civilian and military officials and lawyers in the Department of National Defence, where officials thought of the detainee issue as a nuisance, an obsession of the political class rather than a serious issue."[106] Former CDS Ray Henault remembers things differently. He says that "from the very outset, Jerry Pitzul [the JAG] was very concerned about the whole detainee issue. And he was the one who made it very clear that what we should be doing at the very least is establishing a tracking mechanism for detainees, so that we protect them and ensure they're being treated in accordance with the Geneva Conventions."[107]

Resonating with the concerns emphasized by Henault, Canada signed additional bilateral arrangements with Afghanistan in the lead-up to the Kandahar deployment, and these agreements further stressed the importance of both states' international legal obligations regarding captured individuals. For instance, a technical arrangement between the two countries signed just before the detainee agreement in December 2005 provides that

> Canadian personnel may need to use force (including deadly force) to ensure the accomplishment of their operational objectives [and] the safety of the deployed force … Such measures could include … the detention of persons … Detainees would be afforded the same treatment as Prisoners of War. Detainees would be transferred to Afghan authorities in a manner consistent with international law and subject to negotiated assurances regarding their treatment and transfer.[108]

Similarly, Canada's status of forces arrangement with Afghanistan, which was annexed to the technical arrangement, reaffirmed that the Canadian government would take measures to ensure that all Canadian personnel "will respect international law and will refrain from activities not compatible with the nature of their operations or their status in Afghanistan."[109] Moreover, it stated, "[i]n giving effect

---

104 Interview with Bill Graham, Toronto, 12 Sept. 2011.

105 Ibid.

106 Stein and Lang 2007: 247.

107 Interview with Ray Henault, London, 28 Nov. 2011.

108 Technical Arrangement between the Government of Canada and the Government of the Islamic Republic of Afghanistan, 18 Dec. 2005, cited in *Amnesty*, 2008 FC 336, at para. 47.

109 Article 1.2, Status of Forces Arrangement, cited in *Amnesty*, 2008 FC 336, at para. 50.

to the Arrangements, the Participants will at all times act in a manner consistent with their obligations under international law."[110]

Reflecting the external arrangements above, Theatre Standing Orders 321A and 321, a series of internal orders to Canadian soldiers and Military Police regarding Afghan detainees, provided explicit direction for the treatment and handling of detainees, the procedure for transfer to Afghan authorities, and information to be maintained during the transfer process.[111] Under these orders, the CF commander in theatre decided whether a detainee should be retained, released, or transferred.[112] During the combat phase of Canada's mission in Afghanistan, individuals captured by the CF were held at a temporary detention facility at Kandahar Airfield (a NATO base and the headquarters for Canada's former operations in Kandahar province).[113]

Between 2001 and 2011, when Canada's combat mission ended, 1,073 individuals were reportedly detained by the CF.[114] Of this total, 579 detainees (54 per cent) were transferred to US or Afghan authorities, 488 (45 per cent) were released by the CF, and 6 (0.6 per cent) died from wounds incurred prior to capture.[115] While in Canadian custody, the TSO orders required that detainees be "treated fairly and humanely" in accordance with "applicable international law and CF Doctrine."[116]

As noted in chapter two, we might expect a state like Canada, with fewer resources per area and per capita of the Afghan population and more casualties relative to their allies, to be more likely to use disproportionate force and less likely to be tolerant of fighters who have killed their soldiers. Contrary to such expectations, however, there is limited publicly available evidence to suggest that CF members have mistreated captured individuals in Afghanistan.[117] Indeed, as an official publication on the issue stresses, "In accordance with their obligations under international humanitarian law the Canadian Forces ... treat

---

110 Article 1.4, ibid, at para. 51.

111 Military Police Complaints Commission's [MPCC] *Final Report* of June 2012, at xiv.

112 *Amnesty*, 2008 FC 336, at para. 56.

113 Ibid at para. 57.

114 This total is based on yearly figures listed in Government of Canada, "Canadian Forces Release Statistics on Afghanistan Detainees," Feb. 2013.

115 Ibid.

116 *Amnesty*, 2008 FC 336, at para. 59.

117 Although Canadian soldiers appear to have generally treated detainees humanely, Ahmadshah Malgarai, an Afghan-Canadian who served as an interpreter for Canada's military, told a parliamentary committee in April 2010 that he came across evidence that Canadian soldiers killed an innocent Afghan teenager in 2007 and then tried to cover it up. The Canadian Forces responded by saying they would investigate these "grave accusations." See Steven Chase, "Military Vows to Probe 'Grave' Detainee Accusations," *The Globe and Mail*, updated 23 Aug. 2012.

all detainees humanely."[118] The "standards of protection afforded by the Third Geneva Convention," the publication continues, include the provision of "food, shelter and necessary medical attention."[119]

Further demonstrating restraint where it might not be expected, the CF reportedly transferred suspected Taliban fighters to Afghan authorities even though some of these individuals were known to have killed Canadian soldiers,[120] and one could argue that Canada should prosecute these fighters for their actions. This policy may be due in part to a view that combatants cannot be prosecuted for lawfully killing another combatant in war.[121] If so, this would suggest that – consistent with one of the observable implications posited in chapter two – some Canadian leaders and officials may believe in the reciprocal and equal application of *jus in bello* rules with respect to captured suspected Taliban fighters.[122]

According to NATO and ISAF policy, persons detained by the CF were to be transferred or released within 96 hours of their capture.[123] The CF, however, held people for longer periods due to medical, administrative, and security reasons. The decision to do so was made by a high-level CF commander with input from other government departments.[124] Before transferring someone into US or Afghan custody, the CF had to be satisfied that there were no substantial grounds for believing that there was a real risk that they would be in danger of being tortured or mistreated.[125] The government has maintained that if this standard was not met, a transfer would not occur.[126]

Despite the formal arrangements, orders and policies described above, the *Globe and Mail* reported in April 2007 that detainees transferred by the CF

---

118 Government of Canada, "Canadian Forces Release Statistics on Afghanistan Detainees," Feb. 2013.

119 Ibid.

120 As journalist Neil Macdonald reports from his interviews with two anonymous Canadian intelligence officials, on "several occasions" Canadian forces transferred Afghan prisoners to "their own government" even though Canada knew they "had a role in the killing or wounding of Canadian soldiers." See "The Questions We Are Not Asking," CBC News, 25 Nov. 2009.

121 Indeed, Macdonald argues that the reason for this transfer practice is "[b]ecause Canada, unlike the US, scrupulously *follows* international law" [emphasis added] (ibid).

122 While some Canadian leaders and officials may believe in the reciprocal and equal application of *jus in bello* rules with respect to captured suspected Taliban fighters, the same might not be true regarding captured suspected al-Qaeda fighters, whose legal status is a source of greater controversy. See Byers 2002.

123 *Amnesty*, 2008 FC 336, at para. 61.

124 Government of Canada, "Canadian Forces Release Statistics on Afghanistan Detainees," Feb. 2013.

125 *Amnesty*, 2008 FC 336, at para. 64.

126 Ibid, at para. 65.

had been mistreated and abused by Afghan officials.[127] Following the considerable media attention generated by this article,[128] the Harper government concluded a second detainee transfer arrangement with Afghanistan in May of that year.[129] Supplementing the first arrangement, this agreement aimed to provide Canadian officials and the Afghan Independent Human Rights Commission (AIHRC) with unrestricted and private access to Canadian-transferred detainees.[130]

To facilitate such access, these detainees were to be held in a limited number of detention facilities.[131] Afghan authorities were responsible for treating such individuals in accordance with Afghanistan's international human rights obligations, including the prohibition on torture.[132] They were to notify the CF when a detainee was transferred, sentenced, or released, and Canada could refuse follow-on transfers to a third country.[133] Alleged mistreatment was to be reported to Canada, investigated and, where appropriate, prosecuted.[134]

As with Britain, critics have argued that the formal detainee arrangements between Canada and Afghanistan did not provide adequate substantive or procedural safeguards to ensure that individuals transferred to Afghan authorities, as well as those who may have been transferred on to third countries, were not exposed to a substantial risk of torture.[135] Moreover, it has been suggested, no amount of post-transfer monitoring would have sufficed to protect detainees.[136] To support these views, reference is often made to specific allegations by Canadian transferees and other detainees,[137] and relevant reports by UN agencies, the AIHRC, Canada's own government agencies, and a former justice of Canada's Supreme Court.[138] Again, these reports document, among other things,

---

127 Graeme Smith, "From Canadian Custody into Cruel Hands," *The Globe and Mail*, 23 April 2007.

128 MPCC's *Final Report* of June 2012, at xvi.

129 2007 Detainee Arrangement.

130 Ibid, paras. 1, 2, 8 and 9.

131 Ibid, para. 7. By February 2013, there were seven facilities where detainees could be held (Government of Canada, "Canadian Forces Release Statistics on Afghanistan Detainees," Feb. 2013).

132 2007 Detainee Arrangement, para. 4.

133 Ibid, paras. 3 and 5.

134 Ibid, paras. 3 and 10.

135 *Amnesty*, 2008 FC 336, at para. 7.

136 *Amnesty*, 2008 FC 162, at para. 42. Resonating with this point, Graham notes in his memoirs: "As it turned out, our initial focus on the problems associated with transferring detainees to the Americans had obscured the fact that the Afghan system simply could not manage [the detainee] issue. Whereas the monitoring provisions in the British and Danish agreements were stronger than ours, the distinction made little difference in practice, without an Afghan capacity to fully implement them" (Graham 2016: 397).

137 *Amnesty*, 2008 FC 162, at paras. 85–101.

138 Ibid, at paras. 102–106.

numerous cases of torture and mistreatment of Afghan prisoners, and allege that Afghanistan's National Directorate of Security (NDS) – which reportedly received many Canadian-transferred detainees – has a particularly poor record in this regard.[139]

In light of this evidence, two NGOs argued in the *Amnesty* cases that the government should be ordered to stop detainee transfers until adequate safeguards were implemented, and that Canada's constitutional bill of rights, the *Charter of Rights and Freedoms*, applies to individuals who were detained by the CF in Afghanistan.[140] These NGOs also contended in a related public interest investigation by the Military Police Complaints Commission (MPCC) that certain Military Police failed to investigate Canada's commanders in Afghanistan for directing the transfer of detainees to Afghan authorities in the face of a known risk of torture, and despite compelling first-hand reports that previous CF detainees were tortured by those authorities.[141]

In the *Amnesty* cases, the court found that "[t]he evidence adduced by the applicants clearly establishes the existence of very real concerns as to the effectiveness of the steps that have been taken thus far to ensure that detainees transferred by the Canadian Forces to the custody of Afghan authorities are not mistreated."[142] However, because transfers had already been ceased temporarily, and it was not known "what safeguards may have been put in place" when they resumed, the court did not order the government to stop such transfers.[143] It also found that detainees held by the CF in Afghanistan do not have *Charter* rights, although they do have rights under the Afghan Constitution and the *jus in bello*.[144] The MPCC, for its part, found the allegations against the Military Police to be unsubstantiated.[145] But it also found there was a lack of continuity of knowledge, and problems with accountability and information sharing within the Military Police that should be improved for future missions.[146]

In the 2010 British *Evans* case, the court held that the moratorium on transfers to the NDS facility in Kabul imposed by UK officials should be maintained; and that transfers to the NDS facilities in Kandahar and Lashkar Gah could continue if existing safeguards were strengthened by the observance of three additional conditions.[147] By contrast, the court in the 2008 *Amnesty* cases *declined* to

---

139 Ibid, at paras. 106–107.

140 *Amnesty*, 2008 FC 336, at paras. 7–12.

141 MPCC's *Final Report* of June 2012, at xi.

142 *Amnesty*, 2008 FC 336, at para. 2.

143 *Amnesty*, 2008 FC 162, at paras. 3–6.

144 *Amnesty*, 2008 FC 336, at para. 2. This decision was upheld on appeal. See *Amnesty International Canada et al v. Attorney General of Canada et al*, 2008 FCA 401.

145 MPCC's *Final Report* of June 2012, at xii–xiii.

146 Ibid.

147 *Evans* at paras. 315–322.

order that the existing temporary ban on transfers be maintained until certain conditions were met; to distinguish adequately between Afghanistan's different detention facilities, and the different alleged human rights records associated with these facilities; or to specify what safeguards had to be implemented before transfers could resume. This variance in the two rulings may reflect the fact that additional evidence about Afghan detainees had become available by 2010. But it also suggests that Canadian judges may defer more to government than UK judges regarding executive decisions and issues of "high-policy" such as war.

As with Britain, the extent to which one concludes that Canadian forces in Afghanistan met their international legal obligations regarding the transfer of detainees will turn mainly on the degree to which one thinks transferees faced a risk of torture or serious mistreatment, and the evidence and threshold one believes is needed to establish this risk. It will also depend on whether one thinks the onus is on critics or the government to demonstrate or disprove this risk, and the efforts one thinks Canada needed to make to guard against it.

One challenge to drawing such conclusions is that the *Amnesty* cases focused more on whether Canada's domestic constitutional bill of rights applied extra-territorially to Canada's transfer of Afghan detainees, rather than the arguably more salient question of whether such transfers complied with the relevant *international* law that the government itself acknowledged applied, such as the *jus in bello* and the Convention Against Torture. This suggests that Canadian courts (and public interest litigants) may still feel, as Brunnée and Toope noted in 2003, a "hesitant embrace" towards applying international law, and are perhaps still inclined to avoid deciding cases on the basis of international law.[148]

Another challenge to assessing whether Canada has met its international legal obligations has been the absence of sufficient publicly available information on Canada's policy and practice regarding Afghan detainees. For instance, in the face of renewed public concern over the detainee issue, the Harper government shut down Parliament in December 2009.[149] A key effect of this prorogation was that it suspended the work of a parliamentary committee that was examining Canada's treatment of Afghan detainees.

Prior to this suspension, Richard Colvin, a respected former senior diplomat with Canada's mission in Afghanistan, had told the committee that all detainees transferred by the CF were likely tortured by Afghan officials, and many of these prisoners were likely innocent.[150] Canada was taking six times as many detainees as Britain, Colvin said, and 20 times as many as the Netherlands. Unlike the British and Dutch, however, Colvin claimed that Canada

---

148 Brunnée and Toope 2003: 3–60.
149 Daniel LeBlanc, "Harper to Shut Down Parliament," *The Globe and Mail*, 30 Dec. 2009.
150 "All Afghan Detainees Likely Tortured: Diplomat," CBC News, 18 Nov. 2009.

did not monitor prisoner conditions; took days, weeks, or months to notify the ICRC; kept poor records; and the CF leadership concealed this behind "walls of secrecy" to prevent scrutiny.[151] If Canada did not want detainees to be tortured, Colvin had told an interagency meeting in Ottawa in March 2007, then they should not be transferred to the NDS.[152]

As early as May 2006, journalist Lawrence Martin writes in *Harperland: The Politics of Control* that Colvin had informed senior military leaders of his findings, and noted that they, in turn, would likely have informed General Rick Hillier.[153] But Colvin was then told that Ottawa did not want to hear his reports: two senior officials from the Department of Foreign Affairs warned him to stop writing memoranda.[154] And throughout 2006, the Harper government denied knowledge of any torture of detainees that were transferred.[155] When the issue came up in Parliament in May that year, Defence Minister Gordon O'Connor mistakenly claimed that it was not a problem because the ICRC would have informed him if there were concerns.[156] What O'Connor did not know or understand at the time was that in order to secure access to vulnerable prisoners, the Red Cross only reports to the detaining authority (Afghanistan), and not to anyone else.[157] Moreover, Colvin said later that the organization could not even get its phone calls taken by the Canadian forces in Kandahar.[158]

In response to Colvin's testimony in 2009, the government could have acknowledged in good faith that mistakes may have been made, and/or that the allegations would be investigated. Alternatively, it could have provided evidence to contextualize or challenge the accuracy of the claims. Instead, however, the government responded by attacking Colvin and his credibility.[159] Defence Minister Peter MacKay – who like Bill Graham is also a lawyer – told Parliament that Colvin may have been deceived, there were "incredible holes" in his story, and that none of the allegations had been proven.[160] Former CDS Rick Hillier,

---

151 The individuals, Colvin said, were picked up "during routine military operations, and on the basis typically not of intelligence but suspicion … We … handed over for torture a lot of innocent people." This "strengthened the insurgency" and caused locals to fear us (Martin 2011: 231).

152 MPCC's *Final Report* of June 2012, at xvii.

153 Martin 2011: 231.

154 Ibid.

155 Ibid: 232.

156 HC Debates, Hansard, 31 May 2006, col. 1768. In fairness to O'Connor, a former general and not a lawyer, the statement seems to have been made in good faith, and he clarified it in March 2007.

157 Graham 2016: 397. See also the testimony by government officials and lawyers, academics, and Amnesty International at the Standing Committee on National Defence, 11 Dec. 2006. It is unclear from this testimony whether O'Connor's misunderstanding was corrected by officials at the time.

158 Martin 2011: 232.

159 "All Afghan Detainees Likely Tortured: Diplomat," CBC News, 18 Nov. 2009.

160 Quoted in Martin 2011: 232.

for his part, said he could not recall ever seeing a report from Colvin, and that it sounded like the diplomat was "howling at the moon."[161]

However, when Hillier's successor, Walter Natynczyk, later revealed that military field notes from 2006 did in fact indicate that Canadian forces knew that transferred detainees could be tortured, MacKay "tried to hold firm," and said the government had never knowingly been complicit in torture or any violation of international law.[162] Moreover, Prime Minister Stephen Harper tried to reframe the debate entirely, arguing that the opposition was disloyal and not supporting Canada's troops.[163]

It is thus perhaps unsurprising that when Colvin agreed in 2009 to cooperate with the MPCC detainee investigation, the government sought to block this cooperation by invoking national security concerns, even though the Commission members had security clearance to hear sensitive information.[164] Moreover, the head of the MPCC at the time, Peter Tinsley, was "cut loose" by the government in the middle of his work, effectively halting public hearings on the matter.[165] On leaving, Tinsley said that "the flow of government documents to his commission had all but ended when Peter Mackay became defence minister," and his departure "would send a chill through the other quasi-judicial bodies whose heads were appointed by the government."[166] More generally, as the MPCC observed in its final report of June 2012, rather than cooperating with the Commission and respecting the intent of Parliament, the government instead caused extensive delays and costly obstacles that were "largely unnecessary and avoidable."[167]

Resonating with Colvin's accusations, another former official, Cory Anderson, claimed in the spring of 2010 that, despite implications to the contrary, Conservative Cabinet members such as MacKay had been briefed about the concerns regarding Afghan detainees.[168] Moreover, one of the many documents withheld by the government from the parliamentary committee examining detainees confirmed that former CDS Rick Hillier and another Canadian military leader, Lieutenant-General Michel Gauthier, received legal advice about the issue in May 2007. This widely distributed memo, from then Judge Advocate General Ken Watkin, warned: "Military commanders who know, or are

---

161 Ibid: 233.

162 Ibid: 235.

163 Ibid.

164 "Government Trying to Muzzle Diplomat: Lawyer," CBC News, 6 Oct. 2009; and Martin 2011: 233.

165 Martin 2011: 233.

166 Quoted in Martin 2011: 233.

167 For a description of these numerous delays and costly obstacles, see the MPCC's *Final Report* of June 2012, at xxx–xxxi and 505–521.

168 "MacKay Knew of Afghan Detainee Concerns: Diplomat," CBC News, 31 March 2010.

criminally negligent in failing to know, that a transferred detainee would be subjected to ... abuse have the obligation to take all necessary and reasonable measures within their power to prevent or repress the commission of such abuse. They may also be subject to criminal liability for failing to submit the matter to competent authorities for investigation and prosecution."[169]

If members of the Harper government were genuinely concerned about Canada's international legal obligations regarding Afghan detainees, and about ensuring that adequate public information was available on the issue, it is unclear why warnings from relevant officials would apparently be ignored; why a parliamentary committee examining detainees should be suspended through the arguably anti-democratic practice of prorogation; or why government lawyers would be instructed to adopt such an obstructive and antagonistic approach to the MPCC's public interest investigation. These unanswered questions leave the impression that other leaders, such as former Liberal Cabinet member Bill Graham, have been more committed to ensuring that Canada is seen as trying to meet its international legal obligations regarding Afghan detainees.

On the other hand, it is also the case that, during the tenure of both the Liberal and Conservative governments, Canada employed safeguards regarding transferred detainees, and changed its transfer practices in response to specific concerns. For instance, like Britain, Canada's approach to monitoring transferred detainees improved over time. This is suggested by the earlier observation that, when the second detainee arrangement was signed in 2007, it aimed to provide Canadian officials and the AIHRC with unrestricted and private access to Canadian-transferred detainees. For example, from May 2007, when Canada's monitoring of detainees began, to February 2013, Canadian officials – most of whom were from the Department of Foreign Affairs – conducted more than 430 visits to detention facilities in Kandahar, Kabul, and Parwan (a province north of Kabul).[170] These visits were part of a larger effort by Canada and other ISAF countries to help build Afghanistan's security, justice and corrections sectors.[171]

Canada also responded to specific concerns by stopping detainee transfers for certain periods of time and investigating allegations of abuse. For example, following the report by the *Globe and Mail* in April 2007 that individuals transferred by the CF had been abused by Afghan authorities, transfers were temporarily halted.[172] Once the second detainee agreement was negotiated, however,

---

169 Cited in Richard J. Brennan, "Military Told to Heed Abuse Claims," *Toronto Star*, 25 February 2010.
170 Government of Canada, "Canadian Forces Release Statistics on Afghanistan Detainees," Feb. 2013. It is not clear how many of the 430 visits by Canadian officials were conducted in private.
171 Ibid.
172 MPCC's *Final Report* of June 2012, at xiv.

and the new monitoring regime was established, the relevant Canadian military leaders at the time – Lieutenant-General Michel Gauthier and Major-General Tim Grant – decided that transfers could resume on 19 May. This restructuring of the transfer regime, Grant told the MPCC, was led by himself, his deputy, and people from Foreign Affairs.[173] "The legal test by which ... Grant worked," the MPCC noted, "when deciding to transfer detainees, was that a transfer could only occur where there were not substantial grounds for believing there was a real risk the detainee would face subsequent abuse or mistreatment. In this regard, he had a lawyer providing him advice."[174]

Site visits by Canada between May 2007 and November 2007 revealed several allegations of mistreatment and torture of Canadian-transferred detainees.[175] Officials from Foreign Affairs reportedly investigated some of these allegations.[176] During one visit, on 5 November, to an NDS facility in Kandahar City, a detainee revealed a large bruise on his back, and said he had been beaten with electrical wires and a rubber hose.[177] These items were then found in the interview room.[178] "It was as a consequence of the receipt of this complaint," the court noted in the *Amnesty* cases, that a "decision was made by the Deputy Commander of Task Force Afghanistan to suspend further detainee transfers until such time as the [CF] was satisfied it could do so in accordance with its international legal obligations."[179] Transfers were not resumed, the MPCC noted, "until late February/early March 2008, following the implementation of additional measures, including a significant increase in frequency of visits, an RCMP-led training program for NDS officers, [the] purchase of video cameras for NDS interviews, and evidence that one of the persons responsible for the November 5, 2007 torture allegation was relieved of his duties."[180] Detainee transfers were temporarily stopped again on three occasions in 2009.[181]

In July 2011, NATO's southern command in Afghanistan released a broad directive that ordered all units to stop transferring detainees to the NDS and various Afghan police forces.[182] This directive pre-empted a particularly critical UN report, released publicly in October 2011, which said prisoners handed

---

173 MPCC's *Final Report* of June 2012, at xx.

174 Ibid, at xxi.

175 Ibid, at xiv.

176 Ibid, at xxii.

177 *Amnesty*, 2008 FC 162, at paras. 95–98.

178 Ibid, at para. 97.

179 Ibid, at para. 101.

180 MPCC's *Final Report* of June 2012, at xxii.

181 Government of Canada, "Canadian Forces Release Statistics on Afghanistan Detainees," Feb. 2013.

182 Murray Brewster, "NATO Order Last Year Ended Canadian Transfer of Taliban Prisoners to Afghans," The Canadian Press, 11 June 2012.

over by international forces were subjected to "systematic" torture by Afghan interrogators.[183] The report portrayed prisoner abuse by Afghan officials on a scale far wider than previously thought.[184] Consistent with NATO's order, General Walt Natynczyk, Canada's Chief of the Defence Staff, wrote in a briefing note to Defence Minister Peter MacKay on 15 July 2011 that he "deemed it was appropriate [for] Canadian-captured detainees to be redirected to another facility."[185] The CF quietly stopped transferring detainees that month, and diplomats began negotiations to send prisoners to a US detention facility in Parwan.[186]

These negotiations eventually culminated in Canada signing a third detainee transfer arrangement with the US in November 2011.[187] Although Canada's combat mission in Kandahar ended in mid-2011, it was thought that such an agreement "made sense" in the unlikely event that members of Canada's training mission captured detainees in Kabul.[188] Operating alongside the first and second arrangements, the third agreement allowed Canadian officials to monitor detention facilities, conduct interviews, and assess the conditions under which individuals were detained and treated.[189]

The Harper government did not publicly acknowledge the change in Canada's transfer policy until almost six months after detainee handovers were stopped.[190] Explaining this change, the Department of Defence said in June 2012 that prisoner transfers were halted just before the NATO directive was issued. "In early July 2011," a spokesperson noted, "information concerning the possible mistreatment of Afghan detainees, not Canadian-transferred detainees, raised the Canadian chain of command's concern," and "[w]e ceased transfers as a result."[191]

Commenting on this stoppage, Paul Champ, a lawyer representing the NGOs in the *Amnesty* cases, says that the "Harper government fought us in court and in commissions for five years throughout the duration of [Canada's combat] mission to maintain the right to continue transfers to Afghan authorities and to argue that there was not a risk of torture."[192] However, he says, the fact that

---

183 UN Assistance Mission in Afghanistan, *Treatment of ConflictRelated Detainees in Afghan Custody*, Oct. 2011.

184 Joshua Partlow and Sayed Salahuddin, "Afghan Detainees Tortured in Prison, U.N. Says," *Washington Post*, 10 Oct. 2011.

185 Brewster, 11 June 2012.

186 Ibid. The facility in Parwan is now operated by Afghanistan.

187 2011 Detainee Arrangement.

188 Government of Canada, "Canadian Forces Release Statistics on Afghanistan Detainees," Feb. 2013.

189 Ibid.

190 Brewster, 11 June 2012.

191 Ibid.

192 Ibid.

NATO ordered transfers to be stopped "affirms everything we've been saying all along. It contradicts what Canada had been saying all along about the risk of torture."[193] Perhaps surprisingly, Champ thinks it may have been the US, which was sceptical of the transfer policies of Canada, Britain, and the Netherlands, which pushed NATO to have one position on detainees.

In conclusion, the above section indicates that international law has had a regulative influence on Canada's political and military practice regarding the Afghanistan Conflict. First, as we saw, when the Chrétien government decided that Canada would lead Task Force 151 as part of OEF, its understanding of the legal circumstances at issue helped constrain the nature and scope of the force deployed with this naval group. Second, Canada's policy and conduct regarding Afghan detainees has been governed and controlled in part by its interpretation of its obligations under the Geneva Convention on POWs. However, these perceived obligations appear to have had a stronger impact on members of the Liberal governments of Jean Chrétien and Paul Martin than on those of the Conservative government of Stephen Harper.

3. International Law Helped Permit and Legitimate Canada's Conduct

Canada's military actions in Afghanistan also indicate that, when states use force, international law helps permit and legitimate certain political and military practices that otherwise might not be permitted. As noted in the previous chapter, in response to the terrorist events of 9/11, the US and its allies, including Canada, attacked, invaded, and occupied the sovereign state of Afghanistan, which had not technically attacked them. Again, this response was significantly broader than prior US reactions to earlier terrorist attacks. The broad military response to 9/11 was also strategically different than the reaction some critics say the US and its allies should have focused on, such as addressing the threat posed by al-Qaeda through increased intelligence and law-enforcement activity, and political negotiations with the Taliban.

As will be seen below, international legal considerations were relevant to justifying and explaining Canada's role in the extensive military reaction to 9/11 to the international community and the Canadian public. Further, leaders received legal advice about this role, and this advice helped define and shape the government's account of its use of force in Afghanistan.

For example, on 24 October 2001, Canada sent a letter to the president of the UN Security Council reporting that, further to NATO's invocation of Article 5 of the Alliance treaty, it would be joining with the US in deploying military forces

---

193 Ibid.

into Afghanistan in the exercise of its inherent right of self-defence.[194] Consistent with this view, Defence Minister Art Eggleton stated in a key address to Parliament on 19 November of that same year:

> Six weeks ago, I announced the first of our contributions to the military effort aimed at eliminating the continuing terrorist threat posed by the Al Qa'ida organization, its supporters and followers, including the Taliban. In doing so Canada is acting within, and with the support of, the UN Charter. Article 51 of the Charter preserves the inherent right of individual and collective self-defence. Security Council Resolutions 1368 and 1373 have expressly reaffirmed this right in the context of the tragic events of September 11th. Canada has informed the Security Council that our international military response to terrorism is to collectively exercise the right of self-defence with our allies against the Taliban and Al Qa'ida.[195]

In this statement, note that, like his British counterparts, Eggleton focused on the doctrine of self-defence and did not report that Canada was using force in Afghanistan under the authority of the Security Council.[196] Again, advancing the latter claim would arguably have been possible considering that, as noted in part by Eggleton above, following 9/11 the Council passed Resolutions 1368 and 1373, which condemned the terrorist attacks and regarded them as a threat to international peace and security; recognized the inherent right of individual or collective self-defence in accordance with the Charter; and reaffirmed the need to combat by all means, in accordance with the Charter, threats to international peace and security caused by terrorist acts.[197] Significantly, however, recall that after 9/11, the US did not focus on these resolutions or seek explicit authorization from the Security Council, and instead justified its military actions in Afghanistan as self-defence against a terrorist attack.

As with Britain, the extent to which this US position impacted Canada's justification is unknown. One might reasonably assume American influence in this regard. However, there is limited available evidence that Canadian decision-makers were aware of the US position or its implications for Canada's stance. For instance, no leader or adviser interviewed for this study mentioned the US

---

194 See Security Council doc. S/2001/1005, cited in *Amnesty*, 2008 FC 336, at para. 25.

195 See Department of National Defence, "MND Statement in the House of Commons," Ottawa, 19 Nov. 2001.

196 This point is ignored by some scholars, who suggest instead that Canada was using force in Afghanistan in 2001 under the authority of the UN Security Council (Hendin 2007: 159, and Bratt 2011).

197 See UNSC Resolution 1368 (12 Sept. 2001), [UN Doc. S/RES/1368], *Threats to International Peace and Security Caused by Terrorist Acts*; and UNSC Resolution 1373 (28 Sept. 2001), [UN Doc. S/RES/1373], *ibid.*

position or its impact on Canada's approach.[198] However, there is evidence that the legal context of al-Qaeda's attack and Canada's subsequent military response were analysed and discussed, that this analysis was provided to leaders, and that it helped define and shape Canada's account of its use of force in Afghanistan.

For instance, reflecting on the role played by Jerry Pitzul, the JAG, in the fall of 2001, then CDS Ray Henault noted:

> Jerry was in my office probably every other day, if not every day, talking about Afghanistan, and talking about the legal context of what we were doing and how we were doing it. So, this whole question of international law, and the law of self-def[ence] … the laws of armed conflict, the context of collective self-defence, all of those kinds of things were discussed multiple times. And that was all very much the basis for what we were doing.[199]

As a result, Henault emphasized:

> Any decision that I took in terms of force deployment or the application of force, rules of engagement, any of those kinds of things were reviewed, endorsed and recommended to me by the lawyers. Nothing was done without insuring, before we took action, that we were in compliance with law, in all its forms. So, it was a really important part of our overall make-up.[200]

Similarly, reflecting on the Afghan Conflict in his memoirs, Bill Graham notes, "Whenever Canadian Forces deploy, legal officers are present to advise them that their use of force must be proportional to the military objective so that their actions fit within the constraints of international law. The rule of law gives legitimacy to our operations in the field."[201] Significantly, Henault adds that, consistent with the JAG's statutory mandate to advise both the Armed Forces and the Defence Department, Pitzul gave the same kinds of advisory comments to Henault and Defence Minister Eggleton, and that Pitzul was often in Eggleton's office.[202]

---

198 Interview with Eugene Lang, Ottawa, 8 Sept. 2011; interview with Bill Graham, Toronto, 12 Sept. 2011; phone interview with Paul Martin, 16 Sept. 2011; interview with Art Eggleton, Toronto, 19 Sept. 2011; interview with John McCallum, Ottawa, 20 Sept. 2011; and interview with Ray Henault, London, 28 Nov. 2011.

199 Interview with Ray Henault, London, 28 Nov. 2011.

200 Ibid.

201 Graham 2016: 392.

202 Interview with Ray Henault, London, 28 Nov. 2011. As Henault notes, in accordance with Canada's *National Defence Act*, the JAG is the legal adviser to the Armed Forces and the Department of National Defence (and, thus, to the defence minister).

There are two examples that suggest Pitzul's legal advice helped shape Canada's account of its use of force in Afghanistan. The first is that, contrary to the way some US and UK leaders described 9/11, Canada's military response to 9/11 was portrayed not as a "war" but as a "campaign" against terrorism. The second example is Canada's stated commitment to abide by the international law of armed conflict – the *jus in bello* – in Afghanistan.

Regarding the first example, during the fall of 2001, Henault recalls that Pitzul came to speak with him on more than one occasion, saying, "Remember General, this is not a war, this is a *campaign* against terrorism" [emphasis in original].[203] As a result, Henault says, "we used to have to be very careful how we actually spelled that out, and that [distinction] was something that we made very forcefully understood by people."[204]

To understand these comments, recall that, following 9/11, US President George W. Bush and UK Prime Minister Tony Blair labeled al-Qaeda's attack as an act of war, and described the military response in Afghanistan as part of a broader "War on Terror." By contrast, Henault's reflections indicate that Canada's JAG did not believe that "war" was the most legally appropriate term to describe Canada's use of force in Afghanistan or the broader US-led response to terrorism more generally. And, importantly, this view was reflected in Canada's official statements at the time. For instance, speaking at a key press conference in October 2001,[205] Eggleton did not use the word "war" and instead employed the term "campaign" to describe the US-led response to 9/11, and Canada's military contribution to this response.[206]

Regarding the second example, in the fall of 2001, Henault recalls that Pitzul made it very clear that Canada's military response to 9/11 "was all in accordance with international law as we understood it" and that, notwithstanding the fact that this was not a war but a campaign against terrorism, "the laws of armed combat would likely be applied when we did go into operations [in Afghanistan]."[207] Consistent with this legal opinion, in his address to Parliament on 19 November 2001, noted earlier, Eggleton stated that the actions of Canadian Forces operating in Afghanistan "will fully accord with the laws of Armed Conflict and Canadian Rules of Engagement."[208]

---

203 Interview with Ray Henault, London, 28 Nov. 2011.

204 Ibid.

205 This is the press conference where, as noted earlier in the text above, Eggleton announced that Canada would be contributing special forces as well as naval and air assets to the US-led military response to 9/11.

206 In a press statement consisting of 816 words, Eggleton used the term "campaign" seven different times. See "Speaking Notes" for Press conference, Ottawa, 8 Oct. 2001.

207 Interview with Ray Henault, London, 28 Nov. 2011.

208 See Department of National Defence, "MND Statement in the House of Commons," Ottawa, 19 Nov. 2001.

4. International Law Helped Structure the Development of New Rules and Legitimate Practice

Finally, Canada's participation in the Afghan Conflict suggests that international law helps structure the process by which agents seek to develop and promote new legal rules and legitimate practice for states and other international actors. An important example of this phenomenon is Canada's support for NATO's declaration of Article 5 in response to the 9/11 attacks, and the related perceived change in the customary international law on self-defence.

We saw earlier that, following 9/11, David Wright, Canada's ambassador to NATO, chaired the NAC meeting where the likely applicability of Article 5 of the NATO treaty was first formally discussed. Moreover, Wright took a lead in arguing for Article 5 to be invoked. Following NATO's declaration of this provision, Canadian leaders and diplomats explained in different public forums that Canada was using force in Afghanistan under the right to self-defence recognized in Article 51 of the UN Charter. Again, these arguments are noteworthy from an international legal perspective because the concept of "armed attack" is not defined in Article 5 of the NATO treaty or Article 51 of the Charter, and the provisions do not explicitly say whether the right of self-defence applies only to an armed attack by a state, or to armed attacks by states *and* non-state actors.

Following 9/11, the US legal argument essentially suggested that, if a sufficient nexus exists between a non-state terrorist group and State A, an attack by the terrorist group on State B could constitute an armed attack for purposes of Article 51 of the Charter and/or the customary international law on self-defence, and State B could respond under that law. Further, while variations of this position had been advanced in the past, they had not been accepted by the majority of states. Following 9/11, however, most states appear to have accepted – or at least not publicly criticized – the US argument. Consequently, we saw earlier, Western legal scholars generally believe that customary law changed accordingly.

In hindsight, it may seem that the nature, scale, and target of the 9/11 attacks made the applicability of Article 5 of the NATO treaty logical and inevitable. However, it is important to remember that this provision was drafted primarily in fear of a land invasion by the USSR against Europe during the Cold War, and not a terrorist attack by non-state actors against the US in 2001. The fact that Article 5 could be interpreted and applied to respond to the latter event, and that most states appear to have accepted that the customary law on self-defence changed more generally, offers evidence in support of the observation that, when states use force, international law helps structure the process by which new legal rules and legitimate practice are developed and promoted.

The Understanding of International Law in Canada's Use of Force in Afghanistan

While the foregoing analysis suggests that international law helped influence Canada's involvement in the Afghanistan Conflict, it is less clear the extent to which Canadian leaders understood this law as a distinct and binding set of legal rules, and whether the legal status of these rules impacted their decision-making. As we will see, leaders have tended to view Canada's obligations under the NATO treaty and the UN Charter more in political and moral, rather than expressly legal, terms.

By contrast, some leaders, such as Bill Graham and former CDS Ray Henault, understood the rules of the Geneva Convention on POWs in binding terms. However, Canada's criticized approach to Afghan detainees indicates that the legal status of these rules has perhaps had an uneven impact on the thinking and decisions of other policymakers. It also suggests that state and non-state views of what the prohibition on transferring to possible torture requires in practice are less settled than related shared understandings of other fundamental prisoner protections in international law and armed conflict.

1. Canada's Understanding of the NATO Treaty and UN Charter

When deciding whether and how to participate in the Afghanistan Conflict, some key leaders may have interpreted Canada's obligations under the NATO treaty and UN Charter more in political and moral, rather than distinctly legal, terms. For instance, on the one hand, Paul Martin observes in his memoirs that

> September 11 was simply an attack on our way of life … When the Americans decided to respond to the attack from al-Qaeda with a mission to root out its bases in Afghanistan, and its basis of support among the Taliban, their response was understandable and reasonable. As members of NATO, which is after all a self-defence pact, we had a *moral if not a legal duty* to support them [emphasis added]. We also had self-interest in doing so.[209]

On the other hand, when asked to reflect on the extent to which Canada's NATO's obligations mattered to its policy on Afghanistan, Martin noted: "Well they clearly mattered. I mean, we had a treaty commitment. And … treaty commitments are commitments that you are *honour bound* to live up to" [emphasis added].[210]

---

209 Martin 2009: 390–391.
210 Phone interview with Paul Martin, 16 Sept. 2011.

Like Martin's comments, Bill Graham's reflections also provide mixed insight into whether leaders saw Canada's NATO treaty obligations as legally binding at the time. For instance, Graham has written that after NATO decided on 4 October 2001 to invoke Article 5 of the NATO treaty for the first time, this "*bound* Canada to lend a hand to American-led efforts to hunt down the al-Qaeda terrorists behind the 9/11 attacks,"[211] and Canada was "*obligated* to support" these efforts, including the overthrow of the Taliban regime that allowed al-Qaeda to use Afghanistan as a base of operations [emphasis added].[212] On the other hand, responding to the issue of how leaders interpreted Canada's commitments under Article 5 of the NATO treaty following 9/11, Graham stated in an interview: "I don't know the answer to that question. I wasn't in Cabinet [yet] … I don't know whether Mr. Chrétien saw it as a legal obligation, or a political commitment. I imagine that politics would have trumped the legal, to be quite frank with you."[213]

Like this latter comment, John McCallum's reflections also suggest that leaders may have viewed Canada's commitments to the United Nations and the UN Charter more in non-legal terms. For instance, responding to the question of how leaders understood these commitments at the time of his tenure as defence minister, and why the legitimacy of UN-approval matters to Canada when it uses force, McCallum explains:

> I think it reflects tradition within the Liberal party, certainly since Lester Pearson, who was a major player within the United Nations. It is a view, perhaps starting with Pearson, within the Liberal party that war is a very serious matter. And you can't just have countries off on their own [deciding unilaterally to use force]. There's an international governance mechanism which is what we have bought into with the United Nations. And that is to legitimate war, you should have the agreement of the United Nations. I guess it's almost like a gospel. I'm not even sure that people in the Liberal party ask themselves very often why [UN authorization is needed to use force]. But I think it is a long and strong tradition, at least within our party.[214]

In sum, McCallum's comments indicate that, during the Afghanistan Conflict, some leaders saw Canada's commitments to the United Nations and the UN Charter as a reflection of historical or political tradition within the Liberal party of Canada.

---

211 Graham 2016: 224.
212 Graham 2015: 51.
213 Interview with Bill Graham, Toronto, 12 Sept. 2011.
214 Interview with John McCallum, Ottawa, 20 Sept. 2011.

2. Canada's Interpretation of the Geneva Convention on POWs

After Bill Graham became concerned about the Canadian Forces' practice of transferring detainees to US and Afghan authorities, he helped initiate Canada's first detainee arrangement with Afghanistan in 2005. Again, this arrangement aimed to ensure that transferred persons are treated "in accordance with the standards set out in the Third Geneva Convention [on POWs]." Consistent with other acknowledgments of Canada's international legal obligations regarding detainees, noted earlier in the discussion of the *Amnesty* cases and MPCC investigation, paragraph ten of the first detainee arrangement states that "*[r]ecognizing their obligations pursuant to international law* to assure that detainees continue to receive humane treatment and protections to the standards set out in the Third Geneva Convention, the Participants, upon transferring a detainee, will notify the [ICRC]" [emphasis added].[215] Reflecting this recognition, Graham said the reason he argued strenuously for a coherent detainee strategy was because he saw the need to justify what Canada was doing in Afghanistan "on the highest grounds of behaviour," and "consistent with international legal standards."

Ray Henault's views on this issue resonate with Graham's actions and comments. For instance, when asked how the Geneva Conventions were interpreted during his tenure as CDS, Henault said:

> It seems to me that, over time, it became very clear to people that the laws of armed combat were inviolate, the Geneva Conventions were inviolate … The fact that the rules of engagement needed to be applied with your best judgment [did not change the fact that] by the same token, if you violated the rules of engagement, you needed to know that you may have to suffer the consequences of that.[216]

Notwithstanding Graham and Henault's reflections, however, we also saw critics argue that the formal detainee arrangements between Canada and Afghanistan did not provide adequate substantive or procedural safeguards to ensure that individuals transferred to Afghan authorities were not exposed to a substantial risk of torture. Moreover, it was suggested, no amount of post-transfer monitoring would have sufficed to protect detainees. This view, critics said, was ultimately proven correct by NATO's order in July 2011 that units stop transferring detainees to certain Afghan authorities. Prior to this order, Canadian transferees and relevant reports had documented numerous cases of torture

---

215 2005 Detainee Arrangement.
216 Interview with Ray Henault, London, 28 Nov. 2011.

and mistreatment of Afghan prisoners, and alleged that the NDS has a particularly poor record in this regard.

Members of the Harper government, we saw, were apparently warned of these risks by relevant officials. Moreover, rather than support the work of the parliamentary committee on detainees or cooperate with the MPCC investigation on the issue, this government instead suspended the work of the committee through prorogation and caused extensive delays and costly obstacles to the work of the MPCC. Depending on the efforts one thinks Canada must take to protect against the risk that transferees may be tortured, these details leave open the possibility that the legal status of the Geneva Convention on POWs has had an uneven impact on the thinking and decisions of some policymakers. Assessing this possibility will likely have to wait until more evidence becomes publicly available.

For now, though, it must also be acknowledged that during the tenure of both the Liberal and Conservative governments, Canada employed safeguards regarding transferred detainees, and changed its transfer practices in response to specific concerns. As we saw, Canada's approach to monitoring transferred detainees improved over time, and some of the impetus for these changes reportedly came from military commanders in Afghanistan and Foreign Affairs officials. In addition, Canada also responded to specific concerns by stopping detainee transfers for certain periods of time and investigating allegations of abuse. It is equally possible that these altered practices have been shaped in part by a concern for Canada's perceived obligations under the Geneva Convention on POWs, and that the legal status of these obligations has influenced the thinking and decisions of those individuals involved in bringing about these altered practices.

Key Findings

The aspects of Canada's participation in the Afghan war assessed in this chapter support the argument that, when states use force, international law helps define and shape their possible course of action, and the justifications that can be advanced for their behaviour. More specifically, these aspects help illustrate the four roles that I theorize international law can play in such situations.

First, as was the case with Louis St. Laurent, Lester Pearson, and Brooke Claxton during the Korean War, we saw that in the debate and decisions behind the three phases of Canada's military actions in Afghanistan, international law has helped constitute the identities of key leaders, and shaped the way in which Canada's interests were interpreted and pursued. Regarding the first phase, Canada's perceived obligations under the NATO treaty and its rights under the UN Charter animated the thinking and values of Defence Minister Art Eggleton, Prime Minister Jean Chrétien, CDS Ray Henault, and

Foreign Minister Bill Graham. Such commitments meant that, following 9/11, these leaders thought Canada was obligated to support the US and NATO in the global fight against terrorism, and to participate militarily in this fight. An unstated assumption behind this view is that Canada is the kind of state that honours its prior international commitments and takes action in this regard when necessary.

Moreover, in the debate and decisions behind phase two, Canada's perceived commitments to the UN and NATO continued to help constitute the identities of leaders at the time. While the dominant view is that the government decided in favour of the ISAF operation mainly because it allowed Canada to support the US in its "War on Terror" without having to support its controversial war in Iraq, in fact political leaders appear to have been motivated more by a belief that the UN-authorized ISAF mission was legitimate and more consistent with Canada's identity as a peacekeeper, and that the integrity of NATO was at stake. Finally, we saw that during the initial decisions behind phase three, Canada's perceived commitments to NATO helped constitute the outlook of Prime Minister Paul Martin, and shaped the way in which he interpreted and pursued the country's national interests.

Second, in addition to its constitutive effect, international law also had a regulative influence on Canada's political and military practice regarding the Afghanistan Conflict. Two examples demonstrated this influence. First, when the Chrétien government decided that Canada would lead naval Task Force 151 as part of Operation Enduring Freedom, we saw that its understanding of the legal circumstances at issue helped constrain the nature and scope of the force deployed with this group. Second, Canada's policy and conduct regarding Afghan detainees has been governed and controlled in part by its interpretation of its obligations under the Geneva Convention on POWs. However, these perceived obligations appear to have had a stronger impact on members of the Liberal governments of Jean Chrétien and Paul Martin than on those of the Conservative government of Stephen Harper.

Third, Canada's military actions in Afghanistan also indicate that international law helps permit and legitimate certain conduct that otherwise might not be permitted. As we saw, in response to the terrorist events of 9/11, the US and its allies, including Canada, attacked, invaded, and occupied a sovereign state that had not technically attacked them. This response was significantly broader than prior US reactions to earlier terrorist attacks, and strategically different than the reaction some critics say the US and its allies should have employed. As we saw, international legal considerations were relevant to justifying and explaining Canada's role in the extensive military reaction to 9/11 to the international community and the Canadian public. Furthermore, leaders received legal advice about this role, and this advice helped define and shape the government's account of its use of force in Afghanistan.

Finally, Canada's participation in the Afghanistan Conflict suggests that, when states use force, international law helps structure the process by which agents seek to develop and promote new legal rules and legitimate practice for states and other international actors. An important example of this phenomenon, we saw, was Canada's support for NATO's declaration of Article 5 in response to the 9/11 attacks, and the related perceived change in the customary international law on self-defence.

Although the above suggests that international law helped influence Canada's involvement in the Afghan war, it is less clear the extent to which Canadian leaders understood this law as a distinct and binding set of legal rules, and whether the legal status of these rules impacted their decision-making. On the one hand, we saw that leaders recognized that the use of military force in Afghanistan and the treatment of captured enemy individuals were in part legal issues, in that they were governed by pre-existing rules in the UN Charter, NATO treaty, and Geneva Conventions. Moreover, it appears that leaders discussed the extent to which Canada was legally obligated to consider these rules when deciding whether and how to use force in Afghanistan, and what policy and practices to adopt regarding Afghan detainees.

Further, Canada's practice of transferring detainees – even though some of these individuals were reportedly known to have killed Canadian soldiers – indicates that some leaders or officials may have seen the need to apply relevant *jus in bello* rules reciprocally and equally. Finally, former CDS Ray Henault recognized that violating these rules could lead to "consequences," and Defence Minister Art Eggleton and Foreign Minister Bill Graham saw that Canada's actions would require legal justification at the domestic and international level. The foregoing details resonate with many of the relevant observable implications posited in chapter two, and suggest that a number of key Canadian leaders and advisers felt bound in part by international law.

On the other hand, we also saw that some key leaders have tended to interpret Canada's obligations under the NATO treaty and the UN Charter more in political and moral, rather than expressly legal, terms. By contrast, the rules of the Geneva Convention on POWs have been seen in binding terms. However, Canada's criticized approach to Afghan detainees suggests that the legal status of these rules has perhaps had an uneven impact on the thinking and decisions of some policymakers.

8 Conclusion

Summary of Findings

This book examined important aspects of Britain and Canada's participation in the Korean War of 1950–53 and the Afghanistan Conflict of 2001–14 to better understand how international law influenced this participation, and whether key leaders and officials understood this law as binding and distinct. It drew on constructivist International Relations (IR) theory and "interactional" International Law (IL) theory, and employed a method of historical reconstruction and process tracing. I argued that, contrary to what realist and rationalist IR views might predict, international law helped define and shape each state's possible course of action in the wars, and the justifications that could be made for their behaviour. More specifically, Britain and Canada's involvement in the conflicts suggests that international law can play four main roles when states use force: (1) it helps constitute the identities of actors; (2) it helps regulate their conduct; (3) it permits and legitimates certain actions; and (4) it helps structure the development of new legal rules and legitimate practice.

First, both Britain and Canada decided to support the Security Council resolutions on the Korean crisis and to contribute significant naval, air, and ground forces to the UN mission in Korea, even though political and military leaders thought the country was not strategically important. These decisions suggest that international law can help constitute a state's identity and be used to reorient its political and military objectives. As we saw, UK Prime Minister Clement Attlee, and Canadian Prime Minister Louis St. Laurent, Foreign Minister Lester Pearson, and Defence Minister Brooke Claxton all felt a strong sense of obligation to the United Nations and the conflict in Korea. This perception of obligation, moreover, was partly based on and affected by Britain and Canada's formal membership in the UN, as well as these leaders' belief in the principles of the UN Charter and the idea of collective security. While other leaders, such as the UK Defence Chiefs and former Canadian Prime

Minister W.L. Mackenzie King, did not feel the same sense of responsibility regarding the UN and the Korean crisis, Attlee, St. Laurent, Pearson, and Claxton sought to reorient such thinking and explain their governments' respective actions to the public by reaffirming the importance of responding to aggression, making the newly created world organization effective, and upholding the rule of law in world affairs.

Like Attlee during the Korean War, we also saw that UK Prime Minister Tony Blair felt a sense of obligation towards the conflict in Afghanistan following the events of 9/11. Unlike with Attlee, however, this perception of obligation appears to have been shaped less by Britain's formal membership in the UN and a belief in the international rule of law, and more by Blair's ethical views that mass terrorism must be addressed and that foreign intervention in Afghanistan was needed to do so. More generally, though, during the three phases of Britain's military participation in the Afghanistan Conflict, the UK's perceived commitments to the UN and NATO helped constitute the identities of some leaders and officials, and helped shape the way in which Britain's interests were interpreted and pursued. Further, as the Afghan war became more challenging and US military policy in the region became more controversial, these perceived commitments acted as a site for a "communicative" struggle over Britain's legitimate identity and rightful behaviour with respect to these developments.

Similarly, in the debates and decisions behind the three phases of Canada's military actions in Afghanistan, international law helped constitute the identities of key leaders, and shaped the way in which Canada's interests were interpreted and pursued. Regarding the first phase, Canada's perceived obligations under the NATO treaty and its rights under the UN Charter animated the thinking and values of Defence Minister Art Eggleton, Prime Minister Jean Chrétien, Chief of the Defence Staff Ray Henault, and Foreign Minister Bill Graham. Such commitments meant that, following 9/11, these leaders thought Canada was obligated to support the US and NATO in the global fight against terrorism and to participate militarily in this fight. An unstated assumption behind this view is that Canada is the kind of state that honours its prior international commitments, and takes action in this regard when necessary. Moreover, in the debates and decisions behind phase two, Canada's perceived commitments to the UN and NATO continued to help constitute the identities of leaders at the time. Although the dominant view is that the government decided in favour of the ISAF operation mainly because it allowed Canada to support the US in its "War on Terror" without having to support its controversial war in Iraq, this study found that political leaders were motivated more by a belief that the UN-authorized ISAF mission was legitimate and more consistent with Canada's identity as a peacekeeper, and that the integrity of NATO was at stake. Finally, during the initial decisions behind phase three, Canada's perceived commitments to NATO helped constitute the outlook of Prime Minister Paul Martin, and shaped the way in which he interpreted and pursued the country's national interests.

Britain and Canada's involvement in the Korean War and the Afghanistan Conflict also suggests that international law can have a regulative impact when states use force. We saw two examples of this impact during the Korean War. First, Britain and Canada's non-participation in the US naval blockade of Taiwan was shaped in part by their understanding of the scope of the Security Council's resolutions on the Korean crisis, and the "special legal position" that Britain was in regarding Taiwan and China. Second, Britain and Canada used the Council resolutions and other related international legal instruments to help constrain America's response to the crisis. As we saw, in the discussions leading up to the Council resolutions, both states sought to influence the US negotiating position and shape the outcome of the talks, and their interpretation of the international legal factors at issue played a role in this regard. Britain and Canada also used their understanding of the Council resolutions, as well as other related instruments such as the Cairo Declaration of 1943, to help constrain America's behaviour with respect to Taiwan and China.

We saw two further examples of the regulative role of international law during the Afghanistan Conflict. First, when the Chrétien government decided in 2003 that Canada would lead naval Task Force 151 as part of Operation Enduring Freedom, its understanding of the legal circumstances at issue helped constrain the nature and scope of the force deployed with this group. Second, Britain and Canada's policy and conduct regarding Afghan detainees have been governed and controlled in part by their interpretation of: Security Council Resolution 1386, which created ISAF; relevant basic principles of international human rights law; and their obligations under the Geneva Convention on Prisoners of War. These interpretations, furthermore, have had a significant effect even though other material factors – such as Britain and Canada's interest in gathering intelligence, preventing attacks, and cooperating with Afghan security and intelligence agencies – have arguably conflicted with some of their perceived requirements.

When Britain and Canada responded to the Korean crisis and the 9/11 attacks, international law also helped permit and legitimate certain political and military practices that otherwise might not have been allowed. We saw two examples of this phenomenon during the Korean War. First, Britain and Canada intervened militarily in what was in many ways an ideologically divisive and extremely violent *civil* war, and justified this publicly and privately with reference to the Security Council resolutions on the crisis and the UN Charter's provisions on self-defence and collective security. Second, Britain and, to a lesser extent, Canada ultimately supported the US decision to cross the 38th parallel in Korea in October 1950. Moreover, Britain helped draft the General

Assembly resolution that aimed to provide UN support for this policy of roll-back, and Canada voted for this resolution.

Similarly, in response to the terrorist events of 9/11, the US and its allies, including Britain and Canada, attacked, invaded, and occupied the sovereign state of Afghanistan, which had not technically attacked them. This response was significantly broader than prior US reactions to earlier terrorist attacks, and strategically different than the reaction some critics say the US and its allies should have employed. As we saw, international legal considerations were relevant to justifying and explaining Britain and Canada's role in this exten-sive military reaction to 9/11 to members of the public and the international community.

Finally, Britain and Canada's participation in the Korean War and the Afghanistan Conflict indicates that, when states use force, international law helps structure the process by which agents seek to develop and promote new legal rules and legitimate practice for states and other international actors. An important example of this role, we saw, was the Security Council's novel response to North Korea's attack, and the efforts of UK and Canadian leaders to justify and study this response, and to create new collective security law. Simi-larly, following 9/11, leaders and officials argued that Britain and Canada were using force in Afghanistan under the doctrine of self-defence, and most states appear to have accepted that the customary law on this issue changed. Britain also stressed the importance of the Security Council passing Resolution 1373 in September 2001, which required states to adopt new domestic measures to address international terrorism.

Regarding this book's second hypothesis, we saw that contrary to what IL scholars might predict, the discourse and actions of British and Canadian lead-ers and officials during the Korean War and the Afghanistan Conflict offer mixed support for the idea that policymakers understand international law as a binding and distinct set of legal rules, and the legal status of these rules impacts their decision-making. During the Korean War, British and Canadian leaders recognized that the use of military force in Korea and the treatment of enemy POWs were in part legal issues, in that they were governed by pre-existing rules in the UN Charter and the Geneva Conventions. Moreover, leaders discussed the extent to which Britain and Canada were legally obligated to consider these rules when deciding whether and how to use force in Korea, and what policy to adopt regarding the repatriation of enemy POWs. Finally, leaders recognized that Britain and Canada's involvement in the US-led intervention was subject to international legal critique, and required legal justification at the domestic and international level.

Similarly, during the Afghanistan Conflict, key UK leaders and advisers viewed Britain's obligations and rights under the UN Charter in legal terms, and the legal status of these obligations and rights appears to have impacted the thinking and decisions of policymakers. Moreover, leaders and officials in Britain and Canada recognized that the use of military force in Afghanistan and the treatment of captured enemy individuals were in part legal issues, in that they were governed by pre-existing rules in the UN Charter, NATO treaty, the European Convention on Human Rights, and the Geneva Conventions. It also appears that leaders and officials discussed the extent to which Britain and Canada were legally obligated to consider these rules when deciding whether and how to use force in Afghanistan, and what policy and practices to adopt regarding Afghan detainees. Furthermore, Canada's practice of transferring detainees, even though some of these individuals were reportedly known to have killed Canadian soldiers, indicates that some leaders or officials may have seen the need to apply relevant *jus in bello* rules reciprocally and equally. Finally, former CDS Ray Henault recognized that violating these rules could lead to "consequences," and Canadian Cabinet Ministers Art Eggleton and Bill Graham, and UK leaders Jack Straw, Tony Blair, Geoff Hoon, and Philip Hammond saw that Canada and Britain's actions would require legal justification at the domestic and international level.

The foregoing details from the Korean War and the Afghan Conflict resonate with many of the relevant observable implications posited in chapter two. They suggest that UK leaders such as Clement Attlee, Anthony Eden, and Jack Straw, and Canadian leaders such as Louis St. Laurent, Lester Pearson, and Bill Graham felt bound in part by international law. And this, in turn, responds to Andrew Hurrell's query noted in the introduction, and suggests that the individual policymakers acting on behalf of states *are* capable of feeling a sense of legal obligation when they make decisions regarding the use of force.

On the other hand, insofar as the Security Council "recommended" (as opposed to "decided") that assistance be provided to South Korea, we saw that UK leaders and officials tended to interpret the Council's resolutions on the Korean crisis more in political and moral, rather than expressly binding, terms. Canadian leaders, by comparison, did not seem as concerned about whether the Council had "recommended" or "decided" that help be provided to South Korea. Nonetheless, some of these leaders also viewed the Council resolutions more in political and moral terms. By contrast, a key POW obligation in the Third Geneva Convention, Article 118, was seen by British and Canadian leaders in distinctly legal terms. However, the perceived requirements of this rule conflicted with other political and moral considerations at the time, and these factors appear to have ultimately exerted a greater impact on Britain and Canada than the law at issue.

Similarly, during the Afghan Conflict, key UK and Canadian leaders and advisers saw Britain and Canada's commitments under the NATO treaty more in political terms. Thus it cannot be inferred that the legal status of these commitments impacted the thinking or decisions of policymakers. Further, unlike their British counterparts, Canadian leaders have tended to interpret Canada's obligations under the UN Charter more in political and moral, rather than expressly legal, terms. By contrast, UK leaders and advisers have understood Britain's international human rights obligations in binding terms, and Canadian leaders and officials have viewed the rules of the Geneva Convention on POWs in a similar way. However, the criticized policy and practice of Britain and Canada regarding Afghan detainees suggest that the legal status of these obligations and rules has perhaps had an uneven impact on the thinking and decisions of some policymakers.

Significance of Findings for Theory and Research

There are several reasons why this book's findings are significant for existing theory and research in the fields of IR and IL.[1] And these reasons highlight future investigations that could stem from and build on the work of this study.

First, insofar as this study demonstrated that international law played a role in situations where realists argue that states should be purely interested in maintaining their relative power position – i.e., in decisions about when and how to use military force – then this further supports other IR and IL studies that have sought to show that the relationship between international law and the use of force by states is more complex than realism might suggest, and that law can have an important impact in state decisions regarding war.[2] Future research, however, could examine other cases and assess whether realist predictions about international law are more accurate.

For instance, although I argued that international law influenced Britain's participation in the Korean War and Afghan Conflict, law may have had less impact on the UK's colonial conflicts in Kenya[3] and Malaysia during the 1950s, and on Britain's involvement in the Iraq War of 2003. In contrast to Korea, the colonial crises were likely seen as falling directly within Britain's national interest. If so, this would support the realist idea that the greater the national interest at stake, the less influence international law will have if it conflicts with such interest. Iraq, by comparison, would perhaps offer a more interesting case: Tony Blair led Britain to war there without explicit authorization from the Security Council, but it is not clear that he did so solely because of security concerns or the Anglo-American alliance.[4] Further, despite US pressure, Canada refused to

---

1 I thank Jennifer Welsh for the helpful discussions regarding the broader significance of this study's findings for theory and interdisciplinary research in IR and IL.

2 See e.g. Hoyt 1961, Chayes 1974, Byers 2002, Wheeler 2004, and Brunnée and Toope 2010.

3 During the Mau Mau uprising in Kenya, the abuse and torture of the local population was "widespread, amounting to a systematic pattern of state policy" (Anderson 2012: 700).

4 See e.g. Blair 2010, and the various written and oral evidence of the Chilcot Inquiry.

participate in the Iraq War, and it did so in large part because of the lack of UN authorization.[5]

Second, to the extent that this book outlined the four main roles that international law can play when states use force, then this helps advance existing IR research that seeks to go beyond demonstrating *that* normative factors matter in world politics and can affect state behaviour, to specifying *how* such factors matter.[6] For example, although constructivist research has often focused on the constitutive effects of normative factors,[7] and some constructivist and neoliberal institutionalist work has considered the constraining impact of such factors,[8] this study showed that these factors can have two additional effects – they can permit and legitimate certain political and military practices that otherwise might not be permitted; and they can help structure the process by which agents seek to develop and promote new rules and legitimate practice. The second of these two additional influences, I would suggest, has been comparatively understudied in IR research to date, and is a fruitful area for further interdisciplinary work.[9]

Moreover, and related to the above, by outlining the four roles that international law can play in the use of force by states, this book provides additional evidence against realist and rationalist perspectives that grant law with only weak or functional influence in world politics. Future research could analyse further *why* international law plays these four roles. For instance, employing the "interactional" perspective of Jutta Brunnée and Stephen Toope, one could examine whether there were shared understandings of the principles behind the *jus ad bullum* and *jus in bello* rules that arose in this study, particularly following World War II. One could then assess the extent to which these rules meet Lon Fuller's eight criteria of legality, and the degree to which British and Canadian leaders participated in the creation, maintenance, and evolution of the rules. We saw some evidence in this study, for example, that these leaders were involved in the initial drafting and subsequent interpretation of some of the key rules contained in the UN Charter and Geneva Conventions. Moreover, the POW repatriation rule outlined in Article 118 of the Third Geneva Convention is arguably clear, but – resonating with observations from chapter three – that criterion alone did not predict whether the rule inspired fidelity among leaders and officials. More work on these issues could provide additional insight.

---

5 Chrétien 2008, and interview with Bill Graham, Toronto, 12 Sept. 2011.

6 See e.g. Tannenwald 2007 and Hurd 2007.

7 See e.g. Kratochwil 2000 and Price 2008.

8 See e.g. Goldstein and Keohane 1993, Price 1997, and Tannenwald 2007.

9 For an IL study that analyses the processes by which modern international law is made, see Boyle and Chinkin 2007.

Third, my findings are significant for IR and IL debates regarding the concept of legitimacy, and the historical extent to which this concept has mattered to states when they use force. For instance, it has been observed that international law is now increasingly at the centre of debate over, and justification for, armed conflict. Again, as David Kennedy argues, when states use force, law has become the mark of legitimacy, and legitimacy has become the currency of power.[10] This book, however, found that Britain and Canada were concerned with the legitimacy of their uses of force back in 1950, and explained their actions – both in public and in private – with extensive reference to the international legal principles that they thought were relevant at the time. This, in turn, suggests that research on the concept of legitimacy, and its relationship to international law, should include greater historical analysis of this concept and this relationship.

Fourth, insofar as this study found that international law had an important impact on Britain and Canada's participation in the Korean War and the Afghan Conflict, and outlined the roles that law played in both of these wars, it is difficult to conclude that the influence of law has changed significantly over time for these two states. This observation challenges a working premise noted in the introduction, and may surprise some readers. However, as we saw, the constitutive effect of international law was arguably stronger for Clement Attlee during the Korean War than it was for Tony Blair during the Afghan Conflict. Further, the constitutive and regulative influence of law was significant for Canadian leaders Louis St. Laurent and Lester Pearson during the Korean War, but it is less clear that the government of Stephen Harper has been as concerned about Canada's international legal obligations during the Afghan Conflict. Future research could examine why this kind of variance occurs, whether it occurs with other states, and whether law's influence has changed in ways not observed by this study.

Fifth, insofar as this study found that international law had an important impact on Britain and Canada's participation in the Korean War and Afghan Conflict, and outlined the roles that law played for both of these states in these wars, it is also difficult to conclude that law had a greater or different influence on Canada – a less powerful state – than it did on Britain. In other words, one cannot infer from these findings that law's influence on the use of force varies significantly with the relative material capabilities of a state. And this, in turn, offers further evidence against the idea, noted in the introduction, that powerful states are not constrained by international law when they use force, and the notion that law plays a different role for less powerful states in such matters.

---

10 Kennedy 2005 and 2006.

Sixth, inasmuch as this book found that a number of state leaders interpreted *jus ad bellum* rules more in political and moral terms, and *jus in bello* rules more in legal terms, then this variance suggests that some branches of international law may be seen as binding and distinct phenomena, while other branches may not. This variance also indicates that the legal status of rules may matter less for decisions leading up to war, and more for decisions during it. This, in turn, challenges the common assumption that legal considerations tend to receive low priority in war.[11] Further work, such as James Morrow's research on the traits and impact of POW treaties,[12] could be done to subject this assumption to conceptual clarification and empirical assessment. Such work could also examine a broader range of *jus in bello* rules than this study investigated, to assess whether the impact and understanding of such rules vary within this regime, and to provide further empirical evidence against which the findings of this book can be evaluated.[13]

Seventh, in response to Martha Finnemore's query noted in the introduction, this book found that in some circumstances, policymakers *do* know and *do* care about the legal status of the rules they consider relevant to their decision-making. We saw this when UK leaders and officials discussed, in great detail, whether the Security Council had "recommended" or "decided" under Article 39 of the UN Charter that assistance be provided to South Korea following North Korea's attack. We also saw this when UK leaders and officials recognized that Britain's international human rights obligations were potentially engaged by its policy and practice regarding Afghan detainees, and when Canadian leaders and officials recognized that Canada's obligations under the Third Geneva Convention on POWs were similarly engaged by this issue. This gives us reason to think that, in Finnemore's words, "legalness" can matter in compliance with norms. Future research, however, could assess more comprehensively why and under what conditions policymakers do and do not care about the legal status of the rules they deem relevant to their decisions.

Finally, a number of observers argue that obligation is law's defining feature.[14] This book sought in part to subject this assumption to empirical inquiry. Admittedly, the origin and operation of the concept of obligation are, at best, hard to observe or, at worst, a "mystery."[15] Further, although a sense of obligation

---

11 See e.g. Hoyt 1961: 67.

12 Morrow 2001 and 2007.

13 I thank one of the anonymous reviewers of this book for this observation, and for their insightful and thoughtful comments about examining *jus in bello* rules more generally.

14 See e.g. Byers 1999, Reus-Smit 2003, and Brunnée and Toope 2010.

15 Koskenniemi 2011a. Perhaps for this reason, IL scholars studying customary international law have traditionally focused on examining state practice, and not whether such practice resulted from a felt sense of legal obligation.

may be the main reason states tend to comply with international law, it is also likely one of a few reasons why they do so.[16] Finally, in addition to obligation, law may be viewed more as risk assessment or the enunciation of a standard for behaviour,[17] and it may have other distinct institutional traits or effects.[18] As seen in the discussion of Afghan detainees, courts and legal advisers may affect the way leaders view international law, and the impact that law has. Perhaps consistent with the above reflections, the discourse and actions of Canadian and UK leaders during the Korean War and Afghan Conflict offer mixed support for the hypothesis that, when states use force, policymakers understand international law as a binding and distinct set of legal rules, and the legal status of these rules influences their decision-making. In sum, again, my findings indicate that while international law can play important roles in world politics and the use of force by states, it is unclear whether these effects are ultimately attributable to an obligatory quality in law.

What is clear, though, is that during both the Korean War and Afghan Conflict international law helped define and shape Britain and Canada's possible course of action in the wars, and the justifications that could be made for their conduct. This influence, moreover, was seen in the four different roles that international law played in each conflict. And law played these roles *despite* an environment of US dominance and perceived security threats. Finally, it is also clear that many key UK and Canadian leaders and officials felt bound in part by international law during the two wars. For these reasons, we may conclude that – as this book's title asks – these states are not unbound in armed conflict, and international law continues to affect an area of their activity often assumed to be beyond law's reach: the use of military force and the conduct of war.

---

16 Reus-Smit 2003. The other reasons likely include reputation concerns and, for some regimes, formal sanctioning.

17 From this perspective, law may be seen as concerned more with the evaluation of risk, including the risk of not complying with its international and domestic requirements. Or law may be distinguished from other non-legal factors by its role in enunciating a standard for behaviour within a community, and its use in supporting one's position within that community. I thank one of the anonymous reviewers of this book for these insightful observations.

18 I thank Andrew Hurrell for this point.

Bibliography

Archive Sources

Library and Archives Canada, Ottawa, Canada

- Brooke Claxton Papers
- Lester B. Pearson Papers
- Records of the Department of Foreign Affairs and International Trade
- Records of the Department of National Defence
- Records of the Privy Council Office: (a) Cabinet Conclusions; and (b) Files of the PCO National

Archives, London, United Kingdom

- Records of the Cabinet Office: (a) CAB 128 (Cabinet Minutes), 1950–53; and (b) CAB 129 (Cabinet Papers), 1950–53
- Records of the Defence Department: DEFE 4 (Defence Records), 1950–53
- Records of the Foreign and Commonwealth Office: FO 371 (Foreign Office Records), 1947–53
- Records of the Prime Minister: PREM 8, 1950–53

Interviews

Eggleton, Arthur C. (Canada's Minister of Defence from June 1997 to May 2002), conducted in Toronto, Canada, on 19 September 2011.

Graham, Bill. (Canada's Minster of Foreign Affairs from January 2002 to July 2004, Minister of Defence from July 2004 to February 2006; Leader of the Liberal Party and the Official Opposition from February 2006 to December 2006), conducted in Toronto, Canada, on 12 September 2011.

Henault, Ray. (Canada's Chief of the Defence Staff from June 2001 to February 2005, and Chairman of the NATO Military Committee from 2005 to 2008), conducted in London, United Kingdom, on 28 November 2011.

Lang, Eugene. (Chief of Staff to Bill Graham and John McCallum from 2002 to 2006), conducted in Ottawa, Canada, on 8 September 2011.

Martin, Paul. (Canada's Prime Minister and Leader of the Liberal Party from December 2003 to February 2006; Finance Minister from November 1993 to June 2002), conducted via telephone on 16 September 2011.

McCallum, John. (Canada's Minister of Defence from May 2002 to December 2003; Minister of Veterans Affairs from December 2003 to July 2004; Minister of Immigration from November 2015 to January 2017), conducted in Ottawa, Canada, on 20 September 2011.

Ricketts, Sir Peter. (Political Director of the Foreign and Commonwealth Office from 2001 to 2003, Britain's Representative to NATO from 2003 to 2006; Permanent Under Secretary at the FCO from 2006 to 2010; National Security Adviser to the Prime Minister from 2010 to 2012), conducted via telephone on 26 June 2013.

Sheinwald, Sir Nigel. (Britain's Representative to the European Union from 2000 to 2003; Foreign and Defence Adviser to the Prime Minister from 2003 to 2007; Ambassador to the United States from 2007 to 2012), conducted in London, United Kingdom, on 8 July 2013.

Official Publications, Statements, and Documents

Barry, Donald, ed. *Documents on Canadian External Relations*, v. 18–19, 1952–53 (Minister of Supply and Services Canada, 1990).

Blair, Tony. "Address to the Chicago Economic Club," 22 April 1999. Available online: www.pbs.org/newshour/bb/international/jan-june99/blair_doctrine4-23.html

Bullen, Roger and M.E. Pelly, eds. *Documents on British Policy Overseas, Series 1: Volume II, 1945* (London: HMSO, 1985).

Bush, George W. "Address to Congress," 20 September 2001. Available online: http://archives.cnn.com/2001/US/09/20/gen.bush.transcript/

Butler, Rohan, M.E. Pelly and H.J. Yasamee, eds. *Documents on British Policy Overseas, Series 1: Volume 1* (London: HMSO, 1984).

Canada, Department of External Affairs. *Canada and the Korean Crisis* (Ottawa: King's Printer, 1950).

Canada, Department of External Affairs. *Statements and Speeches* (irregular series, 1950–54) (Ottawa: Dep. of External Affairs, 1950–54).

Canada, Department of Foreign Affairs and International Trade. *Canada's International Policy Statement: A Role of Pride and Influence in the World* (Ottawa: DFAIT, 2005).

Canada, Department of National Defence. *The Canadian Forces' Contribution to the International Campaign AGAINST Terrorism* (Backgrounder) (Ottawa: CEFCOM, 2004). Available online: http://comfec-cefcom.forces.gc.ca

Canada, Department of National Defence. "MND Statement in the House of Commons," Ottawa, 19 Nov. 2001. Available online: www.forces.gc.ca

Canada, Government. *Canada's Mission in Afghanistan: Measuring Progress* (Report to Parliament, February 2007). Available online: www.afghanistan.gc.ca/canada-afghanistan/assets/pdfs/260207_Report_E.pdf

Canada, Government. "Canadian Forces Release Statistics on Afghanistan Detainees," Feb. 2013. Available online: www.afghanistan.gc.ca/canada-afghanistan/news-nouvelles/2010/2010_09_22b.aspx

Canada, Government. "Cost of the Afghanistan Mission: 2001–2011," June 2011. Available online: www.afghanistan.gc.ca/canada-afghanistan/news-nouvelles/2010/2010_07_09.aspx

Canada, Government. "History of Canada's Engagement in Afghanistan 2001–2012." Available online: www.afghanistan.gc.ca/canada-afghanistan/progress-progres/timeline-chrono.aspx?lang=eng

Canada, House of Commons. Hansard, oral debates, 1948 to 1953 and 2000 to 2014.

Canada, House of Commons, Special Committee on the Canadian Mission in Afghanistan, oral and written evidence, 2009–11. Committee's website: www.parl.gc.ca/committeebusiness/CommitteeHome.aspx?Cmte=AFGHandLanguage=EandMode=1andParl=40andSes=3

Canada, House of Commons, Standing Committee on National Defence. *Report 1 – Canadian Forces in Afghanistan,* 12 June 2007.

Canada, Military Police Complaints Commission. *Final Report,* June 2012. Available online: www.mpcc-cppm.gc.ca

Canada, Military Police Complaints Commission. *Final Report,* April 2009. Available online: www.mpcc-cppm.gc.ca

Canada, National Defence Headquarters. *Canadian Military Manual: Law of Armed Conflict at the Operational and Tactical Level* (Ottawa: Office of the Judge Advocate General, 2004).

Canada, Senate. Hansard, oral debates, 1950 to 1953 and 2000 to 2014.

Donaghy, Greg, ed. *Documents on Canadian External Relations,* v. 16–17, 1950–51 (Minister of Supply and Services Canada, 1996).

Eggleton, Art. "Speaking Notes" for Press conference: Canadian military contributions – National Defence Headquarters, Ottawa, 8 Oct. 2001. Available online: www.forces.gc.ca/site/news-nouvelles/news-nouvelles-eng.asp?id=518

European Parliament. 2004 Resolution on Guantánamo.

Farrar-Hockley, Anthony. *The British Part in the Korean War,* v. 1, *A Distant Obligation,* and v. 2, *An Honourable Discharge* (London: HMSO, 1990 and 1995).

Graham, Bill. *The Canadian Forces' Mission in Afghanistan: Canadian Policy and Values in Action* (Ottawa: Department of National Defence, 2005).

Great Britain, HM Government. *UK Policy in Afghanistan and Pakistan: The Way Forward* (Stationary Office, 2009).

Great Britain, HM Government website. "UK Forces: Operations in Afghanistan," online: www.gov.uk/uk-forces-operations-in-afghanistan#page-navigation

Great Britain, House of Commons. Hansard, oral debates and written answers, 1948 to 1953 and 2000 to 2014. The latter are online: www.parliament.uk/business/publications/hansard

Great Britain, House of Commons, Public Administration Select Committee. *Who Does UK National Security?*, HC 435, 18 Oct. 2011, and HC 713, 28 Jan. 2011 (Stationery Office, 2011).

Great Britain, House of Commons Defence Committee. *Operations in Afghanistan*, Fourth Report of Session 2010–12, HC 554, 17 July 2011.

Great Britain, House of Lords. Hansard, oral debates, 1948 to 1953 and 2000 to 2014. The latter are online: www.parliament.uk/business/publications/hansard

Great Britain, Iraq Inquiry (aka. Chilcot Inquiry). Oral and written evidence, available online: www.iraqinquiry.org.uk

Great Britain, Ministry of Defence. *The Manual of the Law of Armed Conflict* (Oxford University Press, 2005).

Hague, William. "Britain's Values in a Networked World," 15 Sept. 2010. Available online: www.gov.uk/government/speeches/foreign-secretary-britains-values-in-a-networked-world

Hermes, Walter G. 1966. *United States Army in the Korean War: Truce Tent and Fighting Front* (Washington, DC: Office of the Chief of Military History).

International Commission on Intervention and State Sovereignty. *The Responsibility to Protect* (Canada, International Development Research Centre, 2001).

Letter Dated 7 Oct. 2001 from the Permanent Representative of the United States of America to the United Nations Addressed to the President of the Security Council, UN Doc. S/2001/946 (2001).

Letter from the Charge d'affaires a.i. of the Permanent Mission of the United Kingdom of Great Britain and Northern Ireland to the United Nations Addressed to the President of the Security Council (7 Oct. 2001), UN Doc. S/2001/947 (2001).

Manley, John, et al. *Independent Panel on Canada's Future Role in Afghanistan* (Ottawa: Minister of Public Works and Government Services, 2008).

North Atlantic Treaty Organization. "About ISAF." Available online: www.nato.int/isaf/topics/chronology/index.html

Statutes of the International Red Cross and Red Crescent Movement, adopted by the 25th International Conference of the Red Cross and Red Crescent, Geneva, 1986. See: www.icrc.org/eng/resources/documents/misc/5vueea.htm

Thorgrimsson, Thor and E.C. Russell. *Canadian Naval Operations in Korean Waters, 1950–1955* (Ottawa: Queen's Printer, 1965).

United Nations Assistance Mission in Afghanistan. *Treatment of ConflictRelated Detainees in Afghan Custody*, Oct. 2011.

United Nations Commission on Human Rights. "2006 UN Report on Guantánamo." Available online: www.un.org/apps/news/story.asp?NewsID=17523andCr=Guant%E1namoandCr1=Bay

United Nations Department of Public Information. *Korea and the United Nations* (United Nations Publications, October 1950).

United Nations General Assembly. *Official Records*, 1947 to 1953 and 2000 to 2012.

United Nations Security Council. *Official Records*, 1950 to 1953 and 2000 to 2012.

United States Department of State. *Department of State Bulletin*, XXIII, 578, 31 July 1950.

United States Department of State. *Foreign Relations of the United States, 1950. Korea, v. VII* (US Government Printing Office, 1950).

United States Department of the Army. *The United States Army in the Korean War*, v. 3.

Wood, Herbert Fairlie. *Strange Battleground: Official History of the Canadian Army in Korea* (Ottawa: Queen's Printer for the Army Historical Section, 1966).

Wood, Michael. "The Role of the FCO in UK Government," written submission for Foreign Affairs Committee (Parliamentary Publications and Records, 24 Jan. 2011). Available online: www.publications.parliament.uk/pa/cm201011/cmselect/cmfaff /writev/fcogov/m18.htm

Yasamee, H.J. *Britain and the Korean War* (London: FCO Historical Branch, 1990).

Yasamee, H.J. and K.A. Hamilton, eds. *Documents on British Policy Overseas, Series II: Volume IV, Korea, June 1950–April 1951* (London: HMSO, 1991).

Memoirs

Attlee, Clement R. *As It Happened* (Odhams Press, 1954).

Blair, Tony. *A Journey* (Hutchinson, 2010).

Chrétien, Jean. *My Years as Prime Minister* (Vintage Canada, 2008).

Goldenberg, Eddie. *The Way It Works: Inside Ottawa* (McClelland and Stewart, 2006).

Graham, Bill. *The Call of the World: A Political Memoir* (On Point Press / UBC Press, 2016).

Heeney, Arnold. *The Things that Are Caesar's: The Memoirs of a Canadian Public Servant* (University of Toronto Press, 1972).

Hillier, Rick. *A Soldier First* (Harper Collins, 2009).

Kennan, George. *Memoirs, 1925–1950* (Little Brown, 1967).

Lie, Trygve. *In the Cause of Peace: Seven Years with the United Nations* (Macmillan, 1954).

MacArthur, Douglas. *Reminiscences* (Fawcett, 1965).

Martin, Paul. *Hell or High Water: My Life in and out of Politics* (Emblem Editions, 2009).

Meyer, Christopher. *DC Confidential: The Controversial Memoirs of Britain's Ambassador to the US at the Time of 9/11 and the Run-up to the Iraq War* (Phoenix, 2005).

Pearson, Lester B. *Mike: The Memoirs of the Rt. Hon. Lester B. Pearson*, v. 2, 1948–57, ed by Munro and Inglis (University of Toronto Press, 1973).

Pickersgill, John W. *My Years with Louis St Laurent* (University of Toronto Press, 1975).

Truman, Harry S. *Memoirs: Years of Trial and Hope, 1946–53*, v. 2 (Hodder and Stoughton, 1956).

Court Cases

Amnesty International Canada et al v. Attorney General of Canada et al, 2008 FC 162.
Amnesty International Canada et al v. Attorney General of Canada et al, 2008 FC 336.
Amnesty International Canada et al v. Attorney General of Canada et al, 2008 FCA 401.
Case Concerning Armed Activities on the Territory of the Congo (Democratic Republic of the Congo v. Uganda), I.C.J., 19 Dec. 2005.
Case Concerning Military and Paramilitary Activities in and against Nicaragua (Nicaragua v. United States of America), Merits, [1986] I.C.J. Rep. 14.
Case Concerning Oil Platforms (Islamic Republic of Iran v. United States of America), I.C.J., 6 Nov. 2003.
Certain Expenses of the United Nations (Art. 17, Para. 2 of the Charter), Advisory Opinion, [1962] I.C.J. Rep. 151.
Hamdan v. Rumsfeld, 548 US 557 (2006).
Hussein v. Secretary of State for Defence, [2014] EWCA Civ 1087.
Legal Consequences of the Construction of a Wall in the Occupied Palestinian Territory, Advisory Opinion, I.C.J., 9 July 2004.
Legality of the Threat or Use of Nuclear Weapons, Advisory Opinion, [1996] I.C.J. Rep. 226.
Legality of the Use of Force (Federal Republic of Yugoslavia v. Belgium), Provisional Measures, Verbatim Record of 10 May 1999 and Order of 2 June 1999.
Mohammed v. Ministry of Defence, [2014] EWHC 1369 (QB).
Questions of Interpretation and Application of the 1971 Montreal Convention Arising from the Aerial Incident at Lockerbie (Libya v. United Kingdom), Preliminary Objections, I.C.J., 27 Feb. 1998.
R (Evans) v. SS Defence, [2010] EWHC 1445 (Admin).

Agreements, Pronouncements, and Treaties

Afghanistan Compact, between the Islamic Republic of Afghanistan and the international community, 1 February 2006. Available online: https://www.diplomatie.gouv.fr/IMG/pdf/afghanistan_compact.pdf
Agreement on Provisional Arrangements in Afghanistan pending the Re-establishment of Permanent Government Institutions (5 Dec. 2001) [aka. Bonn Agreement].
Arrangement between the Government of Canada and the Government of the United States of America concerning the transfer of persons between the Canadian Forces and the U.S. Forces in Afghanistan, 18 Nov. 2011. Available online: www.afghanistan.gc.ca/canada-afghanistan/documents/index.aspx
Arrangement for the Transfer of Detainees between the Canadian Forces and the Ministry of Defence of the Islamic Republic of Afghanistan, Kabul, 18 Dec. 2005. Supplemented by an Arrangement of 3 May 2007. Both documents available at: www.afghanistan.gc.ca/canada-afghanistan/documents/index.aspx

Charter of the United Nations, signed 26 June 1945, 1 U.N.T.S. XVI (entered into force 24 Oct. 1945).

European Convention on Human Rights, signed on 4 November 1950. Available online: http://human-rights-convention.org

Geneva Convention relative to the Protection of Civilian Persons, signed 12 Aug. 1949, 75 U.N.T.S. 287 (entered into force 21 Oct. 1950).

Geneva Convention relative to the Treatment of Prisoners of War, signed 12 Aug. 1949, 75 U.N.T.S. 135, 6 U.S.T. 3316 (entered into force 21 Oct. 1950).

Memorandum of Understanding between the Government of the United Kingdom of Great Britain and Northern Ireland and the Government of the Islamic Republic of Afghanistan concerning the Transfer by the United Kingdom Armed Forces to Afghan Authorities of Persons Detained in Afghanistan, Kabul, 30 Sept. 2006. Available at: www.publications.parliament.uk/pa/cm200607/cmselect/cmfaff/44/4412.htm

Military Technical Agreement between the International Security Assistance Force (ISAF) and the Interim Administration of Afghanistan, 4 Jan. 2002. Text in *International Legal Materials*, 41/5 (Washington, DC, Sept. 2002), at 1032. Text (plus annexes) also available at: www.operations.mod.uk/isfma.pdf

North Atlantic Treaty, signed on 4 April 1949. Available online: www.nato.int

Standard Operating Procedures: Detention of Non-ISAF Personnel, SOP 362, 2nd ed, ISAF Headquarters, Kabul, 23 May 2006.

Technical Arrangements between the Government of Canada and the Government of the Islamic Republic of Afghanistan, 18 Dec. 2005. A Status of Forces Arrangement is annexed to the Technical Arrangement.

Theatre Standing Order 321A regarding the "Detention of Afghan Nationals and Other Persons," Canada's Joint Task Force Afghanistan. Available online: www.cbc.ca /news/pdf/TSO321.pdf

United Nations General Assembly and Security Council Resolutions

United Nations General Assembly Resolution 195 (12 December 1948) *The Problem of the Independence of Korea.*

United Nations General Assembly Resolution 293 (21 October 1949) *The Problem of the Independence of Korea.*

United Nations General Assembly Resolution 376 (7 October 1950) *The Problem of the Independence of Korea.*

United Nations General Assembly Resolution 384 (14 December 1950) *Intervention of the Central People's Government of the People's of China in Korea.*

United Nations General Assembly Resolution 410 (1 December 1950) *Relief and Rehabilitation of Korea.*

United Nations General Assembly Resolution 483 (12 December 1950) *Provision of a United Nations Distinguishing Ribbon or Other Insignia for Personnel Which Has*

Participated in Korea in the Defence of the Principles of the Charter of the United Nations.

United Nations General Assembly Resolution 498 (1 February 1951) *Intervention of the Central People's Government of the People's Republic of China in Korea.*

United Nations General Assembly Resolution 500 (18 May 1951) *Additional Measures to Be Employed to Meet the Aggression in Korea.*

United Nations General Assembly Resolution 501 (5 November 1951) *Question of the Representation of China in the General Assembly.*

United Nations Security Council Resolution 82 (25 June 1950) *Complaint of Aggression upon the Republic of Korea.*

United Nations Security Council Resolution 83 (27 June 1950) *Complaint of Aggression upon the Republic of Korea.*

United Nations Security Council Resolution 84 (7 July 1950) *Complaint of Aggression upon the Republic of Korea.*

United Nations Security Council Resolution 85 (31 July 1950) *Complaint of Aggression upon the Republic of Korea.*

United Nations Security Council Resolution 87 (29 September 1950) *Complaint of Armed Invasion of Taiwan (Formosa).*

United Nations Security Council Resolution 88 (8 November 1950) *Complaint of Aggression upon the Republic of Korea.*

United Nations Security Council Resolution 90 (31 January 1951) *Complaint of Aggression upon the Republic of Korea.*

United Nations Security Council Resolution 1214 (1998) *On the Situation in Afghanistan.*

United Nations Security Council Resolution 1333 (2000) *On the Situation in Afghanistan.*

United Nations Security Council Resolution 1368 (2001) *Threats to International Peace and Security Caused by Terrorist Acts.*

United Nations Security Council Resolution 1373 (2001) *Threats to International Peace and Security Caused by Terrorist Acts.*

United Nations Security Council Resolution 1378 (2001) *On the Situation in Afghanistan.*

United Nations Security Council Resolution 1383 (2001) *On the Situation in Afghanistan.*

United Nations Security Council Resolution 1386 (2001) *On the Situation in Afghanistan.*

United Nations Security Council Resolution 1388 (2002) *The Situation in Afghanistan.*

United Nations Security Council Resolution 1390 (2002) *The Situation in Afghanistan.*

United Nations Security Council Resolution 1401 (2002) *The Situation in Afghanistan.*

United Nations Security Council Resolution 1413 (2002) *The Situation in Afghanistan.*

United Nations Security Council Resolution 1419 (2002) *The Situation in Afghanistan.*

United Nations Security Council Resolution 1438 (2002) *Threats to International Peace and Security Caused by Terrorist Acts.*

United Nations Security Council Resolution 1444 (2002) *The Situation in Afghanistan.*

United Nations Security Council Resolution 1453 (2002) *The Situation in Afghanistan.*

United Nations Security Council Resolution 1455 (2003) *Threats to International Peace and Security Caused by Terrorist Acts.*

United Nations Security Council Resolution 1465 (2003) *Threats to International Peace and Security Caused by Terrorist Acts*.

United Nations Security Council Resolution 1471 (2003) *The Situation in Afghanistan*.

United Nations Security Council Resolution 1510 (2003) *The Situation in Afghanistan*.

Theses and Other Unpublished Secondary Works

Forcese, Craig, et al. *Canada's Detainee Transfers in Afghanistan: An Overview of Potential Legal Implications for Canadian Officials – Brief Submitted to the House of Commons Special Committee on the Canadian Mission in Afghanistan* (University of Ottawa, 2010).

Haggis, Carolyn. *The African Union and Intervention: The Origins and Implications of Article 4(h) of the 2001 Constitutive Act* (D.Phil. thesis, Oxford University, 2009).

Percy, Sarah. *Sons of Iniquity: The Origins, Development and Influence of a Norm against Mercenary Use* (D.Phil. thesis, Oxford University, 2005).

Rapp, Kyle. "Constructing Compliance: Drafting the 1949 Geneva Conventions," paper presented at the International Studies Association conference (9 April 2021).

Richmond, Sean. *Sordid Aggression or Humanitarian Intervention? Why the Kosovo Intervention Divided So Many International Relations and International Legal Scholars* (M.A. thesis, University of British Columbia, 2005).

Truscott, Peter. *The Korean War in British Foreign and Domestic Policy, 1950–52* (D.Phil. thesis, Oxford University, 1985).

Wood, John C.W. *Canadian Foreign Policy and Its Determination During the Korean War* (M.A. thesis, Carleton University, 1965).

Books, Articles, and Chapters

Abbott, Frederick M. "NAFTA and the Legalization of World Politics: A Case Study" (2000) 54/3 *International Organization* at 519–547.

Abbott, Kenneth W. "Modern International Relations Theory: A Prospectus for International Lawyers" (1989) 14/2 *Yale Journal of International Law* at 335–411.

Abbott, Kenneth W., et al. "The Concept of Legalization" (2000) 54/3 *International Organization* at 401–419.

Abi-Saab, Georges. *The UN Operation in the Congo 1960–1964* (Oxford University Press, 1978).

Acheson, Dean. "Remarks," reprinted in *International Rules*, ed by Beck, Arend and Vander Lugt (Oxford University Press, 1996) at 107–109.

Afsah, Ebrahim. "Afghanistan Conflict," in *Max Planck Encyclopaedia of Public International Law* (Oxford University Press, 2009).

Akande, Dapo. "The Role of the International Court of Justice in the Maintenance of International Peace," in *Collective Security Law*, ed by White (Ashgate, 2003).

Akande, Dapo and Marko Milanovic. *Submission to the Iraq Inquiry on the UK's Legal Justification for the Iraq War and Lord Goldsmith's Legal Advice* (October 2010).

Anderson, David M. "British Abuse and Torture in Kenya's Counterinsurgency, 1952–1960" (2012) 23/4–5 *Small Wars and Insurgencies* at 700–719.

Anderson, David M. "Mau Mau in the High Court and the 'Lost' British Empire Archives: Colonial Conspiracy or Bureaucratic Bungle?" (2011) 39/5 *The Journal of Imperial and Commonwealth History* at 699–716.

Arend, Anthony C. *Legal Rules and International Society* (Oxford University Press, 1999).

Arend, Anthony C. "Toward an Understanding of International Legal Rules," in *International Rules*, ed by Beck, Arend and Vander Lugt (Oxford University Press, 1996) at 289–310.

Armstrong, David and Theo Farrell, eds. Special issue on "Force and Legitimacy in World Politics" (2005) 31/S1 *Review of International Studies*.

Armstrong, David, Theo Farrell and Helene Lambert. *International Law and International Relations* (Cambridge University Press, 2009).

Bailey, Jonathan, Richard Iron and Hew Strachan, eds. *British Generals in Blair's Wars* (Ashgate, 2013).

Banks, William, ed. *New Battlefields/Old Laws: Critical Debates from the Hague Convention to Asymmetric Warfare* (Columbia University Press, 2011).

Bassiouni, M. Cherif, ed. *The Pursuit of International Criminal Justice: A World Study on Conflicts, Victimization and Post-Conflict Justice* (Intersentia, 2010).

Beadle, Nick. "Afghanistan and the Context of Iraq," in *The Afghan Papers*, ed by Clarke (RUSI, 2011) at 73–80.

Beck, Robert J. *The Grenada Invasion: Politics, Law and Foreign Policy* (Westview, 1993).

Beck, Robert J. "International Law and International Relations: The Prospects for Interdisciplinary Collaboration," in *International Rules*, ed by Beck, Arend, and Vander Lugt (Oxford University Press, 1996) at 3–33.

Beck, Robert J., Anthony C. Arend and Robert Vander Lugt, eds. *International Rules: Approaches from International Law and International Relations* (Oxford University Press, 1996).

Belt, Walter Stuart. "Missiles over Kosovo: Emergence, Lex Lata of a Customary Norm Requiring the Use of Precision Munitions in Urban Areas" (2000) 47 *Naval Law Review* at 115.

Benitz, Max. *Six Months without Sundays: The Scots Guards in Afghanistan* (Birlinn, 2011).

Bennett, Andrew. "Process Tracing," in *The Oxford Handbook of Political Methodology*, ed by Box-Steffensmeier, Brady and Collier (Oxford University Press, 2008) at 702–721.

Bennett, Gill. *Six Moments of Crisis: Inside British Foreign Policy* (Oxford University Press, 2013).

Bercuson, David J. *Blood on the Hills: the Canadian Army in the Korean War* (University of Toronto Press, 1999).

Bercuson, David J. "Korean War," in *The Oxford Companion to Canadian History*, ed by Hallowell (Oxford University Press, 2004).

Bercuson, David J. *True Patriot: The Life of Brooke Claxton* (University of Toronto Press, 1993).

Berger, Antje C. "Legal Advisers in Armed Forces," in *Max Planck Encyclopaedia of Public International Law* (Oxford University Press, January 2010).

Berman, Franklin D. "What Do We Expect of Lawyers in Armed Conflict?" (2006) 38/3 *George Washington International Law Review* at 627–636.

Berton, Pierre. *Marching as to War: Canada's Turbulent Years, 1899–1953* (Doubleday, 2001).

Besson, Samantha and John Tasioulas, eds. *The Philosophy of International Law* (Oxford University Press, 2010).

Best, Geoffrey. *War and Law since 1945* (Oxford University Press, 2002).

Binder, Christina. "Uniting for Peace Resolution (1950)," in *Max Planck Encyclopaedia of Public International Law* (Oxford University Press, 2006).

Bird, Tim and Alex Marshall. *Afghanistan: How the West Lost Its Way* (Yale University Press, 2011).

Bishop, Patrick. *3 Para* (Harper Press, 2007).

Bjarnason, Dan. *Triumph at Kapyong: Canada's Pivotal Battle in Korea* (Natural Heritage Books, 2011).

Bloomfield, Lincoln P. *The United Nations and U.S. Foreign Policy* (Little Brown, 1960).

Bothwell, Robert. *Alliance and Illusion: Canada and the World, 1945–1984* (University of British Columbia Press, 2007).

Boucher, Jean-Christophe. "Selling Afghanistan: A Discourse Analysis of Canada's Military Intervention, 2001–08" (2009) 64/3 *International Journal* at 717–733.

Boucher, Jean-Christophe and Kim Richard Nossal. "Lessons Learned?: Public Opinion and the Afghanistan Mission," in *Elusive Pursuits: Lessons from Canada's Interventions Abroad,* ed by Hampson and Saideman (McGill-Queen's University Press, 2015) at 59–78.

Boucher, Jean-Christophe and Kim Richard Nossal. *The Politics of War: Canada's Afghanistan Mission 2001–2014* (University of British Columbia Press, 2017).

Bourantonis, Dimitris and Konstantinos Magliveras. "Anglo-American Differences over the UN During the Cold War: The Uniting for Peace Resolution" (2002) 16/2 *Contemporary British History* at 59–76.

Bower, Tom. *Broken Vows: Tony Blair – The Tragedy of Power* (Faber & Faber, 2016).

Bowie, Robert R. *Suez 1956* (Oxford University Press, 1974).

Box-Steffensmeier, Janet M., Henry E. Brady and David Collier, eds. *The Oxford Handbook of Political Methodology* (Oxford University Press, 2008).

Boyle, Alan and Christine Chinkin. *The Making of International Law* (Oxford University Press, 2007).

Boyle, Francis A. *Destroying World Order: US Imperialism in the Middle East Before and After September 11* (Clarity Press, 2004).

Boyle, Francis A. *World Politics and International Law* (Duke University Press, 1985).

Bradford, William. "International Legal Compliance: Surveying the Field" (2005) 36/2 *Georgetown Journal of International Law* at 495–536.

Brady, Henry E. and David Collier, eds. *Rethinking Social Inquiry: Diverse Tools, Shared Standards* (Rowman and Littlefield, 2004).

Bratt, Duane and Christopher J. Kukucha. *Readings in Canadian Foreign Policy: Classic Debates and New Ideas*, 2nd ed (Oxford University Press, 2011).

Brown, Rory S. *Fighting Monsters: British-American War-Making and Law-Making* (Hart, 2011).

Brownlie, Ian. *International Law and the Use of Force by States* (Oxford University Press, 1963).

Brownlie, Ian. *Principles of Public International Law*, 7th ed (Oxford University Press, 2008).

Brunnée, Jutta and Stephen J. Toope. "A Hesitant Embrace: The Application of International Law by Canadian Courts" (2003) 40 *Canadian Yearbook of International Law* at 3–60.

Brunnée, Jutta and Stephen J. Toope. "History, Mystery, and Mastery" (2011) 3/2 *International Theory* at 348–354.

Brunnée, Jutta and Stephen J. Toope. *Legitimacy and Legality in International Law: An Interactional Account* (Cambridge University Press, 2010).

Bull, Hedley. "International Law and International Order," ch. 6 in *The Anarchical Society: A Study of Order in World Politics*, 3rd ed (Palgrave, 2002).

Byers, Michael. *Custom, Power and the Power of Rules* (Cambridge University Press, 1999).

Byers, Michael. *Intent for a Nation* (Douglas and McIntyre, 2007).

Byers, Michael. "International Law," in *The Oxford Handbook of International Relations*, ed by Reus-Smit and Snidal (Oxford University Press, 2010) at 612–631.

Byers, Michael, ed. *The Role of Law in International Politics: Essays in International Relations and International Law* (Oxford University Press, 2000).

Byers, Michael. "Terrorism, the Use of Force and International Law after 11 September" (2002) 51/2 *International and Comparative Law Quarterly* at 401–414.

Byers, Michael and Simon Chesterman. "Changing the Rules About Rules? Unilateral Humanitarian Intervention and the Future of International Law," in *Humanitarian Intervention*, ed by Holzgrefe and Keohane (Cambridge University Press, 2003) at 177–203.

Byers, Michael and Georg Nolte, eds. *United States Hegemony and the Foundations of International Law* (Cambridge University Press, 2003).

Campbell, Alastair and Richard Stott, eds. *The Blair Years: Extracts from the Alastair Campbell Diaries* (Arrow Books, 2008).

Canadian Oxford Dictionary, 2nd ed (Oxford University Press, 2004).

Canestaro, Nathan. "Legal and Policy Constraints on the Conduct of Aerial Precision Warfare" (2004) 37 *Vanderbilt Journal of Transnational Law* at 431.

Carr, E.H. *The Twenty Years' Crisis 1919–1939: An Introduction to the Study of International Relations* (Palgrave Macmillan, 2001).

Carvin, Stephanie. *Prisoners of America's Wars: From the Early Republic to Guantanamo* (Columbia University Press, 2010).

Catignani, Sergio. "'Getting COIN' at the Tactical Level in Afghanistan: Reassessing Counter-Insurgency Adaptation in the British Army" (2012) 35/4 *Journal of Strategic Studies* at 513–539.

Chambers, John Whiteclay. "Korea, US Military Involvement in," in *The Oxford Companion to American Military History*, ed by Chambers (Oxford University Press, online, 2012).

Chapnick, Adam. *The Middle Power Project: Canada and the Founding of the United Nations* (University of British Columbia Press, 2005).

Charbonneau, Bruno and Wayne Cox, eds. *Locating Global Order: American Power and Canadian Security after 9/11* (University of British Columbia Press, 2010).

Charbonneau, Bruno and Geneviève Parent. "Managing Life in Afghanistan: Canadian Tales of Peace, Security, and Development" in *Locating Global Order*, ed by Charbonneau and Cox (University of British Columbia Press, 2010).

Chayes, Abram. *The Cuban Missile Crisis* (Oxford University Press, 1974).

Chinkin, Christine. "Human Rights and the Politics of Representation: Is There a Role for International Law?," in *The Role of Law in International Politics,* ed by Byers (Oxford University Press, 2000) at 131–147.

Churchill, Randolph S. *Winston S. Churchill, v. 8, Never Despair, 1945–1965* (Heinemann, 1988).

Clarke, Michael, ed. *The Afghan Papers* (RUSI, 2011).

Clausewitz, Carl Von. *On War*, translated by J.J. Graham (Routledge and K. Paul, 1966).

Corbett, Percy E. *Law and Society in the Relations of States* (Harcourt, Brace and Co., 1951).

Corbett, Percy E. *Law in Diplomacy* (Princeton University Press, 1959).

Cotton, James and Ian Neary, eds. *The Korean War in History* (Humanities Press, 1989).

Crawford, Emily. *The Treatment of Combatants and Insurgents under the Law of Armed Conflict* (Oxford University Press, 2010).

Cumings, Bruce. "Korean War," in *The Oxford Companion to Politics of the World*, 2nd ed, by Krieger (Oxford University Press, 2001) at 474–475.

Cumings, Bruce. *The Origins of the Korean War: The Roaring of the Cataract, 1947–1950*, v. 2 (Princeton University Press, 1990).

Cunningham, Jack and William Maley, eds. *Australia and Canada in Afghanistan: Perspectives on a Mission* (Dundurn, 2015).

Cunningham, Jack and Ramesh Thakur, eds. *Australia, Canada and Iraq: Perspectives on an Invasion* (Dundurn, 2015).

Currie, John H. *Public International Law* (Irwin Law, 2008).

Deighton, Anne. "Britain and the Cold War, 1945–1955," in *The Cambridge History of the Cold War, Volume 1: Origins*, ed by Leffler and Westad (Cambridge University Press, 2012) at 112–132.

Dickinson, Laura. "Military Lawyers on the Battlefield: An Empirical Account of International Law Compliance" (2010) 104/1 *American Journal of International Law* at 1–28.

Dill, Janina. *Legitimate Targets? Social Construction, International Law and US Bombing* (Cambridge University Press, 2015).

Dinstein, Yoram. *The Conduct of Hostilities under the Law of International Armed Conflict*, 2nd ed (Cambridge University Press, 2010).

Dinstein, Yoram. *War, Aggression and Self-Defence*, 5th ed (Cambridge University Press, 2011).

Dockrill, Michael. "The Foreign Office, Anglo-American Relations and the Korean Truce Negotiations July 1951 – July 1953," in *The Korean War in History*, ed by Cotton and Neary (Humanities Press, 1989) at 100–119.

Dockrill, Michael and John W. Young, eds. *British Foreign Policy, 1945–56* (MacMillan, 1989).

Donaghy, Greg. "The Road to Constraint: Canada and the Korean War, June–December 1950," in *Diplomatic Documents and Their Users*, ed by Hilliker and Halloran (DFAIT, 1995).

Donoughue, Bernard and George W. Jones. *Herbert Morrison: Portrait of a Politician* (Weidenfeld and Nicolson, 1973).

Dorronsoro, Gilles. "The Security Council and the Afghan Conflict," in *The United Nations Security Council and War*, ed by Lowe et al. (Oxford University Press, 2010) at 452–465.

Droege, Cordula. "The Interplay between International Humanitarian Law and International Human Rights Law in Situations of Armed Conflict" (2007) 40 *Israel Law Review* at 310.

Dunlap, Charles Jr. "Lawfare Today" (2008) 3 *Yale Journal of International Affairs* at 146–154.

Dunlap, Charles Jr. "The Revolution in Military Legal Affairs: Air Force Legal Professionals in the 21st Century" (2001) 51 *The Air Force Law Review* at 293–309.

Dunoff, Jeffrey L. and Mark A. Pollack. *Interdisciplinary Perspectives on International Law and International Relations: The State of the Art* (Cambridge University Press, 2013).

Eayrs, James. *In Defence of Canada: Peacemaking and Deterrence*, v. 3 (University of Toronto Press, 1972).

Edmonds, Robin. *Setting the Mould: The United States and Britain, 1945–1950* (Oxford University Press, 1986).

Egnell, Robert. "Lessons from Helmand, Afghanistan: What Now for British Counterinsurgency?" (2011) 87/2 *International Affairs* at 297–315.

Ehrlich, Thomas. *Cyprus 1958–1967* (Oxford University Press, 1974).

English, John. *The Worldly Years: The Life of Lester Pearson, 1949–1972* (Knopf Canada, 1992).

Fairweather, Jack. *The Good War: The Battle for Afghanistan 2006–14* (Vintage, 2014).

Falk, Richard. *The Costs of War: International Law, the UN, and World Order after Iraq* (Taylor and Francis, 2012).

Falk, Richard, Mark Juergensmeyer and Vesselin Popovski. *Legality and Legitimacy in Global Affairs* (Oxford University Press, 2012).

Farrar-Hockley, Anthony. "Korean War," in *The Oxford Companion to Military History*, ed by Holmes (Oxford University Press, 2001).

Farrell, Theo. "Improving in War: Military Adaptation and the British in Helmand Province, Afghanistan, 2006–2009" (2010) 33/4 *Journal of Strategic Studies* at 567–594.

Farrell, Theo. "Review Essay: A Good War Gone Wrong" (2011) 156/5 *RUSI Journal* at 60–64.

Fergusson, James. *A Million Bullets: The Real Story of the British Army in Afghanistan* (Corgi Books, 2008).

Finnemore, Martha. "Are Legal Norms Distinctive?" (2000) 32 *New York University Journal of International Law and Politics* at 699–705.

Finnemore, Martha. "International Organizations as Teachers of Norms: The United Nations Educational, Scientific, and Cultural Organization and Science Policy" (1993) 47/4 *International Organization* at 565–597.

Finnemore, Martha and Kathryn Sikkink. "International Norm Dynamics and Political Change" (1998) 52/4 *International Organization* at 887–917.

Finnemore, Martha and Stephen Toope. "Alternatives to 'Legalization': Richer Views of Law and Politics" (2001) 55/3 *International Organization* at 743–758.

Finnis, John. *Natural Law and Natural Rights*, 2nd ed (Oxford University Press, 2011).

Fisher, Roger. *Points of Choice* (Oxford University Press, 1978).

Fleck, Dieter, ed. *The Handbook of International Humanitarian Law*, 2nd ed (Oxford University Press, 2009).

Foot, Rosemary. "Torture: The Struggle over a Peremptory Norm in a Counter-terrorist Era" (2006) 20/2 *International Relations* at 131–151.

Foot, Rosemary. *The Wrong War: American Policy and the Dimensions of the Korean Conflict, 1950–1953* (Cornell University Press, 1987).

Forcese, Craig, and Kent Roach. *False Security: The Radicalization of Canadian Counter-Terrorism* (Irwin Law, 2015).

Franck, Thomas. "Legitimacy in the International System" (1998) 82/4 *American Journal of International Law* at 705–759.

Franck, Thomas. *The Power of Legitimacy Among Nations* (Oxford University Press, 1990).

Franck, Thomas. *Recourse to Force: State Action Against Threats and Armed Attacks* (Cambridge University Press, 2002).

Fry, Robert and Desmond Bowen. "UK National Strategy and Helmand," in *The Afghan Papers*, ed by Clarke (RUSI, 2011) at 68–72.

Fuller, Lon. *The Morality of Law*, rev ed (Yale University Press, 1969).

Fuller, Lon. "Positivism and Fidelity to Law – A Reply to Professor Hart" (1958) 71 *Harvard Law Review* at 630.

George, Alexander L. and Andrew Bennett. *Case Studies and Theory Development in the Social Sciences* (MIT Press, 2005).

Goldsmith, Jack and Eric Posner. *The Limits of International Law* (Oxford University Press, 2005).

Goldstein, Judith and Robert O. Keohane, eds. *Ideas and Foreign Policy: Beliefs, Institutions, and Political Change* (Cornell University Press, 1993).

Goldstein, Judith, et al., eds. Special issue on "Legalization and World Politics" (2000) 54/3 *International Organization*.

Goodin, Robert E. and Charles Tilly, eds. *The Oxford Handbook of Contextual Political Analysis* (Oxford University Press, 2008).

Gordenker, Leon. *The United Nations and the Peaceful Unification of Korea* (Nijhoff, 1959).

Gordon, Nancy. "Canada's Position on the Use of Force Internationally" (2005–06) 61/1 *International Journal* at 129–134.

Gould, Harry. "Categorical Obligation in International Law" (2011) 3/2 *International Theory* at 254–285.

Graham, Bill. "Afghanistan – Some Lessons Learned," in *Australia and Canada in Afghanistan*, ed by Cunningham and Maley (Dundurn, 2015) at 50–80.

Granastein, J.L. *Canada's Army: Waging War and Keeping the Peace*, 2nd ed (University of Toronto Press, 2011).

Granatstein, J.L. *The Ottawa Men: The Civil Service Mandarins, 1935–1957* (University of Toronto Press, 1982).

Granatstein, J.L. and Dean F. Oliver. *The Oxford Companion to Canadian Military History* (Oxford University Press, 2011).

Gray, Christine. *International Law and the Use of Force* (Oxford University Press, 2008).

Greenberg, Karen J. and Joshua L. Dratel, eds. *The Torture Papers: The Road to Abu Ghraib* (Cambridge University Press, 2005).

Griffin, Christopher. "British and American Military Operations in the Battle of Helmand, 2006–2011" (2013) 26/2 *Cambridge Review of International Affairs* at 411–429.

Griffin, Stuart. "Iraq, Afghanistan and the Future of British Military Doctrine: from Counterinsurgency to Stabilization" (2011) 87/2 *International Affairs* at 317–333.

Guzman, Andrew. "A Compliance Based Theory of International Law," (2002) 90/6 *California Law Review* at 1823–1887.

Hafner-Burton, Emilie, David Victor, and Yonatan Lopu. "Political Science Research on International Law: The State of the Field" (2012) 106/1 *American Journal of International Law* at 47–97.

Hampson, Fen Osler and Stephen M. Saideman, eds. *Elusive Pursuits: Lessons from Canada's Interventions Abroad* (McGill-Queen's University Press, 2015).

Harris, Kenneth. *Attlee* (Weidenfeld and Nicolson, 1982).

Hart, H.L.A. *Causation in the Law*, 2nd ed (Oxford University Press, 1985).

Hart, H.L.A. *The Concept of Law*, 3rd ed (Oxford University Press, 2012).

Hastings, Max. *The Korean War* (Pan Books, 2010).

Hathaway, Oona A. "Do Human Rights Treaties Make a Difference?" (2002) 111 *Yale Law Journal* at 1935.

Hathaway, Oona A. and Harold Koh. *Foundations of International Law and Politics* (Foundation Press, 2005).

Heinbecker, Paul. *Getting Back in the Game: A Foreign Policy Playbook for Canada*, 2nd ed (Dundurn, 2011).

Helmke, Belinda. *Under Attack: Challenges to the Rules Governing the International Use of Force* (Ashgate, 2010).

Hendin, Stuart. "Murphy's Law – The Canadian Treatment of Detainees in Afghanistan: Are Human Rights Law and International Humanitarian Law Obligations Circumvented?" (2007) 26/1 *University of Queensland Law Journal* at 157–178.

Hendin, Stuart. "Unpunished War Criminals: The Shameful Legacy of Canada's Involvement in Afghanistan" (2013) 34/3 *Liverpool Law Review* at 291–310.

Henkin, Louis. *How Nations Behave: Law and Foreign Policy*, 2nd ed (Columbia University Press, 1979).

Heyman, Charles. *The British Army: A Pocket Guide 2005–2006* (Pen and Sword Books, 2005).

Higgins, Rosalyn. *Problems and Process: International Law and How We Use It* (Oxford University Press, 1994).

Higgins, Rosalyn. *United Nations Peacekeeping: Documents and Commentary: v. 2 Asia* (Oxford University Press, 1970).

Hollis, Martin and Steve Smith. *Explaining and Understanding International Relations* (Oxford University Press, 1992).

Holmes, John W. *The Shaping of Peace: Canada and the Search for World Order 1943–1957*, vols. 1–2 (University of Toronto Press, 1979 and 1982).

Hoyt, Edwin C. "The United States Reaction to the Korean Attack: A Study of the Principles of the United Nations Charter as a Factor in American Policy-Making" (1961) 55/1 *American Journal of International Law* at 45–76.

Hull, Isabel V. *A Scrap of Paper: Breaking and Making International Law During the Great War* (Cornell University Press, 2014).

Hurd, Ian. *After Anarchy: Legitimacy and Power in the United Nations Security Council* (Princeton University Press, 2007).

Hurrell, Andrew. "International Society and the Study of Regimes: A Reflective Approach," in *International Rules*, ed by Beck et al. (Oxford University Press, 1996) at 206–226.

Hurrell, Andrew. *On Global Order: Power, Values, and the Constitution of International Society* (Oxford University Press, 2007).

Hurrell, Andrew. "'There Are No Rules' (George W. Bush): International Order after September 11" (2002) 16/2 *International Relations* at 185–204.

Jackson, Robert. *The Global Covenant: Human Conduct in a World of States* (Oxford University Press, 2000).

Jenson, Jane. "Canada" in *The Oxford Companion to Politics of the World*, 2nd ed by Krieger (Oxford University Press, 2001) at 104–106.

Jermy, Steven. *Strategy for Action: Using Force Wisely in the 21st Century* (Knightstone, 2011).

Jochnick, Chris af and Roger Normand. "The Legitimation of Violence: A Critical History of the Laws of War" (Winter 1994) 35/49 *Harvard International Law Journal* at 49–95.

Johnston, William. *A War of Patrols: Canadian Army Operations in Korea* (University of British Colombia Press, 2003).

Jong-yil, Ra. "Special Relationship at War: The Anglo-American Relationship during the Korean War" (1984) 7/3 *Journal of Strategic Studies* at 301–317.

Kahl, Colin H. "In the Crossfire or the Crosshairs? Norms, Civilian Casualties and US Conduct in Iraq" (2007) 32 *International Security* at 7.

Kampfner, John. *Blair's Wars* (Free Press, 2004).

Katzenstein, Peter J., ed. *The Culture of National Security: Norms and Identity in World Politics* (Columbia University Press, 1996).

Kaufman, Burton I. *The Korean War: Challenges in Crisis, Credibility and Command*, 2nd ed (McGraw-Hill, 1997).

Keating, Thomas. *Canada and World Order* (Oxford University Press, 2013).

Keene, Edward. *Beyond the Anarchical Society: Grotius, Colonialism and Order in World Politics* (Cambridge University Press, 2002).

Keohane, Robert. *International Institutions and State Power: Essays in International Relations Theory* (Westview, 1989).

Keohane, Robert. "International Law and International Relations: Two Optics" (1997) 38/2 *Harvard International Law Journal* at 487–502.

Kennan, George. *American Diplomacy* (Expanded edition, 1984).

Kennedy, David. "Lawfare and Warfare," in *The Cambridge Companion to International Law*, ed by Crawford and Koskenniemi (Cambridge University Press, 2012) at 158–183.

Kennedy, David. *Of War and Law* (Princeton University Press, 2006).

Kennedy, David. "Speaking Law to Power: International Law and Foreign Policy" (2005) 23 *Wisconsin International Law Journal* at 173–182.

King, Gary, Robert Keohane and Sidney Verba. *Designing Social Inquiry: Scientific Inference in Qualitative Research* (Princeton University Press, 1994).

Kingsbury, Benedict. "The Concept of Compliance as a Function of Competing Conceptions of International Law" (1998) 19 *Michigan Journal of International Law* at 345–372.

Kirton, John. *Canadian Foreign Policy in a Changing World* (Nelson, 2007).

Kittichaisaree, Kriangsak. *International Criminal Law* (Oxford University Press, 2005).

Klassen, Jerome and Greg Albo, eds. *Empire's Ally: Canada and the War in Afghanistan* (University of Toronto Press, 2013).

Koh, Harold. "Why Do Nations Obey International Law?" (1997) 106/8 *Yale Law Journal* at 2599–2659.

Koskenniemi, Martti. "Carl Schmitt, Hans Morgenthau, and the Image of Law in International Relations," in *The Role of Law in International Politics*, ed by Byers (Oxford University Press, 2000) at 17–34.

Koskenniemi, Martti. *From Apology to Utopia: The Structure of International Legal Argument* (Cambridge University Press, reissued in 2005).

Koskenniemi, Martti. "The Lady Doth Protest Too Much: Kosovo and the Turn to Ethics in International Law" (March 2002) 65/2 *The Modern Law Review* at 159–175.

Koskenniemi, Martti. "The Mystery of Legal Obligation" (2011a) 3/2 *International Theory* at 319–325.

Koskenniemi, Martti. *The Politics of International Law* (Hart, 2011b).

Krasner, Stephen D. "Westphalia and All That," in *Ideas and Foreign Policy*, ed by Goldstein and Keohane (Cornell University Press, 1993) at 235–264.

Kratochwil, Friedrich. "How Do Norms Matter?" in *The Role of Law in International Politics*, ed by Byers (Oxford University Press, 2000) at 35–68.

Kratochwil, Friedrich. *Rules, Norms, and Decisions: On the Conditions of Practical and Legal Reasoning in International Relations and Domestic Affairs* (Cambridge University Press, 1989).

Kratochwil, Friedrich. *The Status of Law in World Society: Meditations on the Role and Rule of Law* (Cambridge University Press, 2015).

Kritsiotis, Dino. "When States Use Armed Force," in *The Politics of International Law*, ed by Reus-Smit (Cambridge University Press, 2004) at 45–79.

Ku, Julian and Jide Nzelibe. "Do International Criminal Tribunals Deter or Exacerbate Humanitarian Atrocities?" (2006) 84 *Washington University Law Review* at 777.

Kunz, Josef L. "Legality of the Security Council Resolutions of June 25 and 27, 1950" (Jan. 1951) 45/1 *American Journal of International Law* at 137–142.

Lauterpacht, Hersch. *The Function of Law in the International Community* (Oxford University Press, 1933).

Lauterpacht, Hersch. "The Problem of the Revision of the Law of War" (1952–53) 29 *The British Yearbook of International Law* at 381–382.

Ledwidge, Frank. *Investment in Blood: The True Cost of Britain's Afghan War* (Yale University Press, 2013).

Ledwidge, Frank. *Losing Small Wars: British Military Failure in Iraq and Afghanistan* (Yale University Press, 2011).

Lee, Steven Hugh. *The Korean War* (Longman, 2001).

Lee, Steven Hugh. "A Special Relationship?: Canada-US Relations and the Korean Armistice Negotiations, January–July 1953," in *Diplomatic Documents and Their Users*, ed by Hilliker and Halloran (DFAIT, 1995).

Legro, Jeffrey and Andrew Moravcsik. "Is Anybody Still a Realist?" (1999) 24/2 *International Security* at 5–55.

Lehmann, Julian M. "All Necessary Means to Protect Civilians: What the Intervention in Libya Says about the Relationship between the Jus in Bello and the Jus ad Bellum" (2012) 17/1 *Journal of Conflict and Security Law* at 117–146.

Levinson, Sanford, ed. *Torture: A Collection* (Oxford University Press, 2006).

Lowe, Peter. "The Significance of the Korean War in Anglo-American Relations, 1950–53," in *British Foreign Policy, 1945–56*, ed by Dockrill and Young (Macmillan, 1989) at 126–148.

Lowe, Vaughan, et al., eds. *The United Nations Security Council and War: The Evolution of Thought and Practice since 1945* (Oxford University Press, 2010).

MacDonald, Callum A. *Britain and the Korean War* (Basil Blackwell, 1990).

MacDonald, Callum A. "'Heroes Behind Barbed Wire': The US, Britain and the POW Issue in the Korean War," in *The Korean War in History*, ed by Cotton and Neary (Humanities Press, 1989) at 135–150.

MacDonald, Callum A. *Korea: The War Before Vietnam* (Macmillan, 1986).

Mackenzie, Hector. "Canada, the Cold War and the Negotiation of the North Atlantic Treaty," in *Diplomatic Documents and Their Users*, ed by Hilliker and Halloran (DFAIT, 1995).

Mahurin, Walker. *Honest John* (Putnam's, 1962).

Maley, William. "Afghanistan," in *The Oxford Companion to the Politics of the World*, 2nd ed by Krieger (Oxford University Press, 2001).

Marston, Geoffry, ed. "United Kingdom Materials on International Law 2001" (2001) 72/1 *British Yearbook of International Law* at 551–725.

Martin, Lawrence. *Iron Man: The Defiant Reign of Jean Chrétien* (Viking Canada, 2003).

Marxsen, Christian. "Violation and Confirmation of the Law: The Intricate Effects of the Invocation of the Law in Armed Conflict" (2018) 5/1 *Journal on the Use of Force and International Law* at 8–39.

McDonough, David S. "Afghanistan and Renewing Canadian Leadership" (2009) 64/3 *International Journal* at 647–665.

McDougal, Myers S. "The Hydrogen Bomb Tests and the International Law of the Sea" (1955) 49/3 *American Journal of International Law* at 356–361.

McDougal, Myers S. "International Law, Power and Policy: A Contemporary Conception" (1953) 82 *Collected Courses of the Hague Academy of International Law* at 133–259.

McLeod, Travers. *Rule of Law in War: International Law and United States Counterinsurgency in Iraq and Afghanistan* (Oxford University Press, 2015).

Mearsheimer, John. *The Tragedy of Great Power Politics* (Norton, 2003).

Mintz, Alex and Karl DeRouen Jr. *Understanding Foreign Policy Decision Making* (Cambridge University Press, 2010).

Moens, Alexander. "Afghanistan and the Revolution in Canadian Foreign Policy" (2008) 63/3 *International Journal* at 569–586.

Moir, Lindsay. *Reappraising the Resort to Force: International Law, Jus ad Bellum and the War on Terror* (Hart, 2010).

Morgan, Kenneth O. *Labour in Power, 1945–1951* (Oxford University Press, 1989).

Morgenthau, Hans J. *Politics among Nations: The Struggle for Power and Peace*, 7th ed (McGraw-Hill, 2006).

Morrow, James D. "The Institutional Features of the Prisoners of War Treaties" (2001) 55/4 *International Organization* at 971–991.

Morrow, James D. "When Do States Follow the Laws of War?" (2007) 101/3 *American Political Science Review* at 559–572.

Morton, Desmond. *A Military History of Canada*, 4th ed (McClelland and Stewart, 1999).

Murphy, John F. "Afghanistan: Hard Choices and the Future of International Law," in *The War in Afghanistan: A Legal Analysis*, ed by Schmitt (Naval War College, 2009) at 79–108.

Murphy, Sean D. "Assessing the Legality of Invading Iraq" (2004) 92/2 *Georgetown Law Journal* at 173–258.

Nossal, Kim Richard. "Rethinking the Security Imaginary: Canadian Security and the Case of Afghanistan," in *Locating Global Order*, ed by Charbonneau and Cox (University of British Columbia Press, 2010) at 107–125.

Onuf, Nicholas. *World of Our Making: Rules and Rule in Social Theory and International Relations* (University of South Carolina Press, 1989).

Osiel, Mark. *The End of Reciprocity: Terror, Torture, and the Law of War* (Cambridge University Press, 2009).

Ovendale, Ritchie, ed. *The Foreign Policy of the British Labour Governments 1945–1951* (Leicester University Press, 1984).

Paige, Glenn D. *The Korean Decision: June 24–30, 1950* (Free Press, 1968).

Palmowski, Jan. "Korean War," in *A Dictionary of Contemporary World History* (Oxford University Press, 2008).

Paris, Roland and Taylor Owen, eds. *The World Won't Wait: Why Canada Needs to Rethink Its International Policies* (University of Toronto Press, 2015).

Pearce, Robert, ed. *Patrick Gordon Walker: Political Diaries 1932–1971* (Historians' Press, 1991).

Peevers, Charlotte. *The Politics of Justifying Force: The Suez Crisis, the Iraq War, and International Law* (Oxford University Press, 2013).

Percy, Sarah. *Mercenaries: The History of a Norm in International Relations* (Oxford University Press, 2007a).

Percy, Sarah. "Mercenaries: Strong Norm, Weak Law" (2007b) 61/2 *International Organization* at 367–397.

Perry, David. "Canada's Seven Billion Dollar War: The Cost of Canadian Forces Operations in Afghanistan" (2008) 63/3 *International Journal* at 703–725.

Petrova, Margarita H. "Curbing the Use of Indiscriminate Weapons: NGO Advocacy in Militant Democracies," in *Democracy and Security: Preferences, Norms and Policy-Making*, ed by Evangelista, Muller and Schornig (Routledge, 2008) at 72–101.

Phythian, Mark. *The Labour Party, War and International Relations, 1945–2006* (Routledge, 2007).

Pickersgill, John W. and D.F. Forster, eds. *The Mackenzie King Record, IV: 1947–1948* (University of Toronto Press, 1970).

Pictet, Jean S., ed. *The Geneva Conventions of 12 August 1949: Commentary*, 4 vols. (International Committee for the Red Cross, 1952–1960).

Pigott, Peter. *Canada in Afghanistan: The War So Far* (Dundurn Press, 2007).

Potter, Pitman B. "Legal Aspects of the Situation in Korea" (Oct. 1950) 44/4 *American Journal of International Law* at 709–712.

Price, Richard. *The Chemical Weapons Taboo* (Cornell University Press, 1997).

Price, Richard. "Detecting Ideas and Their Effects," in *The Oxford Handbook of Contextual Political Analysis*, ed by Goodin and Tilly (Oxford University Press, 2008) at 252–265.

Price, Richard. "A Genealogy of the Chemical Weapons Taboo" (1995) 49/1 *International Organization* at 73–103.

Ragin, Charles. "Turning the Tables: How Case-Oriented Research Challenges Variable-Oriented Research," in *Rethinking Social Inquiry*, ed by Brady and Collier (Rowman and Littlefield, 2004).

Raustiala, Kal and Anne-Marie Slaughter. "International Law, International Relations and Compliance," in *Handbook of International Relations*, ed by Carlsnaes et al. (Sage, 2002).

Razack, Sherene H. "From the Somalia Affair to Canada's Afghan Detainee Torture Scandal: How Stories of Torture Define the Nation," in *Empire's Ally: Canada and the War in Afghanistan*, ed by Klassen and Albo (University of Toronto Press, 2013) at 367–387.

Rees, David. *Korea: The Limited War* (Macmillan, 1964).

Reid, Escott. "The Conscience of a Diplomat: A Personal Testament" (winter 1967–68) 74 *Queen's Quarterly* at 4.

Reisman, Michael. "The View from the New Haven School of International Law" (1992) 86 *American Society of International Law Proceedings* at 118–124.

Reus-Smit, Chris. "Obligation Through Practice" (2011) 3/2 *International Theory* at 339–347.

Reus-Smit, Chris. "Politics and International Legal Obligation" (2003) 9/4 *European Journal of International Relations* at 591–625.

Reus-Smit, Chris, ed. *The Politics of International Law* (Cambridge University Press, 2004).

Richmond, Sean. "Transferring Responsibility? The Influence and Interpretation of International Law in Australia's Approach to Afghan Detainees" (2016a) 17/2 *Asia-Pacific Journal on Human Rights and the Law* at 240–256.

Richmond, Sean. "Unbound in War? International Law and Britain's Participation in the Korean War" (2020) 10/2 *Asian Journal of International Law* at 233–260.

Richmond, Sean. "Why Is Humanitarian Intervention So Divisive? Revisiting the Debate Over the 1999 Kosovo Intervention" (2016b) 3/2 *Journal on the Use of Force and International Law* at 234–259.

Ridgway, Matthew B. *The Korean War* (Doubleday, 1967).

Risse, Thomas, Stephen C. Ropp and Kathryn Sikkink. *The Power of Human Rights: International Norms and Domestic Change* (Cambridge University Press, 1999).

Roach, Kent. *The 9/11 Effect: Comparative Counter-Terrorism* (Cambridge University Press, 2011).

Roberts, Adam. "Detainees: Misfits in Peace and War," in *Prisoners in War*, ed by Scheipers (Oxford University Press, 2010) at 263–280.

Roberts, Adam. "NATO's 'Humanitarian War' over Kosovo" (1999) 41/3 *Survival* at 102–123.

Roberts, Adam and Richard Guelf. *Documents on the Laws of War* (Oxford University Press, 2005).

Rodin, David. *War and Self-Defence* (Clarendon Press, 2002).

Rodin, David and Henry Shue, eds. *Just and Unjust Warriors: The Moral and Legal Status of Soldiers* (Oxford University Press, 2008).

Roth, Brad. "Bending the Law, Breaking It, or Developing It? The US and the Humanitarian Use of Force in the post-Cold War Era," in *United States Hegemony and the Foundations of International Law*, ed by Byers and Nolte (Cambridge University Press, 2003) at 232–263.

Rudderham, M.A. "Canada and United Nations Peace Operations" (2008) 63/2 *International Journal* at 359–384.

Saideman, Stephen M. *Adapting in the Dust: Lessons Learned from Canada's War in Afghanistan* (University of Toronto Press, 2016).

Sassòli, Marco and Antoine A. Bouvier. *How Does Law Protect in War?*, 2 vols., 2nd ed (International Committee of the Red Cross, 2006).

Savoie, Donald J. "First Ministers, Cabinet, and the Public Service," in *The Oxford Handbook of Canadian Politics*, ed by Courtney and Smith (Oxford University Press, 2010) at 172–188.

Scharf, Michael P. "International Law in Crisis: A Qualitative Empirical Contribution to the Compliance Debate" (2009) 31 *Cardozo Law Review* at 45.

Scharf, Michael P. and Paul R. Williams. *Shaping Foreign Policy in Times of Crisis: The Role of International Law and the State Department Legal Adviser* (Cambridge University Press, 2010).

Scheipers, Sibylle, ed. *Prisoners in War* (Oxford University Press, 2010).

Schmitt, Michael N., ed. *The War in Afghanistan: A Legal Analysis* (Naval War College, 2009).

Scott, Shirley V. *International Law in World Politics*, 2nd ed (Lynne Rienner, 2010).

Self, Robert. *British Foreign and Defence Policy since 1945: Challenges and Dilemmas in a Changing World* (Palgrave Macmillan, 2010).

Shue, Henry. "Bombing to Rescue? NATO's 1999 Bombing of Serbia," in *Ethics and Foreign Intervention*, ed by Chatterjee and Scheid (Cambridge University Press, 2003) at 97–117.

Shue, Henry. "Target-Selection Norms, Torture Norms, and Growing US Permissiveness," in *The Changing Character of War*, ed by Strachan and Scheipers (Oxford University Press, 2011) at 464–483.

Simma, Bruno, et al., eds. *The Charter of the United Nations: A Commentary*, 3rd ed (Oxford University Press, 2012).

Simmons, Beth A. *Mobilizing for Human Rights: International Law in Domestic Politics* (Cambridge University Press, 2009).

Simmons, Beth A. and Richard H. Steinberg, eds. *International Law and International Relations* (Cambridge University Press, 2006).

Simpson, Gerry. "The Situation on the International Legal Theory Front: The Power of Rules and the Rule of Power" (2000) 11/2 *European Journal of International Law* at 439–464.

Sinclair, Adriana. *International Relations Theory and International Law: A Critical Approach* (Cambridge University Press, 2010).

Sjolander, Claire Turenne and Kathryn Trevenen. "Constructing Canadian Foreign Policy: Myths of Good International Citizens, Protectors, and the War in Afghanistan," in *Readings in Canadian Foreign Policy*, ed by Bratt and Kukucha (Oxford University Press, 2011) at 96–109.

Slaughter, Anne-Marie. "Governing the Global Economy through Government Networks," in *The Role of Law in International Politics,* ed by Byers (Oxford University Press, 2000) at 177–205.

Slaughter, Anne-Marie, Andrew S. Tulumello and Stepan Wood. "International Law and International Relations Theory: A New Generation of Interdisciplinary Scholarship" (1998) 92/3 *American Journal of International Law* at 367–397.

Slaughter Burley, Anne-Marie. "International Law and International Relations Theory: A Dual Agenda" (1993) 87/2 *American Journal of International Law* at 205–239.

Smith, Raymond and John Zametica. "The Cold Warrior: Clement Attlee Reconsidered, 1945–7" (Spring 1985) 61/2 *International Affairs* at 237–252.

Spencer, Robert A. *Canada in World Affairs, V: From UN to NATO, 1946–1949* (Oxford University Press for the Canadian Institute of International Affairs, 1967).

Stacey, C.P. *Canada and the Age of Conflict, v.2, The Mackenzie King Era* (University of Toronto Press, 1981).

Stairs, Denis. "Canada and the Korean War Fifty Years On" (Summer 2000) 9/3 *Canadian Military History* at 49–60.

Stairs, Denis. *The Diplomacy of Constraint: Canada, the Korean War, and the United States* (University of Toronto Press, 1974).

Stein, Janice Gross and Eugene Lang. *The Unexpected War: Canada in Kandahar* (Viking, 2007).

Stiles, Kendall. *State Responses to International Law* (Routledge, 2015).

Strachan, Hew and Sibylle Scheipers, eds. *The Changing Character of War* (Oxford University Press, 2011).

Stueck, William. *The Korean War: An International History* (Princeton University Press, 1995).

Stueck, William. "The United Nations, the Security Council, and the Korean War," in *The United Nations Security Council and War*, ed by Lowe et al. (Oxford University Press, 2010) at 265–279.

Sylvest, Casper. "Realism and International Law: The Challenge of John H. Herz" (Nov. 2010) 2/3 *International Theory* at 410–445.

Tannenwald, Nina. *The Nuclear Taboo: The United States and the Non-Use of Nuclear Weapons Since 1945* (Cambridge University Press, 2007).

Teigrob, Robert. *Warming up to the Cold War: Canada and the United States' Coalition of the Willing, from Hiroshima to Korea* (University of Toronto Press, 2009).

Terrill, Chris. *Commando* (Century, 2007).

Thomas, Ward. *The Ethics of Destruction: Norms and Force in International Relations* (Cornell University Press, 2001).

Thomson, Dale C. *Louis St. Laurent: Canadian* (Macmillan, 1967).

Toope, Stephen. "Emerging Patterns of Governance and International Law," in *The Role of Law in International Politics,* ed by Byers (Oxford University Press, 2000) at 91–108.

Tootal, Stuart. *Danger Close: Commanding 3 PARA in Afghanistan* (John Murray, 2009).

Towle, Philip. *Going to War: British Debates from Wilberforce to Blair* (Palgrave, 2010).

Turner, Barry, ed. *The Statesman's Yearbook 2007* (Palgrave 2006).

Turse, Nick, ed. *The Case for Withdrawal from Afghanistan* (Verso, 2010).

Trachtenberg, Marc. *The Craft of International History: A Guide to Method* (Princeton University Press, 2006).

Travers, Patrick and Taylor Owen. "Between Metaphor and Strategy: Canada's Integrated Approach to Peacebuilding in Afghanistan" (2008) 63/3 *International Journal* at 685–702.

Tyler, Tom. *Why People Obey the Law* (Princeton University Press, 2006).

United Nations Association in Canada. "The Canadian Contribution to United Nations Peacekeeping." Available online: http://unac.org/wp-content/uploads/2013/07 /CdnUNPkpgBooklet_e.pdf

Van Evera, Stephen. *Guide to Methods for Students of Political Science* (Cornell University Press, 1997).

Vickers, Rhiannon. *The Labour Party and the World: v.1 The Evolution of Labour's Foreign Policy, 1900–51* and *v. 2 Labour's Foreign Policy Since 1951* (Manchester University Press, 2004 and 2011).

Visscher, Charles de. *Theory and Reality in Public International Law* (trans. by Corbett) (Oxford University Press, 1957).

Waldron, Jeremy. "Why Law – Efficacy, Freedom, or Fidelity?" (1994) 13/3 *Law and Philosophy* at 259–284.

Waltz, Kenneth. *Theory of International Politics* (Addison Wesley, 1979).

Warner, Geoffrey. "The Impact of the Second World War upon British Foreign Policy," in *What Difference Did the War Make?*, ed by Brivati and Jones (Leicester University Press, 1993).

Warner, Geoffrey. *In the Midst of Events: The Foreign Office Diaries and Papers of Kenneth Younger, February 1950–October 1951* (Routledge, 2005).

Warren, Aiden and Ingvild Bode. *Governing the Use-of-Force in International Relations: The Post 9/11 US Challenge on International Law* (Palgrave 2014).

Weisburd, A. Mark. *Use of Force: The Practice of States since World War II* (Pennsylvania State University Press, 1997).

Weller, Marc. *Iraq and the Use of Force in International Law* (Oxford University Press, 2010).

Welsh, Jennifer. *At Home in the World: Canada's Global Vision for the 21st Century* (Harper Collins, 2004).

Welsh, Jennifer. "Canada and the World: Beyond Middle Power," in *The Oxford Companion to Canadian Politics*, ed by Courtney and Smith (Oxford University Press, 2010) at 361–377.

Welsh, Jennifer. "Reality and Canadian Foreign Policy," in *Canada among Nations: Split Images*, ed by Cooper and Rowlands (McGill-Queens University Press, 2005).

Welsh, Jennifer. "The 2005 International Policy Statement: Leading with Identity?" (Autumn 2006) 61/4 *International Journal* at 909–928.

Wendt, Alexander. "The Agent Structure Problem in International Relations Theory" (1987) 41/3 *International Organization* at 335–370.

Wendt, Alexander. "Constructing International Politics" (1995) 20/1 *International Security* at 71–81.

Wendt, Alexander. *Social Theory of International Politics* (Cambridge University Press, 1999).

Wheeler, Nicholas. "Dying for 'Enduring Freedom': Accepting Responsibility for Civilian Casualties in the War against Terrorism" (2002) 16/2 *International Relations* at 205–225.

Wheeler, Nicholas. "The Kosovo Bombing Campaign," in *The Politics of International Law*, ed by Reus-Smit (Cambridge University Press, 2004) at 189–216.

Whetham, David, ed. *Ethics, Law and Military Operations* (Palgrave MacMillan, 2011).

White, Nigel, ed. *Collective Security Law* (Ashgate, 2003).

White, Nigel. *Democracy Goes to War: British Military Deployments under International Law* (Oxford University Press, 2009).

Williams, Michael J. *The Good War: NATO and the Liberal Conscience in Afghanistan* (Palgrave MacMillan, 2011).

Williamson, Myra. *Terrorism, War and International Law: The Legality of the Use of Force against Afghanistan in 2001* (Ashgate, 2009).

Windsor, Lee, David Charters and Brent Wilson. *Kandahar Tour: The Turning Point in Canada's Afghan Mission* (John Wiley and Sons, 2010).

Wiss, Ray. *A Line in the Sand: Canadians at War in Kandahar* (Douglas and Mcintyre, 2010).

Wolf, David C. "'To Secure a Convenience': Britain Recognizes China 1950" (1983) 18/2 *Journal of Contemporary History* at 299–326.

Wood, Michael. "Legal Advisers," in *Max Planck Encyclopaedia of Public International Law* (Oxford University Press, April 2008).

Woolsey, L.H. "The 'Uniting for Peace' Resolution of the United Nations" (Jan. 1951) 45/1 *American Journal of International Law* at 129–137.

Wright, Lawrence. *The Looming Tower: Al-Qaeda and the Road to 9/11* (Knopf, 2006).

Young, John W. and John Kent. *International Relations since 1945* (Oxford University Press, 2004).

Publications from Non-Governmental Organizations and Think-Tanks

Amnesty International. "Afghanistan – Detainees Transferred to Torture: ISAF Complicity?" (London, Nov. 2007).

Amnesty International. "Cruel and Inhuman: Conditions of Isolation for Detainees at Guantánamo Bay" (5 April 2007).

Amnesty International. "United States of America: Guantánamo – An Icon of Lawlessness" (6 Jan. 2005).

Canadian Centre for Policy Alternatives. "Canada's Fallen: Understanding Canadian Military Deaths in Afghanistan" (Ottawa, Sept. 2006). Available online: http://www .policyalternatives.ca/sites/default/files/uploads/publications/National_Office _Pubs/2006/Canadas_Fallen.pdf

Sanders, Richard. "Canada's Real Role in Iraq," Canadian Centre for Policy Alternatives (Ottawa, Sept. 2008). Available online: www.policyalternatives.ca/publications /monitor/september-2008-canadas-real-role-iraq

Articles from Newspapers, Magazines, and Online News Websites

Alberts, Sheldon, with files from Chris Wattie. "Six Months and Out for Our Troops: Ottawa: Analysts Warn of Losses," *National Post* (16 Nov. 2001) at A1.

Al Jazeera website. "N Korea under Scrutiny as Obama Visits Border" (25 March 2012).

BBC News website. "Afghan Detainees: UK to Restart Transfers This Month" (6 June 2013).

BBC News website. "UK Forces Begin Transfer of Afghan Detainees" (28 June 2013).

BBC2. *Afghanistan: War Without End?* (22 June 2011) and *Afghanistan: The Battle for Helmand* (29 June 2011).

Brennan, Richard J. "Military Told to Heed Abuse Claims," *Toronto Star* (25 February 2010).

Brennan, Richard J. "Retired Justice to Vet Afghan Prisoner Documents," *Toronto Star* (5 March 2010).

Brewster, Murray. "NATO Order Last Year Ended Canadian Transfer of Taliban Prisoners to Afghans," The Canadian Press (11 June 2012).

CBC News website. "Afghan Mission Could Cost up to $18.1 Billion" (9 Oct. 2008).

CBC News website. "All Afghan Detainees Likely Tortured: Diplomat" (18 Nov. 2009).

CBC News website. "Government Trying to Muzzle Diplomat: Lawyer" (6 Oct. 2009).

CBC News website. "In the Line of Duty: Canada's Casualties" (31 Oct. 2011).

CBC News website. "MacKay Knew of Afghan Detainee Concerns: Diplomat" (31 March 2010).

Chase, Steven. "Military Vows to Probe 'Grave' Detainee Accusations," *The Globe and Mail* website (updated 23 Aug. 2012).

Fraser, Blair. "Backstage at Ottawa," *Maclean's* (1 Sept. 1950).

Hickey, Michael. "The Korean War: An Overview," BBC (21 March 2011). Available online: www.bbc.co.uk/history/worldwars/coldwar/korea_hickey_01.shtml

Keeston. "International Law and Korea," *Manchester Guardian* (29 and 31 July 1950).

Kelly, Jeremy. "NATO Stops Sending Prisoners to Afghan Jails Over Torture Fears," *The Guardian* (6 Sept. 2011).

Laghi, Brian. "Eggleton Plays Down Combat Role for Troops," *The Globe and Mail* (16 Nov. 2001) at A1.

LeBlanc, Daniel. "Elite JTF2 Goes into Kandahar War Zone," *The Globe and Mail* (20 Dec. 2001) at A1.

LeBlanc, Daniel. "Harper to Shut Down Parliament," *The Globe and Mail* website (30 Dec. 2009).

LeBlanc, Daniel and Jill Mahoney. "Going to War: Canada Opts for Combat Role in Kandahar Region," *The Globe and Mail* (8 Jan. 2002) at A1.

Macdonald, Neil. "The Questions We Are Not Asking," CBC News website (25 November 2009).

McKenzie, Lewis. "Go Big, Go Bold and Get It Done," *The Globe and Mail* (22 Nov. 2006) at A25.

National Post website. "Over 2,000 Canadians Were Wounded in Afghan Mission: Report" (1 Feb. 2012).

Partlow, Joshua and Sayed Salahuddin. "Afghan Detainees Tortured in Prison, U.N. Says," *Washington Post* (10 Oct. 2011).

Rashid, Ahmed. "Afghan Peace at Stake in Bonn," BBC News website (4 Dec. 2011).

Schiller, Bill. "The Road to Kandahar," *Toronto Star* (9 Sept. 2006) at F1.

Smith, Graeme. "From Canadian Custody into Cruel Hands," *The Globe and Mail* (23 April 2007).

The Guardian website. "British Dead and Wounded in Afghanistan, Month by Month" (updated June 2013).

The Guardian website. "'We Should Have Talked to Taliban' Says Top British Officer in Afghanistan" (28 June 2013).

Thompson, Allan. "Sailors Would Not Hand Over Iraqis," *Toronto Star* (9 April 2003) at A12.

Thompson, Allan. "Six-Month Relief Mission Eyed," *Toronto Star* (16 Nov. 2001) at A6.

Thorne, Stephen. "'Our Job Is to Be Able to Kill People,' Top Soldier Says," *Edmonton Journal* (16 July 2005) at A12.

Travers, James. "Graham Still in the Picture," *Toronto Star* (22 July 2004) at A21.

Ward, Olivia. "Where the Taliban Breeds," *Toronto Star* (18 Feb. 2007) at A10.

Warner, Albert L. "How the Korea Decision Was Made," *Harper's* (June 1951).

Work, Clint. "How to Constructively and Safely Reduce and Realign US Forces on the Korean Peninsula," 38 North (25 Aug. 2020).

Index